THE TRAVEL DIARIES OF
THOMAS ROBERT MALTHUS

The Rev. Professor Thomas Robert Malthus, from an engraving, after the portrait by Linnell, 1833.

THE TRAVEL DIARIES OF
THOMAS ROBERT MALTHUS

EDITED BY

PATRICIA JAMES

CAMBRIDGE
AT THE UNIVERSITY PRESS
FOR THE ROYAL ECONOMIC SOCIETY
1966

PUBLISHED BY
THE SYNDICS OF THE CAMBRIDGE UNIVERSITY PRESS

Bentley House, 200 Euston Road, London, N.W. 1
American Branch: 32 East 57th Street, New York, N.Y. 10022
West African Office: P.M.B. 5181, Ibadan, Nigeria

Printed in Great Britain at the University Printing House, Cambridge
(Brooke Crutchley, University Printer)

LIBRARY OF CONGRESS CATALOGUE
CARD NUMBER: 66–16667

Contents

List of Illustrations

vi

Foreword

The place of Malthus in the history of economic thought—his position as the author of the famous *Essay on the Principle of Population*, as one of the originators of the classical theory of rent, as a participant with Ricardo in the most celebrated epistolary dialogue in the literature of the subject—is such that anything that throws light on his life or the genesis of his ideas is valuable. Together with Adam Smith, Ricardo, John Stuart Mill and Marshall, he is one of the select company of nineteenth-century British economists of which even the least fragment of literary remains is to be welcomed.

The main diaries here reproduced have an importance transcending the interest of mere association, fascinating though that may be: they are the authentic record of a stage in the evolution of Malthus's thought on population which is of critical significance. The contrast between the first and second editions of the *Essay*, the first a brilliant *a priori* polemic, the second a weighty empirical treatise, has long been recognised. Indeed, it was pointed out by Malthus himself. In the preface to the second edition he relates how, in the course of the reflections on the application of the ideas of the first edition, he was led to 'an historical examination of the effects of the principle of population on the past and present state of society', so 'that by illustrating the subject more generally and drawing those inferences from it, in application to the actual state of things which experience seemed to warrant, I might give it a more practical and permanent interest.' In the first edition he had stated more or less dogmatically that population was confined within the limits of subsistence by checks all of which involved either misery or vice. In the second edition he inquired what these checks actually were and was disposed to admit the possibility of checks which were neither miserable nor vicious. This involved detailed inquiries and travel in a number of countries.

The result, as he says in the preface, 'was in effect a new work' which, in Marshall's words, was based on so wide and careful a statement of facts as to claim for the author 'a place among the founders of historical economics'.

These records of his travels in Scandinavia show the investigation actually in progress. Some at least of the events of the journey are related in the *Travels in Various Countries of Europe* by one of Malthus's companions, Dr Edward Clarke, to whom he had lent his manuscript diaries. But here we have their original impact entered up presumably more or less as they occurred. Mrs James's Appendix 1 sets out the passages, in the definitive edition, which resulted from these observations. In their context in the daily records, we can see how they arose in the actual process of travel, how for instance, the information regarding the effects of military service in Norway on what Malthus calls 'popn' first emerged after a meal in a bedroom which started badly with 'dried salmon undress'd & spinage', a circumstance leading almost to 'despair', but which improved considerably when 'a fine roasted turkey made its appearance which set our minds & our bodies at rest'. We become privy to some of the difficulties of research in the report of the awkward interview with the unfortunate Professor Thaarup who, when they made him 'understand that we had heard of his fame as a Statistic writer, & had purchased his work in Copenhagen even tho we did not understand Danish or German,—& that we wished to beg the favour of an answer to a few questions on the subject of his enquiries, he was so much alarmed, & seemed to feel so awkward that we were rather in pain for him'—an interview, however, which was eventually cheered by 'plenty of strawberries and cream' which 'afforded us great relief'.

But it is not only for the occasional entries on 'popn' questions that the diaries are notable. Both in the main Scandinavian narrative and in the supplementary records of other excursions here reproduced, they afford valuable evidence of general temper of the author's mind in its focus on the economic aspect of things—his patient empiricism, his concern with the mundane details of institutions and customary behaviour, his persistent interest in the costs and amenities of living in different environments. From the arrival at Hamburg, where he learned that 'the war, by raising prices of all articles in so extraordinary a manner, had greatly oppressed those who had fixed incomes' to the last few entries of the Scottish holiday where it is noted that 'the farm next to Mr Jeffrey lets for a boll of wheat, a boll of barley, and £3. 15. an acre' and that Mr Naismith had an 'invention for securing the safety of High Pressure Engine', he is ceaselessly observing—the prices of goods, the wages of labour, the fertility of soils, the milk yield of reindeer, the institutions of inheritance....

Behind all this, we have the man. All Malthus's contemporaries who knew him, testified to the serenity and sweetness of his disposition. And here he is in person with his speculative interests, his very human curiosity and his wholesome delight in the small good things of life—a cheerful travelling companion, a perceptive observer, and a courteous, inquiring guest. Surely we must all be grateful to Dr McCleary for his scholarly initiative, to Mr Robert Malthus for his generosity with family treasures, and to Mrs James for her dedicated care with the difficult and protracted labours of editorship.

Since the discovery of these diaries, I have often thought of the pleasure which they would have given to Maynard Keynes who wrote so eloquently of their author and who valued so highly the ways of living and thinking for which he stood. How he would have relished the piquant details of travel and the agreeable parties at which such serious questions were discussed. It is a fitting thing that they should now be published by the Royal Economic Society whose fortunes he did so much to establish and whose meetings for so many years were made memorable by the liveliness of his wit and fancy.

ROBBINS

Preface

Research today is becoming more and more a matter of team-work, and this book is no exception. Never can a grateful editor have owed so much to so many, beginning with the first exacting task of typing the literal transcription of the MS journals, for which I cannot adequately thank Miss Prince and her assistants, always cheerful and ingenious, even when faced with difficulties which seemed beyond the scope of any machine.

As far as the editorial matter is concerned, the British Museum must have pride of place, where the staff of the Reading Room, Map Room and Manuscript Room were, as always, models of competent helpfulness. First in time, however, came the Golders Green Branch Library, and for some of the essential unpublished information about Malthus I am indebted to the Hertfordshire County Record Office, the Borough Muniment Room of Guildford, and the Bath Municipal Library, which contains the City's archives: the help given to research by the librarians and archivists of local authorities is not perhaps as well known or as much appreciated as it should be.

As the standard life of Malthus still remains to be written, some field-work was necessary to establish the basic facts. I am therefore extremely grateful to Prebendary H. W. Beck, the rector of Wotton, where Malthus was born and where his parents and two of his five sisters are buried; the Rev. G. R. Whitcombe, vicar of Harrow, where there is a memorial to another sister and to Malthus's maternal grandfather; the Rev. the Hon. F. A. R. Richards, vicar of Okewood, where Malthus was curate; the Rev. D. Harvey, rector of Claverton, where Malthus was married and where his only son was christened; and Prebendary G. Lester, rector of Bath Abbey, where Malthus was buried.

For the use of unpublished material in private ownership I

must thank the Master and Council of Jesus College, Cambridge, for permission to quote from the letters of E. D. Clarke, and mention with more than formal gratitude the kindness of Dr Brittain, the Keeper of the Records, and Mrs Freda Jones, the archivist. For the Recollections of Malthus's niece, Louisa Bray, my warmest thanks are due both to Mr John Barclay of Shere, the owner of the MS, and to Miss Helen Lloyd, who lent me a copy of it. To Miss Lloyd, a Malthus cousin who still lives at Albury, and is a perfect guide on any Malthusian pilgrimage between Guildford and Dorking, I—and his future biographers—must be for ever grateful.

With regard to the Scandinavian Journal, I have to thank Dr T. K. Derry for indispensable help with history, topography, and individual biographies: I am also very grateful to him for assistance and advice concerning the work as a whole. For all the help and hospitality I was given in Norway, I should like to express my gratitude to the staff of the Royal Norwegian Embassy in London, and to Kontorsjef S. S. Nilson of the Cultural Relations Department of the Norwegian Ministry of Foreign Affairs; I am also particularly indebted to Fru Boye of the Town Museum, and Fru Greftegreff of the National Gallery, in Oslo, and Fru Kagan and Fru Belsaas of the Museum and Library in Trondheim, as well as to the staff of the Folk Museums at Oslo, Trondheim, and Lillehammer. The interest they all showed in Malthus, as well as their generous kindness to me, will remain among my happiest memories.

More formal acknowledgement is due to Messrs Allen and Unwin for permission to quote from T. K. Derry, *A Short History of Norway*, and to Messrs Longmans Green and Co. for permission to quote from Michael Joyce, *Edinburgh: The Golden Age*. For permission to reproduce the plates acknowledgement is due to the following: to the Marshall Library of Economics, University of Cambridge for the frontispiece; to Nasjonalgalleriet, Oslo, for Plate 2; to Portrettarkivet, Riksantikvaren, Oslo, for Plate 3; to the Cambridge University Librarian for Plate 5; to the Kongelige Norske Videnskabers Selskab, Trondheim, for Plates 6 and 7; to the Trustees of the National Portrait Gallery for Plates 8 and 9; and to the rector of Albury and the curator of Guildford Museum for Plate 11.

In a work of this sort, the publisher who turns an annotated transcription into a book is faced with innumerable problems, scholarly, aesthetic, and financial, and I cannot leave unsaid the admiration and gratitude which anyone must feel who comes into contact with the Cambridge University Press. I am also extremely grateful to Professor Robinson, Secretary of the Royal Economic Society, for all the help he has given me, especially with the complications of the cash accounts and the letter in Appendix 3. Of course all errors and omissions remain my own, but without the patient and sympathetic assistance of everyone concerned, there would be a great many more of them.

It would be impossible to thank individually all those friends and relations who have helped with the index and proof-reading, often at much personal inconvenience, but I must mention especially the work done by Mr and Mrs Frank Hopkins, kind neighbours of Dr McCleary, who were the first people to read the transcript; their encouragement and criticism in the early days of the undertaking, as well as at the end, were invaluable.

Finally I must record my heart-felt gratitude to Mr Robert Malthus and Lord Robbins: to the former, for so generously allowing me to transcribe and publish the diaries, and to the latter, for bringing them to the attention of the Royal Economic Society; they have both been most sympathetically prompt with practical help, in every kind of crisis: but for their enthusiasm and unfailing support, this work could never have been accomplished at all by the present editor; still less could it have been, intermittently, the most absorbing and enjoyable of occupations for nearly four years.

June 1965   P. D. J.

Introduction

There can be few educated people who would admit to never having heard of Malthus and his *Essay on the Principle of Population*, first published in 1798. Those more closely concerned with his work or his period, economists and historians, have long known that in the following year he travelled extensively in Scandinavia, which was then seldom visited by Englishmen other than merchants. He went with two friends, Otter and Clarke, and Clarke's nineteen-year-old pupil Cripps; the three older men, just in their thirties, were all Fellows of Jesus College, Cambridge. Malthus referred to this tour in the second edition of his *Essay*, which appeared in 1803, and some account of their journeys had been published both by Otter, in his *Memoir of Robert Malthus*,[1] and by Clarke in his *Travels in Various Countries of Europe, Asia, and Africa*: Clarke had, indeed, reason to be grateful to the Rev. Professor Malthus, who 'allowed the use of his own Manuscript Journal for the description of Norway'.[2] Not unnaturally, it had been taken for granted that these journals were irretrievably lost.

They came to light through the enterprise of the late Dr G. F. McCleary, whose book, *The Malthusian Population Theory*, was published in 1953. In 1960, at the age of ninety-two, Dr Mc-Cleary was still hoping to collect further material for a second edition, and so made an expedition to the Isle of Wight to visit Mr Robert Malthus, a descendant of Sydenham, the elder brother of Thomas Robert Malthus, and the only surviving member of the direct male line in this country. Dr McCleary was too blind to see for himself the Linnell portraits, but was delighted to be able to handle a small riding-switch which had belonged to 'Old Pop'. Nothing was discovered at the time,

---

[1] Attached to the second and posthumous edition of Malthus's *Principles of Political Economy* (1836). It is anonymous, but there is little doubt that it is Otter's work.
[2] Vol. v (1819), p. x.

but a year later he received a parcel from Mr Malthus, containing the two main volumes of the Scandinavian Journal, and also a much smaller notebook with some odd jottings on economic matters and a short record of a continental tour which Malthus made in 1825 with his wife and two of their children. Mr Malthus knew what pleasure these would give to Dr McCleary, and told him to make what use of them he wished, asking only that they should eventually be given to Cambridge, to be deposited with other Malthus manuscripts which are already there.

Dr McCleary shared the excitement of his discovery with his friend Lord Robbins, and it is largely due to Lord Robbins that the Royal Economic Society has taken the responsibility for this publication. I myself became associated with the work as one of the group of honorary nieces who read to Dr McCleary in the last years of his blindness, and as his companion on the memorable trip to the Isle of Wight. When Dr McCleary died early in 1962, it became my task to transcribe the manuscripts and prepare them for publication. Mr Malthus not only readily gave permission for this to be done, but ransacked his shelves to see if he could find any more notebooks: he discovered the first two sections of the Scandinavian Journal and the diary of the Scottish holiday of 1826.

The diaries show that writing did not come easily to Malthus: they are full of crossings-out and interpolations, sometimes due to changes, mid-way, in the construction of a sentence, sometimes to avoid repetition, especially of adjectives, and occasionally to clear up ambiguity. I have left the text almost exactly as Malthus wrote it, with his erratic spelling and peculiar use of capital letters; all that has been done is to break up some of the longer passages into paragraphs, and to add a very few punctuation marks where the sense was not immediately clear. The words crossed out have been omitted (as otherwise the work would have been unreadable) except where they have some special significance; then they are given in footnotes.

Footnotes have also been used for references, factual statements, and short comments. Where a fuller explanation was needed, or where it seemed appropriate to quote at some length from the works of other writers, the editorial matter has been printed with the text in the body of the page, but in smaller type, and separated from it by horizontal lines. This arrangement, it is hoped, will not only give the reader the assistance he needs when reading the journals for the first time, but will also enable him, if he wishes, easily to skip all editorial comment, and read the diaries straight through just as Malthus wrote them. To make the diaries easier to follow, I have standardised the form in which the dates appear at the beginning of each entry.

While Malthus's spelling is erratic, his handwriting, once one is accustomed to it, is not difficult to read. The page that is reproduced as Plate 1 shows a typical extract. The text has been very carefully checked and I believe that what is here printed can be taken to be an accurate transcription of Malthus's journal. One must always remember that he wrote these diaries for his own use and not for publication, and that he possibly wrote late at night after he had been gathering information at a party, or during a tedious wait for horses at a farmhouse.

The main part of this book consists, therefore, of the very detailed journal which Malthus wrote of his Scandinavian travels in 1799, from his arrival at Cuxhaven on 25 May up to the time of his crossing the border from Norway to Sweden on 3 August. We know that he and his friend Otter went to Stockholm, Viborg, and St Petersburg, and that he kept up his journals, because he also lent this part of them to Clarke, in 1820, but the diaries from 4 August onwards are lost.

Although much of the journal is taken up with information which Malthus published almost verbatim, four years later, in the 1803 edition of the *Essay*,[1] it has also a human interest for anyone concerned with him as a person: it reveals a lovable young man (he was thirty-two when the first edition of the *Essay* was published, and possibly rather young for his age) who had just brought upon his head an unprecedented eruption of fury and prejudice. In his *Memoir* of him, Otter was to write of the tenor of Malthus's life as 'one of the most even, serene and peaceful that can well be imagined';[2] Malthus himself told Harriet Martineau many years after, in 1832, that he had suffered in spirits from the abuse lavished on him 'only just at first', and that it had never kept him awake a minute 'after the first fort-

[1] See Appendix 1.
[2] Written as an introduction to Malthus's *Principles of Political Economy* (London, 1836), p. xiii.

night'.[1] One cannot help pondering, as one reads these journals, on what that searing fortnight (if fortnight it was) must have meant to this young country parson, very susceptible to the opposite sex, fearing to make a poor figure at a waltz,[2] and feeling all the shame of an adolescent at being considered the owner of a shabby cart.[3]

All who met Malthus are unanimous in agreeing with his niece Louisa Bray, that no one could know him without loving him, and something of this seems to have continued since his death, as has also the opprobrium of those who have never tried to know him. No editor or biographer could have had his way opened up before him with more warm interest and hospitality than I have had: talking about Malthus, even now, seems to generate the cheerful serenity and kindliness of the man himself. Malthus emerges from these diaries as the perfect travelling companion, unselfish and good-humoured, prepared always to accommodate himself to the customs of the country, and eager for every kind of experience and information.

[1] Harriet Martineau, *Autobiography* (London, 1877), I, 211.

[2] See pp. 108–9.   [3] See p. 93.

Biographical Sketches

Dr McCleary had a whole chapter in his book devoted to 'Mistakes about Malthus',[1] and a complete collection would certainly fill several volumes. It is unlikely that the present writer will escape.

The mistakes, as far as we are concerned, begin with his memorial tablet in Bath Abbey, where Thomas Robert Malthus is said to have been born on 14 February 1766. He was indeed baptised on that day, 'at the Rookery' at Wotton in Surrey, but the Parish Register is quite clear that he was 'born 13th'.[2]

When Robert was born ('Thomas' was never used) his parents, Daniel and Henrietta Malthus, already had five children: Sydenham who was 12 and Henrietta Sarah (Harriet) who was 9, then Eliza Maria aged $4\frac{1}{2}$, Anne Catherine Lucy aged $3\frac{1}{2}$, and Mary Catherine Charlotte who was only 19 months.[3] A fifth daughter, Mary Anne Catherine, was born in 1771; she married Edward Bray, a lawyer, when she was 19, and it is from the unpublished recollections of her daughter, Louisa, who was born in 1801, that we get some insight into Malthus's unusual childhood. Louisa Bray's reminiscences are muddled, and she is not always accurate, but her account of Daniel Malthus has the authenticity of family tradition.

'My Grandfather Malthus', wrote Miss Bray, 'was a great admirer of Rousseau and his works, which no doubt contributed to his eccentricities. He would not allow his wife to wear her wedding ring. My grandmother would not have been supposed a happy woman by those who knew her, yet towards the close of her life, she said she would willingly pass it over again.' Daniel Malthus, so Mrs Bray told her daughter, was 'a person

---

[1] G. F. McCleary, *The Malthusian Population Theory* (London, 1953), p. 94.
[2] Wotton is some $3\frac{1}{2}$ miles west of Dorking. The church is well worth a visit.
[3] See the family tree at the end of this book.

whose will was imperative, and to whom everything gave way'.
'With a highly cultivated mind and very fascinating manners,
he was cold and reserved in his own family, except towards his
eldest daughter of whom he was very fond, and his youngest
son, whose talents probably early attracted his attention.'

Mrs Daniel Malthus, née Henrietta Catherine Graham, was
'a most affectionate and indulgent Mother, and all her children
loved her in the tenderest manner. She was likewise a devoted
wife. They all took after her rather than Mr Malthus, for never
was there a set of more amiable and unselfish beings than my
uncles and aunts.' Mrs Malthus must indeed have had a hard
time of it with her difficult husband, and without even the
usual solace of home and neighbours; her grandchild wrote:
'I have heard my Mother say she did not know where she was
born, for my grandfather after building the Rookery, and
making it a delightful place according to his own excellent
taste, left it and wandered about for some years before finally
settling in Albury.' Strictly speaking, Daniel Malthus did not
build the Rookery, but converted a farm-house into a gentleman's seat, round about 1760. He re-named it very aptly,
for the rooks are calling there still; it has been once more converted, into flats this time, but there is still a terrace reminiscent
of a former, rather grandiose, elegance.

We have no idea where 'home' was when Robert Malthus
was a little child, or when he returned, for the holidays, from
school—probably to a number of different places. All we
know from Louisa Bray is that his eldest sister Harriet, 'among
her other accomplishments, was very musical, and when they
lived at Cookham on the Thames, they often went on the river,
and she would sing the beautiful airs from the Messiah with
only the accompaniament of a flute or guitar'.

There is a memorial tablet over the south door of the church
at Harrow to HENRIET. MALTHUS VIX. AN. XXVIII DAN. ET
HENRIET. MALTHUS FILLAE [sic] DULCISSIMAE. The bottom half of
the tablet has been left quite blank. Near it is a memorial to her
maternal grandfather Daniel Graham, who was buried there
on 17 March 1778, and is described in the register as 'of Pall
Mall, London'. His son-in-law, Thomas Ryves, Malthus's
maternal uncle by marriage, was also buried at Harrow, on
1 August 1788, and is described as being 'of Easher'. There

seems to be no particular reason why this church was chosen by the family, and we are left little the wiser by the entry relating to Harriet among those 'Buryed 1785': it runs, 'July 14. Henrietta Sarah Daugh^t of Daniel Mothus of Maidenhead Berks.'. Malthus would have been 19 then, and had just finished his first year at Jesus College, Cambridge.

This is not the place to quote again the family letters relating to Malthus's school and university days, from which extracts can be found in the works of Otter, Bonar, and Keynes,[1] but whose present whereabouts are unknown. From 1776 to 1782 'Don Roberto', as his master affectionately called him, was a pupil of Richard Graves, then in his sixties, the rector of Claverton, near Bath, and author of *The Spiritual Quixote*, described in the *D.N.B.* as 'a coarse satire upon the Methodists'. According to local tradition there were some forty little boys at Mr Graves's school in Malthus's time, and as there was not room for them all at the Rectory, he rented Claverton Manor and housed them there. Before he went up to Cambridge, Malthus was coached by the Unitarian, Wakefield, at Warrington, so that he could hardly have failed to think seriously about religion.

The evidence we have from the family letters of Malthus's life at Cambridge shows that, as at school, he worked hard and enjoyed himself at cricket, swimming and skating, just as at home in the country he enjoyed a day's shooting. Otter describes his 'taste for humour', which was 'often a source of infinite delight and pleasantry to his companions', and 'wont to set the table in a roar'.[2] Louisa Bray wrote that Uncle Robert 'must have been a very handsome young man'; she continues, 'and I have heard that when at Cambridge he let his fair hair, which curled naturally, hang in ringlets on his neck, which in those days of powder and pigtails must have looked singular'.

Malthus took Orders as soon as he left Cambridge, as 9th Wrangler, in 1788. He had written to his father on 19 April 1786 of an interview with the Master of Jesus, Dr Beadon: 'He seemed at first rather to advise against orders, upon the

---

[1] William Otter, *Memoir of Robert Malthus*, printed as an anonymous introduction to the *Principles of Political Economy* (London, 1836); James Bonar, *Malthus and His Work* (London, 1924); J. M. Keynes, *Essays in Biography* (London, 1951), p. 81.

[2] Otter, *Memoir of Robert Malthus*, pp. xxx–xxxii.

1-2

idea that the defect in my speech would be an obstacle to my rising in the Church, and he thought it a pity that a young man of some abilities should enter a profession without at least some hope of being at the top of it. When, however, I afterwards told him that the utmost of my wishes was a retired living in the country, he said he did not imagine that my speech would be much objection in that case, that, for his own part, when I read or declaimed in chapel he scarcely ever lost a single word.'[1]

As far as I know, Harriet Martineau is our only written authority for stating categorically that Malthus had a hare-lip,[2] though this is visible in the Linnell portrait. She was nervous of meeting him (in 1832) because of her deafness, and 'his hare-lip which must prevent my offering him my tube', but to her relief the ear-trumpet was unnecessary. 'Of all people in the world, Malthus was the one whom I heard quite easily without it;—Malthus, whose speech was hopelessly imperfect, from defect in the palate.'

Malthus did get his quiet country living, but its exact whereabouts have not hitherto been known. Bonar, both in an article on Malthus in Palgrave's *Dictionary of Political Economy* and in *Malthus and His Work*,[3] had assumed that he held a curacy at Albury. This proved not to be the case; the actual church is some eight miles as the crow flies from Albury, where the family seems finally to have settled in 1787.[4] Two marriages linked the family closely with this pleasant country, where descendants of Daniel Malthus live to this day: on 10 August 1789, at Albury, Anne Catherine Lucy Malthus, who was then 27, married Samuel Godschall; on 28 September 1790, Mary Anne Catherine Malthus, who was 19, married Edward Bray at Shere. The Godschalls were childless, but the Brays had twelve children, including our Louisa.[5]

[1] Quoted by Bonar, *Malthus and his Work* (London, 1924), pp. 409–10.
[2] Harriet Martineau, *Autobiography*, I, 327.
[3] *Malthus and His Work*, p. 413.   [4] Otter, *Memoir of Robert Malthus*, p. xxv.
[5] Both fathers-in-law kept diaries in which there is much to interest Malthus's biographer. These diaries (unpublished) are in Guildford Museum, references William Bray 85/1/1–76 and William Man Godschall 52/1/2. William Bray, the Surrey historian, was an extremely busy lawyer; William Man Godschall was a landowning justice. Both were well-informed, active and conscientious. Malthus visited them both and it is clear that he learned much from them about the day-to-day working of what we now call 'the establishment', and particularly of the Poor Law.

Samuel Godschall acted as curate at Albury in the summer of 1789 and the autumn of 1790, and it is perhaps because he was married to a Malthus and because there were so many Malthuses in the district that Malthus appears in the *D.N.B.* and elsewhere as curate of Albury. He never was. According to Louisa Bray her Uncle Sam Godschall (who became rector of Ockham), although gifted in many ways, 'had neither religious nor moral principles, and a temper over which he had no control'. Perhaps that is why William Polhill, who was rector of Albury from 1780 to 1822, gave up the idea of keeping a curate altogether, until old age forced him to have one in 1814; Louisa Bray's description of him is worth giving here, partly because he is such a contrast to the poor Norwegian pastor so cruelly patronised by Mr Anker,[1] and partly because his habit of taking an annual holiday in the autumn, from 1785 to 1795, provided the essential clue which led to the discovery of the truth about Malthus's curacy.

'Mr Polhill, Rector of Albury, was a good specimen of the old fashioned race of clergy, now nearly extinct. He and his wife were perfect pictures in their neat and pretty parsonage, and when on Sundays, he descended from his respectable Chariot, in his full bottomed powdered wig, Dingle hat, and flowing silk gown, and walked up the Churchyard with his lady by his side dressed in white with black silk cloak, he made a most imposing figure to my mind. Yet his teaching was not such as I should value now, and he did not scruple in his younger days to join the Hunt on his sleek steed, which was used for farm work and riding in the week, and with its companion drew the couple to Church on Sundays.[2] They were thoroughly respected. Mr and Mrs Duncombe of Shere, were of the same class, but a step lower, though he was descended from an old and respectable family, to whom the Advowson of Shere had belonged for some generations. They were connected with the Brays by marriage.'

It was through an event at Albury, nonetheless, that it became possible to trace the whereabouts of Malthus's curacy. It hap-

---

[1] See p. 100.

[2] This church, which now stands within the grounds of Albury Park, is closed; near it are two cottages, once an inn, which are all that remains of the centre of the village of Albury as Malthus knew it.

pened that William Lowick, who came of a large Albury family, and his future wife Hannah Noyes, described as also of Albury, wished to be married on Thursday, 3 October 1793, while Mr Polhill was away; for some reason Mr Duncombe could not take Mr Polhill's place, as he had done on the occasion of October and November weddings in previous years; there must have been nothing for it but to send for Mr Robert Malthus.

One can but hope that the marriage service was not as confused as the entry in the register: Mr Polhill's clerk was obviously not used to managing on his own without the rector, and Malthus was not used to marrying people at all, as his chapel was not licensed for marriages; he wrote 'by me Robert Malthus' where he should have written 'by banns', and had to cross it out and write again in the proper place, 'Robert Malthus, Curate of Okewood Chapel' (see Plate 11).

But for the marriage of Mr and Mrs William Lowick, we might never have known that it was to Okewood that Otter referred when he said that Malthus 'undertook the care of a small parish in Surrey'.[1] He was not strictly accurate, as Okewood was then only a chapel of ease at the southern extremity of the strip-like parish of Wotton; people also came to the little church from Rudgwick, Ockley and Abinger—in fact, according to the eighteenth-century register, 'Abinger Parish claims the Privilege of burying for the same fee as Wootton'. Congregations cannot have been large, for the 1801 census shows that the whole parish of Wotton only contained 441 inhabitants, Abinger 632, and Ockley 592.

I have not been able to find out when Malthus became curate of Okewood. It was not then an ecclesiastical parish,[2] and the officiating Clergyman was not inducted or instituted, but merely appointed, probably by the rector, in consultation with the Evelyn family who were the patrons. Nor do we know with any certainty when Malthus ceased to serve Okewood: the entries in the register are usually in the hand of the clerk rather than the curate, so that the negative evidence is inconclusive. Malthus's modesty does not make matters easier for us; unlike many of his predecessors and successors, he did not sign his name at the foot of each page of the register. The four entries in Malthus's

[1] Otter, *Memoir of Robert Malthus*, p. xxxv.
[2] It became one in 1853.

6

handwriting are baptismal entries in July, September and October 1792, and in November 1794, but the absence of entries in his hand after that date does not necessarily mean that Malthus did not serve as curate for some years after 1794.[1]

The little thirteenth-century church stands on a knoll so completely surrounded by trees that it appears, when one comes upon it, like a discovery in a fairy-tale (see Plate 10). The grave-yard gives the impression of being an almost perfectly circular clearing in the wood, somehow more pagan than Christian, and it seems quite natural that there should be a local tradition of druids and Roman temples; it is very large for so small a church, and it is not surprising to read an indignant entry in the register, 'The grass in the Yard belonging to the Chappel is worth Ten Shillings per Year at least, though now let for but five.' That must have been but one of Malthus's practical problems. At the same time it is impossible not to believe that he loved the place, and found it 'picturesque'—a word he was not at all afraid of using in his journals.

But there is one fact about Okewood more important than any other, a fact which has been noticed by a number of vicars who knew nothing whatever about Malthus: Okewood was truly remarkable, throughout the eighteenth century, for its enormous number of baptisms and its small number of burials. To take but the three calendar years 1792–4, there were at Okewood fifty-one christenings and only twelve funerals; during the same period at Wotton Malthus's rector, Mr Taylor, had twenty-four christenings and thirty-four funerals. Statistically, of course, as Malthus himself would have known, these figures are of no importance, but who can deny their emotional impact on the curate?

It is possible, by comparing the baptisms with the burials, to deduce that Malthus himself buried three of the babies he christened in these three years. To ascertain exactly how many elder brothers and sisters stood round the font while Malthus baptised each new arrival might be a rewarding piece of research; even a cursory glance at the entries shows that, in

[1] In his *History of Surrey* (Dorking, 1841–8) E. W. Brayley says that Thomas Robert Malthus, A.M., was appointed curate of Okewood on 5 April 1824 (v, 48). This is obviously nonsense, but it would be interesting to know what lies behind it.

these three calendar years alone, no fewer than seven couples came twice with infants to be baptised; the record is held by James and Sarah Pellet who, in 1794, brought Sarah to be christened on 19 January and Mary on 28 December.

There is no need to stress the importance of all this to the man who was to make the principle of population a public issue for the first time. It is worth noting, however, that at Okewood Malthus must also have seen for himself the unreality of much that was said and written about 'the children of the poor'. 'Indeed,' he wrote, 'it seems difficult to suppose that a labourer's wife who has six children, and who is sometimes in absolute want of bread, should be able always to give them the food and attention necessary to support life. The sons and daughters of peasants will not be found such rosy cherubs in real life, as they are described to be in romances. It cannot fail to be remarked by those who live much in the country, that the sons of labourers are very apt to be stunted in their growth, and are a long while arriving at maturity. Boys that you would guess to be fourteen or fifteen, are upon inquiry, frequently found to be eighteen or nineteen.'[1] One of the most endearing characteristics of the Scandinavian Journal is the light it throws on Malthus's interest in the care of children, and his knowledge of the condition of the cottagers of his own country.

On 10 June 1793 Malthus had been appointed to a Fellow-ship at Jesus College, Cambridge—the college where he seems to have been so happy as an undergraduate. He held the Fellowship until he forfeited it by marriage in 1804, but it would appear that he did not actually reside in Cambridge for much of the time. The Conclusion Book of the College, which records the decisions of the Master and Fellows, contains Malthus's signa-ture on a number of occasions—as a rule, once in each academic year—and in most years he is given leave of absence at the meet-ing at which he signs the book, usually in December or January. There are a few exceptions to this pattern: in April 1801 he attended two important meetings at which the Society gave its consent to several inclosures, and at the first of these Malthus signed next after the Master; on 20 November 1799, he was given leave of absence without signing the book, which suggests that he was not yet back from Russia, the final stage of the Scandi-

---

[1] *Essay on the Principle of Population* (1798), pp. 72, 73.

navian tour; there are also no signatures when he was granted his leave of absence in December 1802 and December 1803.[1]

Thus it would seem that Otter is right in saying that Malthus was only 'occasionally residing in Cambridge upon his fellowship, for the purpose of pursuing with more advantage that course of study to which he was attached'.[2] Malthus himself tells us that the 1798 version of the *Essay on the Principle of Population* 'was written on the impulse of the occasion, and from the few materials which were then within my reach in a country situation',[3] so Otter probably means the further study needed for the second, more inductive, edition, which had been completed by June 1803, while Malthus was still a fellow. Although we have no definite knowledge of where Malthus was living between 1794 and 1804—an important decade—I feel certain that he stayed mostly with his family in Albury; his parents died early in 1800,[4] but Albury was to remain the home of Malthus's elder brother Sydenham (and of Sydenham's son and grandson) as well as of his two unmarried sisters. This is borne out by the fact that when he married, in the spring of 1804, he is described as 'The revd Robert Malthus of the Parish of Aldbury [*sic*] in the County of Surrey'.

At this time Malthus was rector of Walesby, near Market Rasen, in Lincolnshire; he held the living from 1803 until his death in 1834. He solemnised three marriages there, on 21 and 22 May 1804, and 1 July 1805, but otherwise the parish was served by curates.[5] In justice to Malthus, it should be pointed out that at this period a non-resident incumbent was not considered as anything out of the ordinary, any more than was the non-resident fellow of a college; livings and fellowships, although they could be corruptly bestowed, were generally regarded as a means of providing scholars with a livelihood, and also as rewards for literary merit.

We know that late in 1800 Malthus paid a visit to the Eckersall

---

[1] I am indebted for this information to Dr Brittain, of Jesus College, Cambridge.

[2] *Memoir of Robert Malthus*, p. xxxv.

[3] The second sentence of the *Author's Preface to the Second Edition* of the *Essay on the Principle of Population* (London, 1803).

[4] Their graves may still be found in Wotton churchyard, bowered in ivy; Louisa Bray might have some comment to make on the way Daniel Malthus's headstone has sunk into the earth, so that it now seems but half the height of his wife's.

[5] This information was kindly supplied by the Rev. F. M. Massey, rector of Walesby. See also J. M. Keynes, *Essays in Biography* (London, 1951), p. 96.

family. His cousin, John Eckersall, had sold Burford Lodge, near Dorking, in 1791, and moved to Claverton Manor, where Malthus had been at school; Richard Graves, then 87, was still rector, and still walking up Bathwick Hill, but he no longer took pupils. The close relationship between the Malthuses and the Eckersalls is best studied from the family tree at the end of this book. John Eckersall and his wife Catherine were both first cousins to Malthus and to each other, their mothers both being sisters of Daniel Malthus, with the additional complication that their grandmothers were also sisters, Anne and Jane Dalton, who, early in the eighteenth century, had married respectively Sydenham Malthus and James Eckersall.

No anxiety about consanguinity seems to have troubled Malthus, who wrote to a friend, 'Your letter was sent to me to Bath, where I have been on a visit to a family of pretty cousins and could not therefore look down long enough to write a letter.'[1] Two of the pretty first cousins once removed, Anne Eliza and Clara, would have been still in the schoolroom; and the baby of the family, Charles, was only three: he was later to become a clergyman; the only other boy, George, was 18: after two years in the army, preceded by an even briefer career at Jesus College, Cambridge, he seems to have settled down to doing nothing at all. Kitty Eckersall had married, four years before, the Rev. Henry Wynne, rector of Killucan in Westmeath, but Harriet, Lucy and Fanny, aged 23, 20 and 19 respectively, were presumably all at home.[2]

In 1802, following the Peace of Amiens, a party of Malthuses and Eckersalls set out, like so many other English people, on a tour of France and Switzerland. We know from Harriet Eckersall's diary that the tour lasted from Sunday 2 May, when the party crossed from Dover to Calais, until Wednesday 13 October, when they reached London in time for dinner;[3] we can guess that she already had an understanding with 'Mr M.'. Her account of an amusing episode which Malthus used in the 1803 edition of the *Essay on Population* is given as Appendix 2 of this book (see Plate 8).

Some ten months after the publication of the second version

[1] Quoted by Bonar, *Malthus and His Work*, p. 418.
[2] Burke's *Landed Gentry* (1952). See under Wood of Hollin Hall.
[3] Unpublished. The property of Mr Robert Malthus.

of the Essay, Malthus and Harriet were married at Claverton, by Robert Cropp Taunton, on 12 April 1804; the date is wrongly given in the *Gentleman's Magazine* as the 13th.[1] Their first child and only son, Henry, was born prematurely on 16 December 1804, at 37 New King Street, Bath:[2] the tall, narrow house still stands, although the street is now no longer inhabited by admirals and generals and ladies of title as it was in Malthus's time.[3]

In April 1805 there must have been a great family party at Claverton. On the 16th Henry Malthus, exactly four months old, was christened, and on the 22nd Lucy Eckersall was married to the same Rev. Robert Taunton who had married Malthus and Harriet the year before. The officiating clergyman was Henry Wynne, who had come over from Ireland, and it seems likely that he was accompanied by his wife and children.[4] Sentimentalists should be warned, at this juncture, that the present Claverton Manor, which houses the American Museum, has no connection with Malthus; the old house was completely pulled down in 1819, Richard Graves's rectory was demolished in 1852, and the church entirely rebuilt in 1859.

The Malthuses must have left Bath in 1805, for him to take up his appointment as Professor of History and Political Economy at the East India College, then domiciled, while Haileybury was being built, in the dignified but cosy red-brick Tudor Castle of Hertford. Here Malthus's two daughters were born and his small family circle completed. They were both christened at St Andrew's Church (not the present building, but the walk across the green and the little bridge might have been much the same), Emily on 31 July 1806—she had been born on the 5th—and Lucy on 9 January 1808, 'aged 5 weeks'.[5] Lucy died of 'a rapid decline' at the age of 17; Henry and Emily both married after their father's death, but had no children (see Plate 9).

[1] The date given in the Claverton Register is confirmed by the *Bath Chronicle* for Thursday, 19 April 1804.
[2] A letter written by Malthus on this day is printed as Appendix 3 of this book. It was Jane Austen's 29th birthday; she was a near neighbour at 27 Green Park Buildings.
[3] Rate Books of the Parish of Walcot, now in the Bath Municipal Library.
[4] See Burke's *Landed Gentry of Ireland* (1958).
[5] The register is in the County Record Office at Hertford.

With the family's removal to Haileybury Malthus's life ceases, to a certain extent, to be a personal biography, and becomes more the concern of historians of economic theory. We print here the notes he made on a northern tour in 1810; we know from his answers to questions about Ireland from the Emigration Committee of 1827 that the Malthuses visited the Wynnes in Westmeath in 1817;[1] in 1820 Maria Edgeworth met both him and Mrs Malthus in Paris;[2] we have the diaries for his continental tour in 1825 and his Scottish holiday of 1826. But these little books are mere fragments compared with the Scandinavian Journal of 1799, and for a full account of the last half of Malthus's life the biographer would have to draw on Malthus's own published works, and on the letters and memoirs of innumerable literary and political figures of the period, as well as on those of the economists.

Many of them stayed at Haileybury. For those coming from the north, it was a most convenient stopping-place, and Malthus must have written many letters such as the one dated 5 February 1827 to T. F. Kennedy:[3] 'If you can put up with our scanty accommodation, we should be most happy if you could take us in your way to town...' The accommodation may have been scanty but the atmosphere must have been delightful and the surroundings, undulating and rich with trees, were full of charm (see Plate 12). There is something in the architectural simplicity of the old buildings at Haileybury, the satisfying proportions and the great sloping quadrangle, which make one understand why Malthus did not wish to leave the College for any other office or preferment in the Church.[4] Also, perhaps, the memory of his uneasy, peripatetic childhood made him want to give his own wife and family a settled home, and he would certainly not have minded if some of his friends, like Sydney Smith, regarded him as rather a stick-in-the-mud.

One of Malthus's last visitors was Harriet Martineau, who

---

[1] Third Report, *Minutes of Evidence*, p. 311. The questions relative to the Irish holiday are 3186 and 3225, but students of Malthus will find all his evidence of very great interest.

[2] *Memoir of Maria Edgeworth* by her step-mother (privately printed 1863), II, 69, 85.

[3] *The Letters of Henry Cockburn* (London, 1874), p. 481. See also pp. 264–6 of this book.

[4] I have to thank Mr A. E. Melville for most kindly showing me round Haileybury, which is full of treasures, and where Malthus is still warmly remembered.

has left an attractive account of 'the pleasant house where I had spent such happy days'. She wrote, 'On my arrival, I found that every facility was indeed afforded for my work. My room was a large and airy one, with a bay-window and a charming view; and the window side of the room was fitted up with all completeness, with desk, books, and everything I could possibly want. Something else was provided which showed even more markedly the spirit of hospitality. A habit and whip lay on the bed. My friends had somehow discovered from my tales that I was fond of riding; and horse, habit and whip were prepared for me. Almost daily we went forth when work was done—a pleasant riding-party of five or six, and explored all the green lanes, and enjoyed all the fine views in the neighbourhood.... Now they are all gone.... The subdued jests and external homage and occasional insurrections of the young men; the archery of the young ladies; ... the somewhat old-fashioned courtesies of the summer evening parties, all are over now, except as pleasant pictures in the interior gallery of those who knew the place—of whom I am thankful to have been one.'[1]

Two years after Malthus's death William Empson wrote an account of him in the *Edinburgh Review* which is a perfect supplement to Otter's *Memoir*. Empson joined the staff at Haileybury, as Professor of General Polity and the Laws of England, in 1824, when he was 33 and Malthus a celebrity of nearly 60 with an almost grown-up family; they were colleagues for ten years. How well they got on together can be shown in a single sentence of Empson's: 'But as for hating, Mr Malthus could hate nobody—which, considering the strength of his feelings, public and private, and the provocations which for forty years he was perpetually receiving, was almost as wonderful a circumstance, as that anybody could be found capable of hating him.'

Perhaps the most interesting aspect of this article is that Empson seems to have been more conscious than anyone, certainly more than any of Malthus's older friends, of the curate of Okewood who had preceded the professor: 'Mr Malthus', he wrote, 'owed the discovery, which will immortalize his name, mainly to his benevolence. Instead of his speculations on population having hardened his heart against the interests of

[1] *Autobiography*, I, 328–9.

the poor, it was the earnestness and the perseverance with which he set himself to work in behalf of those very interests, that first fixed his attention upon these particular speculations.' At the very beginning of his essay he makes the point which he stresses throughout: 'Mr Malthus was a clergyman—a most conscientious one, pure and pious. We never knew one of this description so entirely free from the vices of his caste.'[1]

The story ends in 1834, when the Malthuses left Haileybury to spend Christmas with Harriet's parents;[2] they had moved from Claverton to Bath in 1815, and lived at 17 Portland Place. The house, now made into pleasant flats, is still there and, as it stands on a hill, the rooms at the back still have a good wide view of the country he loved. Here Malthus was taken suddenly ill, and died on 29 December. He was buried in Bath Abbey on 6 January 1835, in the north aisle, but the grave has since been covered by pews. His memorial tablet, believed to be Otter's work, is now in the north porch at the west end of the Abbey,[3] and is a far better summing-up than epitaphs usually are, of 'a serene and happy life...supported by a calm but firm conviction of the usefulness of his labors'. The inscription may contain a 'mistake' about his birth, but it is the truth about the man.

OTTER, CRIPPS, CLARKE AND HIS 'TRAVELS'

The history of Malthus's Scandinavian journey really begins with a letter, written in the spring of 1798, by Edward Daniel Clarke to 'The Revd. William Otter, Jesus College, Cambridge'. They had been undergraduates there together, and friends and contemporaries of Malthus. When they came down, their ways parted; Otter took Orders, and became a curate at Helston, in Cornwall, where he also taught at the grammar school; Clarke, who had astonished the College by making a balloon, and sending it up from Cloister Court bearing a kitten, embarked on a more adventurous life by becoming a tutor in

---

[1] William Empson, 'The Life, Writings, and Character of Mr Malthus', *Edinburgh Review* (January 1837), pp. 481–2.

[2] Both Malthus's parents-in-law outlived him. Catherine Eckersall died on 16 January 1837, and her husband on 2 December of the same year, aged 89.

[3] It is given in full as Appendix 4 of this book.

great houses. He was thus able to spend ten years in almost continuous travel, touring his own country, including Scotland, Italy (twice), Switzerland and the Rhine: in 1798 he was living at Uckfield, in Sussex, with all his cases from Italy lying 'open and half-ransacked' about the house of his widowed mother and, according to Otter, caring for nothing but her and shooting.[1]

Otter was by then in residence as a Fellow of Jesus and concerned to get Clarke to stop frittering away his life and return to College; this Clarke was the more inclined to do when he found that the alternative was to be called up in the Sussex Militia. (The perceptive reader will have seen by now that Clarke was a completely different young man from Malthus, and it says much for Otter's character that he remained a cherished friend of both of them until they died: it is clear from what we know of all three that Clarke and Malthus were far more attached to Otter than they were to each other.)

Thus, on 15 March 1798, Clarke wrote to Otter the news which is still having its effect on the lives of a number of people: 'A young Man of 19 years of age, is just come into possession of a large fortune—about two thousand five hundred a Year—and has applied to me to be his private Tutor for three Years, at any terms. Hearing I intended & wished to go to College, he offered to go there also, and to travel with me, where I pleased, during the Vacations...Certainly I shall not take less than £300 a Year...'

The pupil whose sudden accession to wealth was to have such remarkable consequences was John Marten Cripps. We know very little about him except that the money came from a maternal uncle, and that his previous education had been, according to Otter, 'indifferent'. Clarke's account of Cripps in his published *Travels*, of which this pupil was the 'cause and companion', naturally contained nothing but praise; but in his letters to Otter, to whom he wrote extremely frankly, he is equally enthusiastic about Cripps's energy and endurance (both were highly necessary when travelling with Clarke), his cheerfulness and good manners, and his devotion to his tutor whenever the latter was ill or depressed. He was also extremely

[1] William Otter, *Life and Remains of Edward Daniel Clarke* (London, 1824), p. 333.

liberal with his money in the purchase of every kind of museum piece which Clarke discovered, from lumps of rare minerals to manuscripts and statuary, and it is perhaps rather unfair that by about the end of the last century his name had faded away from all the catalogues, and their joint acquisitions are listed everywhere as 'presented by the late Professor E. D. Clarke'.[1]

In 1799, as Clarke wrote, 'Englishmen were excluded from almost every part of the European Continent by the distracted state of public affairs', and a journey to Denmark, Sweden, Norway and Lapland possibly appealed to him not only because these countries were, 'at this time, less liable than any other to those political convulsions which agitated more frequented regions', but because they were 'seldom seen by literary men'.[2] As all concerned were probably in Cambridge when the journey was decided upon there is unlikely to be any record of the discussions which took place. We know that the tetrarchy, as they called themselves, travelled together for a month, and then decided to separate, by the Venner Lake in Sweden: Malthus and Otter journeyed—as we shall see—in a comparatively leisurely way, on a tour that, as Otter wrote, 'could be comprehended within the extended limits of a long summer vacation'; Clarke and Cripps vigorously explored not only Scandinavia, visiting Röros and Trondheim, Christiania and Kongsberg, a few weeks later than Malthus and Otter, but went also to Russia, Tartary, Turkey, the Holy Land, Egypt and Greece, extending their itinerary as circumstances suggested, and not returning to England until November 1802.

The loot of this $3\frac{1}{2}$-year tour was certainly enormous. Cripps brought back more than eighty packing cases, Clarke had seventy-six, and also the two-ton statue, then believed to be of Ceres, which he had obtained at Eleusis, somewhat against the wishes of the inhabitants. It is not surprising to read in the *D.N.B.* that, with all this cargo, they were shipwrecked off Beachy Head, but it is astonishing to learn that this catastrophe occurred 'not far from the home of Mr Cripps, whose father saved what he could from the wreck'.

---

[1] I am indebted for this information to Dr Nicholson of the Fitzwilliam Museum.
[2] E. D. Clarke, *Travels in Europe, Asia, and Africa* (London, 1819), v, 1.

Cambridge made Cripps an honorary M.A. On New Year's Day, 1806, he married Charlotte, the third daughter of Sir William Beaumaris Rush, and settled down at Novington Lodge in Sussex to a life of 'practical horticulture', his chief contribution being the introduction of the kohlrabi from Russia. He died in 1853, and was succeeded by his eldest surviving son.[1]

Cripps's connection with Clarke was not severed but made closer after their travels, for they became brothers-in-law. Clarke had written to Otter from Mount Hamus in April 1802 (there had been an embarrassing entanglement with a lady in Constantinople), 'My greatest Happiness would be to marry,' and when, towards the end of 1804, he fell passionately in love with 'the little Rushlight', his sufferings were acute. He would have been 35, and Angelica Rush 17, when they were making up their minds. In the end Sir William dowered his daughter handsomely, although Clarke uncharitably remarked that Cripps, with his 'long head for £. s. d.', got more out of their father-in-law. Clarke called £. s. d. 'le sacré diable', and never did any accounts at all for the first seven years of his married life—with what disastrous results can easily be predicted.

But this is looking ahead. Since Clarke, who had become Senior Tutor of Jesus, had to resign his Fellowship on marriage, there was no alternative but to take Orders, which he did at Christmas, 1805; he became vicar of Harlton, near Cambridge, and later rector of Yeldham in Essex. In 1808 he became the first Professor of Mineralogy at Cambridge—a subject which interested him just as much as classical antiquities or chemistry —and in 1810 and 1812 the first two quarto volumes of his *Travels* were published, dealing with his peregrinations in Russia and Greece.

At this time he was living at Trumpington, and in April 1813 Maria Edgeworth persuaded her father to call on the great Dr Clarke on their way from Cambridge to London. Her superb description of the whole visit is too long to quote here, but I cannot resist her account of Clarke himself: 'From the print I had imagined he was a large man, with dark eyes and hair, and a penetrating countenance. No such thing: he is a little, square, pale, flat-faced, good-natured-looking fussy man, with very intelligent eyes, yet great credulity of counte-

---

[1] I can find no trace of this family after Burke's *Landed Gentry* for 1882.

nance, and still greater benevolence.'[1] It is amusing to find that
Maria Edgeworth was one of the first women to be deceived
by the engraved portrait of himself which Clarke had as a
frontispiece to the first volume of his *Travels*: how many romantic ladies must have been inspired to attempt at least one
of the six quartos, some 800 pages thick, after gasping at this
sensitive, wilful and utterly Byronic face, which they would
naturally assume belonged to a man as tall as he was handsome.

Otter, meanwhile, seems to have been living quietly at his
rectory at Chetwynd, near Newport in Shropshire, with his
growing family. He had married Nancy Bruere on 3 July 1804
and he was staying with his father-in-law in London when
Clarke wrote to him at 'No. 6, Argyle Street, Oxford Road'
on 25 January 1811: 'Let me beg of you not to suffer the copying of your Journal to stop—it will soon be wanted. As to
that of Malthus, he seems to swell a little about it—as if it
contained intelligence to make a fuss about—therefore I have
resolved to consign it to that peaceful repose whence it will
never awaken—at least I will ask for it no more.—I am vain
enough to believe that if my lambent flame be fed with a little
of your Oil, it will cast a lingering Light upon our Graves.'

Poor Clarke! The reason Otter's journal had to be copied
was that his handwriting was illegible to everyone except his
wife, who must have spent much of her time acting as his
amanuensis. But why did the good-natured Malthus swell a
little? The answer may well be that he distrusted the Clarke
brothers' approach to the truth, particularly with regard to
documents. Edward Clarke's brother, James Stanier Clarke
(immortalised by his correspondence with Jane Austen), had
published in 1809 a life of Nelson which, according to the
D.N.B., 'loses much of the value it should have had from the
lax way in which it is written; official as well as private letters
and documents having been garbled to suit the editor's idea
of elegance, and hearsay anecdotes mixed up indiscriminately
with more authentic matter'.

This was to be exactly the technique Clarke used with other
people's diaries, and Malthus's doubts must have been more
than confirmed in 1812 when Clarke, with tremendous enthusiasm, decided that a private letter of Otter's to him should

---

[1] *Life and Letters of Maria Edgeworth*, ed. A. J. C. Hare (London, 1894), p. 205.

be published as a pamphlet in defence of the British and Foreign Bible Society. The controversy does not concern us: what is fascinating is the liberty Clarke and a group of like-minded divines (including the Bishop of Bristol, who was very useful for franking letters) were quite happy to take with another man's work. As the pamphlet was being printed by Watts of Brox-bourne,[1] 'Malthus could read every Sheet, as it issued from the Press',[2] and his different approach to the matter is made very clear in a letter Clarke wrote on 7 August 1812: 'Malthus will "read the sheets, and mention anything that strikes him: but he will neither correct nor transpose"—Those are his Words.' No wonder Malthus did not want to trust Clarke with his journal.

In the midst of the correspondence about the Bible pamphlet (Clarke wrote twenty-nine letters in nine months) there is another appeal to Otter: 'I wait in earnest expectation of your promised MS Diary do not delay it!'[3] Then the subject is not mentioned again until $3\frac{1}{2}$ years later; on 27 November 1815 Clarke wrote at great length to Otter about his never-ending financial troubles, a bitter quarrel with his in-laws (who had stopped his wife's quarterly 'salary'), Angelica's having still-born premature twins, and a great deal of amusing gossip, finishing up, when there was scarcely any paper left: 'Here comes the end of my letter, more important than any other part of it.—It relates to your Journals. Send them instantly for I have begun my fifth Volume. You promised that Mrs Otter should copy them. Pray tell her if she can do this, and send them by piece-meal it will do; but I am already at Hamburgh.'

Ten months later, on 5 September 1816 (we have three other letters in between), Clarke wrote:

My dear Otter,

I can only give you an idea of the loss I sustain in not having your Journal (which you so long ago assured me Mrs Otter would have the goodness to transcribe) by telling you that I am at this instant sending to Press my account of Hamburgh—and I am quite sure that in the description of its Bank, I stand in great need of such a

---

[1] He printed for Cadell, who published Clarke's *Travels*.
[2] Clarke to Mrs Otter, 18 February 1812.
[3] Letter of 1 July 1812.

Prop in the margin. I have all along hoped that in this *third part* of my Travels I should see very often—'*Mr Otter's MS Journal*'—as I have seen *Mr Heber's* and *Mr Walpole's*. I am however constrained to go to Press; but as a *last dying Squeak* I send forth this letter that if there be even yet a possibility, you will be so good as to forward it in Scraps, one after another.

The second half of the letter, that which Otter printed in his *Life and Remains of E. D. Clarke*, tells how happily he 'sacrificed the whole Month of August to Chemistry'. Thereafter there are no more requests and reproaches: one can only assume that the diaries were useless as they were, and that Mrs Otter, who had seven surviving children, did not have time to copy them out.[1]

It must have been after this that Clarke again approached Malthus—and Malthus responded by sending the two chunky leather-bound books which describe the whole of his time in Norway. It is not hard to see why he did so. Clarke had his first financial panic in 1813: in January 1814, as a result of this, he moved from Trumpington to a much smaller house in Cambridge; thereafter many of his letters to Otter are extremely pathetic. He worked unceasingly, as a J.P. as well as a clergyman and a professor, being carried to his lectures in a sedan chair when he was too ill to walk,[2] and slaving at his *Travels*: two more volumes on what we would now call Greece and the Middle East came out in 1814 and 1816. Malthus might well have felt that Clarke's financial crises were due as much to his own mismanagement as to the principle of population (Angelica had ten sons—of whom only five lived—and then two daughters), but his kindness triumphed over his distaste for seeing his work mangled. One feels that he also responded favourably to an amusing letter from Clarke dated 4 February 1817 asking for Malthus's support in his election as University Librarian—which he duly became.

The preface to the fifth volume of the *Travels* was dated 15 December 1818 and on p. x Clarke wrote, '*Professor Malthus* allowed the use of his own *Manuscript Journal* for the description of *Norway*: the extracts, it is true, consisting frequently of short and detached passages, are not separated

---

[1] But see also p. 168.   [2] Letter of 3 April 1815.

from the body of the text, but they will not, on this account, be the less conspicuous.' Clarke must have returned the Norwegian diaries to Malthus as soon as he had finished his account of Christiania—the opening chapter of the posthumously published sixth volume—which was probably early in 1820; the two little books have page after page scored with a bold diagonal pencil stroke, showing the passages Clarke had incorporated in his own work.

When the fifth volume was published Malthus must have winced at what Clarke had done, for in spite of using quotation marks to indicate Malthus's contributions, he had altered and elaborated the language in a manner that would today be regarded as quite outrageous. An example is given on p. 183 n. As the sixth volume was going to press, in the piecemeal fashion of the time, Malthus did what he could to save the situation, for on 4 December 1820 Clarke wrote to him, 'Already Watts has orders to omit all inverted commas in this Vol. so you will find your injunctions strictly adhered to.'

Poor Malthus! One longs to know how he framed these injunctions so as not to hurt Clarke's feelings; what we do know is that he most nobly sent Clarke his Swedish Diaries at the same time, for Clarke writes in the same letter, 'Your Journals came safe. How valuable! I capered for Joy...I thought I should have died with laughter at some of the Scenes you describe with Otter—especially the visit to the *Patron* who spoke only Swedish...and again when the old Doctor seized you and Otter and kissed you on both cheeks in spite of your Latin.[1] It is really quite curious that upon entering Westmania (where you found them all black) you make the same reflections that I have done & nearly in the same words —ascribing to that general mourning the impress upon y^r mind as to the wretchedness of the Country...'

It is obvious that these Swedish journals must still have been in Clarke's possession some fifteen months later when he died (like Malthus, at the house of his father-in-law) on 9 March 1822. He was buried in his College Chapel. He left his Angel, as she was deservedly called, with seven children, the eldest only fifteen, and his friends at once set to work to finish the sixth volume of the *Travels*, so that it could be published post-

---

[1] Kissing was obviously a problem. See p. 172.

humously for the benefit of the family. In such circumstances Malthus was not the man to press for the return of his diaries; one cannot wish him to have been other than he was, but it is tantalising to think that Malthus's Swedish journals have perhaps been lost to posterity as the result of his kindness to this exasperating old friend.

Otter published his quarto edition of *The Life and Remains of Edward Daniel Clarke* in 1824, and it was so successful that a three-volume octavo edition came out a year later. He drew largely on the letters (carefully bowdlerised) which are now at Jesus College. The work was advertised in the posthumous volume of the *Travels* as being in preparation, in order to raise money for the education of Clarke's children; the Rev. Professor Malthus put his name down for two copies, and George IV headed the list with a subscription for fifteen: James Stanier Clarke was his librarian.

Twelve years after the publication of Clarke's *Life and Remains*, Otter was writing another memoir of an old friend for another widow—only this time the object was not to raise money, but 'to lessen the weight of those calumnies, which, though they passed lightly over his family while he was alive, are calculated to aggravate their grief now they are deprived of him', and also to vindicate 'the truth itself, by procuring for his writings a calmer and more impartial hearing than they have hitherto received'.[1] After Otter's devoted work as the biographer of Clarke and Malthus, it is a little sad to think that he had no old friend left to write about him; he is, however, not without his memorial, for the Bishop Otter Training College, for teachers, still flourishes; it was founded in his memory by public subscription in 1850.

Otter seems to have altered the course of his career after the death of Clarke, for in May 1822 he went with his family to Oxford, as private tutor to the third and last Lord Ongley, who was up at Christ Church. In 1825 Otter was rector of St Mark's, Kennington, and in 1830 he became the first Principal of King's College, London; six years later, at the age of 68, he was made Bishop of Chichester. He died in 1840, but during his episcopate, which lasted less than four years, he had amongst other things instituted weekly

[1] *Memoir of Robert Malthus*, p. xv.

communion services in the Cathedral, established the diocesan association for building churches and schools, and for augmenting the incomes of poorer livings and curacies, and founded both a theological college and a training college for schoolmasters.

Before he died, Otter's eldest daughter, Sophia, had married Henry Malthus, who was vicar of Effingham. They had no children, although all three of Sophia's married sisters did: from the worldly point of view, they all 'married better' than Sophia. It was at the vicarage at Effingham that Nancy Otter died in 1860.

The Scandinavian Journal, 1799

The Scandinavian diaries which are printed here were written in four notebooks: the first two, measuring $7\frac{1}{2}$ in. $\times 4\frac{1}{2}$ in., have greyish blue marbled paper covers; the first contains 64 pages, the second 68, but except at the very end of the second book, when paper was running short, Malthus only wrote on one side of each sheet, using the verso for interpolations and rough sketches.

The first book seems originally to have been intended for rather elementary Greek notes. There are two illegibly pencilled pages which must have been accounts: 'Coach to bury [Bury St Edmunds] & 1 man—£3. 0s. 0d.' has been written in ink at the top of one of them; at the bottom is written 'Fees of office for luggage &c:— £1. 9s. 0d.'. It is also possible to make out the pencilled words Waiter, Breakfast, Turnpike, and Chaises. In the 'front' of the book, when it is turned upside down, Malthus has written:

'Sm's. Qns.[1]
Interest of money.
Corn laws. Inland merchants & at the Ports.
Recompence of labourer.
Relative prices of provisions & manufactures at different times.
Bills & Bankers.
Religious establishments & sects.'

Malthus goes from the first to the second book in mid sentence, describing the caps worn by the women of Lubec,[2] and also from the second to the third, when he is reporting a discussion with Professor Abildgaard in Copenhagen.[3] The third and fourth books are leather-bound volumes, $6\frac{1}{2}$ in. $\times 4$ in., about an inch thick, each containing 280 pages, written on both sides except for some thirty-five which are blank or almost blank, and which Malthus obviously

---

[1] 'Smith's Questions'; topics from Adam Smith's *The Wealth of Nations*. Malthus used to set questions on Adam Smith to his class at Haileybury. One such set of questions (taken down by his pupil J. D. Inverarity) is in the Marshall Library of Economics at Cambridge, and is mentioned in *The Works and Correspondence of David Ricardo*, ed. Piero Sraffa, VI, 159 n.

[2] See p. 43 n.   [3] See p. 59 n.

meant to fill up later, but never did. The books have small brass clasps, and he used them vertically, as we should use a writing-pad.

It is plain from both Clarke's and Malthus's accounts of their Scandinavian tours that they had studied two books beforehand, Bishop Pontoppidan's *Natural History of Norway*, and the relevant parts of Archdeacon Coxe's five volumes of *Travels*, describing the Scandinavian journeys he made in 1779 and 1784.[1]

Eric Pontoppidan, Bishop of Bergen (1698–1764), published his great work in Danish in 1751, and an anonymous translation appeared in London in 1755. Clarke describes this enchanting, illustrated folio as 'The History of Norway, a very jejune performance, and unfortunately the only one that has been translated into English'. Pontoppidan not only believed the most fantastic folk-lore about well-known animals; he dealt perfectly seriously with leviathans, sea-serpents, mermen, mermaids, and a species called Marmaele, 'of the bigness of an infant of half a year old', though some were larger—'the upper part was like a child, but the rest like a Fish'. Yet this good bishop was Malthus's sole guide to the fauna of Norway.

It is interesting to consider, by the way, the great advances made in scientific observation between the publication of the *Natural History of Norway* in 1751 and Darwin's *Origin of the Species* in 1859. Darwin's first inspiration had come in 1838, when he 'happened to read for amusement Malthus on *Population*',[2] though what Darwin drew from Malthus was, of course, the general idea of the struggle for existence.

Archdeacon William Coxe (1747–1828) is still well regarded as a historian; he was the son of a court physician, and educated first at Marylebone Grammar School, and then at Eton and King's, where he became a Fellow in 1768, and took Orders in 1771. He became tutor to the Duke of Marlborough's eldest son, and then made a tour of Switzerland with the son of the Earl of Pembroke; this was trebly lucrative, for he wrote it up afterwards, and later on the Earl gave him a very good living. His most famous travels were in 1784–6, when he toured Poland and part of Russia, as well as Scandinavia, with his most famous pupil, Samuel Whitbread.

Malthus had obviously read Coxe attentively (it is quite possible that they may have met) and I have quoted both him and Bishop Pontoppidan in cases where their works throw some light on Malthus's experiences or reactions.

---

[1] William Coxe, *Travels into Poland, Russia, Sweden and Denmark* (4th ed., London, 1792).

[2] Charles Darwin, *Autobiography*, ed. Nora Barlow (London, 1958), p. 120.

Some account is necessary of the political condition of the Scandinavian countries for which the 'four Gentlemen of Jesus College, Cambridge, left their University'[1] in 1799. It should be remembered that Denmark, Norway and Sweden were all united in 1397 by what was called the Union of Kalmar; this was largely the work of a formidable woman, Margaret, daughter of Waldemar IV of Denmark, whose own son (by the King of Norway) had died, and who had her great-nephew Eric of Pomerania crowned King of all three countries. Sweden broke away in 1523, under her hero-king Gustav Vasa, but Norway remained united to Denmark for over 400 years, until the Treaty of Kiel in 1814; then the victorious powers transferred her crown from Denmark to Sweden.

The union of Norway with Denmark was complete, and the two countries were ruled from Copenhagen as if they were one; it was not, however, a conquest, in the sense that the Norwegian farmers did not have their land taken from them and given to Danes. Officials, administrative, military, and judicial, were inclined to return to Denmark after their service in Norway was over, which is one of the reasons why Norway has few buildings comparable with the French château or the English gentleman's seat; some Norwegians deplore this, but the foreign visitor, enchanted by the timber farm-buildings and the elegantly painted houses of the merchants, just as they were in the eighteenth century, is unconcerned. The union of Norway with Sweden, which lasted from 1814 until 1905, was much less close: Norway had her own Storting, or Parliament, for internal affairs, on the lines of the Constitution drawn up at Eidsvoll in 1814, on 17 May—still the Norwegian national festival. At the time of Malthus's visit, however, it is helpful to think of Norway as being, politically, united with Denmark.

The King of Denmark in 1799 was the mad Christian VII, and the government was carried on by his son, the Crown Prince Frederick, who became Regent in 1784 at the age of 16: he reigned as Frederick VI from 1808 to 1839. From 1660 the Danish monarchy was, quite constitutionally, the most absolute in Europe: the cynical may enjoy the reflection that it was based on Hobbes' *Leviathan*. Much therefore depended on the character of the monarch, and Malthus writes a great deal about this unlucky Prince, the son of a mad father and a mother (a sister of George III of England) who was exiled for adultery when he was only four years old. He was to have a hard time of it, as he had a great admiration for Napoleon, as well as sympathising with his merchants' dislike of the behaviour of the British navy, and his punishment for

[1] Clarke, *Travels*, v, 1.

backing the wrong horse was having to cede the crown of Norway to Sweden in 1814.

The King of Sweden in 1799 was Gustav IV, then 20 years old; he had succeeded his father, Gustav III (who was assassinated in 1792) at the age of 13. Gustav IV seems to have been mentally unbalanced, and was in any case made a scapegoat for the troubles of the Napoleonic wars and the unhappy half-starved condition of Sweden generally: he was deposed in 1809, and his uncle was made first regent and then King, as Charles XIII; this poor man, then already senile, adopted as his heir Jean-Baptiste Jules, Marshal Bernadotte, who became Crown Prince Regent under the name of Charles John, and reigned as Charles XIV John from 1818 until his death in 1844.

In 1799 England's war with revolutionary France was still being waged against the Directory, five men who had nominally been governing the country since November 1795; General Bonaparte's military successes, however, were already making him the most powerful man in Europe, although his fleet had been defeated by Nelson in the Battle of the Nile, and Sir Sidney Smith had checked him when he besieged Acre in the spring of 1799. Pitt's second coalition against him, with Russia, Austria, Naples, and Turkey, was formed while he was in the Middle East: unknown to Malthus, Napoleon, having heard of this, was hastening back to France in the late summer of 1799, to be made First Consul before the year was out.

It could therefore be said that this party who, 'upon the 20th of May, took leave of a society whose members might truly be said to live together in fraternal harmony' were not lacking in courage: there was always the risk of being attacked at sea by a French privateer. They spent the first night of their journey at Bury St Edmunds, which Clarke said was 'a place no less remarkable for its ecclesiastical antiquities, than for the polished manners of its inhabitants'. According to him, they explored the Abbey before going to bed. The next day they reached Yarmouth, which Clarke thought resembled Genoa, 'in its narrow alleys full of shops'; as Yarmouth–Cuxhaven was the only 'avenue to the continent', 'its inns were crowded, and its haven thronged with ships'. On the 23rd the party boarded the packet *Diana* at 9 a.m.; the master, Captain Osborne, came on board at about noon.[1]

Clarke described their passage to Cuxhaven in 47 hours as 'uncommonly expeditious', but in fact another party had taken just the same time some eight months earlier. They were Coleridge (also

[1] Clarke, *Travels*, v, 1–7.

at one time a member of Jesus College, Cambridge) and William and Dorothy Wordsworth, who went to Hamburg immediately after the publication of the *Lyrical Ballads*, a book as epoch-making in its own sphere as Malthus's *Essay on Population*. They left Yarmouth at 11 a.m. on Sunday 15 September 1798 and reached Cuxhaven at ten on Tuesday morning. Dorothy thought Cuxhaven an 'ugly, black-looking place'.[1]

Clarke wrote to his mother from Hamburg on 28 May: 'What think you now of our flight? At Cambridge on the 20th; at Hamburg on the 25th. We had few alarms in the passage. Rather a stout gale, as you may suppose by our progress; but not more than the sailors desired. Twice we received signals to hoist our colours; and once we were boarded by the crew of an English-hired armed cutter. Otter suffered most in the voyage. Malthus bore it better than any one. Cripps made a good seaman, being always upon deck.'[2]

Thereafter let Malthus's Journal take up the story.

May 25. 1799. We arrived after a most favourable passage in 47 hours at Cruxhaven. As the wind & tide were in our favour, we were advised to embark immediately on board a Blankaness boat that we might reach Hamburgh the same evening before the gates were shut. Our passengers on board the packet were about sixteen, & consisted of French, German, Swiss & Italian. They all talked french well. Most of them had travelled & were well informed & entertaining. The Italian told us that when he first entered England, it appeared to him quite a new world; & superior to that which he had left. He said that we should not change for the better by travelling & that we should heartily wish our[selves] back again in 2 or 3 months.

A Swiss who had been lately at Paris gave us a reason for the conquest of Egypt by the French which I had not heard before. He said it was a plan of the directory to procure an asylum for themselves if the republick should fail. For without such a place; as all nations were so inveterate against them,[3] they could have no possible hope of escaping in the case of a counterevolution. I thought the idea rather ingenious.

At the entrance of the Elbe the shores are so extremely flat,

---

[1] Dorothy Wordsworth's *Journals*, ed. William Knight (London, 1925), p. 21.

[2] Otter, *Life and Remains of E. D. Clarke* (London, 1824), p. 345.

[3] Malthus started to write *nations of Europe*, altered it to *nations of the Earth*, and finally crossed out both.

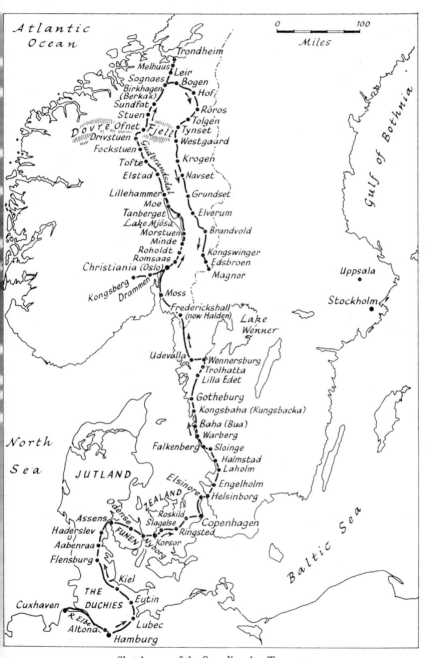

1   Sketch-map of the Scandinavian Tour, 1799

29

& the river so broad, that there are no marks by which a vessel can steer in the night. Had we arrived at the mouth of the Elbe at 10 oclock at night, the Captain told us that he must have waited till the morning before he could enter it. In hazy weather they are sometimes obliged to lie to for many days. The River opposite to Cruxhaven is about 10 leagues across, and the Shore on the side of Denmark so flat that we could not distinguish it. Almost all the party embarked on board the Blankaness vessel at about ½ past eleven. The wind had been high & cold, & the weather showry during the passage, (the Thermometer about 48). As we advanced up the river in our boat, the sky cleared & the wind sunk, which made our sail extremely pleasant.

We reached Hamburgh about half past 8 in the evening. The distance from Cruxhaven is about 70 english miles, which with the tide in our favour we completed in nine hours. We were told that there was a packet which generally attended passengers that arrived at Cruxhaven; the price is rather lower, but the Blankaness boats in going to Hamburgh outsail them by 2 or 3 hours. They are reckoned the fastest sailors on the river. They have one strong mast on which they carry a very large sail in the shape of a parrallelogram, the longest side in the direction of the mast. Towards the evening when the wind sunk lower they put out a three corner'd sail by the side of the mainsail. The prow runs extremely high, and they are sharp at both ends. The little cabin they have is forwards.[1]

When we were sufficiently advanced up the river to be able to see both shores distinctly, the banks on the side of Denmark appeared to be verdant to the water's edge, but very flat & with very few trees. Those on the Hanoverian shore were flat, but better wooded. On both sides, but particularly on the side of Denmark the villages, & separate cottages had an air of great neatness. They appeared to be built of brick, with many transverse wooden beams (what I believe is calle'd in England Brick nogin, only with more wood than is usually seen in such houses with us).[2] The roofs were very very large

---

[1] On the opposite page there is a small pencil drawing of a 'Blankaness boat'.

[2] According to the *O.E.D.* 'nogging' is 'brickwork built up between wooden quarters or framing'. The date of the noun is given as 1825; of the verb 'to nog' the date given is 1805.

& some of the gable ends of the houses painted green. About 14 or 15 english miles from Hamburgh the shores of the left bank began to rise. At first they were chiefly covered with heath, afterwards more trees were interspersed.

On arriving at the village of Blankaness, from which the boats which I have mentioned take their name, we were particularly struck with its picturesque beauty. It is situated on the Denmark side of the Elbe about ten English miles from Hamburgh. The shore is here of considerable height, & very well wooded, & the neat houses of the village seperated from each other by trees & gardens, & hanging as it were upon the cliff, formed a very delightful view. We were near the shore & saw many groups at their various occupations. One merry party seemed to be drinking under a tree. The dresses of the women, from their novelty, appeared to us picturesque,[1] the petticoats blue or red, of a different colour from the body, and very short. The master of our boat, who was a blankaness man, hailed his wife from the shore & brought forwards two or three of the groups to see us pass. It is difficult to judge of the happiness of a people through a telescope, which by the by we used to bring them near to us, but, influenced perhaps by the fineness of the evening & the beauty of the scene, we could not help fancying from the air of neatness & cheerfulness that seemed generally to prevail among the cottages, that the inhabitants were happy.

The master of our boat was a very good natured man. We amused ourselves with talking to him in English & found that there were many words which we could make him understand. He had a very foreign countenance, but not disagreeable, wore large dutch breeches, a tight waistcoat, a kind of cloth turban, & slippers. It was observed by some on board that he had a little the air of a chinese. His companion looked as foreign as himself & much more ugly; but his son, a boy about 10 or 12 yrs old, might have passed for a very handsome English boy.

The Hanoverian side of the Elbe opposite Blankaness, at some distance from the shore, rises into hills of moderate height covered with wood. All the way from Blankaness to Altona, the left bank of the river was thickly dotted with the country houses of the merchants of Hamburgh, & some we

---

[1] Malthus wrote, but crossed out, *& a little a la greque.*

understood had been built by the fortunes that had been made during the war. The shore continued of some height, & many of the houses appeared to be very agreeably situated. I could not help observing that the foliage of the trees appeared to be forwarder than in Cambridgeshire & Norfolk, thro which we had passed in our way to Yarmouth. I had observed, however, that the foliage in these counties seemed to be full a week later than in Surrey & about London. As we are travelling to the North just as the trees are coming into leaf, it appears to be a good opportunity of observing the comparative forwardness of the spring in the difft. countries thro which we pass, & I mean to pay some attention to this subject.

The sun was setting very beautifully just as we came within sight of the crouded shipping of Altona & Hamburgh, and the view both up & down the river was truely enchanting. Altona from the river appears to be a very neat & well built town, the houses high with a profusion of windows. The commerce of Altona & Hamburgh has increased so much since the war that their shipping, which joins, appears almost like the shipping in the Thames; but the river is much wider & finer.

After passing thro the crouded vessels we arrived at a boom which serves as a barrier, where were stationed three miserable looking soldiers, who desired us to give our names & characters. This we complied with, and when we arrived at the Inn a similar request was made, & papers were given to each of us to fill up. One of our passengers in the boat said his name was Moses, on which one of the soldiers asked him what was his religion; the man seemed to be a little puzzled by the question; but desired that he might be put down a christian.

On our arrival at the Inn we were introduced to a suite of three rooms in each of which was a bed in a recess. Another bed was to be placed in one of the rooms to make up the number wanted; and we were to make one of them our eating & sitting room. The price for the 3, was a guinea a night. We were told that every thing was very dear in Hamburgh & so indeed it appeared. The porters who brought our luggage from the boat in two barrows asked half a guinea for their trouble; but this was so exorbitant a demand that we refused to comply with it. We found the bedsteds so short, & the beds made so high at the head, that it was impossible to stretch oneself out

We heard in the Town that many of the poor were frozen in their houses. The government lays in a store of Corn & sells it to the poor at a reduced price during the winter. The price of corn in general has by no means risen in proportion to the price of other articles. Houses & Lodgings have increased almost five times. Meat about twice at present Mutton & beef are ~~about~~ 6 & 7 veal 10¼. We heard in the Town that there had been an accession of strangers since the war of 60 or 70 thousand, & that the pop^n of Hamburgh was nearly double what it was before the war. Dr M. thinks that there are great exaggerations on this subject, & that the pop^n does not perhaps amount to more than 120000. In the year 1790 the pop^n was estimated at 100000. The price of labour has risen ~~perhaps~~ higher in proportion, ~~than~~ the price of provisions. The lower classes of people seem to be in a good state, &

1. Page 17 of the first book of the Scandinavian Journal (actual size). It contains part of the entry for 29 May 1799. (See p. 36.)

2. Bernt Anker, from the portrait by Jens Juel, c. 1795.

3. John Collett, from the portrait by Carl Fr. von Breda, 1790.

4. Gudbrandsdal peasant dress from J. F. Eckersberg's book of
Norwegian costume (1852).

5. Cataract and bridge near the pass at Kringlen, from a sketch by E. D. Clarke, reproduced from his *Travels* (vol. v).

6. Mrs Lysholm, from the portrait by P. H. Kriebel.

7. General von Krogh (artist unknown).

8. Mrs Malthus, from the portrait by Linnell, 1833.

9. Emily Malthus, from the portrait by Linnell, 1833.

10. Okewood parish church, 1965.

Banns of Marriage between _Walter Riddal Bachelor & Ann Howell Spinster_
both of this Parish were publish'd on 16th Septr 2d & 9th 1792 by me W. Tothill Rector

No 116

Walter Riddal — — of this Parish _Bachelor_
and _Ann Howell_ — — — of this
Parish _Spinster_ — — were
Married in this _Church_ by _Banns_
this _twentieth_ — Day of _September_ in the Year One Thousand Seven
Hundred and _ninety two_ by me _W. Tothill Rector_

This Marriage was solemnized between Us { _Walter Riddal_
Ann Howell

In the Presence of _John Parker_
Ring Mayer

Banns of Marriage between _____

No 117

James May — — — of _this_ Parish _Bachelor_ — —
and _Catherine Mason_ — — of _this_
Parish _Spinster_ — — were
Married in this _Church_ — by _Licence_ — —
this _fourth_ — Day of _October_ in the Year One Thousand Seven
Hundred and _ninety two_ by me _W. Tothill Rector_

This Marriage was solemnized between Us { _The mark of × James May_
The mark of × Catherine Mason

In the Presence of _Richard Tarbott_
James Keen

Banns of Marriage between _Daniel Ranger Bachelor of this Parish & Martha Edsor_
of the Parish Ewhurst Spinster were publish'd April 21st & 28th & May 5th 1793 by me W. Tothill Rect

No 118

_____ and _____ of ___
Parish _____ were
Married in this _____ by _____
this _____ Day of _____ in the Year One Thousand Seven
Hundred and _____ by me _____

This Marriage was solemnized between Us { _____

In the Presence of _____

Banns of Marriage between _William Lowick Bachelor & Hannah Noyes Spinster_
both of this Parish were publish'd Sept 8th 15th & 22d 1793 by me W. Tothill Rect

No 119

William Lowick of this Parish _Bachelor_
and _Hanah Noyes_ of _this_
Parish _spinster_ were
Married in this _Church_ by _Bans_ _Robert Malthus Curate of Okewood_
this _third day_ Day of _October_ in the Year One Thousand Seven
Hundred and _ninety three_ by me _Robert Malthus Curate of Okewood Chapel_

This Marriage was solemnized between Us { _William Lowick B_
Hannah Noyes

In the Presence of _John Noyes_
Ann Francis

---

11. Page of the parish register of Albury. (See p. 6.)

12. Haileybury, from the London Road, reproduced from *Memorials of Old Haileybury* (Constable 1894).

in them, a luxury which we wished for after passing two nights without pulling off our cloaths.

Malthus's sociability on this, his first trip abroad, is in marked contrast to the behaviour of Coleridge and the Wordsworths. On the way up the Elbe, Dorothy wrote, 'We drank tea upon deck by the light of the moon. I enjoyed solitude and quietness, and many a recollected pleasure, hearing still the unintelligible jargon of many tongues that gabbled in the cabin.'[1]

May 26 [Sunday]. After breakfast which was served up a l'anglois, we took a walk in the Town. The houses are very high with a great number of windows, the gable ends generally placed towards the street, & the windows run up into the point. We often counted seven rows from the bottom to the top. The caps of the lower classes of women were formed of a broad stiff frill like a fan placed perpendicularly to the head, and passing the middle of the crown, leaving a great part of the head and hair uncovered in front, having upon the whole a very odd effect.[2] They appeared more various with regard to height, but in general rather shorter than English women— very fair, rather broad, & most of them marked with the small pox. The Town from the height of the houses, the narrowness of the streets, & the rows of dirty trees which are in them, has a sombre appearance, and the houses have an air of old fashioned magnificence. There is a fine bason of water to the North of the Town formed by the Alster, a small river which afterwards empties itself into the Elbe. By the side of the bason is the prettiest walk in the Town, which seems to be a kind of publick mall. The dresses of the men have nothing very peculiar in them; but you see continually many very odd figures, some with very large hats. The people in general look paler & more unhealthy than in England—this we remarked particularly with regard to the soldiers, & that they have in general high shoulders short necks & stoop a little.

We dined at the table d'hote of the Inn. The table was long,

---

[1] Dorothy Wordsworth, *Journals*, ed. E. de Selincourt (London, 1941), I, 19.
[2] On the opposite page there is a pencil drawing of the left profile of a woman wearing a pleated cap; the sketch just shows her head and shoulders, and a shopping basket on her left arm.

but the party small, and the dishes were handed round to us one after another, and not placed down the table. The eating part lasted near an hour and a half.

In the afternoon Otter & myself lost ourselves in the Town & had some difficulty to find our way to the Inn. We met with no persons who talked English or French. French is not so common in Hamburgh as I expected to find it.

We met the guard of the citizens on the ramparts. It consisted of the most miserable set of lame and old people that I ever beheld. The ditch that surrounds the town is very broad, but the fortifications much neglected.

Forenoon fine, afternoon rainy. Thermometer at 3, on a North window in the Town, 57. The Wych Elms which on the 20th at Cambridge had not opened their buds, were here very generally in small leaf. The limes round the Town had about half their full foliage—heard a nightingale.

May 27 [Monday]. Called upon Dr Mumssen whom I did not find at home, but met him in returning from Altona. He seems to be in great practice, & to have little leisure. Heard that the prices of most articles at Hamburgh had risen two hundred per cent since the war. Dined at the table d'hote, & went to the French Comedie in the evening where we were very much pleased with a mademoiselle Sevigné who played the part of Joseph in the two little Savoyards, very much in the style of Mrs Jordan. The comedy of the Conciliateurs ou l'homme aimable by Moustier we thought well acted. I expected to find the rhyme of the french comedie very disagreeable, but scarcely perceived it. The music was good. The leader of the band did not play upon any instrument himself, but merely beat time with much significant gesture. The little box just before the lamps for the prompter, does not much molest the audience, & is certainly much more convenient for the actors. Frequent hard and cold showers all day. Therm. at 2, 54.

Dorothy Wordsworth's account of the French theatre is very different: 'The piece a mixture of dull declamation and unmeaning rant. The ballet unintelligible to us, as the story was carried on in singing. The body of the house was imperfectly lighted, which has a very good effect in bringing out the stage, but as the acting was not very amusing, I should have been glad to have had a better view of the audience. We returned home in the 2nd Act of the Ballet.'[1]

May 28 [Tuesday]. Walked about the Town. It is full of narrow streets & close alleys, which makes it very difficult not to lose one's way—Went to the top of St Michael's Church, from which we had a good view of the Town & adjacent country. On the other side of the Elbe opposite Hamburgh, (a part of Lunenburgh) the country is extremely flat & marshy, & must be continually subject to inundations. The little girl that shew'd us the church had a very pretty face, & a most pleasing countenance, particularly when she said in her german, I dont understand you. Went to the French comedy in the evening, & was very much pleased with the performance of Pizarro. Madamoiselle Sevigné, & the performer of Pizarro, were excellent.

Cloudy all day with a few drops of rain. Therm. at 2, 51. Wind high, S.W.

May 29 [Wednesday]. Walked to Altona to call on Dr Mumssen —had an hour's very agreeable conversation with him before he went out to visit his patients. He told me that the profession of a phisician was by no means in high repute at Hamburgh & its invirons, that the fees were so low that it was impossible for a man, without other funds, to support a family upon them, unless he would consent to give up the society of gentlemen; which was the reason that very few men of liberal minds were to be found in the profession.

He observed that the war, by raising the price of all articles in so extraordinary a manner, had greatly oppressed those who had fixed incomes, & that the liberality of the Hamburghers had by no means increased in proportion to their riches. A great quantity of corn is imported into Hamburgh, from Dantzick & other parts of the Baltic, & much again exported. The Hamburghers, being rich, can always retain what they want.

During the last hard winter (harder than was ever remembered) no distress was suffered for want of provisions, tho

[1] *Journals*, ed. E. de Selincourt (London, 1941), I, 23.

much for want of fuel. We heard in the Town that many of the poor were frozen in their houses. The government lays in a store of Corn & sells it to the poor at a reduced price during the winter. The price of corn in general has by no means risen in proportion to the price of other articles. Houses & Lodgings have increased almost five times. Meat about twice. At present Mutton & beef are 6*d*. & 7*d*., veal 10*d*. Fine sugar is now 2*s*. & 2*s*. 1*d*. per pound. Five years ago it was only 7 or 8. Coffee has risen in the same proportion. It is now 2 marks a pound. Butter was formerly 7*d*. & 8*d*., now a marc—(1*s*. 4*d*.).

We heard in the Town that there had been an accession of strangers since the war of 60 or 70 thousand, & that the popn of Hamburgh was nearly double what it was before the war. Dr M. thinks that there are great exaggerations on this subject, & that the popn does not perhaps amount to more than 120,000. In the year 1790 the popn was estimated at 100,000. The price of labour has risen higher in proportion, than the price of provisions. The lower classes of people seem to be in a good state, & are in general dressed clean & neat, particularly the women. Many of the common maid servants look as if they were always in their sunday apparel. In my walk to Altona & back, I met many very agreeable faces. The country girls have a little of the Flanders make in their persons, & are sleek and plump like the horses of the country. We remarked, by the by, a great number of very beautiful horses in the carriages.

Dr Mumssen observed that the government of Hamburgh was almost a model & that a citizen has as much liberty as could be desired. One proof of its excellency was, that there had been no dispute between the people & the Senate for the last century. The content & satisfaction which the people feel in the government was the reason, he said, that from the beginning they were in general averse to the french revolution. Not feeling themselves oppressed they did not conceive that the French were, & concluded therefore that the revolution proceeded solely from a foolish desire of Change. He said that the Emperor of Russia had certainly been completely misinformed in supposing that Hamburgh was the foyer of Democrats. This affair however is now said to be on the point of being settled.

Much distress has been felt in all the adjacent country from the wet spring, particularly in Jutland, where they have been obliged to drive all their cattle to the heaths to save them from the inundations. The lower parts of Hamburgh itself have often sufferred much from floods.

Accepted an invitation to dine on thursday at Mr Voght's in company with Dr Mumssen.

After returning from Altona took a walk by the side of the great Bason or lake that is formed by the Alster. It is a very fine piece of water, but of a colour as if the river had run over moors. The gardens on the borders are laid out in the dutch style. We walked in some of them, & heard a great many nightingales, which appeared to be less shy than with us. As a base to the nightingales we heard some frogs croaking in a most extraordinary manner. The note was so distinct & almost articulate, that it was a long while before we could persuade ourselves that it could proceed from a frog. It was most like the quacking of a duck.

Dined at a french Restaurateur's. Went to the French comedy, & saw a new ballet very well performed for the benefit of the principal female dancer Rose Colinet. Supped at the Caffé Chinois where we had a fine view of the lake, which was enlivened by many boats sailing on it. A fete of Freemasons on the other [side] of the water, with fireworks, contributed to our entertainment; but we paid pretty dearly for our supper. 3 marks a head besides wine. The man proposed four marks, tho we told him that we were no supper eaters. In the summer when the lake is covered with boats, the scene must be very beautiful.

Fine all day. Therm. at half past 2, 63.

May 30 [Thursday]. Call'd upon Dr Mumssen at 2 to go to Mr Voht's; found that he had put off his party. Dined at a Mr Thornton's instead, who received us, tho totally unexpected, with great hospitality.[1] His wife, a very lively little

---

[1] It seems likely that 'Mr Thornton' was one of the members of the firm of Thornton and Power, Hamburg merchants and members of the Right Worshipful Company of Merchant Adventurers Residing in Hamburg. Richard Thornton of that firm was Deputy Governor of the Company, 1788–98, and it may well have been he who entertained Malthus. (See *Works and Correspondence of David Ricardo* (ed. P. Sraffa), III, 430–1, and H. Hitzigrath, *Die Compagnie der Merchants Adventurers und die englische Kirchengemeinde in Hamburg, 1611–35, passim.*)

woman with a folatre manner, sung german, Italian & French airs to the Piano Forte.

Heard from Mr T. that the interest of money had lately been 11 or 12 per cent. The merchants of Hamburgh were obliged to borrow money at any rate to pay for goods consigned to them from England. This extraordinary rise of interest had only taken place during the last five or six months, and is expected to be merely temperary. The cause of it is supposed to be, the purchase of a great quantity of Hamburgh bank money by the English Government, to send to the Emperor.[1] This Banco money has been purchased by consignment of English goods, & till these are sold & the bullion again placed in the bank, money will continue very scarce at Hamburgh and the interest very high. The bank of Hamburgh is merely a bank of deposit, & transfer, & issues no paper whatever. A merchant places a certain quantity of pure silver in the bank, and has credit for a certain number of marks banco. The transfer of this capital forms the grand medium of circulation in the purchase of merchandise. A high penalty is attached to overdrawing, so that there are no merchants' bills in circulation that are not actually represented by bullion in the bank. It follows that if this bullion be drawn out of the bank and sent away, (as is said to be the case lately) capital must be scarce, & the interest of money rise.

A mark banco is the weight of a mark in pure silver, & therefore banco money is always above currency. Spanish dollars or bars of silver are the most common form of the bullion in the bank. Currency is sent very rarely as it must be melted & assayed before it be admitted. The bank gains no kind of profit whatever. The expences of the clerks &c are paid by a small per centage when the money is drawn out. At present 3 marks banco are worth 3 marks 12 sou's currency. Banco is 25 per cent higher than currency. Before the late extraordinary rise, the interest of money was only 3 or 4 per cent, & had not been much affected either way, by the war.

The government of Hamburgh is rather complicated. The executive power & much of the Legislative resides in the Senate, which consists of 4 Burgomasters, 24 senators & 4

---

[1] Pitt was subsidising both the Hapsburg Emperor and the Czar against the French.

syndicts. The Burgomasters are in turns presidents of the Senate & act as magistrates in the Town. The Syndicts are in a manner secretarys, and have the department of foreign affairs. The Burgom^s are elected from the Senate, & the Senators are elected for life by themselves, according to a particular process. When a senator dies, four electors are named, who each mention one person.

Morning fine, warm. Therm. at 10, 65. Thunder shower at 3, afternoon rainy. The therm must have been high at 2., but I did not see it. In returning from dinner, we saw a very beautiful place by the side of the Elbe about half a mile beyond Altona, laid out with much taste. I observed the oak & the ash both in small leaf. I had seen none so forward about Hamburgh. The wych Elms in this country seem to be forwarder in propn to the other trees than in England. The Lombardy poplars in the garden by the lake were but little forwarder than those at Albury when I left it. The beeches nearly in the same state. The ashes on the ramparts of the Town were to day just beginning to open their buds. I have not remarked any of our common elms.

The therm. on Xmas day last winter was, according to Dr Mumssen, 18 Reaumur. This was the lowest during the winter. In the summer of 1793 the therm was 25 Reaumur.[1]

The gentlemen who have houses along the banks of the river beyond Altona are subject to the King of Denmark;[2] but the taxes are extremely moderate, and a little understanding with the Bailly settles matters very easily. It seems to be agreed that the King of Denmark, tho by law the most despotic monarch of Europe, has the least power of exercising that despotism.

Dr M. is publick physician to a district adjacent to Altona, for which he receives however only a salary from Government of 25£ per annum. He is obliged to attend in case of any

[1] Malthus should, of course, have written '−18 Reaumur' or '18 degrees below zero'; he was very careless about this throughout his journals, except on p. 113. (−18° R = −8·5° F and 25° R = 88° F.)

[2] It will be remembered that at this time the Duchies of Schleswig and Holstein owed allegiance to the King of Denmark as their Duke. Many of the inhabitants (especially the Holsteiners) were of German origin, and spoke German, and German influence generally was very strong throughout the whole of the Danish kingdom.

epidemic, & when any person dies a violent death (something like our Coroner's inquest). He visits also all apothecarys' shops to see that their medicines are good.[1] The regulated fees of a physician, are only a shilling a visit.

May 31 [Friday]. Cloudy with few drops of rain. Therm. at 2, 62.

Police extraordinarily good. Murder scarcely ever heard of—robbery very seldom. The precautions against fire very effectual.[2]

Dorothy Wordsworth also admired the good order of Hamburg; in her diary she comments unconsciously on the state of English towns at the end of the eighteenth century: 'During my residence in Hamburgh I have never seen anything like a quarrel in the streets but once, and that was so trifling that it would scarcely have been noticed in England. I have never seen a drunken man, nor a woman of the lower orders who was not perfectly decent and modest in her appearance and manners.' Later on she did see a drunken man, and a beggar, and on the following day a man beating a woman 'in the public street'.[3]

June 1 [Saturday]. Left Hamburgh at 8 in a post waggon with four horses, the driver riding on the near wheel horse, & managing the other two with a small cord rein & a long whip —the cord traces between the wheel horses & foremost pair extremely long. The first village we came to about 2 english miles from Hamburgh—extremely neat—houses low with large roofs. The people sitting at the doors & windows looked very clean & comfortable. Flat corn country—a little like Cambridgeshire. Observed rye in ear.

Country afterwards more barren, with much heath interspersed. Soil sandy. Road a sand with deep ruts & a most exercrable pavement in the middle. Observed the oak pretty generally in small leaf—ash hardly opened. Therm at 9, held in my hand in the waggon, 64. Wind. S.E. The cattle appeared

---

[1] Malthus first wrote, *to see that their medicines do good*.

[2] Malthus wrote the word *Police* in ink, but continued his jottings again in pencil. Three whole pages of the notebook are then left blank; he must have meant to write an account of what the party did on 31 May, but never had time to set it down.

[3] *Journals*, ed. E. de Selincourt (London, 1941), I, 25.

very small and poor. Sheep less than the welsh breed & lambs very backward. The Viola tricolor, the viola Canina, the ranunculus aquaticus were larger & finer than they usually are in England; and Otter observed some plants in a flourishing state that had been out of flower some time before he left Cambridgeshire, tho the trees did not appear to be later in leafing.

Before we came to Schoenberg the place where we baited & dined, the country changed & became a little like parts of Surrey. Hills, Sandy roads, Heath & beech woods,[1] and here & there a large pond or little lake interspersed. The houses are large barns with immense thatched roofs & folding doors, & an inclosed part at the end for the family. The horses, cows, pigs, fowls &c live in the barn part, & the people themselves sit there in the summer. The degree of poverty among the people seemed to be nearly the same as in the general run of villages in England. Some of the children with stockings— some without. Common price of labour 1s., & a marc, or 1s. 4d. a day. The common bread used is made entirely of rye, & is rather black. The driver of our waggon baited his horses almost every german mile with large slices of this bread.[2]

The wells to most of the houses are worked by a large lever, which looks rather picturesque, & seems to be convenient enough for shallow well, but would not do for a deep one.[3]

At Schoenberg where we stopped to dine we found a large party of travellers, all in waggons, except one english post-chaise. We had our dinner at a mark a head in a room with four beds in it, but as it had plenty of windows it was tolerably airy. Pretty good old Hoc at 2 marks. Our host talked french & english. The women shuffle about in slippers that but just cover their toes, & do not come to the end of their heels.

Most of the cottages have gardens and orchards to them, & the houses in the villages are scattered—none joined. We saw two or three storks flying & afterwards one on her nest at the top of a house. It is reckoned a very fortunate sign. Many

---

[1] Malthus put an asterisk here, and wrote on the opposite page, 'The beech woods were almost in full foliage, but a great many of the oaks not out, & hardly any of the ashes.'

[2] A German mile was 4⅛ English miles.

[3] On the opposite page is a rough sketch in ink of a well with a lever.

of the villages were without churches. We met some waggons drawn by six horses, three abreast, & the driver riding on the near wheel horse. With a very heavy load they sometimes put another pair before. We saw a very picturesque mother walking with short petticoats & bare legs & neck, with ten children round her. The country near Lubec grows again flat, & has some fine pasture land—The cattle large.

The fortifications of Lubec seem to be in better preservation than of Hamburgh. On entering the Town we came into a fine broad street, with the houses built a little in the same style as those of Hamburgh; but handsomer—the tops of them looking almost like Gothic spires. We had been most thoroughly jolted—almost all the way more than on the box of a mail coach over the worst pavement in London; but did not feel much fatigue the next morning.

Fine & fair. Wind S.E. Therm. at 1, in shade, 67.

June 2 [Sunday]. Walked a little about Lubec. Went to the Cathedral, a handsome Gothic building plain in architecture but much ornamented with guilded monuments, a very brilliant organ, & old pictures, the grounds of many of which are Gold. There is also a most extraordinary clock dated 1404, with a curious perpetual almanack below, & above a figure of our saviour. When the clock strikes twelve, the 12 apostles come out of a folding door, walk round the figure of our saviour, bow as they pass him, & enter into a folding door on the opposite side.

There are many old & superb monuments of the consuls of Lubec, among the rest one of the name of Gotscald, pro-cunsal, dated 1683.

We met with the greatest hospitality from a Mr Paisly, to whom we had no other introduction than one of Sir Robert Herries's notes. He insisted upon our all four dining with him at his garden without the ramparts, where we met a party of 21 people. We heard that the government of Lubec was quite upon the model of Hamburgh, & that the people had as much liberty as could be desired. The greatest part of the inhabitants are in politics highly averse to the French. There are some young men however of another way of thinking. The port of Lubec has been purposely stopt up so as to prevent the admission of Ships of War. It is generally thought that the King of Prussia could take possession of Lubec whenever he pleased. Some goods from Lubec are sent to Hamburgh up the River Steiknitz which falls into the Elbe; but the route is circuitous, & the river Steiknitz only navigable for very small vessels. The greatest part of the goods is sent by land in waggons with sometimes 9 horses, 3 abreast.

The caps of the women at Lubec, which are a kind of muslin bonnet with the prominence behind instead of before, have their cauls almost covered with a broad lace of gold.[1] We saw a woman coming out of a cottage, looking very poor in other respects, who yet had this ornament to her cap.

At a little after four we left Lubec for Eutin. The first village we came to, about a mile english from Lubec, was extremely neat. Many of the houses appeared to be new & many more building. They mix the bricks with the woodwork, so that the pointing forms lines and angles in various directions, which gives the houses an odd dutch-like appearance. Soon after we left this village the road became extremely bad—very deep holes of muddy sand. Had it not been for the length of the waggon we should certainly have been overturned. We had four very fine black horses with long tails, which wherever the road was tolerable, got on at a very good rate. The country soon became uneven, a little like parts of Surrey, only with more pasture & less heath. On the banks of the hedges we observed a great many wild currants. The farm houses were very large, & many of them new. The kind of barn & cottage together, which we had remarked all the way from Hamburgh to Lubec, & which continued with slight variations, on this road, must be much more expensive in building than our cottages in England. We saw the frames of some of them before the bricks were added, & they appeared to take a great deal of timber, & some workmanship. Some of the houses on this road were contiguous. When we were about a german mile from Lubec we drove with our waggon & four into one of these large halls, to bait. We found a party at cards tho it was

---

[1] The second of the Scandinavian paper-covered journals starts in mid sentence with the words *cauls almost covered with a broad lace of gold*. At the end of the first book there are two sketches, one in ink and one in pencil, of the left profiles of women wearing the caps described—they look a little like sou'westers. There is a third sketch, in ink, labelled 'a back view'.

sunday, all in their nightcaps & with pipes. They seemed very intent upon their game, & tho we had created some kind of stare in the village, they would hardly vouchsafe us a single look, tho we stood behind their chairs some time. We saw a great number of healthy fine looking children in the village. As we proceeded, the country improved & was interspersed with lakes, beech woods, & hills. The hills however were not high, & some of the lakes might perhaps deserve only the appellation of marshy ponds. As we approached Eutin we came to lakes of a different character; but we had left Lubec rather too late & it was hardly light enough to see their particular beauties; but perhaps more was gained than lost by what was supplied by imagination. We heard many nightingales, and a continual chorus of frogs from the lakes & small pounds. The noise was like the quacking of innumerable broods of ducks. The first view of the Town of Eutin is very pretty, & the lake a noble piece of water. Slept at a neat Inn on the borders of the lake—did not find any body that spoke french or english, but contrived to make ourselves understood.

Fine & fair except a slight thunder shower about half past four.

June 3 [Monday]. Rose at half past five; but could not get off before 8 on account of disputes about the Denmark paper money, which the waggon master would not take. Passed thro a beautiful country for two or three miles, with fine views of the lakes of Eutin & [the next word is illegible but was probably *Plön*]—woody & irregular shores. After we left the two great lakes the country had a little the air of parts of Kent —short woody hills with well cultivated fields interspersed— much rye that was just coming into ear.

About 11 we reached Prae's, the half way Town between Eutin & Kiel.[1] It is remarkably neat & clean. The gable ends of the houses all towards the street & the pointings of the bricks making lines & angles in all directions. Many of the houses were new, and there were fewer poor looking houses than in the generality of our towns of the same size. The features of the women appeared to be changing, & not to be so much marked

---

[1] This was probably Preetz (called by Clarke *Pruz*). It is in fact much nearer to Kiel than to Eutin.

by the characteristic features which we had generally observed
—the broad face, nose rather small & turned up, blue eyes, &
light eyebrows. At Praes I understood that the price of labour
was 1s. & 16d. The farms are very large, & the peasants not all
yet liberated, tho the work is going on. There were some women
without stockings, but hardly any signs of squalid poverty.
After leaving Praes we went thro a fine forest of beech wood
interspersed with oak—some very fine timber. All the way
from Eutin to Kiel there was nothing characteristic in the
appearance of the country. In the mode of cultivation, in the
hedges & ditches, & in the kind of trees in the hedge-rows, it
resembled exactly many parts of England.

Dined and slept at Kiel, situated on an inland bay of the
Baltic. The bay is so land-locked that it appears like a lake.
The shores are irregular & in some parts finely wooded, so as
to make the environs of Kiel very beautiful. Walked to the
old Palace of the Duke of Holstein, part of which is at present
inhabited by the Commandant, & part forms an auditory, &
lecture rooms for Anatomy &c belonging to the college. There
is an inscription over one of the doors, purporting that the
building was restored in 1766 by Catherine the 2nd, Empress
of Russia.[1] The gardens are well situated by the side of the bay
but are in a formal style. They seem to be the public promenade
of the Town.

In the evening we took a walk to see the famous canal. We
were told that it was only half an hour's walk, but found it near
an hour and a half. Feeling rather fatigued, we wished that
we might be so fortunate as to find a boat that would take us
to Kiel by water, as it was a most delightful evening, & the
bay had presented to us in our walk some very beautiful views.
We had some difficulty in making ourselves understood; but
at last were introduced to a sailor who talked English, & who
was just going to take two gentlemen by water to Kiel. We
accepted with great joy places in the boat; but were told that
we ought not to return to Kiel without seeing the sluice which

---

[1] The ducal palace and the university buildings of Kiel were completely demolished in the Second World War. Kiel was the seat of the Dukes of Holstein-
Gottorp from 1721 to 1773, and was inherited by Paul, the son of Catherine the
Great of Russia; she, however, had ceded Holstein-Gottorp to the King of Denmark in 1767—the year after her restoration of the buildings of the seventeenth-
century university.

45

was about a quarter or half a mile from the mouth of the canal. The gentlemen promised to wait for us.

The sluice is a fine compact well constructed work, but has nothing in it very peculiar, as it consists of only one lock, the fall of water not being above 12 or 14 feet. There is a side sluice to let off the superfluous water, & from an opening in this cut the lock is filled in 5 minutes. The Canal is ten feet in depth, & admits vessels of three hundred tuns burden, so that there is no necessity, except in very particular cases, for unloading & loading again. The same vessels that navigate the german ocean & the Baltic can pass the canal. We had heard that the banks of the Canal had often suffered, and the navigation been interrupted, but it appears that the number of vessels that pass the canal is increasing every year. The tolls are very trifling, only 8 shillings & fourpence for every vessel, which is paid either at Kiel or Rentsbergh. This money is laid out in paying the persons who attend, & other expenses relating to the canal. The return to the King of Denmark is solely from the Customs, & these are rather high.

We did not set off to return to Kiel till near nine oclock; this was rather late for a water party; but the bay was so still & serena, the evening so enchanting, and the bright streaks of twilight gave such softness to the picture, that we could not regret the expedition tho we did not arrive at Kiel till eleven.

Fair & fine except a heavy shower at 5 in the morning. Therm. at 9, 61; at half past 12, 63.

June 4 [Tuesday]. We left Kiel at six. Past thro a flat country —soil chiefly sandy with many new inclosures sown with rye. Saw a stork at the top of a low house feeding her young, she let us come near her without alarm; 2 or 3 more passed pretty near us on the wing. We observed that the houses were smaller and not so neat as those from Lubec to Kiel. Fewer were built with the large barns that have been mentioned. We met some women about Kiel & on this road without stockings, but looking rather neat. About a mile before we reached Eckenburgh we passed thro a fine forest of beech interspers'd with oak. Some of the oaks were large & the beeches the finest, & with the tallest and straitest stems, that I have ever seen.

The opening on the bay of Ekenberg is very pretty, tho the town itself is not a very picturesque object, being covered with red tiles.[1] At Eckenbergh we made an early dinner & took horses for Flensburgh, $7\frac{1}{2}$ german miles. We had hitherto travelled in one waggon & four horses; but here we were recommended to take two waggons with a pair each, for fear of breaking down. We put all our luggage in one & ourselves in the other & proceeded very comfortably. We had observed that the features of the people had been rather changing, and at Ekenbergh we were particularly struck with a great number of faces so perfectly english that we could hardly persuade ourselves that we were not in an English Town.

After leaving Eckenburgh we passed over some hilly ground interspersed with heath and down—the soil sandy & rather barren. Houses smaller & shabbier, much like middling English cottages. We saw many peasants with wooden shoes made in a very awkward manner, and very low at the heel in proportion to the toe. In about [blank] miles from Eckinbergh we passed a pretty arm of the sea at the end of which Sleswick is situated. The passage was not above 40 yrds over. The country after crossing was pretty; moderate hills well wooded. The mode of cultivation & enclosures exactly like many parts of England, and the roads sandy, & as good as the generality of private roads with us. Wooden shoes became more general and the women sometimes shuffled along in wooden slippers into which they could put only the point of the foot. No appearance however of great poverty.[2] We arrived at Flensbergh in a hard shower of rain which had wetted us through, & found a tolerable inn, tho not remarkably clean.[3]

Morning fine. Therm. at 6, 57; at half past 12, 60. After-noon hard rain. Wind cold, S.W.

June 5 [Wednesday]. We set off early for Abenrae. The Town of Flensburgh is prettily situated on one of the numerous bays of the baltic, and carries on some commerce, which appears

[1] 'Ekenberg' is Eckernförde.
[2] Malthus first wrote *squalid poverty*.
[3] Clarke wrote of Flensberg, '. . . a dirty inn. The next morning, we observed other public houses, with an outward appearance of cleanliness, and even of elegance.' According to him, they left before six the next day to go on to 'Apenrade', now Aabenraa (*Travels*, v, 51).

now to be increasing, from the number of new houses that we observed building. The bricks were small & almost white—not very well made—the houses built in the English fashion. Not long after leaving Flensbergh we passed a very extensive desolate heath, with only a shabby inclosure here & there. They appeared to be new. By the side of the road at certain intervals were erected polls about 20 feet high with large lamps upon them, which we supposed were meant to direct the post waggons in the snows.

After quitting so barren a heath we were much struck, upon breaking all at once on the beautiful Bay of Abenrae, surrounded by high banks of fine wood, chiefly beech. All the bays that we passed were nearly landlocked and appeared like so many fine lakes. Took two waggons for Adersleben.[1] The waggons were growing smaller and it became always necessary to have two. About half way up the hill from Abenrae the view back was extremely beautiful and you seemed to look on a fine lake encircled by hills and woods in the finest shapes. The prevailing tree was beech which was nearly in full foliage; but the oaks and the ash had hardly any appearance of green.

The country afterwards to Hadersleben was rather pretty but not in any respect particular. At Hadersleben, as the wind was favourable for crossing the nearest passage of the little belt, we determined to go on to Assens the same evening. We embarked 2 german miles from Hadersleben at about half past six, and had a very delightful sail to Assens where we arrived about 8.[2] In the vessel we met with a gentleman who talked english & french and seemed to be well informed as to the state of Holstein & Sleswic. We had been particularly struck with the neat & cleanly appearance of the peasantry and the goodness of the houses in Holstein, and we were informed by this gentleman that they were at present in a remarkably good state, and that you might drink a dish of coffee with them, in as neat a manner as at a good inn. The riches that have poured into this country from its neutrality during the

---

[1] On modern maps 'Adersleben' is spelt Haderslev.

[2] Clarke said that the passage from Arroe-sund across the Lesser Belt (from Jutland to Fünen) was nine English miles, and took two hours with gentle but favourable winds (*Travels*, v, 55).

war has diffused itself among the peasants, & many of them he said, possess'd plate.[1] All traces of slavery had, he said, for some time been abolished in Holstein & Slewick; & more lately in Jutland and the other parts of Denmark. The emancipation at first entirely depended on the will of the nobles, but latterly it has been a measure of Government.[2] Holstein and Sleswick seem at present to be very thriving provinces. Last year from Holstein, Sleswic & Jutland were exported 20,000 horses.

Therm at 5, 50; at half past 12, 53. Frequent slight showers. Evening fine. S.W.

June 6 [Thursday]. At Assens we found a tolerable good inn. The house was capacious; but the room rather dirty. We left Assens at a quarter before five, & proceeded for Odensee the capital of Funen. The country was, during the first part of the road, a large common field; after wards there were inclosures made merely of banks, the summits of which were in serpentine curves, following the shape of the ridges of the lands. Through the whole way the country was remarkably bare of trees. The cottages were exactly like English cottages formed of mud or brick, whitewashed with thatched roofs, & much smaller & less neat than those of Holstein & Sleswic. Our Danish Ancestors were probably a stout race as their descendants here still retain a very robust make. The men had most of them very broad shoulders and good countenances; and the women were a little in the same way. Men, women & children wear wooden shoes which from their awkward make prevent them from walking with any tolerable ease.[3]

Odensee seems to have no other great marks of antiquity about it than its name, which imports that it was the seat of Oden. We walked to the Church, which is rather handsome, to look for the tomb of Christian the second, but as the clerk could not understand us, & as we could not read the Danish inscriptions, we did not find much to interest us.

[1] Malthus put an asterisk here, and wrote on the opposite page, 'This I found afterwards to be a mistake.'

[2] Serfdom was formally abolished in Denmark in 1788, and in the Duchies between 1797 and 1805.

[3] Malthus at first wrote *prevent them from walking with much grace.*

The Church at Odense would have been the thirteenth-century brick Cathedral, described in the guide-books as the largest and most beautiful Gothic building in Denmark.

Christian II was King of Denmark, Norway and Sweden from 1513 to 1523; in 1531 he was captured by a rival faction, led by his uncle who became Frederick I of Denmark and Norway, and survived for twenty-seven years in castle dungeons. He is famous for having executed, in the most treacherous way, eighty-two Swedish noblemen who had assembled for his coronation; this 'bloodbath of Stockholm' was one of the incidents which led Sweden, under Gustav Vasa, to break away from the rule of Denmark.

According to Archdeacon Coxe, the 'cruel and unfortunate' Christian II is 'entombed near his father under a plain grave-stone, somewhat raised, but without any inscription'.[1]

The common people seem to be very fond of red, & most of them wear red woollen bodies & sleeves & blue petticoats, or blue bodies & red petticoats, which gives them rather a neat appearance. On their heads they wear large broad white fillets, generally very clean, with the ends hanging on their shoulders. This costume extends over part of Sleswic, & through Funen & Zealand. It is pretty general, but not worn by all.

We left Odensee about 2 and passed thro the same kind of country, tho rather more diversified by inclosures, to Nyburgh, 4 miles, where we arrived about 6, in a beautiful afternoon with not much wind; but what we had was fair for crossing the great Belt. In Nyburgh a great number of new houses were building—the Inn seemed to be new & pretty good.

We embarked about seven, and in a short time had the sea as smooth as glass.[2] The apprehension of being becalmed did not prevent us from enjoying the beauty of the scene & of the evening. Many parts of the shore were woody tho flat; and to beguile the time during our slow progress we had one of the finest sunsettings that I had ever seen. We were much pleased with the expressions of rapture which a young lady from Berlin [?] made use of, who had never been on the sea before, & who seemed enchanted with the beauty of the scene. When

---

[1] Coxe, *Travels*, v, 282–3.

[2] Clarke recorded that crossing the Greater Belt, from Fünen to Zealand, took four hours. He gave the distance as 18 miles (*Travels*, v, 59).

the sun was set, the wind freshened, & we arrived after a very pleasant passage at Corsoer, where Otter & I determined to pass the night; but Clarke & Cripps not much liking their beds & being in haste to get to Copenhagen ordered horses to go on.[1]

The[r]m at ½ past four, 48; at 9, 62; at 2, 67. Fine. S.

June 7 [Friday]. Intended to have left Corsoer early; but on account of some difficulties about our passport, which we thought we had lost, did not get off much before 8. Proceeded to Slagelsee 2 miles thro an open country, & scarcely a single enclosure—soil a moist & in parts tolerably rich sand, mostly in Corn—the barley and oats not 3 inches high.

Paid for the waggon & 2 horses, 2 dollars, and gave the driver 2 Danish marks equal to 1s. 4d., which we found was more than was customary. From Slagelsee proceeded to Ringstead, 4 miles, thro the same kind of country, except about midway where we passed two lakes, the first of which was almost entirely surrounded with beech woods & the second was enriched with them on one side. For about an english mile before we came to these lakes, we had seen some extensive woods at a distance on each side, & they appeared to meet here. Having passed so uninteresting a country, the lakes appeared to us very pretty. After another interval of bare country, the woods which we still saw at a distance again met, and we passed for half a mile through some pretty forest scenery, chiefly of beech. Here we observed 2 or 3 storks' nests, on the tops of some old oaks. A male & female on an oak not far from us were standing in their nest, & feeding their young. They looked very large when they were on the wing near us. The oaks in small leaf, rather forwarder than the oaks near Hamburgh, tho in parts of Funnen & Sleswick many of the oaks had no appearance of green.

We took a slight dinner at Ringsted while our waggon was preparing, for which with a bottle of common wine they made us pay 2 rix-dollars which we thought very exorbitant. We had

---

[1] Clarke's published account of the split in the party at Korsör is a little different: 'The long twilight of the *North* began already to allow of our travelling with equal convenience by night as by day: we therefore left Corsoërs two hours after midnight, in a large open waggon, which also carried all our luggage' (*Travels*, v, 59).

travelled the four german miles, about 18 english, for the same sum. Proceeded thro the same kind of open uninclosed country to Roskild. The cottages were very poor built, chiefly of mud, & some tumbling down; and the peasants had much more an air of poverty than any we had hitherto remarked.

In three out of the four stages across Zealand we had drivers that were very good specimens of Danish louts. Their countenances were completely expressive of their stupidity, & even the promise of a good Drinkgelt could not rouse them from their lethargy. At Slagelsee we had met with some Frenchmen who were travelling, & who said that if you meant to describe all the ill qualities that a man could possess, it was sufficient to say that he was a Danois; but till we were in Zealand we had observed nothing of the kind, & then, nothing that could make us draw so very unfavourable an inference against the whole nation.

As there are scarcely any inclosures thro that part of Zealand which we passed, & as corn & pasture are in consequence necessarily mixed, all animals are tethered. The cattle were in general small & poor, and the horses of the same character. The Roiston crow with a brown back was frequent here. In Sleswick & among some of the paysannes of Funen & Zealand we observed a form of bonnet very much like one that was lately in fashion among our ladies.[1] We observed black cattle, sheep, pigs, geese, all tied either by the head or the legs— generally by the head. The road from one side of Zealand to the other is very good, except the last stage to Copenhagen which is marked with a number of shallow ruts. It is elevated considerably, & must have been made at a great expence, as the soil is in many parts wet.

At Roskild we went to see the tombs of the Kings of Denmark. The coffins in the vaults are very superbly ornamented with velvet, gold, and silver. Some of them, particularly four children of the present Prince royal, are very fresh, and look very handsome; but others exibit only the tattered remains of Grandeur. It seems absurd to form of such perishable materials objects that are meant to be shewn to posterity. We saw the

---

[1] Below this passage are two pencil sketches of the left profiles of women: one has her face completely hidden in a sort of poke-bonnet, the other is wearing a head-dress more like a veil or hood.

tomb of the famous Margaret of Valdemar & expressed our surprise at its being in such high preservation; but were told that an artist was paid to repair it every year. There are two handsome Alabaster monuments of Christian the 3rd & Fredc. the second, executed in Italy, the sculpture of which seems to be good, & two of Fredc. 4th & his wife, by Danish sculptors, that are not bad.

The twelfth-century Cathedral of Roskilde is the most important national monument in Denmark; it stands on the site on which the first Danish Christian church was built in 960. Today it contains the coffins of thirty-six kings and queens, and a hundred other people of royal blood.

'Margaret of Valdemar' was the daughter of Waldemar IV of Denmark, who was married at the age of ten, in 1363, to Haakon VI of Norway; it was she who had her great-nephew, Eric of Pomerania, crowned King of Denmark, Norway and Sweden at Kalmar in 1397.

A little old gentleman that Clarke had found out & to whom he recommended us served as an interpreter in bad french; but he was so tedious, & found in his heart to bestow so much of it upon us, that we set off from Roskild but just in time to save the gates of Copenhagen, where we arrived a little after 12. The customs-house officers came with us to the Inn, the Royal Hotel, and as they did not seem disposed to be very civil, we let them rummage our trunks & portmanteau's, determined not to give them a farthing. They went away with an air rather capot. We had been so completely broiled by the hot sun & white roads during the last two days that our faces were allmost flead, & my eyes were so inflamed that I determined to give myself a whole day's rest, and not to look at anything till I could see a little clearer.

Therm. at 8, 55; at 9, 62; at 3, 67. Wind S.W.

June 8 [Saturday]. Rested ourselves the greatest part of the morning—dined at the table d hote where we found rather a large & noisy party, among others were one or two frenchmen with national cockades. They spoke of the great liberty every person enjoyed here of saying what they please. One of these gentlemen, we found afterwards, was much averse to the directory in his real sentiments, tho he was a violent democrat in publick.

Walked about the town in the evening which has been improved and the streets made wider since the great fire.[1] The grand palace which, as the inscription imparts, was built by Christian the 6th for the residence of the future Kings of Denmark is a melancholy object. Chris. 6th. Regiam hanc intra septem annorum spatium, abque subditorum onere exstructam suaeque ac successorum habitationi dicavit occupavit.[2] It is a vast pile of building, and was I believe more remarkable for extent & grandeur, than taste. We understand that there is at present no intention of rebuilding it, as the King has fitted up another palace for his usual residence in Copenhagen, & the royal family seem to prefer living in the most quiet manner. The palace was burnt in [blank] the year before the Town, & the ruins afforded shelter to a number of persons who were without houses. The demand for workmen to rebuild the houses that were destroyed has raised the price of labour very high. The most common workman can earn 7 or 8 danish marks a day. The Prince permits the soldiers to work who are in consequence very well off. The great demand for labour to rebuild the town is one of the reasons given for not rebuilding at present the palace, the Prince wishing in the most patriotic manner that his subjects should be served before himself.

Two English gentlemen at the table d'hote told us, that they were detained at Kiel by floating ice in the Baltic on the 12th of May, & were obliged to come to Copenhagen by land.

Fine. Sun very hot, but Therm at a north window in the Inn only 63 at 2.

June 9 [Sunday]. Called upon Ld Rt Fitzgerald who received me very agreeably, invited the party to dine with him the next

---

[1] In the great fire of 1795 Copenhagen lost 950 buildings. Many of the new buildings which Malthus saw were destroyed during the British bombardment eight years later. The grand palace was Christiansborg.

[2] Archdeacon Coxe, who saw Copenhagen before the great fire, wrote: 'The royal palace...was built by Christian the Sixth in seven years, as the inscription informed me, without laying a single tax on the subject' (*Travels*, v, 127). It was rebuilt in 1828, and again after a second fire in 1884.

day, & offered us all the assistance in his power.[1] Went to deliver one of my letters to a merchant, but did not find him at home. Walked to the observatory, the ascent to which, up the tower, is without steps, & so very easy that a coach might drive up it. There was nobody to show us the instruments; but by what we could see of them thro the windows, they appeared to be in very bad condition & very little used.

Dined at the table d'hote & in the afternoon went to the gardens of Frederiksbergh, where we saw much company; but chiefly of the lower & middling classes.[2] The women seemed to imitate at some little distance the English—they are now in the extremity of the short waists. The men in general, particularly the military, wear coats with short waists & long skirts which, being a vulgar fashion among us, gave them in our eyes a vulgar appearance. There were some few paysannes dress'd as we supposed in the old style, with much variety of colour & profusion of ornament. They looked old fashioned; but not unpicturesque. We observed one with a blue silk body, red cloth sleeves, black cloth or black velvet girdle, brown silk petticoat &c &c. & each of them trimmed with gold. She appeared to have no pretensions above a paysanne. We were told that the caps ornamented with gold lace which we saw so common at Lubeck generally cost a guinea.

We walked over the Palace which is the common summer residence of the King; but saw nothing whatever to interest us. The rooms are very small & ill-furnished, & there is not a single good picture. The gardens are about to be laid out more in the English taste & are now in a state of great untidiness. From the eminence on which the palace is situated the shores of Sweden may be seen distinctly; but the other views are flat & marshy. We drank tea at a house near the gardens & afterwards returned to walk in the King's gardens near the Town where we met with the same kind of company. The Danish features & countenances are entirely English; but

---

[1] Lord Robert Stephen FitzGerald (1765–1833), an almost exact contemporary of Malthus, was the sixth of the nine sons of James, first Duke of Leinster; the duke also had nine daughters. Lord Robert was British Minister in Copenhagen at the time.

[2] 'The gardens of Frederiksbergh' are still a public park, but the palace is now used by the Military Academy.

upon the whole not so handsome or so well made. At Copenhagen we observed very few of the same stout make that we had remarked in Funen.

Fine. Sun very hot. Ther. at 3, 65. Wind S.

June 11 [Monday *June 10*]. Went to the Museum & chamber of natural history, in which there appeared to be some curiosities, but very ill arranged.[1] There is one very long gallery consisting chiefly of the pictures that were saved when the small palace was burnt. A few of them are by the best masters. Among these is a very fine historical piece of Salvator Rosa representing Jonah preaching to the Ninevites. The countenance of Jonah is very fine, & the attitudes & expressions of the different auditors beautifully expressed. The King's head is bowed down to the earth. The historical pieces of Salvator are so scarce that they are most highly valued; but independant of its rarity this is certainly a very beautiful picture. Cain killing Abel, by Luca Jordano; and Adam relating the story to Eve, by the same; appeared to me very good paintings and the passions well expressed.

Dined at Lord Robert Fitzgerald's where we met a party of English naval officers, who were very agreeable, and invited us on board their ships at Elsineur if they were there when we arrived. Captain White, the Senior Officer, informed me that he never perceived any tide in the sound, but that there were strong currents both in & out of the Baltic which appeared to depend entirely upon the winds.

We heard that the climate of Copenhagen was reckoned in geneial very wet & changeable, & the people much subject to Epidemics. Lady R F. assured us that during the last spring there was scarcely any family in Copenhagen without the ague.[2] There are canals that cross the Town in different

---

[1] Coxe thought that the Royal Museum, or Cabinet of Rarities, merited the first place 'among the curious collections in Copenhagen'. It was 'deposited in eight apartments...animals; shells; minerals; paintings; antiquities; medals; dresses; arms and implements of the Laplanders' (*Travels*, v, 131).

[2] Lady Robert FitzGerald was Sophia Charlotte Fielding, the daughter of a naval officer. They were married in 1792, when he was 27 and she 19. She died in 1834 at the age of 61. When Malthus met her, she already had six children, the eldest just six years old, and the youngest, twin girls, barely three months; she was to have three more babies, and only one of the nine died in infancy (*Debrett's Peerage*, 1849).

directions, which from the filth thrown into them, generally are very offensive after hot weather.[1]

The extraordinary laxity of the Danish Government, & the very great liberty of speaking & writing, that all persons enjoy, is attributed rather to want of activity, & energy in the government than to great liberality of sentiment.

The Prince however is very active in everything that relates to the army; & in state affairs is his own prime minister. He professed his intention of acting from himself, as soon as the old Count Bernstoff died.[2] The son who succeeds to his father's public office as minister for foreign affairs, and possesses much of the Prince's confidence, has still but little of the power of his father. He can never give an answer to any state questions himself but receives every thing of that kind ad referendum. A little coldness at present subsists between our court and Denmark, on account of the improper use that has been made of the neutral flag. The P is not esteemed a man of talents.

Lady R F has six children, the two last twins, and appeared to us a very agreeable & domestic woman. Ld R F was very polite & attentive.

Fine. Sun very hot. Therm. at 2, 67.

June 11 [Tuesday]. Spent almost the whole morning in walking over the docks & Arsenals with the English officers, accompanied by Ld R F & a Danish officer. To those who have seen the English dock yards the sight is not very interesting. The motto to the Arsenal is qualitas quantitas et ordo; I was told that the first & last may be generally seen; but that the second sometimes fails. The buildings are all very neat & the arms, tho clumsy themselves, orderly arranged. There are 28 2 deckers, some of which are of 80 guns. A few seemed to be preparing for service now, in order, as we understand, to support the neutrality of the Danish flag, which suffers both

---

[1] Malthus wrote first that the canals generally *stink*.

[2] The old Count Bernstorff was Andreas Peter, who died on 21 June 1797 at the age of 62. His uncle, Count Johan Hartwig Ernst Bernstorff, was memorable for having begun the emancipation of the Danish peasantry and the abolition of the communal village system, described by Malthus on pp. 63–5, but his nephew Andreas Peter was managing his estates at the time, and is generally believed to have inspired the reform. The son, Christian Gunther, was 28 at the time of his father's death.

from the English & French, tho most from the French. It is generally acknowledged that the Danish neutral flag has been much prostituted during the war, and that many large fortunes have been made by the merchants in an illegal manner. Some ships have lately been seized by the English bringing home dutch property to a very large amount from Batavia.

In the store houses, all the rigging belonging to every ship is kept seperate with the name of the ship affixed. The whole island on which the small arsenals & storehouses are built was entirely water 80 yrs ago; & must therefore have been made at a great expence. There is but one dry dock, which on account of there being no tide is very difficult & expensive to work. When empty it may be fill'd almost immediately by pulling up the sluices, but when the ship is in, it takes 24 hours with 8 horses to pump the water out. Another cause of expence is that the bottom is unsound & the salt water is continually breaking up thro it; & can only be kept down by great weights of iron all over the foundation.

Denmark, to the honour of her kings & ministers, has not been at war for the last 70 yrs, except the little affair in 88, which was so immediately terminated that it cannot be considered as any thing.[1] The Danish officer that accompanied us said that they were doing all in their power to preserve the smaller states from being swallowed up, & preserve the republic of Europe; but that appearances seemed to indicate that in a short time there would be only 2 or 3 great powers.

Fair, except a few drops of rain. Therm at 3, 61. Wind S.E.

June 12 [Wednesday]. Called upon Professor Abilgaard, head of the Veterinary College, to whom I had a letter from Dr Mumssen—had a conversation of some time with him in French; and he appeared to be a very well informed man.[2] With regard to the College itself, he said that his great object was cheapness, as he thought that if he could not cure the

---

[1] The 'little affair in 88' was when Denmark most reluctantly and half-heartedly declared war on Sweden; Russia (under Catherine the Great) was at war with Sweden, and Russia at that time was Denmark's ally.

[2] Professor Peter Christian Abildgaard (1740–1801) was the brother of a well-known painter, and a much travelled man; he was known as a scientist outside Denmark, especially as a veterinary expert. Malthus first wrote that he appeared to be *very clever*, but changed it to *well informed*.

animals at a small expence the institution would be of very little general use. He cares little about the cattle of the rich, & has very few of them, except now & then from a more informed man who is able to overule the prejudices of his servants. The institution supports itself, except the salary from the King to the Professor. I mentioned our institution in London, & he said it would be a long time in its infancy from the little respect that was generally paid to the Study, and from the bad preparatory education of the pupils.

I understood from the Professor that all the peasants in Holstein were not yet emancipated. The peasants in the royal lands are; but many of the Seigneurs would not consent to it; and the King has not a great deal of power in Holstein, or at least does not chuse to exercise it. I mentioned the remarks we had made on the neatness of the houses & the apparent richness of the peasants in Holstein; and he seemed to think that in the parts we had pass'd thro, the peasants were all free. In Sleswic, Jutland & the Islands the general emancipation took place in 88, fortunately just before the breaking out of the French revolution. Had the measure been delayed a little longer, probably it would never have taken place; as the government would not have ventured upon it, after the popular commotions in France. All people do not give the Prince the whole credit which such a measure deserves. They say he was in fact influenced by the trouble he found in recruiting his armies, owing to the difficulties which the Seigneurs made in sparing their peasants.

At present the peasants may go where they please without leave of their Seigneurs; and as every peasant or farmer's son that has no property in land, is a soldier from his birth, & must serve seven yrs, if he is call'd upon, the armies are always fully supplied. This inscription in the army from birth is, I understand, to cease with this century. A peasant after he is 28 years old is not liable to be call'd upon, whether he has actually served his seven years or not. Marriage therefore is generally delayed till this period is past, which forms a kind of preventive check to popn.[1] The lower classes are seldom distressed for

---

[1] Here Malthus passes from the second of the paper-covered books to the first of the leather ones. He wrote the words *this period is* twice, at the end of one book and the beginning of the next.

subsistence, tho what they have is coarse. They eat always the black rye bread which the professor does not think very wholesome. The Norwegians who are used to the flad brod made of oatmeal always find the rye bread disagree with them. He seemed to think that the peasants were not often prevented from marrying from the fear of not being able to support a family.

Agriculture has advanced very rapidly within this last ten years. The value of estates has been doubled; and the great demand for labour has placed the lower classes in a good state. The common price of labour in the country as far as I could inform myself is about 2 Danish marcs or 1s. 4d. a day. Workmen in the town earn much more. Corvées have not been entirely abolished on account of the losses that the seigneurs would thereby have sustained, but they have been obliged to take an equivalent in money. It is supposed that in Holstein the peasants will all be emancipated next year as the seigneurs are now convinced that it is their best interest. The professor spoke of the state of agriculture in Norway as very miserable, on account of the very few people of education that there are there. It is now however thought to be improving.

The P is admired more as a K than as a man. He is rather vif and emporté, and likes to have his own way. He has little general knowledge himself & is no great encourager of science; but the professor said that they were now marching on the road that Fredk 5th had raised; & that the arts and sciences, tho not publickly encouraged, still held on their place. The P, tho he may not do much, has at least the great merit of not hindring anything. There is the most perfect freedom of opinion allowed. The professor observed that if he was to declare himself a Mahometan, it would not in the smallest degree affect him in his place which is appointed by the King. In the libraries we observed the works of Th. Paine in French & German.[1] None but particular or personal libels are pro-

---

[1] Malthus might have been especially interested in Tom Paine (1737–1809), as his effigy had been burnt on Market Hill, at Cambridge, on 31 December 1792; he had escaped to France after being prosecuted for treason in England, following the publication of *The Rights of Man*, in which he had advocated republicanism. He had previously been in America, and fought for the colonists in the War of Independence. In 1793 he wrote *The Age of Reason*, in which he defended deism against both atheism and Christianity. In 1799 he was still in France, but he returned to America in 1802.

secuted. The crown never interferes with the courts of justice. A man was lately prosecuted for a direct attack on the court, & afterwards published his procés from his prison which sold very rapidly; & no measures were taken to prevent it. The fines even for personal libels are very light.[1]

The Professor shewed me his school of anatomy & his cabinet of mineralogy, which were both worth seeing. Mineralogy is his favourite pursuit at present. He promised to get for me before I left Copenhagen some meteorological observations from Professor Bogner.[2]

Went to the Glassen Library, a present to the public from a Mr Glassen who made a great fortune at the Iron foundery of Frederick's wash.[3] He has left a sum to pay all the expences attached to it, and the attendants are remarkably civil. It is open four days in the week from 10 till 2. The collection is not large, and is confined chiefly to Agriculture, Natural history, & Antiquities. I talked with an intelligent man in the library who confirmed what Pro. Abilgaard had said about the rapid increase of agriculture within the last ten years. He mentioned that the value of many farms had been doubled. This is chiefly attributed to the emancipation of the peasants, which has rendered them so much more industrious.

Morning cloudy. Afternoon showry. Therm at 3, 60.

June 13 [Thursday]. Showry. Therm at 2, 59. Saw the King's library which consists of upwards of 300,000 volumes. It contains many scarce books & valuable manuscripts; but we were too much pressed for time to examine them with any attention. Talked to a man who had published a book on Statistics. According to his calculations, 1 in 40 die in Norway, 1 in 38 in the islands, 1 in 37 in the dutchies. He said that Professor Thaarup had stolen from him.[4]

---

[1] The free expression of opinion was especially important in a country like Denmark, where the people had no constitutional means of influencing their government. However, some degree of censorship was restored by an ordinance of September 1799.

[2] This may have been Thomas Bugge (1740–1815), Professor of Astronomy since 1777.

[3] Johan Frederik Glassen (1725–92) made his fortune in armaments at Frederiksvaerk; his own collection of 20,000 books formed the nucleus of the library, housed in a building designed by his son.

[4] On pp. 208–10, Malthus gives a most amusing account of his meeting with Professor Thaarup at Kongsvinger on 1 August.

Call'd upon Monsr. Wad, professor of natural history in the University, a great mineralogist, & saw some curious specimens relating to the formation of coal & amber, a new semimetal & some new crystals & c. & c.[1] We have found all the professors that we have seen extremely polite, & ready to give every kind of information. The King's library is open every day from 10 till 12, & a professor generally attends.

There are no corn laws in Denmark & no publick store except a small one for the army. The Bank is entirely a government institution but in great credit. The notes are as low as 1 rix dollar. Silver must be paid at the bank when demanded. These notes bear a discount in Holstein. I heard, but do not know whether from good authority or not, that there was a discount on these notes in the islands about 10 yrs ago. The Bank is said now to be very rich in silver, & it is thought probable that in a few years the notes will be destroyed & that there will be only a silver currency.

Every thing is remarkably dear at present in Copenhagen. Beef & mutton 6d., Fresh butter 1s. Common labour in the environs of the town 2s.—in the country 1s. 4d. There is a very great demand for labour at present, and labourers are scarce. Every thing in the shops is remarkably dear, & books particularly so. Only four years ago labour in the country was 1 danish marc or 8d. a day. This rapid rise in the price of labour has placed the lower classes in a very good state, and it is expected that there will be a very rapid increase of population.

In the afternoon went to see the review, which upon the whole went off very well, tho it was unluckily a showry afternoon. The soldiers at a distance appeared to be handsomely drest, but on a nearer view their cloathing was very coarse. The horses small, but handsome, & in good order—all with long tails. Towards the end of the review I got near the King's tent & saw him quite close. He is treated quite as an idiot. The officers about the court have all orders not to give him any answer. Some of the party observed him talking very fast & making faces at an officer who was one of the sentinels at the tent, who preserved the utmost gravity of countenance & did not answer him a single word. Just before the royal party

[1] Gregers Wad lived from 1755 to 1832; he had become Professor of Mineralogy and Zoology in 1795.

left the tent the Prince rode up full speed, & his father made him a very low bow. I could not well distinguish the Prince's countenance, and could only see that he had a thin pale face & a small person. His father has the same kind of face & person, but is reckoned a better looking man.

We observed the French minister with his national cockade. He had an interesting, tho rather fier countenance, and seemed to look on what he saw as a poor farce not worth his attention. When he addressed any person his features relaxed into mildness & he seemed to be perfectly well bred in his manner. The Princess Royal is rather pretty, and is, I understand, a most agreeable & valuable woman. Lady R F spoke in the highest terms of her—She is a daughter of the Prince of Hesse who lives in the palace at Sleswic. We saw the Princess get into her carriage with her daughter, the only remaining child of five, who is now about five yrs old.[1] There was a large party of nobility in the King's tent, but Ld R F was not there. The King drove off first, accompanied by the Princess Royal & her daughter, in a gilt chariot with six very handsome grey horses.[2]

June 14 [Friday]. Showry. Wind rather high. N. Therm. at 3, 52. General green. Chestnuts in full bloom. Lilac open.

After a morning spent in the most complete confusion of packing up & separating the things that were to be sent to Stockholm, left Copenhagen for Elsineur. For about a Danish mile after leaving the town,[3] we pass'd thro Count Bernstoff's estate, towards the extremity of which is the Pillar erected to him by his grateful peasants for their liberty. He was the first that emancipated his slaves. When he called them together & told them that they were at liberty to go where they pleased it is said that they beg'd he would let them remain in their former state—he replied, that if they continued in the same opinion after five years were elapsed they should have their wish. When the term was expired, he called them together again and asked them if they chose to return to their former state. With earnest entreaties they beg'd that they might not,

---

[1] The Princess Royal was Princess Sophia Frederica of Hesse-Cassel; she had a second daughter who also survived.

[2] On the next page Malthus wrote nothing but *On the burning of the palace the Prince*, and the three following pages are completely blank.

[3] A Danish mile is 4⅗ English miles.

acknowledged that they did not at first know the value of liberty; but that they were now about to erect a monument to him, to perpetuate the memory of his wisdom & benevolence & their gratitude.

Coxe saw the Pillar in 1784, and described it as a column of Norwegian marble, 'ornamented with a wheat-sheaf, a spade, and a pick-axe, the emblems of agriculture'. After transcribing the Latin inscription—there was also one in Danish—Coxe gives an English translation in a footnote:

'To the affectionate memory of John Hartvic Ernest, Count of Bernstorff, who in 1767 rendered free his hereditary estates, and thereby imparted industry, wealth, and every blessing, as an example to posterity. Erected by his grateful peasants, 1783.'[1]

It is possible that Malthus confused this Count Bernstorff with his nephew, Andreas Peter, who died in 1797; Hanoverian in origin, uncle and nephew were leading statesmen in Denmark throughout the second half of the eighteenth century.

This anecdote I had from a gentleman who farms an estate about 20 miles from Copenhagen, and who accompanied us in the waggon to Elsineur. He also gave me some information with regard to the former & present state of the peasants. Before their emancipation, the farmers were still more oppressed than the labourers, as the Seigneurs had their horses & cattle at command as well as themselves. This was in general so disheartening that they exercised no kind of industry. Their cattle almost constantly died in the winter, and the lords were absolutely obliged to assist them in the spring. The farmers or boors would then have parted with their farms almost for nothing,—now they valued them most highly. The farmers possess still about the same quantity of land as they did before, calld five barrel of heart corn, which consists of more or less acres according to the richness of the land, for which they pay to their lords about 6 pounds a year. It is not lawful at present for any farmer to possess more than 3 of these parcels of land.

A boor (or farmer) who possesses one of these parcels of land has it almost in fee, & may sell it to whom he pleases, provided

[1] *Travels*, v, 134–5.

25 or thirty acres remain attached to the farm house, which is considered as sufficient to secure the tax to the Landlord. Whoever possesses this house & land must pay 6 pounds to the landlord. Before the emancipation the boors were equally at liberty to sell their farms; but nobody would buy them, as the purchaser immediately became a slave & was bound to the same services as the boor whose farm he bought. The seigneurs have not the power of resuming any part of their lands that have been apportioned in farms to the boors; & the chief advantage which they gain at present is the certainty of their rents, & their exemption from the necessity of assisting their boors in bad seasons.[1]

Count Bernstoff's estate is now beginning to be inclosed; and farm houses are scattered about in different places which were formerly all confined to one village; and the boor had perhaps a danish mile to walk before he reached the land which he was to plow. The first part of the country from Copenhagen is flat,—corn, & rich pasture land. In about a danish mile & a half we came to the country house of Prince Frederic, where he lives most of the summer in a very domestic and private manner. The house is very poor but there are some fine woods near the gardens. In these gardens saw the Lilac in flower. Soon after pass'd Mr de Conig's seat, a rich merchant in Copenhagen.[2] It is at some distance from the road; and as far as we could judge seemed beautifully situated, being on the borders of a fine lake surrounded by woods, and having another lake at some distance behind, bordered in the same manner by banks of fine wood. Pass'd thro some pretty beech woods & some heathy uneven country. Stopped about half way to see the palace of Hirsholm. The exterior looked poor & desolate; but the interior shewed that the rooms had formerly been very magnificent. Upon the whole however it was hardly worth the trouble & expence of seeing, the latter of which cost 2 rix-dollars.

The rest of the country to Elsineur was waving ground with corn, pasture, heath, varied with woods of beech, oak & alder,

[1] Malthus left two pages blank after this, obviously for more information which he never had time to write down.
[2] Frederick de Coninck (1740–1811) was a Dutchman who settled in Copenhagen in 1763, and at this time had the fifth-largest of its shipping concerns. His country seat was Dronningsgaard, near Lake Fureso.

& a distant view of the sea to the right. After leaving Count Bernstof's estate, the lands for the rest of the way to Elsineur, we heard, belonged to the King, except some estates to the right near Elsineur. The King possesses the greatest part of Zealand. There are not above two or three estates besides his. The palace of Hirsholm is situated in a bog, & many parts of the lowlands from Copenhagen to Elsineur are rather marshy. We had a remarkably brilliant tho stormy sunsetting, & a curious appearance in the opposite part of the heavens called by sailors a sun dog, which seems to be a small segment of a rainbow. During the six days warm weather, while we remained at Copenhagen, the spring had made rapid advances. The oaks were almost in ¾ foliage.

The Castle of Hirscholm is now the National Hunting Museum and Forestry Industry Museum.

Clarke agreed with Malthus that it was not worth seeing—it 'exhibited no marks of a good taste'.[1] It was, however, the 'favourite palace of the Queen Matilda', and Coxe had written a romantic account of it: 'The dining-room is a very large appartment, and remarkable for a *jet d'eau*, and twelve fountains, which sprouted from the sides... The place is so entirely neglected, that the court-yard is covered with weeds, and the moat is a green mantled pool.'[2]

Caroline Matilda was a sister of George III of England, and married the mad Christian VII of Denmark. In 1770 the King was completely dominated by his German doctor, Struensee, who, although he could speak no Danish, virtually ruled Denmark and Norway for about eighteen months. Matilda became his mistress, apparently without any objection from her husband. A conspiracy was formed against Struensee, who was seized after a fancy-dress ball and later executed in public. There was much indignation in England over what was regarded as the ill-treatment of Queen Matilda, who was imprisoned at Elsinor, and after strong representations from her brother she was allowed to leave Denmark; she died soon afterwards, of scarlet fever, in Hanover.

Malthus would have read Coxe's touching account of the disgraced queen's departure from 'Elsinoor':[3]

'A few months before her imprisonment she had been delivered of a princess, whom she suckled herself. The rearing of this child

[1] Clarke, *Travels*, v, 83. [2] Coxe, *Travels*, v, 224–5.
[3] Coxe, *Travels*, v, 112–15.

had been her only comfort; and she conceived a more than parental attachment to it, from its having been the constant companion of her misery. The infant was at that period afflicted with the measles; and having nursed it with unceasing solicitude, she was desirous of continuing her attention and care. All these circumstances had so endeared the child to her, rendered more susceptible of tenderness in a prison than in a court; that when an order for detaining the young princess was intimated to her, she testified the strongest emotions of grief, and could not, for some time, be prevailed upon to bid a final adieu...She remained upon deck, her eyes immoveably directed towards the palace of Cronborg, which contained her child that had been so long her only comfort, until darkness intercepted the view.'

June 15 [Saturday]. Elsineur. Walked to Cronberg Castle where poor Matilda was confined. The man who shewed it remembered her, but was too stupid to give any rational answers.[1] The rooms within the tower are rather dreary; There is a fine view of the Swedish shore from the top, particularly of a high and rocky part of the coast called Kullen, which looks at the distance of about 20 miles quite mountainous.[2] Dined with Captain White on board the Vestal and we saw an instrument that he had invented for spherical trigonometry.

In the afternoon crossed the sound to Helsinbourgh; and proceeded in two small waggons to Engelholm, 2½ swedish miles.[3] Helsinbourgh is a shabby town, and the cottages surrounding it appeared much less neat than on the other side of the water. Allmost all the women without stockings & dressed very poorly. The country from Helsingbourgh to Engelholm was chiefly a flat, consisting of very extensive heaths & commons, interspersed with young trees & scrubby oaks, and with very little mixture of corn or grass land. We had a very fine sunsetting, & it was quite light till ten oclock.

Fair and fine. Wind North. Therm at 12, 52. Wind quite cold in the evening.

[1] The man may have been cautious rather than stupid. Adultery in a queen is treason, and sympathetic answers to the Englishmen's questions might have meant life imprisonment for their guide.
[2] The highest point is only 615 feet.
[3] A Swedish mile was about 6½ English miles.

June 16 [Sunday]. At the inn at Engelholm had bad rooms, but good beds, 2 in each, only eggs & bread & butter for supper; yet they charged us six dollars.[1] The posting is 8 pence a horse for a swedish mile equal to about 6½ english miles. The first stage to Margaretstorp, a swedish mile, chiefly consisted of heath, large commons & shabby trees. On the commons we observed a number of poor horses & some small cattle feeding—the country for the most part flat.

Understood from the driver that the wages of common farmer's labour were 8 pence with victuals & 16d. without. Spring is the time that the people are most distressed. Their store generally lasts them well thro the winter. A great many of the cattle died last winter; but the people were not distressed for want of corn. They begin to feel the want a little now. Forage was so extremely scarce that the straw of their thatched houses was chopped for their cattle.

From Margaretstorp we soon mounted a rocky hill covered with wood; and as the foreground was wild and picturesque, the view back to the sea & the Kullen rocks was very beautiful. On the hill we entered a pretty forest of young beech, which lasted with a very good road winding thro it for 2 english miles. The road afterwards was chiefly heathy, interspersed here & there with trees, & small rocks, till we began again to descend the hill, when we had a fine view of a bay of the sea, & a wide champaign country terminated by hills at a distance. The descent of the hill was steep, & the sides dotted with small rocks, & oaks. The village of Karup was prettily situated at the bottom by the side of a small stream; and the hill that we had descended look'd high & well wooded from below. The house was small & poor. We could get nothing but eggs & very coarse rye bread full of sand by way of luncheon, & were obliged to wait near two hours for horses. From Karup to Laholm 1¼ miles the road was flat & uninteresting, chiefly heath & commons, but with a few spots of cultivation.

Dined at Laholm indifferently. In the streets we saw a great number of peasants dressed very neatly, & afterwards a caval-cade of near twenty carts, that went out of the town together. We were told that a wedding had just taken place which had

---

[1] Clarke wrote of Engelholm, 'The inn here was small, but we had cleanly accommodation.' They got up at five the next morning (*Travels*, v, 90).

caused so gay an appearance.[1] It was sunday & all were in their best apparel which was very neat & clean, tho coarse. The men wore chiefly common blue coats & waistcoats, & the women in general red woollen bodies & blue ditto petticoats. Many were in their shift sleeves. The cap was red, blue or green, setting quite close to the head & apparently by way of bonnet, they tied a large, clean, white handkerchief on their heads—one end hanging low down behind. The town was but poor and straggling; but the scene altogether very lively and pleasing. We had met many women walking to church in the morning without shoes & stockings, & all their petticoats tuck'd up, leaving only their shifts which reached a little below their knees. They were most of them tall & rather large women & look'd very picturesque figures.

On going out of Laholm we pass'd a good pretty fall of the River near which the town is situated.[2] The fall is not deep; but there is a considerable body of water—dark as if it came from moors. Passed over a dreary country to Halmstadt. The few spots which we saw in cultivation seemed to be tolerably well ploughed & sowed & to be very free from weeds. The rye pretty generally in ear—the barley about 2 inches high. I saw no wheat, & understood that there was seldom any sown.

Halmstadt, the next stage, is rather prettily situated on a river that runs into the sea.[3] On leaving Halmstadt the country immediately became more varied and the soil better tho light. Heard that the price of labour at Halmstadt was 1*s* a day. In the country, farmers' labourers had 4*d* a day with victuals. The 16*d*. pence a day that I heard of was probably incorrect. Butter 6*d*. the pound. Rye is reckoned now extremely dear—6 dollars the tun (consisting as our swedish servant told me of 250 pounds). In common years a tun is bought for 3 dollars.

Towards the end of the stage to Quibille the country became very pretty, birch & oak woods with fine dark hills to the right;

---

[1] Clarke describes at Laholm 'garlands suspended upon upright poles, adorned like our May-poles. There was also an arch made of the stems and branches of green birch-trees. Around the poles, and through this arch, a new-married couple, followed by the bridemaids and friends of the bride-groom, had been dancing' (*Travels*, v, 94).

[2] The river at Laholm is the Lagan, famous for salmon. Laholm is 13½ miles from Halmstad.

[3] The river at Halmstad is the Nissan, which flows into the Kattegat.

& cottages with their white chimnies peeping thro the trees. From Quibille to Sloinge, 1¼, the country was beautiful. Fine rocky hills thrown about in various shapes & shaded by oak, ash & birch. The wooden cottages in picturesque shapes scattered among the rocks & trees with pretty white churches at small distances, and the whole picture warmed by a fine sunsetting, made our evening's drive appear very delightful. The oaks & ashes were forwarder a little than in Zealand; answering about to the two days since we had left Denmark. The stage before I had remarked some oaks that had been out in leaf, & had been since shrivelled by a frost. They look'd almost as if they had been burnt. In some of the more barren parts that we had passed over the ashes did not appear to have been out above 3 or 4 days.

The next stage to Falkenbergh was a little of the same kind, but not quite so pretty. We got to Falkenbergh about half past eleven & found all the people in bed.[1] After some knocking we were introduced into a large room next to the kitchen, where a woman was in bed & fast asleep. She lay very quietly for some time; at last when the room was full of men, & there had been a great noise for some time, she got up as quietly, put on a petticoat & walked out, seemingly very little molested by our intrusion.

After supping on one of Clarke's custards, went to bed 3 in one room.[2] Near Sloinge I observed a very fair field of rye very forward.

Fine. Therm at 6, 52; at 1, 60. Wind N.W., rather high & cool in the middle of the day, tho the sun was hot. Wind sunk in the evening.

June 17 [Monday]. Left Falconbergh at 6. The country began immediately to change to barren heaths & commons dotted with rugged stones, with but few spots of cultivation. Changed waggons at Morup, 1¼ of a mile. From thence to Warbergh 1⅝. We passed near the coast & a great part of the two last stages presented as desolate & noir a picture as could well be

---

[1] The distance from Angelholm to Falkenberg is about 68 miles by road, a long day's journey in a horse-drawn waggon.

[2] Clarke did not remain with the rest of the party 'halting for repose at Falconberg', but continued the journey for a few stages alone and on foot (*Travels*, v, 95).

seen. The soil seems to produce nothing but stone. From Warbergh to Baha, 2 miles, the same kind of country & some-times worse continued. Warberg has a fortified castle & a toler-able port. There are some large good wooden houses in it. Between Warbergh and Baha we pass'd many small bays & observed a great number of small cattle near their shores. The cottages, which were more frequent than could be expected in so barren a country, were almost all of wood, with inclosures of stone walls round them. The ground in some of these inclosures seemed to be but little used.

From Assa to Kongsbaha the country rather improved, the flat parts were more cultivated, & frequent windmills appeared on the rocky eminences. The ploughs that we observed had only one handle, & a strait beam, or sometimes shafts in which was one horse, which the man drove with one hand & held the plough in the other. There was no wheel & nothing to turn under the clod, & the man seemed to direct his plough with so little regularity that it appeared to be a little like the grubbing of a hog. When the work is quite completed, however, it looks very well.[1]

We dined at Kongbaha, & merely for Bacon & eggs, a custard & a bottle of beer were charged two dollars.[2] There were three of us & a servant. Clarke was gone on before to order horses. Konsbaha is prettily situated in a flat valley surrounded by rocks; with two or three small hamlets at the same time in view. The land in the valley seemed to be good & the cultivation better than any we had observed. We remarked a great number of peasants in the fields at work. The cottages were frequent, all built of wood & most of them very neat.

For the greatest part of the stage to Karra, $1\frac{3}{4}$ of a mile, the country continued of the same kind—green & cultivated vallies sometimes enriched by a stream, & surrounded by a wall of rugged rocks interspersed with cottages & trees. Some parts were very picturesque The cattle were larger than those we had seen before, & we observed some cows that might be admired in England. Some ploughs were drawn by small oxen & we remarked one which was drawn by four small oxen & 2 horses; but none had more than one handle, tho in other

[1] Malthus made a very small diagram of this plough.
[2] Kungsbacka, 50 English miles from Falkenberg.

respects they were improved from those we had seen in the wilder part of the country.

Slept at Karra. The sun had been very hot, the wind high & the roads so dusty, that our faces & eyes were much inflamed.

Fine. Therm at 6, 57; at 1, 65. Wind N by W—rather high.

June 18 [Tuesday]. Fine. Wind N by E. Therm. at 2, 68.

Arrived at Gotheburgh to breakfast. View from the ramparts over the river pretty. Many new good houses have been built since the fire. Dined at a Merchant's. Heard that Sweden imported annually 800,000 barrels of corn. Complain much of a want of hands. They calculate that during the Russian war from disease & other causes near a hundred thousand men were lost.[1] Before the war they were in a very prosperous state, & the paper then in circulation was as good as specie. The present banc-notes still retain their full value; but the current paper which was issued to pay the expences of the war, & for which there is no solid security, now bears 40 per cent discount. They were issued from the treasury, & guaranteed by the Diet. The price of labour has risen greatly of late years, but the price of provisions nearly in proportion, so that the labourer is not much better off than before, which prevents the increase of popn.

For near 20 miles, however, before we reached Gothenburgh, there were many new houses building & much appearance of an advance in riches & population, particularly among the labouring classes. We did not see many gentlemen's houses.

The tenures of land are very complex, & are supposed, in conjunction with the prodigal use of brandy, to be the cause of the slow increase of popn. The women do not in general marry before 25 & have seldom large families. Little outdoor work can be done in the winter, and they generally employ themselves during that part of the year either in sleeping, or some home manufactory, at which most of them are able to work.

---

[1] The Russian war was that waged by King Gustav III of Sweden against Catherine the Great from 1787 to 1790. Sweden almost lost the war, but on the day on which the Russians had decided to hold victory celebrations, Gustav won a decisive naval battle at Svensksund. The King's adviser on naval matters was an Englishman, Sidney Smith, who had served under Rodney; it was he who, in May 1799, commanded the east Mediterranean squadron which forced Napoleon to abandon the siege of Acre.

People complain of the power & influence of the nobles, and of the difficulties thrown in the way of the purchasers of land. It is expected that at the next diet something will be done in favour of burghers & peasants. The late King is thought to have favoured the peasants & burghers more in words than deeds.[1] The door to all employments in the state is open to them; but they are never suffered to enter.

Almost all the peasants are weavers, & employ themselves during the long nights of winter in making their own cloathing. Their shirts are of the coarseness of sail cloth. The washing is performed in Sweden as in most of the country we have passed thro. The women stand in the water, or sit upon a raft, & beat the linen after dipping it, with a flat piece of board. At Copenhagen we saw little frames or boxes upon a large raft for each woman, on which she sat and did her work very comfortably.

At Gotheburgh we met with a clerk to a merchant who had been at Tornea & Drontheim & had travelled much, very far north, collecting rock moss for an English company. It appears to be a lichen, and is used for a scarlet die. When it was first discovered the price was only 3£ the tun, & is now 28. Formerly there was much of it about Gotheborg; but it is now nearly all picked, & it seems to grow very slowly.

June 19 [Wednesday]. Left Gotheburgh at 8 for Lahall, 2 miles. The country of the same character as that we had passed thro in the two last stages to Gotheburgh, but richer, & with more trees. The river Gother was to our left, running thro a flat valley of fine rich meadows, & closed in on all sides by rocks, sometimes in very fine shapes, particularly the rocks on the right, which here & there, when well enriched by trees, formed spots highly picturesque. The river is in parts marshy in its margin which detracts much from its beauty. Cottages were frequently interspersed, & here & there some gentlemen's houses; both of which from their situation would have look'd more agreeable, but for the common custom of painting the

---

[1] The late King, Gustav III, was assassinated on 16 March 1792, at a masked ball at the Opera House in Stockholm. He had patronised poets and painters, and modelled his court on Versailles; the conspiracy against him was believed to have been inspired by the French Revolution. On his deathbed the King nominated his brother to act as regent for his thirteen-year-old son, Gustav IV, who came of age in 1796.

wooden houses red.[1] Before the end of the first stage the country began to grow rather more bare & barren. We pass'd a ruined tower & fortifications to the left, on the other side of the river. It is situated on an island formed by two branches of the river, & was formerly in possession of the Danes.[2]

From Lahall to Kattlebergh, $1\frac{1}{4}$ of a mile, the country continued of the same kind, but not so pretty. From Kettleburgh to Edet, $1\frac{3}{4}$, the country continued much the same till within 3 miles of Edet, when we entered the finest valley of pines that we had seen. The shores of the river became more bold, the rocks were covered with firs, & the bases of them enriched by various other trees. The road winding thro the pines & rocks, & opening occasionally on views of the river presented some very beautiful scenery, which C. said very much resembled some of the roads in Swisserland.[3]

Edet is very pretty, situated near a fall of the Gotha; but is rather spoilt by the litter occasioned by three or four saw mills.[4] On the opposite shore we saw the ha[n]dsomest country seat that we had yet observed in Sweden. It was white & had some little appearance of architecture.[5] From Edet to Forss, 1 mile, we pass'd a pretty country, hills chiefly covered with pines.

At Edet for a cold dinner they charged us 6 rix dollars.[6]

Soon after leaving Edet we mounted one of the steepest & longest hills that we had yet met with. In general the roads have been remarkably level. The cottages were not now painted red, & were in very picturesque shapes, the slope of the roof being so small as to look much in the proportion of a simple Grecian temple. Many of the roofs were covered with turf, & look'd like plots of grass. The windows in general small & few.

[1] The red paint is known as Falu Red, made from a red ochre originally mined at Falun. It is much admired by many Swedes today, for its beauty as well as its preservative qualities.

[2] The ruins were probably those of the fortress of Bohus, built about 1300, and the seat of the governor of Bohuslän until 1700.

[3] C. is Clarke, who wrote in his account of this journey: 'The author had been for ten preceding years almost constantly engaged in travelling...His companions were, for the most part, novices in such pursuits...' (*Travels*, v, 35).

[4] Lilla Edet is now an important power-station and famous for paper-mills.

[5] The country seat may have been Ström, which Muirhead says was 'occupied in the 18th cent. by Baron G. Maclean'.

[6] Clarke wrote: 'Here they made us pay four shillings each for a little cold meat' (*Travels*, v, 103). Malthus first called this meal *a cold snap*, then altered it to *dinner*.

The enclosures for many stages past had been principally of wood, in small pieces 4 or 5 feet long, laid upon one another in a sloping direction & kept together by uprights.

From Forss to Gurdelesm 1 mile; the first part continued pretty, particularly some piny hills with a small lake to the right. The last stage to Trolhatta was more heathy & bare of wood.

The wooden houses are generally built with the planks put upright, & another plank over the cracks, tho we saw a few with weather boards. The roofs are very frequently of wood; but many are of thatch & turf.

We arrived at Trolhatta about 9, and walked to the nearest fall before supper. It is a fine torrent in a very fine shape; about 23 feet. A more complete view of it, we left for the morning.

Fine. Therm at 2 under the shade of a tree in the road, 74. Wind N by E.

June 20 [Thursday]. Went to see the cataracts & canal. There are 3 principal falls near Trolhatta.[1] The highest is the broadest and in the most picturesque shape. I had seen none so fine myself; but Clark held it very cheap, & thought it very much inferior to many of the falls in Scotland, & not to be named in the same day with those of Italy. The second fall is about 30 feet, is more perpendicular than the first, but is not so broad & does not roll into such fine shapes. There is a great body of water, & it falls with very great force. The present King of Sweden about 6 years ago came with a large party to see the works, & ordered a strong built wooden house, & afterwards 2 geese & 2 pigs to be floated down the stream. The house was dashed to atoms—the geese were never seen more; but strange to tell the pigs escaped unhurt, & were sold afterwards at an advanced price on account of their good fortune.[2]

The opposite shore of the river is a fine bold rock thinly spread with pines; the near shore is rock but not so high, & now much spoilt by the works. The new canal, the plan of which

[1] These waterfalls now operate Sweden's greatest hydro-electric power-station.
[2] If 'the present King', Gustav IV, visited Trolhättan '6 years ago', he would have been fourteen years old at the time. He was deposed in 1809, when he was thirty, after a disastrous war with Russia, in the course of which Sweden lost Finland, a connection that had lasted for 650 years.

was formed when Cox was here, is now near its completion.[1] It is calculated that it will certainly be fit for navigation by the end of next year, and it was begun only six yrs ago. The ill success of the former enterprises at Trolhatta seems to be owing to the plans being ill laid & attempting too much. The cut which is working at present, & of the success of which no doubts are entertained, is about 2 miles & a half long, & at the shallowest part will be 7 feet deep. It passes at some little distance from the banks of the river on the side of Trolhatta, and is to have five locks for a descent of about 200 feet. The chief difficulty of the work arises from the hardness of the rock that is to be cut thro, which for the most part consists of solid granite.

When Polheim attempted to make a dam against the whole river in a narrow part below all the falls; first five, & afterwards, 80 were swept away by the torrent during the work. The river rose 12 feet & then the whole dam was torn up by the weight of the water. It was his intention to have raised it 34 feet, to make it smooth up to the cut that is called Polheim's sluice, which was to communicate with the Ekerbrad sluice.[2] The guide who conducted us round the works could only speak German & Swedish, so that our only means of conversation was through our Swedish servant.

Went into some saw mills, & were pleased with the simplicity of the machinery. I dont recollect any saw mills in England; but suppose there must be some, as they save so much time & expence. Four or five saws may work on a piece of timber at once, & they are set near or further apart according to the thickness of the plank required. The whole machinery is set in motion by a common undershot weel, the two handles of

---

[1] The new canal was successful, and the first ship passed the falls on 14 August 1800. 'Cox' was Archdeacon William Coxe (1747–1828), who was last at Trolhättan on 26 August 1784, and took as much interest in the works as Malthus did. His first visit was on 10 March 1779, and is described in detail in his *Travels* (IV, 302–19).

[2] Kristoffer Polhem (1661–1751) first tried to build locks round the waterfalls at Trolhättan in 1749. The destruction of his dam in 1755 may have been deliberately caused, by the local peasants sending a mass of timber down the river against it: they naturally did not wish to lose the money they earned by carting cargoes round the falls. Polhem was known as the Archimedes of the North; Malthus may not have known that his interests included the study of obstacles to the increase of population.

which move up & down the saws. An iron weel at the side moves the frame on which the timber is placed, gradually forwards to meet the saws, & another weel as simple draws the timber that is wanted out of the water.

Took a cold dinner at Trolhatta at one, & went up the river in a boat to Wennersburgh, where we arrived about 6. The banks of the river, tho not very bold, are pretty, & in parts well wooded. We passed one or two gentlemen's seats agreeably situated near the banks. The River, before it reaches the Wenner lake, is full of shoals & rocks which has occasioned the navigation to be carried on by the Carlsgraf canal, which joins a little bay of the Wenner. At the entrance of this cut from the river there are two fine locks, for a descent of about 40 feet.

After getting our rooms at Wennersburgh we walked down to the lake, & in a lovely afternoon had a most agreeable bathing in the Wenner, with which we felt ourselves much refreshed. At this end of the lake the shores on each side are not very distant, perhaps about 7 or 8 miles, but in front no land was visible. The shores on the eastern side of the lake are of perpendicular rocks that have the appearance of basaltic columns; but are rather too even at the top to look very picturesque. The lake is upon the whole however a very fine object, & as we had a delightful evening with a most brilliant sunsetting, we passed an hour or two wandering on the shores & upon the lake with much pleasure.

All the rooms in the inns of Sweden we have found sprinkled with Juniper or Jin or both, which in the bed rooms is not pleasant to the feet, & the smell is rather faint.[1]

Fine. Therm at 2 on the water, 61; at 6, in the deep shade of a house, 64. Wind in the morning N by E. In the evening S.W.

We remarked on entering Sweden that the men were much more lively than the Danes. Our drivers, instead of hanging their heads down in stupid apathy like most of those that we had seen in Zealand, were singing and laughing all the way.

---

[1] Clarke wrote: 'There is a custom, all over this country, of strewing the floors of their apartments with sprigs of *juniper*; and upon this strew is often scattered a considerable quantity of sand—a practice once common in the presence-chambers of Sovereigns. It is a practice that conduces much to uncleanliness; and the reek of dying vegetables in close rooms is not wholesome' (*Travels*, v, 108).

The men were in general well looking both in person & face, but the women by no means so, & we were particularly struck with their all appearing old. In the villages thro which we passed, we remarked very few young women that looked to be from 17 to 22. The children generally speaking did not look healthy. We hardly ever met with tolerable butter, and it always appeared dirty.

Wennersborgh is an airy little town with a large square & some good wooden houses in it; but many of the cottages in the out-skirts looked very poor & miserable, yet we heard that the price of labour in the town was 16 scillings. We saw many women digging in their gardens with their petticoats tuck'd up & their ragged shifts appearing below. I have seen however as bad cottages & as poorly dressed people in some English villages. The fishermen near the lake, as is usual, have large families. The immediate shores of the lake are all rocky—no marshiness appeared in any of the parts that we saw; & we found the finest place for bathing imaginable, with hard rocky margin & sandy bottom.

July 21 [Friday *June 21*]. As after much deliberation we determined to separate—Clarke & Cripps for Tornea & Otter & myself for Norway, we pass'd the morning in settling our accounts before parting & then had a delightful bathe in the lake Wenner which we took leave of with regret.

About 2 we set off on an mineralogical & antiquarian expedition to the mountains of Halleburgh & Hunneburgh, where Mr Hailstone had heard that trap was to be found in the greatest plenty [1]—the same hills which we understood at Gotheborgh had ranges of Basaltic columns. We set off on our last party together in 3 of the most miserable carts that could well be conceived. We had not proceeded above 300 yrds when

---

[1] The mountains of Hunneberg and Halleberg, whose heights are 505 and 509 feet respectively, are still popular for what are now called geological expeditions.

The Rev. John Hailstone (1759–1847), Fellow of Trinity College, Cambridge, was Woodwardian Professor of Geology from 1788 to 1818; he corresponded and collected, but never lectured, though in 1792 he did publish 'A Plan for a Course of Lectures'. In 1818 he married and became vicar of Trumpington, where he worked for the education of the parish poor, and 'kept for many years a meteorological diary'.

trap (Swedish *trapp*) is a dark-coloured igneous rock, which often has a 'stair-like appearance' (*O.E.D.*).

the equippage in which Clarke & I were seated broke down, & as Clarke was going forward to tell the story, he saw Otter & Cripps sprawling in the road about fifty yrds further on, the wheel of their cart having come off. Nobody was hurt. We managed matters as well as we could, & having sent one cart back to be mended, proceeded slowly to our mountains which were not above 4 or 5 english miles from Wennerburgh.

We entered a pretty valley shut in by two high cliffs the sides of which, where absolutely perpendicular, had a basaltic appearance, & every other part was thickly covered with firs, chiefly the spruce. Under the hill on our left, called by the people of the country Eckerfiel, & sometimes Yetterstrop, (Giants leap) we saw some large stones placed a little in the shape of Stone Henge. They were seven in number, & the area they enclosed which was circular, about 17 yrds. diam. Height of the stones 8 or 9 feet, & breadth & thickness about a yard. In a part where one seemed to be wanting, a flatter stone has been erected since by Gustavus Frederick, to commemorate a visit which he & his Queen made there in 1754.[1]

From the range of perpendicular rocks which rises not far from the stones, tradition says that the Giants in old times used to leap when they were tired of life & wished to go to Valholl. Their brethren below used to pick them up, wash them in a little pond at the bottom of the cliff which is now grown marshy, burn their bodies & bury their bones inclosed in urns. This tradition we heard from the countryman who shewed us the spot; but he said that orders were given by Adolphus Fried'k to dig for these urns, but none were found.

On examining the cliff near, it appeared that there was a great similarity to Basaltes in the formation of the stones, but they wanted that regularity with which Basaltes are usually accompanied. Clarke took with him a specimen for examination at Stoc[k]holm, & also a specimen of what he thought was trap. From the top of the loose rocks that had fallen from the cliff, the scene appeared a fine amphitheatre of rocks fringed with fir.

[1] Malthus has made a slip here about Gustavus Frederick: the King of Sweden from 1751 to 1771 was Adolphus Frederick, the father of Gustav III.

Clarke regarded the royal stone as 'a most preposterous addition', and thoroughly disapproved of 'the *Swedish* Monarch who thus violated a Celtic coemetery' (*Travels* v, 122).

Here we parted, Otter & I to return to Wennersburgh & Clark & Cripps to proceed to Stockholm.

Clarke and Cripps went on from Stockholm to Uppsala, and along the west coast of the Gulf of Bothnia to Tornea; thence they came south to Röros and Trondheim, and down the Gudbrandsdal to Christiania, which they reached on 14 October. Their tour was extended to Russia, Tartary, Turkey, the Holy Land, Egypt, and Greece; they did not come back for three and a half years: see p. 16.

Clarke was "'feverishly impatient" about his travels. In his journey from Lake Werner to Torneá, which, including a stay at Stockholm, occupied about eighteen days, he was "never in bed more than four hours out of forty-eight". Malthus and Otter soon dropped off, but Clarke and Cripps pressed on.'[1]

In our way from Wennersburgh we had pass'd over the upper part of the river Gotha by a bridge; & in its rocky bottom & frequent falls saw the reason why the navigation is carried on by the Carlsgraaf sluice. While we were near Hunneburgh we went into a peasant's wooden cottage to get some milk, & found every thing very clean & neat about it, with a weaving machine in the middle. A little field of hemp adjoining.

At the inn at Wennersburgh, on our return, we met with a gentleman who had been at school in England, & had a farm 3 or 4 miles off. He told us that we could not have travelled at a worse time with regard to horses; for that they had been almost all half-starved by the hard winter, & there was now scarcely anything for them to eat. He himself was travelling with his own horses, & could find neither corn, hay or grass for them. The only thing he could get was a little rye bread, which he did not consider as very good nourishment for them. He told us that the price of labour was 1s. & 16d., & dearer in general than at Gotheburgh. The married labourers of the farmers have generally a house & land enough to keep 1 or two cows, found them; for which they may be called upon to work at all times, & any time, even sundays. The servants that live in the houses of the farmers are seldom married. They are paid about 50 or 60 dollars, a year. I asked him if the

[1] Quoted from *D.N.B.*

lower classes of people in general married young—he said yes; but upon enquiry it appeared that only those who had some property did so.

The horses & cattle in Sweden had not bean in so bad a state for these last 50 years; and indeed we found that the post horses looked very thin & miserable; and tho they went better than their appearance indicated, yet they travelled much slower than we had heard was the common rate of posting in Sweden. We found in generall very small horses very much like those bred on our commons.

Fine, except a few clouds in the evening. Therm at 10, 69; at 2, 72. Temperature of lake Wenner at 11, 61. Observed at Wennerburgh an apple tree in full blossom—rather late.

Otter & myself left Wennerburgh about half past 7 for Udevalla, with the same horse that we had taken to Hunne-burgh, not having been able to procure any other. We left the Swedish servant with the other party, thinking 4s. a day too much for us; & determined to make our way as well as we could to Christiania without an interpreter, hoping to find a cheaper one there.

For the first stage to Almro,[1] 1 mile, we were obliged to walk almost all the way, our horse being quite knocked up. The other two stages we got on rather better, but did not arrive at Udevalla till 1 o'clock—found a hospitable chambermaid, & by the assistance of our own sheets had tolerable beds. The road from Wennersburgh to Udevalla is not particularly interesting, consisting chiefly of rocky ground, not high, thinly sprinkled with young firs, & here & there some grass, & poor cultivation. On our road we met & overtook a great number of small carts; but did not know what goods they carried. Many of them indeed seemed to be returning empty.

June 22 [Saturday]. Left Udevalla about 8, & soon after mounted a steep hill from which the view back was extremely pretty, a small arm of the sea reaching nearly to the town & the shores of it being high rocks, sprinkled with firs.[2] From Udevalla to Horiston,[3] ¾ of a mile, the country all the way is

[1] Almas on Pontoppidan's map of 1785.
[2] The 'small arm of the sea' at Uddevalla is the Byfjord.
[3] Horiston is Härsta.

pretty, bold rocks with woods in the bottoms, some grass fields not unfertile, & now & then a very fine field of rye in full ear. From Horiston to Quistrum, 1½ miles, country of the same kind; but not quite so fertile. Quistrum itself beautifully situated. From Quistrum to Swarteburgh,[1] 1¼ mile, rocks lower & more bare. From Swarteburgh, 1 mile to Rabalshee, a still more barren country. From Rabalshee to Hede, 1¼, one of the most dreary & desolate scenes that could well be conceived. For the two last stages rocks seem to be the only produce of the soil; but they wanted height & shape to give them any picturesque appearance.

Snow ploughs by the road side are common every where in Sweden. They are large triangular frames drawn with the point foremost along the roads, to remove the snow that has last fallen, by which means the roads are kept passable in the winter. From Wennersbergh we had travelled entirely in carts, some of which had no other bottoms than 2 or 3 sticks, to which a trunk might be strapped. We regretted much not having bought a cart or waggon at Gotheborgh, as those that we now found on the road were so very bad that we could not sit on them with tolerable ease, & were perpetually losing the small parts of our baggage. From a waggon without a bottom I lost my cloak a little before we reached Gothenburgh. In general however the waggons were much better than the carts.

From Hide to Skyallired,[2] ¾ mile, some rocky country not quite so bare. To Wik, 1 mile, similar. To Erit, 1 mile. Country improved, & more cultivated spots. To Hogdal 1 mile, a very hilly stage—towards the end pass'd thro a very fine rocky valley. At Hogdal, having overtaken our avant-courier, & finding two tolerable beds, we determined to sleep, instead of going on to Swinesund.

The house was of timbers formed of firs almost whole, at least only a little flattened, and the seams stopped well with moss. This forms a wall of considerable thickness which looks as if it would be very dry & warm. Most of the houses in this part of Sweden are built in the same way. In general nothing further is done to the inside of the room; but the boards are left in their natural state. For our beds & breakfast we paid

[1] Svarteberg.   [2] I think this must be Skallerod.

24 schillings (2s. English) the cheapest bill we had had. In general we had found our living dearer than in London for the same fare, which we supposed to be owing to their wish to get as much as they could out of Englishmen.

We had in general caused some staring; but this morning more than usual. A party among which were 2 or 3 women collected at the door of our room which was accidentally open & seemed to be exceedingly diverted with all our gestures. They had the politeness sometimes to turn aside their faces that we might not see them burst into a laugh.

Cloudy—few drops of rain. Therm at 9, 62; at 7, 65. Wind S.W.

June 23 [Sunday]. From Hogdal to Swinesund 1 mile—steep hills & fine bold rocks with some small lakes. To Swinesund we descended by a steep rugged hill to the water that goes up to Frederickshall, which is here inclosed by dark rocks rising almost perpendicularly out of the water. As the custom house officer on the Swedish side was not very civil we took a boat on the other side for Fredericksall (for which we were to pay a dollar) & had a pleasant row to the Town.[1] The shores widen after leaving Swinesund; but the same rockiness continues; & the river is certainly beautiful.—The only fault is too great a smoothness on the tops of some of the rocks.

Morning cloudy—afternoon showry. Therm at 1, 60. Wind S.

Arrived at Frederickshall very hungry having had nothing but eggs & milk the preceeding day, & not having been able to eat the bread they gave us with our breakfast in the morning— Got some tolerable cold veal which we relished much. Sent our letter to Mr Niels Ancher, who called upon us in the afternoon & obligingly invited us to a dance & supper, which was to take place that evening.[2] We rather wished to see some Norwegian dancing & tho a little tired accepted of his invitation.

[1] Halden is the modern and also the original name of the Norwegian border town of Fredrikshald. After repulsing Swedish attacks in 1660, it was granted municipal privileges by Frederick III, and called after him for over 250 years.

[2] Niels Anker (1764–1812) was a member of a large family, described by Coxe as 'the richest and most commercial' in Norway (*Travels*, v, 38). Niels had received his commercial education in Holland and England, and took over an important sugar-refining business from an uncle.

The ballroom was not very elegant or large, nor were the ladies in general very pretty;[1] but both ladies & gentlemen danced very well, particularly the Walse, at which we made a very awkward figure. Their time is slower; but there is more variety both in their tunes & figures than in the English country dances. Sometimes a minuet air & step were introduced. We could not help making the same remark as at Copenhagen with regard to the provincial appearance of the ladies & gentlemen. They had no foreign air whatever;—the company looked exactly like an assembly in a small country town in England, only the ladies not quite so pretty. Some of the ladies spoke french tolerably well; but the first that I danced with could only speak Norwegian, so that we could converse only by signs. Short waists both in men & women prevailed in the extreme. The very long skirts of the men's coats, & the narrowness of the buttons behind, contributed to their vulgar air.

The dance was given by a society composed chiefly of the military—very few of the merchants besides Mr Ancher belonged to it. He told us that the other society to which the military were not admitted had a much more brilliant ballroom. This room was only large enough to hold about ten couple & the walls were left in the natural state of the rough wood except being painted white. Each of the societys has a ball once a week—the ladies are extremely fond of dancing. They told us that they sometimes begun at 7 & continued till 7 the next morning.

Mrs Ancher we found a very pleasant & well informed woman—she talked french very fluently & english a little.[2] She was the daughter of a general officer at Christiania, & had received a much better education than the ladies of the country in general; though we understood that a great many of them spoke both french & german—german more frequently than

[1] Henry Brougham, who was at a similar party on 22 December of the same year, did not agree with Malthus about the ladies of Fredrikshald; he wrote, 'The women struck us as very pretty.' He was, however, only twenty-two (*Life and Times of Henry, Lord Brougham*, by Himself (Blackwood, 1871), I, 211).

[2] Mrs Niels Anker would have been 23 years old at this time, having married Niels when she was 20 and he 32. He was to die when he was only 48, in 1812, but she lived until 1855. Her name was Annette Beata, and her father was General August Fredrik von Wackenitz.

French. In the winter the ladies & gentlemen of Frederickshall act Danish plays & some of them we were told were tolerable proficients. We did not hear of many plays that were written by Norwegian poets.[1] Our supper lasted a considerable time, & consisted of soup, turkey, fish & veal, in the order in which they are mentioned. We have observed in general ever since we have been out that the fish always comes in the middle or towards the end, & never at the beginning as in England.

In the course of the evening we were introduced by Mr Ancher to General Mainsbach, the Governor of the fortress,[2] who was very polite, & asked us to breakfast with him the next morning, when he would shew us the fortress, & take us a very beautiful ride.

Mr Ancher was very goodnatured & hearty, & pressed us to drink much claret at supper & much punch both before & after. He had been much in France & seemed to be no great enemy to republican principles. He complained with some warmth of the conduct of the English towards the Danish trade; & seemed to think that it would be wise in Denmark to fit out a fleet of 20 sail to assert her rights. War he thought would be better than the suffering such repeated outrages against their trade.[3]

The ball was on sunday—a proof that they have not the same notions about the manner of keeping it that we have.

June 24 [Monday]. Went in company with Mr Ancher to breakfast with the Governor where we found a set out of dryed

[1] The passage about Danish plays and Norwegian poets would be ironically received by a Norwegian patriot. The greatest 'Danish' playwright of the eighteenth century was Ludvig Holberg (1684-1754) who was born in Bergen, but left Norway at the age of twenty-two. He has been compared with Molière, and twenty-six of his comedies were acted in Copenhagen in the years 1722-7. Norway had no theatre, just as she had no national bank, and no university.

[2] Johann Friedrich von und zu Mansbach was born at Mansbach in Hesse in 1744, but became a naturalised Dane in 1776. He was Commandant of the fortress of Fredriksten from 1790 until his death in 1803, but in 1801 he commanded troops in Vestfold (the west side of the Oslofjord) for protection against a British landing.

[3] Danish-Norwegian warships, in charge of convoys, were resisting the British 'right of search', which was formally reasserted by sending a squadron to Copenhagen in August 1800. The sequel was the second Armed Neutrality of the North, formed in December, and Nelson's victory at Copenhagen in April 1801.

salmon, raw ham, a kind of sausage, & a very fine bird, cold, which they call'd an aarehen, a species of game which is common in the country, & is bought generally of the farmers & peasants who kill them in the woods. It is a large bird, & from the description given us, we thought it might be the black cock. There are no game laws—any person may shoot; but an owner of land who wishes to preserve his game may do it by giving notice.

The only liquors which we found to drink at breakfast were wine & rum—not a drop of water on the table. We eat heartily of the bird & drank a glass of wine, determined to accommodate ourselves to the customs of the country. After breakfast we walk'd round the ramparts. The fortifications are very irregular, partly from having been made at different times, but chiefly perhaps from being accommodated to the irregularity of the hill. There are very strong casemates; and every accommodation for a garrison, bomb-proof. The fortress will hold near 2,000 men. The garrison of Frederickshall at present is about six hundred, which with the national troops in the neighbourhood would amount to about 2,000; but in a case of necessity the general told us that an army of 8,000 could be collected in 7 or 8 days. The fortifications have been much improved since the siege of Charles the 12th,[1] & have lately been kept in a constant state of preparation, particularly during the reign of the late King of Sweden.

General Mainsback was asked by a Swedish officer as from the King, why he appeared to be so extraordinarily cautious, as the army of Sweden was by no means in a state fit for attack. He answered Je ne crains pas votre armee mais Je crains la tete de votre Roi. It was thought that the King would be rather pleased with the answer. General Mainsbach had before

---

[1] Charles XII of Sweden was killed besieging Fredrikshald in 1718. One of the claimants to his throne was his sister Ulrica Eleanora, who was married to Frederick, Prince of Hesse. There was a strong belief that Frederick of Hesse was responsible for Charles XII's death; his wife was duly crowned, and then in 1720 Ulrica abdicated in favour of her husband.

Charles XII was a highly romantic personage, of much interest to many Englishmen, including Dr Johnson. During the latter part of the Great Northern War, in which Sweden virtually lost her Baltic empire to Peter the Great of Russia, Charles went to Turkey to seek help from the Sultan. For years he was kept more or less as a prisoner, but finally escaped disguised as a horse-dealer, and rode back across Europe to his kingdom after an absence of fifteen years.

often seen the King of Sweden & conversed with him—he spoke of him as a man of great abilities & great insight into the characters of others; but a little too romanesque and bizarre. They had talked on the subject of Charles the 12th's death, & it was the King's opinion that he was not killed by a ball from the fortress.[1] The General seemed to have the same idea. We saw the spot at a little distance, where Charles was killed. The Danes had erected rather a boastful monument upon it; but afterwards when the two courts were on a friendly footing it was pulled down, in compliment to Sweden. We saw a part of the broken pillar at the house of a Mr Tank, & copied the inscription from a print of it, but unfortunately lost it the next morning.

The hill on which the fortress stands is composed chiefly of rock, & is about 500 feet high, (according to the Governor) but only 360 according to Mr Ancher.[2] It seems to be rather higher than any in the neighbourhood from which a judgement may be formed of the height of the rocks on the shores of the river. They were high for rocks but had no pretentions to be mountains. Sometimes they were in fine craggy shapes, but more frequently had the appearance of hills formed of rock instead of earth. The spruce fir which we observed in the greatest abundance often makes too smooth a covering.

After seeing the fortress we took a ride, mounted on 2 of Mr Ancher's horses, about 2 or 3 miles to the lake from which the fall of Tiesdal flows, & the river that runs to Frederickshall. The general talked french remarkably well, & appeared to be a man of much information. He is a cultivator as well as warrior, & farms himself a considerable quantity of land which belongs to the castle. He said that the summer was too short & the soil in general too moist for corn to thrive well. Pasture he finds succeed best. We saw some good fields of grass, & a few of corn. The General is no friend to commerce. He thinks

---

[1] Archdeacon Coxe was obviously fascinated by the mystery of Charles XII's death: he writes about it at length, and quotes an eyewitness whom he actually met; this man, then in his 94th year, convinced Coxe that the bullet which pierced the King's skull had come from the fortress, and not from an enemy nearer at hand—but Malthus seems to have kept an open mind (Coxe, *Travels*, v, 24–9).

[2] According to a modern Norwegian guide-book, the 'unconquered fortress' of Fredriksten is 394 feet above Halden.

that it enervates & corrupts the common people, & spoils the soldiers. He seemed to look with a little jealosy on the rich commercial upstarts & complained that the point of honour was nearly lost. Of all folie, he thought the cultivating folie was the most useful.

After a pretty ride, thro grass fields & fir woods mixed with rocks, we came to the fall of Tiesdal, from a wooden bridge over which, & from a house situated higher up the hill where the general had once lived, we had a delightful view down a narrow rocky valley, at the extremity of which we saw Fre-Frederickshall. The fall is altogether two or three hundred feet; but is divided in many places, & wants weight of water, to give it all the grandeur which we were told it sometimes possessd in the spring after the melting of the snows. The scenery, which would otherwise be very beautiful, is a little spoilt by the number of saw mills on the cataract, & the litter they occasion. The water after falling winds along the valley to Frederickshall, & is seen with all its winding from the house. At the back of the house is a fine view of the large lake which furnishes the stream. The shores are rocks covered with firs, but not very high.

This lake joins others which, by the help of some intervening streams, forms a communication by water for near 20 norway miles,[1] by means of which the timber in all the neighbourhood is floated down to the saw mills with little or no expence. The greatest part of the timber that we saw was small—between half a foot, & a foot in diameter. Mr Ancher told us that some of it was not above 10 or 12 years growth; but he seemed to talk loosely sometimes. We returned along the valley by the side of the river, & were very much pleased with our ride. The rocks on each side were in the finest shapes, & their bases well-wooded by other trees besides firs. After we were out of sight of the saw mills, the valley appeared a most romantic & secluded spot.[2]

Without returning to our lodgings, went to Mr Ancher's

[1] A Norwegian mile was about 6¾ English miles.

[2] Coxe also enjoyed the 'most delightful prospect', from 'a villa called Vake', above the village of Tistedal. He did not agree with Malthus about the ugliness of the saw-mills. He writes of the 'beautiful cataract of the Tiste, which precipitates itself in continued but irregular falls for a considerable way, and turns several saw-mills that form very picturesque objects, impending over the torrent of waters' (*Travels*, v, 29).

to dine, who told us that we must lay our account to a very poor dinner, as he had given no orders about it before. The first dish was dried salmon undress'd & spinage, which we could not relish at all, & as we expected only a cold dinner we were beginning to despair, when a fine roasted turkey made its appearance, which set our minds & our bodies at rest. We observed at dinner, and before at the supper, that the plates were changed, but not the knives & forks. Though there were two other very good rooms in the house, yet we dined in a bed room. We heard that meat was 5*d.* a pound. Their beef & mutton are generally thin, but their veal sometimes well fatted, & of a proper age. Mrs Ancher told us that baking, brewing & every thing must be done at home, which required rather a large household of servants, particularly as the servants were rather proud, & would not turn their hands to different sorts of work. She had only one child & was obliged to keep six maid servants.

From the Governor & Mr Ancher I learnt that a change had just taken place in the laws relating to the enrollment of the peasants for the army. Every man in Denmark & Norway born of a farmer or labourer is a soldier. Those born of sailors are sailors. Formerly the officer of the district might take them at any age he pleased and he generally preferred a man from 25 to 30 to those that were younger. After being taken the man could not marry without producing a certificate signed by the minister of the parish that he had substance enough to support a wife & family, & even then it was at the will of the officer to let him marry or not. This, & the uncertainty in respect to the time of being taken has hitherto operated as a strong preventive check to population in Norway, & accounts for their increasing so slowly, tho the people live so long.[1] No man could consider himself as perfectly free to marry, unless he had solid possessions, till he had served his time which, from their being taken sometimes at thirty, might not happen till he was 40 years old.

Clarke here shocks the modern reader. In his own book he quotes Malthus almost verbatim, beginning 'From the Governor

[1] According to the first census, in 1769, the population of Norway was 728,000; by 1801 it had increased to 883,000.

and Mr Anker we learned...', as though the conversation had taken place with Clarke and Cripps and not with Malthus. Worse still, he shifts the scene of the conversation from Fredrikshald to Christiania, so that 'the Governor' is not General Mansbach, who in fact expressed the views which Malthus recorded, but Colonel Bielefeldt, and the Mr Niels Anker of Fredrikshald, from whom Malthus actually received the information, is turned into Mr Bernt Anker of Christiania.[1]

The only excuse for Clarke must be that this report occurs in the volume of his travels which was published posthumously, and he was already ill when he was working on this part of it.

I took some pains to enquire whether the certificate of having enough to support a family was a civil or military institution. From what I could learn it appeared to be entirely military, & to have arisen from the fear that the children of soldiers might fall upon the publick or starve. It has however without doubt had a very strong influence in a civil point of view, & is in my opinion the cause why the lower classes of people in Norway are in a much better state than could be expected from the barreness of the country. These laws however are just now at an end.[2] The liberty of marriage is allowed without any certificate, or permission of the officer, & all the young men of 20 are taken first, & if that is not enough all of 22, & so on, & it is no longer in the breast of the officer to chuse the men at what age he likes. Formerly any person under 36 might be taken; & the oldest were generally taken first. One proof that the certificate is entirely a military institution is, that a peasant before he was taken might marry without one; but then he exposed his wife & family to the danger of being starved, if he was taken, unless he could leave behind him a sufficiency to support them; and it is probable that parents would not let their daughters marry without some prospect of that kind.

The General disapproved of the new regulation, & said that the peasants would probably now marry without any prospect of being able to maintain a family, & that the consequence

[1] *Travels*, VI, 8–10.
[2] The laws governing military service in Denmark were changed at the time of the emancipation of the serfs in 1788; the new system of enrolment in Norway was established by a decree dated 1 November 1799.

would be that more would be born than the country could support. He said that the old laws on the subject had been put in force very loosely lately, & that the effect was that they had more jeux than ever. A great many children, he said, died between birth & five years old. He thought that 20, tho it might suit very well France, was too young for a Norwegian, as the northern peasant was much later in attaining maturity.

All born in the districts along the coasts, & all in the inland towns born of parents who get their living by fishing are enrolled as sailors. All born in the inland districts in the country are soldiers. Those born of tradespeople in the towns are free except with regard to the services they are obliged to perform as burghers.[1]

In the evening we went to sup with a Mr Tank, a merchant, who had a house very prettily situated by the water half a mile out of the Town.[2] He took us into his garden which was laid out perfectly in the dutch style, & kept us near two hours explaining the several means he had used to deform the fair face of nature. We were pretty well tired with summer house after summer house, & box after box, turks' heads, guns, batteries, & a long etcetera of absurdities. The only tolerable thing was a Hermit very well done in wax, which upon touching a spring on the floor moved forwards in a manner rather to startle one.

After our walk in the gardens he took us into his museum of curiosities, where he appeared rather in a more favourable point of view, having a tolerable collection of books in different languages. He shew'd us the print of the monument erected on the spot where Charles the 12th was killed, from which we copied the inscription. The only thing besides that we thought worthy of remark was one of the vertebrae of a whale, the skeleton of which was found entire near the falls of Tiesdal, one among the many proofs of the convulsions that the earth has sustained.

The supper, at which were about 20 people, lasted a long time. Every-thing was carved at the bottom of the table, &

---

[1] Malthus left the next three pages blank.
[2] Carsten Tank (1766–1832) was a leading timber merchant with important political contacts in Sweden. His fine house and park are still to be seen at Röd, on the outskirts of Halden; they passed to the Anker family when Tank's business failed in 1829.

dishfull after dishfull was handed round almost without end. We were rather hungry & thought we played our parts pretty well; but some of the ladies beat us hollow. I had an old lady who spoke french on one side of me & Mr Tank's son, a well informed young man, on the other. Mr T informed me that the first vessels sail'd from Frederickshall the 20th April; but that the frost was not completely over till the 1st of May. The thermometer on the coldest day was between 26 & 27 Reaumur. The governor had told me only 22.[1]

Most of the merchants seemed to be a little inclined to republicanism. They extoll much the liberty they enjoy under their own government; & say that in England we are comparatively slaves. Mr T complained in the same manner as Mr Anker of the conduct of the English government towards the neutral powers.

The interest of money on landed security is 4 per cent. On simple bond the common interest is 5. 4 is the legal interest of money throughout the Danish dominion.

Formerly there were many different religious sects in Norway, some like our methodists; but at present all are united.[2] Mr T seemed to talk as if a good deal of indifferentism prevailed on religious subjects, tho he did not expressly say so.

On coming first into Mr Tank's house we were introduced into a room with a bed in it, where were about a dozen men smoaking. This custom is universal. The Governor told me that he smoaked about 20 pipes a day. Speaking of the climate the Governor said that they had huit mois d'hiver & quatre mois de mauvais temps, but from what we have seen our selves we certainly should not make the same remark. He said that he had been only four days this summer without his great coat. We had heard the same expression of huit mois d'hiver & quatre mois de mauvais temps at Copenhagen.

On entring Norway I observed that all the trees were in full foliage, ashes, oaks & c. The Lilacs in Mr Tank's garden were fully out—every bud was blown, so that in a day or two they would begin to go off.

---

[1] Malthus has again omitted the words 'below zero'. ($-26°$ R $= -27°$ F and $-22°$ R $= -17°$ F.)

[2] The people 'like our methodists' were led by Hans Nielsen Hauge, the 'Wesley of Norway', who by 1799 had several thousand followers. They remained within the State Church, although their lay preachers were bitterly persecuted.

I had no opportunity to day of looking at the thermometer. We returned to our lodgings between 12 & 1.[1]

June 25 [Tuesday]. After a second breakfast at Mr Ancher's, which was forced upon us, we left Fredickshall in two most miserable carts. Having been treated so handsomely in the Town we were rather ashamed of so shabby an exit, & therefore walked forwards hoping that the carts would not be thought to belong to us. From Frederickshall to Skieberg, 1½ miles, we passed a rocky country sprinkled with firs, & here & there some spots better cultivated than the greatest part of Sweden. The cottages were built in the same form & of the same materials; but occurred rather more frequently.

From Skiebergh to Thunde,[2] 1½, country flatter & more cultivated. On our way we made a little detour to see the grand waterfall of Sarp.[3] The scenery around is not nearly so beautiful as at Tiesdal; but the fall itself is much finer. The body of water is greater than that of Trolhatta & the fall much higher. It is not however quite in so picturesque a shape, & the effect of it is much spoilt by the number of saw mills which prevent its being seen in the best point of view. The old general told us that it was the grandest fall in the World after that of Niagara in America; but it appears to us that he could not be very well informed upon such subjects, to make such an assertion.

Soon after leaving the fall we passed the Glommen, the river that forms it, by a ferry, & found the stream very strong. The breadth at the ferry might be about 70 or 80 yards. Before the end of our stage we passed another river, more than half as large, by a bridge. The valley thro which it flowed was very pretty in the style of the prominent features of the country— rocky hills covered with pines.

From Thunde to [blank] 1½ miles, we pass'd some piney hills, with one or two pretty lakes at a little distance. At Thunde we met with a Scotch-man who kept the post house. He looked very dirty & ragged but said he was very well off, & had lately taken a farm there which he expects would

---

[1] Malthus again left two pages blank.
[2] Possibly Kjölberg and Lundby.
[3] The Sarpsfossen falls are 68 feet high.

answer. He was very civil & seemed to be an honest man which we hardly expected, having in general found that those who could speak English, were inclined to make us pay for the convenience. Before the end of our stage we were caught in a shower, and saw by far the most brilliant rainbow that I ever saw in my life. It appeared to be double, particularly towards the upper part of the arch, and to consist of twice the number of stripes usually observed, all marked in the most distinct manner. It was near sunsetting, & the arch remarkably large & in every part complete & vivid.

From [blank] to Moss 1½ mile. Same kind of country. Towards the end of the stage we passed a very fine lake to the right, at some little distance, which seemed to extend far into the country, & to be covered with many islands. We did not reach Moss till after 12. It was quite cold but fine & clear. We read a small print at 12 with perfect ease. Got tolerable beds at Moss.

Fine & fair except a shower in the afternoon. Therm at 2, 57; at 10 at night, 42. Wind S. by W.[1]

June 26 [Wednesday]. Wishing to go to Christiania by water instead of journeying in our miserable carts, we did not order horses overnight, and had some difficulty in finding a boat. We passed the morning in walking about the invirons & seeing Mr Ben't Anker's iron works.[2] The country about Moss is pretty & the river a fine object. It has some commerce in wood & iron; but a peninsula that juts out into the river just before the town, & extends some way upwards, is a great disadvantage to its navigation as it makes two opposite winds absolutely necessary to get out—a south wind to weather the head of the Peninsula, & a North wind to go down the river.

At the inn we met with a pleasant young Norwegian officer

---

[1] Here Malthus left almost a whole page blank.

[2] Bernt Anker had owned the Iron Works since 1776; the main building is from the second half of the eighteenth century and is today one of the 'sights' of Moss: the Convention of Moss, which arranged the union with Sweden, was signed there on 14 August 1814. The Mosseelv river was used to operate saw-mills as early as 1503.

Archdeacon Coxe also went round the Iron Works at Moss, breaking his overland journey from Fredrikshald to Christiania in order to do so. At that time (1784) they employed about 150 men, and had only lately begun 'to cast cannon, which are mostly exported to Copenhagen' (*Travels*, v, 32).

94

who spoke English remarkably well.[1] He seemed not much to like the army—spoke of the brutality & want of education in the greatest part of his companions, and expatiated with much feeling on the starving condition of the inferior officers, & the hopelessness of promotion. All officers, except for some particular merit during actual service, rise by seniority, which makes promotion during a peace most extremely slow. An education during four years at least at the Military academy, either of Copenhagen or Christiania, is previously necessary to a commission; & after that, those that are not noble often serve for some years as non commissioned officers, before a commission can be given them. He said there was hardly a captain in his regiment that was under 60 years old. He seemed to think that the Prince, with all his attention to the army, had not done much to increase the comforts of the soldiers & officers.

We walked together to see Mr Anker's iron works, & were pleased with an ingenious slitting machine, the plan of which was brought here by an Englishman, & also by the manner of making nails a process which I had not seen before. All the hammers, & every other part of the machinery are worked by water. On a cannon which was cast in the presence of the Prince, when he made the tour of Norway in 89, was inscribed 'Non ullo tantum tellus jactabit alumno'.[2] The young officer desired us to construe it & seemed to think it too high a compliment.

There are many saw mills at Moss which also belong to Mr Anker.

For beds without supper, coffee in the morning & a very miserable dinner at the table of our host & hostess, we were charged 4 dollars to the great astonishment of the young officer, who said that he could not conceive how the bill could amount to one dollar. We were glad, in this instance, to know from good authority, that the very high charges that had been made to us during our journey, did not arise from the actual dearness of provisions in the countries thro which we had

---

[1] Clarke makes a paragraph out of this young army officer, using Malthus's words, but letting it appear that he had met him at 'a rout and supper in Christiania' (*Travels*, VI, 6, 13).
[2] 'Earth will not boast so much of any other offspring.'

passed; but from the desire of the people not to lose an opportunity of making as much of strangers as possible. We made
some remonstrances, but found they were of no avail. We had
before been at a loss to conceive how people of small fortunes,
& all are certainly not rich in Sweden & Norway, could con-
trive to live.

Soon after 2 we set off in a small boat with a favouring wind
for Christiania, 6½ miles. There is no tide of any consequence
in the river, tho the water is salt up to Christiania.[1] A little
rise & fall of 2 or 3 feet sometimes takes place from the currents
formed chiefly by the wind. The river is very irregular in its
breadth, being in parts confined in one & sometimes 2 narrowish channels 3 or 4 hundred yards wide, & in other parts
extending itself to one or two miles. The shores are perfectly
clear. Rocky hills covered with pines rise immediately from
the water & their only fault is that they sometimes form too
smooth a surface. We pass'd 2 pretty villages on the right hand
shore, on almost the only spots indeed on which villages could
be placed, the greatest part of the shore being too rocky &
perpendicular for the habitations of men. In one of the villages
particularly were some very neat houses. As we approached
Christiania the hills increased in height & the river had the
appearance of a large & beautiful lake, studded with numerous
islands, & bounded by hills in very fine shapes, which now for
the first time had the blue cast of mountains upon them. It
was the most beautiful view that we had yet seen. We were
much pleased with our sail, & arrived at Christiania about 10
where we got a comfortable room & a veal steak dress'd in a
better manner than we had met with since leaving England.

Fine & fair. Therm. at 3, 61. Wind a fresh breeze.[2]

We are now introduced to the 'great Mr Anker'. See Plate 2. This
was Bernt Anker (1746–1805) whose fortune came from shipping,
timber and mines. He sold timber to the British Navy, and knew
England well; at one time he was expected to become Danish
Minister in London. The firm came to an end in 1819, after a fire
in the timber-yards at Christiania.

[1] The 'river' is, of course, the fjord. Malthus is continually handicapped in his
descriptions of fjords through not knowing this word.
[2] Here Malthus left another blank page.

Malthus would have known about him from Coxe's book: he was 38 when Coxe met him in 1784, 'Fellow of the Royal Society, speaks English nearly as well as a native, possesses an excellent house in Christiania, elegantly furnished in the English taste, and ornamented with a good collection of pictures which he purchased in Italy. He lives in a stile of elegant magnificence, and receives all travellers with unbounded politeness and hospitality.'[1]

Clarke describes him in some detail; he and Cripps were 'feasted' in Christiania, in the middle of October, by the same set of people who entertained Malthus and Otter in the summer. 'Being Chamberlain to the King of Denmark, Bernard Anker wore the Danish court badge—a large key and riband, fastened to the button of his coat behind. In his person, he was above the common size, of athletic form, and well-looking. His hair, decorated in the old Parisian taste, was highly frizzled and powdered: and, during the whole of his conversation, he stood opposite a large mirror, attentively surveying and adjusting the different articles of his dress: but in all this there was nothing of mere vanity, or of affectation...We soon found, in the conduct of this exemplary individual, a lesson against judging too hastily from outward appearances. His heart was possessed by the best qualifications of human nature; and his mind, well stored with intelligence and full of resources, poured forth, in every conversation, such general knowledge of the world, and of the springs of human actions, whether in court cabinets or in private life, as made all who became acquainted with him eager to join his company.'[2]

In this connection it is interesting to note that Bishop Pontoppidan of Bergen (1698–1764) commented on the 'magnificence' of the Norwegian merchant in his *Natural History of Norway*, first published in Danish in 1751. He wrote of 'the Norvegian's desire to distinguish himself in his station by fine cloaths, elegant houses & c. This is very conspicuous in most of the trading towns, where commerce gives them an opportunity of conversing with foreigners, especially the English, whom they chiefly endeavour to imitate; but for want of abilities to equal that nation in splendor, magnificent entertainments, furniture, and equipages, a great many ruin themselves.' He adds in a footnote, 'Our Bergen merchants, who are most of them descended from the frugal Dutch, or Germans, continue still in that plain way, like good sober tradesmen.'[3]

The Bishop, however, is not quite consistent; he is surely boasting a little when he writes that 'most of our merchants live in a more

---

[1] Coxe, *Travels*, v, 38.   [2] Clarke, *Travels*, vi, 3, 4.
[3] Erik Pontoppidan, *Natural History of Norway* (London, 1755), p. 255.

elegant manner than the noblesse in other countries'.[1] It would appear that elegance was closely related to the consumption of wine.

June 27 [Thursday]. Sent our letters to the great Mr Anker, who returned an answer that he should be glad to see us at 2. We called at the time appointed & found him very polite & obliging tho rather great. We had an hour & a half's conversation with him, but he sent us back without a dinner, promising however to send his carriage for us at six to take us to his seat in the country about half a Norway mile off, where he is generally resident in the summer.

During our conversation the character of the Prince was started; and Mr A observed that his character was not well known & seldom greatly appreciated. He believed him to be the most moral man that could well exist, and of the most strict & impartial justice. He was not indeed generous; but it could hardly be attributed to him as a fault, arising as it did from the very small sum which he took for his own expences—not more than 12,000 dollars—a little above 2,000£ a year.

He never would confer the rank of nobility, & was always most extremely cautious in granting any office or favour of any kind. His extreme fear of being partial sometimes carried him too far, & prevented him from granting anything, to a person who he might even think deserved it, if it was asked for.

He was very silent in company & partly Mr A thought from the fear of having some proposition made to him or some favour asked. If a man had once made a request of him, the Prince seldom spoke to him afterwards, tho he might still continue to like him. Mr A said that the P talked often very familiarly with him, which he attributed to his never having once asked a favour of him. The P is disliked at Copenhagen because the people about the court are all poor & beggars. Mr A seemed to think that he had good natural talents & particularly a good memory; but that his education had been much neglected, of which he was fully sensible, & sometimes complained himself. Unfortunately he was not fond of reading, which prevented him from repairing what was deficient.

He has no favourite whatever. Count Bernstoff, Mr A

---

[1] Pontoppidan, *Natural History of Norway*, p. 267.

thought, had no particular influence. He is only secretary of state & not of the Grand council; and is by no means considered as prime minister.

The King is very fond of the parade of royalty, & appears extremely displeased when any thing like a want of proper respect is shewn to him. It is an order of the Court that nobody should speak to him. He is to be answered only by a bow, & this rule is kept with great strictness.

Mr A thinks that the liberality of the Prince's government, and his contempt for libels, proceeds from principle & from his consciousness of rectitude of conduct, added perhaps to his opinion that it is the wisest & safest plan to let those things quite alone. A libel was some little time ago prosecuted by one of the courts, & the consequence was that the book which had before been neglected sold in the most rapid manner & 3 or 4 large editions were successively published.

At six we went to Mr Anker's country house & drank tea in the garden. The house is very charmingly situated among some very fertile grass fields, surrounded by hills covered with firs and some fine views of the river and its surrounding mountains.[1] Mrs Anker seems to be a motherly good sort of woman much older than her husband.[2] During our walk round the garden & grounds Mr A expatiated with no small degree of vanity on his own magnificence, & the largeness of his establishment. He said indeed that it was absolutely necessary for a man to have every thing within himself in Norway; for that scarcely any thing could be bought. Those who live handsomely in this country must collect a store themselves from all parts of the world, for the whole year; which makes living in Norway more expensive perhaps than any other part of the world. He keeps thirty servants & told us that his brother kept 60.

The fire wood consumed by his establishment, in the number of different stoves required in the winter, amounted to above 4 times as much as a nobleman's family would consume in Copenhagen, & we were rather surprised to hear him say that

---

[1] This was Frogner, now the Oslo Town Museum.

[2] Mrs Bernt Anker (Mathia Collett), nine years older than her husband, was 61 at this time. She was a widow when he married her in 1773: he would then have been 27 and she 36. She died in 1801, and her husband only lived another four years. They had no children.

fire wood was an expensive article. But the article of the greatest expence to a gentleman in Norway was his horses on account of the dearness of hay in general; but particularly this spring. As well as we could calculate, the common price of hay seemed to be about 5£ a tun—this spring it has been double, and indeed not to be had for money; but Mr A was in no want, always taking care to secure a very plentiful stock. He keeps 20 horses for pleasure; & 8 or so carriages.

As we were returning from a Grecian Temple that he had been shewing us,[1] we met a gentleman who seemed very submissively to ask to see it—this Mr A condescendingly granted, telling us at the same time with a half contemptuous wave of his hand, that it was one of the parsons of the Town. After having seen the Temple the poor parson returned & walked at an humble distance by the side of the great man, who did not vouchsafe him a single word or even look. When we returned to the ladies, they received him rather more graciously. He was dress'd in a lightish brown coat, with black buttons, and I must confess did not look much like a gentleman.[2]

Having sufficiently seen & admired the gardens Mr A, after enumerating his various kinds of carriages that were left in Town, ordered the Holstein waggon to take us to Mr Collet's, a friend of his who lived about an english mile off. He had married an eleve of Mrs Ancher's, & Mr A told us that he had given him the estate. Mr Collet's house was situated higher & commanded a more extensive view than Mr A's; but upon the whole I preferred Mr A's. In all the environs of Christiania there is much softness—none of the more rugged features of the country appear.

Mr Collet received us with great heartiness, & seemed much pleased to shew his grounds that he had laid out, & his lands that he improved.[3] He is a great farmer & has nearly four

---

[1] There is a Grecian Temple there still, built in 1840, but on exactly the same little knoll as Bernt Anker's was, as can be clearly seen from contemporary paintings.

[2] Compare this pastor with Mr Polhill of Albury, p. 5.

[3] John Collett (1758–1810) was English by origin, and well known for his large model farm in what are now the suburbs of Oslo, where he practised and popularised the improved English methods of agriculture. He had studied for a time at Oxford, and was in business in London from 1780 to 1792. His farm at Ullevaal was famous for its English equipment and bloodstock; his parties were famous, too. See Plate 3.

hundred acres of land in his own hands. He treats rye in the same manner as we do wheat, and prepares the land for it by 2 or 3 other crops successively, so as to get a good crop of rye on the same land once in 3 or 4 years. His first crop of clover was cutting & some of it in cock. He feeds his cows in the winter with turnips & carrots preserved in cellars, 6 different sorts of food every day. He kills his veal at about 6 weeks or 2 months old. The price of labour, he told us, was 1s. in summer & 10d. in winter, without victuals. Potatoes thrive remarkably well. They have been introduced into Norway about 30 years, and are coming daily more into use.

When we got into his garden, which in some parts is laid out pretty well, in others too much in the dutch taste, we thought we should never get out of it again. In one little retreat we found liqueurs, oranges & sweetmeats, in another pipes, tobacco & beer, in another, which was up in a tree, some very fine champaign &c: &c: It was a most delightful evening, and tho we were rather incommoded by too much fussing, yet we could not help being much pleased with the novelty & beauty of the scene.

Mr Collett's hospitality suited Clarke better than Malthus. Clarke and Cripps were invited to dine with the Colletts on 15 October 1799 and Clarke wrote: 'Such was the magnificence of the feast to which we had been invited, that it would hardly be possible for our own Sovereign to afford a more sumptuous entertainment. We had every delicacy of the country, and all the wines of Europe, together with every species of costly liqueur and confectionary...According to the custom of the country, we remained many hours at table: but we did not wish to move; for the most cheerful conviviality, and the liveliest conversation, was maintained the whole time, without dispute or intoxication. The only anxiety on the part of our host and hostess, arose from a fear lest their guests should not be as well fared, and as merry, as it was possible to make them.'[1]

Henry Brougham had a different point of view. He joined a house-party of thirty-five people at Mr Collett's country place, Flädebije, just after Christmas, 1799, and was distressed at finding his host and hostess the 'slaves' of their company, constantly running hither and thither.[2]

---

[1] *Travels*, VI, 18.
[2] *Life and Times of Henry, Lord Brougham*, by Himself (Blackwood, 1871), I, 217.

Mrs Collet was a very agreeable woman & is reckoned a pattern to all the wives in Norway.[1] Mr C looked as if he had been very well taken care of. With some difficulty we got away, to return to Mr Anker's to supper at a quarter past ten; but we even then left Mr Col. in the act of opening another bottle of champaign, & murmuring against our unkindness in going.

We supped at Mr A's & came to our lodgings in his chariot at half past 12.

Fine. Therm in a deep shade at 4, 71. Wind S.[2]

June 28 [Friday]. We were engaged to dine with Mr Ancher at half past 2, & to go to his brother's in the evening. In the morning, walked up to the Castle with the daughter of the landlord of our Inn as an interpreter.[3] She speaks french, is a little of a coquette, & is much celebrated in the neighbourhood for the gracefulness of her manners; but she has not much pretension to beauty. On account of her superior accomplishments she is admitted into the first circle at Christiania. Mr A praised her highly & said that she was one of their best actresses. They have private theatricals at Christiania as well as at Frederickshall, & Mr A himself often takes a principal part—sometimes indeed that of author as well as actor. He told us of a tragedy that he had written on the subject of the death of Major André, which he performed before the Prince Royal, playing himself the part of the Major.[4] The Prince, he told us, was highly pleased.

We were much delighted with the view of the river & the country from the ramparts. The river is so landlocked that its general appearance is that of a fine extensive lake ornamented with islands, & surrounded by blue mountains in fine shapes; but as far as I can judge the mountains are not as high as those about the lakes in Westmorland & Cumberland. The fortress seems to be strong & there are some fine brass cannon on the

[1] Martine (Tina) Christine Sophie Elieson married her first cousin John Collett at Bernt Anker's house in 1783, when she was 19 and John 25. They had no children. She died in 1826, having been widowed for 16 years.

[2] Malthus left two pages blank before starting the entry for the following day.

[3] 'The Castle' is Akershus, the fortress of Oslo.

[4] This performance had taken place as long ago as 1788, when the Crown Prince Frederick had been Mr Anker's guest at his 'palace' in Christiania. Major John André (1751–80) was hanged by the Americans as a spy during the War of Independence.

ramparts. The garrison at present at Christiania does not consist of one entire regiment; but there are some chasseurs besides, which make up altogether the number of a whole regiment, or 1,200 men, & four companies of artillery.

At 2 the chariot came for us to go to Mr Anker's, where we met among others an english lady, the wife of a merchant in Christiania, & Colonel Bielefeld, commander of all the artillery in Norway, who distinguished himself much when the Prince of Hesse entered Sweden in 88 & was near taking Gotheburgh.[1]

In conversation with Colonel Bielefeld I found that he did not approve of the new regulations respecting the enrollment of the peasants. He thought that very young men did not make good soldiers, & he had besides apprehensions that they would all be tempted now to marry so early, that they would not be able to provide for their families, & the country be much more distressed than formerly. They were now however to make the trial, & events would determine respecting the utility of the measure. He said the lower classes of people were very much delighted with it.

The English lady who sate by Otter expatiated much on the inconveniences which persons of moderate fortunes were subject to, from not being able to lay in those stores which Mr Ancher spoke of. She said that nothing was to be bought, if you had ever so much money; & that she was really sometimes ready to cry with vexation. She had lived in Norway about 2 years, & said she was very happy, having only one wish, and that was to live in England. She was rather vulgar, & not a very agreeable person—we had not much reason to be proud of our countrywoman.

We had a good dinner; but not the roast beef which Mr A promised us, having forgot to mention it to his wife in time. He says he kills a fat ox generally once a fortnight. They drink much at dinner but not afterwards. We had a bowl of bishop made of burgundy;[2] & one of champaign—madeira & claret

---

[1] Carl Frederick Bielefeldt (1752–1825) had become a Lieut.-Colonel in 1796; in 1807 he was to be second-in-command during the siege of Copenhagen, and to be court-martialled and cashiered as a scapegoat after its surrender to the British.

[2] According to Clarke, 'Bishop' (which he drank at Mr Collett's house) was 'a favourite beverage...served in copious bowls of rich porcelain: it consisted of Burgundy and claret, mixed with sugar, spices, and Seville oranges' (*Travels*, VI, 17).

in profusion. We dined in an harbour in the garden. We rose from dinner before five, took our coffee, & set off in the Holstein waggon with four very handsome horses, to Mr Peter Ancher's, who lives up the country about half a Norway mile from his brother. On our way we called at a place of Colonel Bielefeld's which he had lately taken, & which was very prettily laid out, & commanded some delightful views of the river. I rather preferred it to either Mr A's or Mr Collet's. Mr A told us that the Colonel rented it of his brother Mr Peter Ancher. It had been laid out by Mrs Collet's sister who was a widow, & had now left it in order to marry & follow a young officer of 22.

Mr Peter Ancher's house we found to be much the most magnificent of any we had yet seen—the suite of apartments was quite princely, & fitted up in a very elegant style.[1] The gardens were laid out a l'Anglois—the situation on the borders of a lake at the foot of a rocky mountain covered with pines. The lake however, tho very pretty, was not so fine as the river, & as there was a little flatness, with some red houses in the front of the house, I preferred upon the whole the situation of the Colonel's & Mr Ancher's. The mountain close to Mr P Ancher's is reckoned the highest in the neighbourhood of Christiania. I could not get at the measure of it, but it appeared to me not to be high as a *mountain*; I should rather have called it a high hill.[2]

Mr & Mrs P Ancher were out when we arrived; but we were furnished with tea in the gardens by the governess, an agreeable woman who spoke french well.[3] When Mr P. A. returned he received us with great hospitality & gave us all sorts of invitations, which we had it not in our power to accept.

---

[1] Both Coxe and Clarke were very impressed by Bogstad, the seat of Peder Anker (1749–1824). He was one of the richest men in Norway, had travelled in England, and known Linnaeus. From 1789 to 1800 he was Superintendent of Roads in southern Norway; his most important work in this connection was the improvement of the road to Dovre, along which Malthus was shortly to travel.

[2] The summit (Tryvasshögda) is 1,710 feet above sea level.

[3] Mrs P. Anker was formerly Anna Elizabeth Cold, and was married to Peter Anker in 1772, when they were both 23; when Malthus met them they would both have been 50. She died in 1803. They had two sons who died in infancy, and the governess would have been in charge of their only child, Karen, then 9½ years old. Bogstad was owned by her descendants until 1955. The house and grounds, now open to the public, are much as they were in Peder Anker's time.

Colonel Bielefeld had engaged us to dinner with him the next day, & Mr P. A. said he would meet us there.

On our return we had a long conversation with Mr A on the subject of Nobility. He said that some time ago (in 84 or 86 if I recollect right) a proclamation was issued by the court of Copenhagen, that all persons who claimed the rank of nobility should prove their just title, by regular descent. Mr A proved his descent from a noble Swedish family; but they made some difficulty in granting him the arms of that family, as he had not himself a title, and the arms interfered with some of the Danish titles. However, he gained his point at last, & has got the arms, & about 3 years since, without applying for it, received the key of chamberlain, which gives him the highest rank in Norway, even above the Governor. His brother Mr P Ancher has the rank of general—wears the uniform, & is Intendant General of the roads in Norway.

There are but 2 titled estates in Norway. Count Larvigs, & another whose name I forget;[1] but there are many other estates that have certain priviliges of Nobility attached to them. Any person nobly born may purchase any of these estates & possess all the privileges belonging to them. If it was a Count's estate he would become a Count. A person not nobly born cannot purchase them. A commission from the King confers the same privilege as noble birth. An ensign might purchase a noble estate and possess all the rights & honours attached to it. All civil offices, as in Russia, have a certain military rank. The title of Count gives a certain rank in the army; but a simple ensign would take place of a nobleman born, with the largest possessions, if he had no title, & held no civil office from the Crown.

Norway imports 300,000 quarters of corn yearly. Principal exports, deals & iron. Mr A possesses 250 priviledged saw mills, chiefly in the Glommen which runs to Frederickstad.[2] Mr A. & Mr de Rosencrantz almost possess the port of Frederickstad between them;[3] & Mr A says that it is more advantageous to

[1] Laurvig was a county from 1671 to 1805, when it was sold to the Crown. It had been inherited in 1791 by Frederik Ahlefeldt-Laurvig (1760–1832).
[2] A total of 664 saw-mills in southern Norway were privileged in 1688 to saw prescribed quantities of timber for export or any other non-local use.
[3] Marcus Gjöe Rosenkrantz (1762–1838), a strong sympathiser with the American Revolution, had acquired three big estates by his marriage in 1796 to Maren Juel.

him than all his other possessions, on account of the facility with which all the timber is floated. Those who have forests up the country are obliged to have the wood transported on sledges in the winter, which makes a great difference in the expence, & a delay of a year. A saw mill cannot be erected without a privilege from the King. There are no publick stores of corn, except small ones for the garrisons, which however are sometimes opened in times of distress.

Mr A spoke of the connection of Norway with Denmark as most fatal to the interests of Norway. If it was connected with England, & the trade left perfectly free, it is thought it would soon rise to a flourishing state. The project was once held by Mr Pitt, & not totally discouraged in Norway. Copenhagen is thought to be the sink of all the riches of Norway.

Fine. Therm. at 1, 74. I believe it was higher afterwards.

Mr Peter Ancher told me that a short time ago he had a horse who would trot a Norway mile in a quarter of an hour with a sledge.

July 29 [Saturday, *June 29*]. Dined with Colonel Bielefeld who gave us some of the best claret I ever tasted. Col. B. lives with a lady that is not his wife, but we find that she is generally received into all companies. His wife lives at Copenhagen.[1] Mr P. Ancher told me that he kept 50 cows & consumed their produce in his own establishment. He complained of the scarcity of cream which he found when he was in England in the best houses. A great qty of cream is used in Norway, for strawberries, the season for which lasts 6 weeks. They prefer the white alpine's & think their wild strawberries very superior to our garden strawberries in England.

We went in the Holstein Waggon to drink tea at a little garden of Mr A, about half a mile from the town, where he has fitted up two rooms very elegantly.

In the course of the evening we understood that there were four principal courts of justice in Norway, one in each Government in which the Grand Bailiff or Governor presides. From these however an appeal lies to the superior court at Copenhagen. In the trial of every cause a jury of six men assists,

---

[1] In 1782, when he was thirty, Carl Frederick Bielefeldt had married a doctor's daughter called Margrethe Jensenius.

not chosen as with us, but for life. There are inferior courts in the different Bailliages, from which an appeal lies to the superior. There is also in every parish a commission of conciliation, before which every cause must be stated, previous to its coming into a court of justice; and it is the office of the commissioners to mediate between the parties & if possible compromise matters. The party refusing to abide by the opinion of the commissioners is condemned to all the costs if it does not afterwards appear upon trial that he was in the right.

Before we went to Colonel Bielfield's we called upon Mr A, & were introduced into his study & interior apartments, where he considers himself as free from all interruptions, & where he only introduces his particular friends. We found rather a large room with a good library & philosophical apparatus. At the end was a kind of pulpit from which he sometimes gives philosophical lectures to the ladies & gentlemen in the neighbourhood, and there were seats placed below for the audience. He walked with us to Colonel Bielfield's.

Fair. Therm at 2, 64.

Clarke gives this account of Bernt Anker's library, which he saw in October: 'The following words were inscribed in large letters over the door of this apartment: DOCENDO DISCIMUS. Here we saw a complete apparatus for philosophical and mechanical purposes, the work of Nairne and Blunt of London; astronomical instruments, globes, and a museum of antiquities, and of natural history, containing minerals, shells, &c. "I must send to England", said he, "for almost every thing: all the linen of my family is sent annually to London to be washed." And when we observed that the stock of linen must be very large to admit of such an arrangement, he added "that it was absolutely necessary to have a large stock of every thing in Norway".'[1]

Clarke then repeats, almost in Malthus's own words, the information given on pp. 99–100.

July 30 [Sunday, *June 30*]. Passed most of the morning in writing. Mr A called upon us in his coach at 2, to take us with him to dinner & a ball which he was to have in the evening.

In our way we called to take up the Treasurer and his lady.

[1] *Travels*, VI, 14–15.

He was a remarkably meek & innocent looking man, & Mr A told us that he had not been long enough treasurer to keep his carriage. While we were in the carriage Mr A opened upon us in all sorts of quotations, & verses of his own to Countesses, Princes &c: &c: As we did not understand the Danish in which they were written, it was chiefly for the harmony & cadence that he exacted our admiration. We did as well as we could, but must have come far behind the critics & princesses who had judged of his compositions, if his account of their praises was just. After our arrival he told us a number of his bons mots, with which we were much entertained, but not exactly in the way he would wish.

At dinner I sate by a Mrs Skilstrop who had been married only ten days to a young phisician at Christiania.[1] She had a most elegant person & a very pretty face, & something so particularly naive & pleasing in her manner that before the evening was over both Otter & myself were half in love with her. The dancing began about 9—the company had been coming in since six, & formed really a brilliant assemblage, particularly the ladies, who were much superior both in beauty of person & elegance of dress & manners, to those we had seen at Frederickshall. There were full as many handsome women in proportion to the number as would be seen at an assembly in England.[2] Otter & myself, finding that we made but a poor

[1] Mrs 'Skilstrop' was twenty: she was formerly Eleanore Clauson-Kaas, and had married Magnus Andreas Thulstrup on 19 June. This doctor, born in Copenhagen in 1769, became famous in Norway as a surgeon and obstetrician, and a street in Oslo is called after him; he was as much loved in his way as his wife was in hers. Mrs Thulstrup was described as the most elegant lady in the capital and the prima donna of the Dramatic Society. Although there were a number of ladies of high rank present, King Charles John of Sweden (Marshal Bernadotte) chose Mrs Thulstrup as his partner to open his coronation ball in 1818 (Jacob S. Worm-Müller, *Christiania og Krisen efter Napoleons Krigene*. Kristiania, 1922, p. 28). She died in 1823, and her husband in 1844; they had no children. For all this information I am indebted to Kontorsjef S. S. Nilson, of the Norwegian Ministry of Foreign Affairs, who is Mrs Thulstrup's first cousin three times removed.

[2] The delightfully proportioned little ball-room in which this dance took place may still be seen at Frogner. Clarke was also enthusiastic about 'the beau-monde of Christiania...among which we observed...a number of beautiful women in elegant and fashionable dresses, exhibiting the latest modes of London... Indeed, to English eyes, there was nothing foreign in the appearance of the company: the manners, abating only the smoking and spitting, were those of our own country; and we found the English language very generally understood' (*Travels*, VI, 6, 7).

figure at the Walse, did not dance much. The supper was not regular, but in the form of sandwiches &c &c.

Thunder shower at 3. Therm at 2, 70. Fine & fair other parts of the day.

July 1 [Monday]. As we did not leave Mr Ancher's till past 2 and as some few preparations were necessary in the morning, we did not set off on our expedition to Kongsbergh till near ten. Mr A had insisted on our taking his small poney phaeton, not having yet procured a vehicle of our own. From Christiania to Rafnsbergh, 1¾ miles,[1] we passed a very delightful country with frequent charming views of the river, & abrupt rocky hills covered with firs—the river alway looking like a lake with many islands. The bottoms consisted chiefly of rich grass fields, & only here & there a spot of corn. Farm houses & neat cottages were frequent; but from the wood with which they were built, being painted red & being covered with red tiles they did not look so picturesque as some of the Swedish houses.—Paid two dollars & some odd stivers for the 3 horses. It is the custom always in Norway to charge double posts from all the large towns.

To Gullbeck 1¼ miles.[2] Country of the same kind—high bold rocky hills covered with firs—in the valley the firs mixed with other trees, birch, alder, ash, mountain ash, foresty ground —no oak or beech. Observed that the leaves of the ashes were particularly large & fine. Remarked some may—the first I had seen. I had observed no white-thorn before either in Sweden or Norway. It was pretty generally in blossom, but all the buds not open. After leaving Gullebeck we ascended a high hill on the top of which are some marble quarries; but the marble is not very good, & is therefore not much used. From the hill is a very fine view of the valley in which Drammen is situated, enclosed by dark rocky mountains. A bay of the Christiania River looking like a lake extends to the town, & receives into it the river Drammen, about the size of the Thames above Putney.[3] The valley seems to be rich land which

---

[1] Clarke, being more punctilious over foreign names, as we shall see later, calls 'Rafnsbergh' Ravensbörg.

[2] Clarke calls 'Gullbeck' Gillejebek.

[3] In comparing the Drammen with 'the size of the Thames above Putney', Malthus is following the example of Archdeacon Coxe, who must have been

is chiefly in pasture. In going into Drammen we were overtaken by one of the hardest showers I ever saw in my life, & in
driving along the streets it was with great difficulty that we
could keep clear of the water spouts pouring like cataracts
from the houses.

In setting off again from Drammen to Hogsund, 2 miles, we
were stopped in the street some time on account of a dispute
about the horses, the people wishing to make us pay double
shutes (double postage) tho they had not waited the appointed
time. The argument was carried on by means of a french barber
who acted in the double capacity of interpreter & mediator.
We at length went to a Magistrate & with some difficulty &
the loss of much valuable time gained our point & another
piece of information besides, namely, that it is better to submit
to all impositions with becoming patience, than to have recourse
to law.

It rained at times during the rest of our way—the clouds
were low, & hung in various fantastic shapes upon the mountains, sometimes increasing their beauty. Hogsund is prettily
situated on the river near a cataract which turns some saw
mills. From Hogsund to Kongsbergh, 2 miles, a very hilly
road which appeared to us very long, as we were rather late,
a little wet & cold, & our horses very dull. We ferried over
the Dram immediately from Hogsund, & pass'd a fine country
with bold hills & one fine small lake to the left. Towards
Kongsbergh the mountains became higher & more bare at
top. We descended a very long & steep hill to the Town, &
passed the river Lave by a wooden bridge, just before we
entered it.[1] We found but a middling inn, & a Landlord who
did nothing but bow & shake us by the hand. There was only
one room & one bed; but after some discussion on the subject,
a box of moss was brought in and a bed made upon it, which
was not so soft in reality, as a mossy couch generally is
in idea.

Fair till 11, afterwards rainy, with one very hard shower.
Therm at 12, 60; at 2, 57.[2]

familiar with the Thames at London, Putney, Richmond, and Henley, as he
used these comparisons continually.
[1] The river is the Laagen. Malthus first wrote *Lavage*.
[2] Malthus left a blank page after this day's entry.

July 2 [Tuesday]. Sent Mr Ancher's letter to the Intendant of the mines, Professor Brunnick, and called upon him according to his appointment, at 11, but found that we were too late to see the mines that day, as soon after we could get to them the men would be leaving their work. Determined to see them the next morning at five.[1] Walked with Monr. Brunnick, who talked English, to the smelting houses &c:[2] Heard from him that about 100,000 dollars are coined from the mines yearly. 2,300 men are employed & in general earn a dollar & a half a week, or 1*s.* shilling a day. This seems very little; but in addition, the King always supplies the miners with corn at a fixed price much below the average value. At present the price of rye per tun is 6½ dollars & the miners have it at 2 dollars 80 scillings or near 3 dollars.

The mines have been for some time in a poor state. There is a regular annual loss; & the King is wishing on that account to contract the works, & employ fewer men; for which purpose every miner or young man in a miner's family is encouraged to leave Kongsbergh by the praemium of a year's pay after he is gone.

Clarke, who visited the silver mines with Cripps later on, in October, was 'everywhere struck by the proofs of the same inconsiderate expenditure of public money, and the same waste among the works. There can be little doubt but that these mines would become very profitable, if they were in private hands: and perhaps the best thing the Government can do, is to farm them out to individuals.'[3]

As in other cases, Clarke made full use of Malthus's diary in writing his own account of the mines.

The mines were closed down completely between 1805 and 1815; this was a disaster, as Kongsberg at the time of Malthus's visit had the second largest town population in Norway, being exceeded only by Bergen.

---

[1] Silver was discovered at Kongsberg in 1623, and production reached its maximum in about 1770. The mines are no longer worked, but are visited by 10,000 people annually for conducted tours on a miniature railway.

[2] Morten Thrane Brünnich was a native of Copenhagen, where he died in 1827 at the age of ninety. He had visited the Cornish mines in 1765. He was first sent to Norway in 1772, on a commission to inquire into the complaints of the miners at Kongsberg. From 1789 to 1814 he had charge of all Norwegian mines. He was a zoologist as well as a mineralogist.

[3] *Travels*, VI, 56.

Formerly the mines were much richer. The professor remem-
bers when 200,000 dollars were coined yearly; & still earlier
300,000 dollars were coined, 4,000 men employed. The ore is
melted generally 3 times with Mundic before the last melting
with lead.[1] Boys are employed to seperate those pieces of ore
that have any appearances of silver in them, & these go immediately to the smelting houses. The poor ore is stamped in
stamping houses, & washed, & a considerable quantity of
native silver is sometimes found in pieces that shewed no marks
of it before.

The miners work from five to one, summer & winter. When
they work in the afternoon, as they sometimes do, they are
paid extra. The business of mining is confined to the same
families. No strangers are taken, & there is generally employment for the children of the miners at 12 years old. They are
now, however, increasing rather faster than the employment
for them. We saw many children in the streets, & much
apparent distress & poverty; but the houses are tolerably neat.
Many beggars both of children & grown persons.

Clarke wrote: 'This place, like Christiania, swarms with beggars;
who beset the door of the inn at which travellers arrive, forming
together a mob of most disgusting objects; each endeavouring to
extort money, as in France and Italy, and as it used to be in Ireland,
especially in the streets of Dublin, by exposing to view distorted
limbs, and deformity, and open sores; thrusting these revolting
sights in the very faces of every stranger they meet. We were glad
to get away from them.'[2]

Mr Brunnick invited us to sup with him, & we were to call
at 3 o clock on Monr l'assesseur Estmark to see the mineralogical school & a collection of minerals. After dining at a
kind of table d'hote at the Inn without being able to understand a word of what was said, we called upon Mr Estmark,
who spoke very bad french, & could hardly understand us, but
was very civil & obliging. We heard from him that the school
was a royal institution, for the instruction of the children of the
miners in mineralogy, chemystry, physic, mathematics &c:

[1] According to the *O.E.D.* Mundic is the Cornish miners' name for pyrites.
[2] *Travels*, VI, 67.

There are three professors—Mr Estmark is in the mineralogical & geological department. Any of the miners or children of the miners attend that please. 2 days in the week, & 2 hours each day, are generally dedicated to the miners, & the same to other persons who chuse to attend. Nothing is taken for the lectures.

We saw a large collection of minerals from different parts of Europe, among which were some very beautiful specimens of native silver from the Kongsbergh mines.

Jens Esmark (1763–1839) was described by Clarke as 'the most scientific mineralogist, perhaps, in all Europe. This gentleman is well known in all Foreign Academies, for the works which he has published...His collection of minerals is one of the most *geognostic* we ever saw...Professor Esmark conducted us to the grand chamber of the Kongsberg Academy, where we saw a collection of minerals, in beautiful order, and most scientifically arranged. The very sight of such a collection affords of itself an edifying lesson for mineralogists; but we were willing to forego some of the advantage which might be derived from its inspection, that we might enjoy the valuable conversation of the Professor.'[1]

The mountain on which are the mines nearest the town is about 1,295 french feet (1,498 danish feet) above Kongsbergh, which is 926 feet above the level of the sea. Many of the mountains in the neighbourhood are much higher, but Mr Estmark had not measured them himself. The base of the mountains in which the silver mines are found are chiefly Hornblend & Mica. We saw a range of Granite mountains to the East on which were still some spots of snow.

Mr Estmark keeps a regular account of the thermometer & told me that on the 8th of Feby last at 5 in the morning the therm. was at 26 below 0 Reaumur. Some day last week at 3 in the afternoon Reaumur's therm. was at 24, but Mr E had not then his book by him to refer to the day. Mr E has only been at Kongsbergh a year—he means to measure all the mountains by the barometer—he has measured some of the mines in that way & finds that his account does not differ more than ten or twelve feet from the accurate depth.

In the evening, after taking a walk with Mr Brunnick, to see

---

[1] *Travels*, VI, 64–5.

the strong box opened, in which the hoards of native silver are kept, we were introduced to his family, & sate down to supper with a large party. Mrs Brunnick seemed to be a vulgar good sort of woman & a great manager.[1] She gave us an excellent supper which lasted near 2 hours; but it did not appear tedious to me as I had the good fortune to sit by one of her daughters who was very pretty & very agreeable, & talked french with tolerable fluency, & English a little.

Mrs B told me before supper that except in the articles of house rent & wood, everything was dearer than at Copenhagen. She has her stores for the year from Copenhagen. At Kongsbergh, however, veal & mutton are only 4d. a pound. Beef is rarely to be got. No apples grow at Kongsbergh. It is reckoned a fortnight later than Christiania, from its being so much higher & the soil poorer. Veal is kill'd young. The cows, when they do not go out to pasture, have their meat boiled for them every morning—chiefly straw and leaves.

Rainy the greatest part of the day. Therm at 1, 57.

At Kongsbergh in the summer the soil is in want of rain every seven or eight days.

We heard from Mr Brunnick that there were no privileges attached to any estates but those of the two Counts Larwig & Yalsbergh;[2] & that noble birth was of no consequence whatever, and did not even exempt a person from serving in the national army. We have received many contradictory accounts of this kind.

Mr B shewed us a scale of ranks, which consisted of 6 or 7 different classes. We observed that the rank of Chamberlain was in the same class with the Major Generals; but at the head of it. In the class above were the full generals & Admirals & the Counts who possess'd estates annexed to their titles. Those who did not were in the class below.

July 3 [Wednesday]. Went to see the mines at 5 in the morning accompanied by Mr l'Assesseur Estmark. We descended the

---

[1] Mrs Brünnich was Wibecke Shou (1746–1820), a native of Jutland. She married Morten Brünnich in 1776, when she was thirty and he forty-one. Malthus wrote to begin with that she *was a vulgar good sort of woman*, and altered it later.

[2] *Laurvig* and *Jarlsberg*. For Laurvig see p. 105 n. The County of Jarlsberg came into the Wedel family in 1684, and was inherited in 1811 by Hermann Wedel Jarlsberg (1779–1840), who played a leading part in Norwegian political life. Titles of nobility were abolished in 1824.

one that was nearest to Christiania. The strata of earths lye East & West, the veins of silver N. & S. The richest veins are those which descend towards the south, & particularly when they are found in a stratum with Mundic or pyrites. The veins of silver that we saw were very small, & very poor, & would scarcely be perceptible but to the eye of a connoisseur. We descended by ladders nearly perpendicular, with resting places at no long intervals. Being rather pressed for time we did not go much lower than a hundred feet; being assured that we had then seen all that could be seen, the lower parts being perfectly similar to the higher.

The ore & rocks were drawn up by a wheel which was worked by water at the distance of four or five hundred yards from the place; the communication was carried on by cumbrous machinery connected all the way.

From the place where the mines were situated we had a very fine view of Kongsbergh & the surrounding country. The fog which had been rather thick in the morning was just breaking away & opened to us some grand prospects of the mountains which appeared higher from being seen indistinctly, & mixed with the clouds.

We returned to our inn to breakfast, paid our respects to Monr Brunnick & set off on our return about ten. Mr Brunnick acts as civil Governor throughout the district in which the mines are situated, & two, who are called Assesseurs, are joined with him. They have each a key of the strong chest in which the silver is kept, & it cannot be opened without the consent of all. The salary of the Intendant is 2,400 dollars a year. Monr l'assesseur Estmark is married to one of Mr Brunnick's daughters.[1] He is a very goodnatured & well informed man; but he appears too much of a philosopher & too dirty to please the ladies. We were rather surprised at the young lady's choice, & were inclined to believe Mrs Brunnick when she told us that there was a great scarcity of men in the neighbourhood.[2]

[1] The wedding of 35-year-old Jens Esmark and 20-year-old Wibecke Brünnich had taken place eight months before, on 14 November 1798. Wibecke died only thirteen years later, but was the mother of two well-known men, Hans (1801–82), a pastor and another mineralogist, and Laurits (1806–84), a zoologist.

[2] Mrs Brünnich was probably right about the shortage of suitable men in what the Danes must have regarded as something of an outpost: on 1 August 1802 her

At Hogsund on our return we had another dispute about horses in which we thought ourselves extremely ill used; but submitted according to our determination at Drammen. We had ordered horses at Hogsund & arrived there full an hour before the time that they are obliged to wait. We were rather surprised not to find the horses ready—They had been either sent home or somebody else had taken them. We waited an hour & a half for fresh horses grumbling at being treated so ill. But just as I was setting off (Otter had walked forwards) thinking that we had been much more sinned against than sinning, they stopt the carriage, & actually would not let me go till I had paid, not only for the horses I was going to use, but for the others which we did not find on our arrival. All remonstrances were vain—the woman of the post house took the bridle out of the horses' mouths; & I was forced to submit with patience to all that was demanded before I was permitted to depart, & I thought Otter would be almost at Drammen before I could overtake him.

In the Church yrd of Drammen I observed that almost every tomb stone was made with a bed of flowers on the top of it, some of which were growing very prettyly. Other tombs had gathered flowers scattered over them. There are many good houses in Drammen & a considerable trade in wood is carried on there. The whole valley from Hogsund to Drammen along the course of the Dram is very beautiful; and the soil seems very good. The mountains are all covered with firs.

We did not arrive at Christiania till 2 in the morning, having been detained at Drammen 3 hours for horses, besides our fracas at Hogsund. But the greatest evil was yet behind—our little portmanteau which had been placed at the bottom of the carriage had in some unaccountable manner fallen out, and it contained a number of things of the first necessity to us. We have sent back for it; but have not much hopes of finding it.

In our journey to Kongsbergh & back we met a great number of fine looking country girls on the road—most of them large & handsome. In Sweden we had remarked that the men were

23-year-old daughter Nicoline Christiane married the Professor Wad whom Malthus had met in Copenhagen; he would then have been 47, more than twice the age of his bride She did not die until 1864, having been a widow for thirty-two years.

much superior to the women. Here we should make the contrary observation, & particularly amoung the higher classes. At Mr Anker's we had met with many pretty elegant looking women; but scarcely a single man that had the air of a gentleman. The custom of smoaking among the men so universally prevalent here greatly contributes to make them look dirty. The women have not in general good teeth; but at Mr Anker's assembly we saw many that had.

In our journey to Kongsbergh we observed that most of the houses have little porches, which are generally ornamented with birch boughs. The country women when working wear nothing upwards but their shifts—which are made higher than those in England—sometimes a coloured handkerchief is thrown over their shoulders; but there are no stays or other covering to the waist. The women in Sweden worked in the same manner, & looked exactly like men working in their shirts.

Fine & fair. Therm at 2, 70; at half past 6, 67.

Near Drammen Otter found the Linnea Borealis in great plenty.[1]

July 4 [Thursday]. Our departure for Drontheim delayed on account of our loss.—Dined at Mr Ancher's—after dinner in the garden had some conversation with Mrs Collet whom I found the best person for examination that I had yet met with. In general I have found the gentlemen whom I have talked with either unable, or unwilling to answer the questions I have asked; but very willing to run on into long discussions of their own.

Mrs Collet informed me that the general food of the labourers who worked for Mr C. was Black rye bread & salt butter or cheese for breakfast, & boiled barley & a herring or some other fish with beer for dinner. Once a week, & sometimes twice, they have fresh meat. The common people in general live nearly in the same way, only not quite so well, & instead of beer they use sower milk. Some who have large families are often in great distress. The men who work for gentlemen or farmers have generally a house found them rent free, for which they are always obliged to work for the master from whom they

---

[1] After this day's entry, Malthus left one page blank.

receive it in preference to any other. These receive 10*d*. a day in summer & 8 pence in winter; in Harvest 1*s*. or 1*s*. 2*d*. Those who have no houses are paid 1*s*. in summer & 10*d*. in winter. Mrs C thinks that the state of the common people is improving & that they are not so dirty as they were, & that consequently not so many children die young.

There is not a pound of fresh butter to be bought at Christiania. All persons use what they make themselves or salt it for keeping. The farmers who live higher up the country go for two months, from June to August, up into the mountains to pasture their cattle. The[y] live in little wooden sheds built at the time, & it is during these 2 months that they make the greatest part of their butter, which is salted, & brought to the fair at Christiania in the winter on sledges. This butter is bought by the families in the neighbourhood for their servants, but the better sort of people use butter imported from Holstein for themselves. So little has the custom of selling fresh butter prevailed, that if a person wished to dispose of any he would hardly find purchasers.

The cattle in the winter, besides hay & straw, where they are to be got, are fed very much on the leaves & small branches of a species of poplar which are gathered at the end of the summer and laid by for winter provision. I was told by a gentleman present that these leaves stripped from the branches were excellent food for horses, & gave them a very fine coat.

There is no provision for the poor except a hospital for old men & women, which is very limited in number. There are many beggars at Christiania; but by what I could hear & see the common people appeared to live as well as those in England, with the difference of rye bread instead of wheaten, and they are here so much accustomed to rye that they prefer it to wheat, & it is reckoned a heartier food. Wheat is sometimes cheaper than rye. A Flat cake made of rye, & sometimes of oatmeal, call'd flad bru, is much in use. The Housemen about Christiania have very seldom land to keep a cow.[1]

---

[1] The Housemen or Husmenn of Norway were cottars or smallholders, whose rent was paid to the farmers in the form of services performed by themselves, their families, and even their horses. By the end of the eighteenth century housemen were believed to constitute one quarter of the rural population, and landless labourers another quarter, one half being owners or in some cases substantial leaseholders (T. K. Derry, *A Short History of Norway*, p. 111).

At supper I talked with a Mr Nielsen who was a great Democrat & admirer of Thoms Paine.[1] He abused a great deal the English government for their interference with the French—thought that Kings were now receiving a proper lesson, & that the light of the French revolution could never be thoroughly extinguished. He said that K in general thought only of getting taxes. Complained of the taxes in Norway, which are certainly not very heavy—said that it was treated as a conquered province; but acknowledged that the Danish government did not exercise the power which it possessed by law. He owned that it was mild & in some respects liberal; but without knowledge & activity. He was a little inconsistent in talking of the old King of Prussia as a model of Kings.[2]

I learned from him that the peasants, before they are called upon to serve, have no occasion to ask permission to marry of the officer, or to have a certificate from the priest. He said in general that the asking permission of the officer was merely a ceremony, & that it was hardly ever refused. The regiments that are in constant service are raised by enlisting for a certain term of years. The peasants are never forced to go with them. It is reckoned rather a disgrace not to be called upon to serve in the national army, and is considered sometimes as implying that they were too good for nothing, to be taken. The officers however when they had the liberty of taking any person under 36 were often bribed to let off the negocians & rich farmers, which may be one reason of their dislike to the Change.

Fine. Therm at $2\frac{1}{2}$, 75; at $5\frac{1}{2}$, 73; at $7\frac{1}{2}$, 72; at $9\frac{1}{2}$, 62. Wind S.
In enlisting, only housemen, not farmers, may be taken.

Mrs Collet told me that the housekeeping in Norway from its peculiar nature, & the largeness of the establishments

---

[1] Peter Vogt Nilson (1761–1837) was an uncle of the beautiful Mrs Thulstrup. He commanded a detachment of Danish hussars, which had been moved to Norway in March 1799. As a boy he had been sent to England to learn the language. In 1804 he married a niece of Bernt Anker, Karen Dorothea Martine (1783–1846), the daughter of Jess Anker and his wife Karen Elieson. Jess Anker was the black sheep of the family, and in 1798, when in England, in Bath, he shot himself on finding that he could not meet his gambling debts in time to save his honour. (Information kindly provided by Mr S. S. Nilson, great-great-great-nephew of Peter Vogt Nilson.)

[2] Frederick the Great (1712–86), King of Prussia as Frederick II from 1740, generally considered as the model of an enlightened despot, as well as a first-rate soldier.

necessary, took up so much time, that the ladies had not leisure for many other employments after marriage.[1] In their house in the country they make up eleven servants' beds. We have heard from many authorities, that the servants are very idle, & never like to do any thing out of their peculiar department, so that more are required than for the same work in England.[2]

July 6 [Friday, *July 5*]. Heard no tidings of our portmanteau— Determined however to make all possible efforts to get off the next day; but were so completely in the power of Mr Anker with regard to money matters, letters &c &c: that we could not get away without his full permission. He had promised to get us a Swedish Cart; but there was no tolerable one to be found in the town, & we were obliged to buy a small poney phaeton for which, with harness, we gave a hundred dollars. At Mr Anker's, who gave us a batchelor's dinner at his house in Town, we also heard of a servant & agreed with him for a guinea a week—to keep himself. The man had lived with one of Mr Anker's brothers and Mr A assured us he could answer to his character.

After settling all these matters & getting our notes changed, Mr A took us to see his deal yards, which were indeed prodigious. The present stock in them was worth 50,000£. Otter understood him that from Christiania, Frederickstadt & Moss he exported altogether deals to the amount of 180,000£ yearly, above a hundred of which were from Christiania. The deals that are sold in one year, are cut three years before, and as everything is paid for in ready money, an immense capital is required to carry on the deal trade which is the reason that it is so profitable & in such few hands. At Frederickstadt, from the facility of floating the timber to the saw mills, & from the saw mills immediately to the port, a whole year is saved, & the clear profit consequently much greater. The timber that comes to Christiania is brought in the winter by sledges.

Mr A's outgoings are immense—he keeps 40 stewards or clerks, who on an average have 1,000 dollars a year each. He professed himself so much of a philosopher that he should like

---

[1] Clarke wrote of Norway that 'literary female characters are unknown' (*Travels*, VI, 76).
[2] Here Malthus left one and a half pages blank.

to give up the whole if he could find any person of *sufficient* capacity to *undertake* it; in which case he would consent to lose 50 per cent. Mr A has 3 copper mines, on one of which he has sunk a great qy of money;—it promises now to answer very well; but the specimens which he shewed us did not appear very rich.

The carrying timber on sledges forms one of the principal employments of the farmers & housemen (who keep horses) during the winter.

After drinking tea with Mrs Clareson, the English lady we had met at Mr Anker's, we returned to Mr A's again, & took leave of him with many thanks for his polite attentions. We could not help lamenting as we walked to our inn that a man of such acknowledged talents & of so much real merit, should be so spoilt by vanity.

Morning fine. Afternoon thunder showers—from 9 till 12 very heavy. Therm at $\frac{1}{2}$ past 1, 78; at 2, after a slight thunder storm, 68.

To day we saw the first wood strawberries ripe; but I believe they had been brought to Christiania some days before.[1]

In his own book, Clarke has a dig at Malthus here on the subject of Bernt Anker's character. He writes: 'Some travellers have spoken of his vanity: to us, this foible, if it deserved so harsh a name, served only to render his company the more amusing: not that we were amused at his expense, but because we discerned, through all his supposed egotism, a playfulness of disposition, which seemed to say, "I will be any thing, from the loftiest statesman to the merriest member of a party at blind-man's buff, sooner than my guests shall suffer *ennui* for want of conversation or amusement!"'[2]

Bernt Anker's vanity, in his own country, is regarded as an endearing characteristic, however laughable: when he became Chamberlain, he had two candles set in a conspicuous window of his town house, and sat between them for a whole evening, with his key of office in front of him.[3]

July 6 [Saturday]. Not being aware that a passport was necessary we had neglected to send in time for one & were delayed

[1] Malthus has again left one and a half pages blank at the end of a day.
[2] *Travels*, VI, 76.
[3] I am indebted for this information to Mr Erik Anker, a descendant of Bernt's brother Jess.

in the morning on this account. Did not set off till about eleven. Tho we had almost begun to despair about ever leaving Christiania, & were rather glad to get off at any rate; yet we could not help feeling some regret at leaving so beautiful a country, where we had been treated with much kindness & hospitality.

From Christiania to Romsaas 1 mile. We mounted a high hill soon after leaving Christiania from which were some fine views back on the town & river. We found the roads quite heavy from the late rains—the soil blacker than those we had in general met with. The latter part of the stage was among high hills covered with firs, & fertile vallies chiefly in pasture.

	m	stivers
For horses & driver 1st stage paid	3	8

From Romsaas to Schedsmoe 1½ miles. Cross'd a fine rich valley with a small river running thro it—land apparently rich & well cultivated—farms & cottages frequent. Some part of the stage very hilly. The hills covered with pines, & in the vallies the pines mix'd with other trees—enclosures of wood, rather large—trees & shrubs interspersed among the grass fields—some good patches of barley & oats.

	m	sti.
For horses & driver paid	2	6

From Shedmoe to Moe 1 mile   Road better. Rich waving ground—trees & shrubs interspersed among the grass fields—pass'd another river.

At Moe eat some eggs with the bread & butter that we had brought—found the laying in a store an excellent plan. At Moe we saw a man grinding salt in a hand mill—a flat stone moving horizontally—he said he could grind about 2 pecks in the hour; but it seemed to be very hard work. All the women & boys & most of the men were without stockings—The women with only their shifts—a little handkerchief round their necks, & apparently but one petticoat. On their heads they wore either a small coloured cap, or handkerchief setting quite close to the head, or a large straw bonnet very prominent before.

From Moe to Dragvold 1 mile—good road not so hilly. Some foresty ground, principally of young fir.

From Dragwold to Roholdt 1¾ miles—excellent road—much foresty ground of young fir, & many patches where the firs had been cut & burnt. In this & the last stage we passed many spots of this kind, some of which had been sown to rye, others had tolerable grass upon them, & others had returned again to firs. I was informed that it was a common practice to cut the firs in this manner, leaving the stumps about one or two feet above the ground; to burn all the branches as they lye on the ground, and in the ashes, without ploughing, to sow rye. Only one crop can be obtained in this manner. The cattle are afterwards turned in & the land either gets a covering of grass or returns again to firs, according to its quality.

We had intended to go another stage but finding that we should not get horses in less than 2 hours—we determined to remain here all night—found moderate beds, & cooked a custard ourselves for supper.[1]

Fine & fair. Therm at 3, 67.

July 7 [Sunday]. Paid a dollar & 12 stivers for our supper beds & breakfast—the woman asked 2 dollars, but our servant told her it was too much. From Roholdt to Minde 1½ miles. Road excellent—Pass'd many of the spots where the fir woods had been taken into cultivation. The stumps are a long while rotting, & the plough cannot well be used before. The bodies of the trees that do not burn with the branches are split & cut up to make the wooden enclosures. Some of the new inclosures had tolerable grass, but many had returned again to fir, & other trees. No pains seemed to be taken to grub up the young trees as they rise.

Pass'd under a fine mountain, which we had long had in view, call'd something like Muberry,[2] at the foot of which was a house & some saw mills, which belonged to Mr Anker's youngest brother. One of Mr A's Stewards lives there at present, but we had only time to accept a draught of milk. At Minde we came down upon a large & beautiful river, & pass'd the narrowest part of it by a ferry. It is called the Minsen &

[1] 'Here' is Raaholt, about 38 miles from Oslo, on the road to Trondheim by way of Lillehammer and the Gudbrandsdal.
[2] This mountain might be Mistberget, 2,181 feet. The large and beautiful river is Lake Mjösa, 62 miles long, and in some places 10 miles broad; the land round it is still some of the most fertile and best cultivated in Norway.

communicates, as we understand, with the Glomme, which runs to Frederickstadt, by which means timber is floated down from a great distance up the country. About 3 Norway miles below Minde, the two rivers join.

The River at the ferry has a very strong stream & is not very broad, but above, the breadth extends from half a mile to two or three miles, & the shores are almost every where formed of fine wooded mountains. On the banks on the other side of the ferry were litterally two complete beds of roses. They were just of the height to reach the nose of a person reclining, & the beauty of the day & the scenery together, almost tempted us to spend some hours in so poetical a situation.

From Minde to Moerstrue $1\frac{1}{4}$ mile. When we had crossed the water, the road turned to the left in the direction of the river. When we had proceeded a little way, we had a fine range of Alpine hills rising almost perpendicularly on our right; & on our left delightful views of a fine broad river, the opposite shore of which rose into bold mountains, among which Muberry that we had passed made the most respectable figure. The road sometimes ran close to the river, sometimes a part of the way up the hill, in short, steep ascents & descents. The pines, that covered the tops of the steep hills to our right, were mix'd with clumps of beautiful birches, & nearer the bottoms, a great quantity of aspens, with alders & wild cherries added to the variety. These woods, for the extent of 13 or 14 miles, belong to Mr Anker. Cottages were here and there prettily interspersed—houses all detached—some very small, & many without gardens; but observed one or two with a patch of potatoes near them. When we arrived at Moerstrue, many people were assembled about the inn. It was sunday & all looked very neat. Most of the men wore red woollen caps.

To Rorsegaarden $1\frac{1}{4}$. Cliffs on the right rather more bare— a fine rocky mountain on the other side of the river called Crawberry rising directly out of the water. Cottages thinly scattered in picturesque shapes—flat roofs—some very fine views of the opposite mountain towards the end of the stage. On the water we saw two large divers almost as big as geese with long, large bills. They dived each time to a great distance. Many people were assembled at Rorsegaarden, a very neat house.

To Nocklebye 1 mile. In this stage we lost sight of the river & of our beautiful scenery.—Country flatter, rather foresty, some distant views of the mountain behind us. To Biellum, $1\frac{1}{2}$, more cultivated.[1] Toward the end a fine valley with very neat houses & farms thickly scattered.

To Bierke $\frac{7}{8}$ mile. Fine cultivated country, with many hamlets & neat churches with spires. The churches generally built of wood in the form of a cross with the spire nearly in the middle. Cottages with flat roofs covered with grass, moss or wood. Under the covering of grass or moss I understand they place the bark of the birch or fir. Some are covered with pieces of wood in the shape of tiles. Toward the end of the stage, we came again to some pretty views of the river.

To Tangberget $1\frac{1}{8}$ mile—A little the same kind of country— small clusters of farms & cottages on the sides of the hills— mountain on the other side of the river. Towards the end of the stage the road pass'd under a very high cliff of fir & birch. A branch of the river only runs by Tangberget, & is then contracted, to the breadth of the Thames at Putney.

To Moe $1\frac{1}{4}$ mile. Came again to the full body of the river— fine varied hilly country, a little in the same style as the last. For the three last stages the country had appeared very well peopled & the soil by no means unfertile. We pass'd many fields of barley, rye and oats that looked very well; but pasture lands with a fine verdure predominated; & appeared more picturesque from being mixed with trees. We had observed the mountain ash very frequent. [A long passage is crossed out, concluding with the words *which looked like the mountain ash. We found it to be the Lotus Concuparia, a kind of fruit tree. I believe we have it not in England.*]

Since we passed the ferry of Minden, we had seldom left its shore for any long time together. The weather had been delightful & the impression on our minds was that the river Minden, & its shores, would not probabley suffer in the comparison with any river in Europe.

Therm at half past 3, 75. Fine. No wind. No chill in the evening.

We had passed no Towns or even what could be called villages; but clusters of houses, three or four together (tho not

[1] Biellum was probably Hjellum.

joined) & cottages sprinkled here & there on the sides of the hills, were more frequent, particularly during the 3 last stages, than in most parts of England. We understood that it was one of the most cultivated, & best peopled parts of Norway.

Found at Moe tolerable beds with the assistance of our own sheets.[1] If one arrives late at any house, the people do not appear to be in the least molested by it. They tumble out of bed with the utmost facility, & are ready in an instant.[2] The men put on a pair of breeches & the women a single petticoat, which on these occasions forms the whole of their dress. When we came to Moe, tho it was not late, the maid was gone to bed. The mistress called out Matty, the maid answered, Strax,[3] & in 3 seconds tumbled out of her loft in her single petticoat, & waited upon us so attired.

For beds & Coffee & custard for supper, paid a dollar.[4]

July 8 [Monday]. To Thang $1\frac{1}{2}$ miles. We passed under some most beautiful cliffs rising almost perpendicularly on our right, 2 of them were covered to the top with fir & clumps of birches, & the other a perpendicular dark rock, of a peculiar kind, enclosing flints; but every where where the rock was not absolutely perpendicular were firs & birches. The river was here extended to 2 or 3 miles broad, the road sometimes close to it & sometimes at a little distance from it, & the interval filled up with grass fields ornamented with birch, aspen, alder, ash & c: but no oak or beech. Road excellent.

To Lillehammer $1\frac{1}{2}$. Foresty hilly country, the first part away from the river. The road quite green, as if very little used; but excellent. Came soon again to the river. Great variety of ground & of trees—foliage luxuriant, the birches very beautiful. Heard that Orehens & wild turkeys breed in all the woods about.[5] They are seldom killed by the farmers

---

[1] Moelv is now a little industrial town with 2000 inhabitants, 102 miles from Oslo.

[2] Bishop Pontoppidan wrote, 'I do not think there is any country in the world where the people are so hospitable, liberal, and willing to serve and oblige strangers as they are in Norway' (*Natural History of Norway*, p. 256). This was equally true in 1965.

[3] *Straks*, immediately, at once.

[4] Malthus left the next page blank.

[5] The Orehen (of which we shall hear more) is spelt *urhane* by the translator of Pontoppidan's *Natural History of Norway*. He also calls it the Aarfugl, Urogallus, Tetrao Minor, and Growse. It is 'shaped not unlike to a common cock, but

but in the winter, when they can be kept & sent to Christiania. The common price of an Orehen (which from description I suppose to be the same as our black game) is 8*d.*, of what they call a wild turkey 3 shillings in the winter. Woodcocks also breed in all the woods;—yesterday evening I saw one flying over my head. There is not one of them left during the winter. Towards the end of the stage, the hills on the opposite side of the river, which for some way had rather decreased in height, rose again into a mountain. The clouds were low & the tops of most of the fells covered.

At Lillehammer the river contracts suddenly & loses the name of Miosen.[1] It is then about the size of the Thames at Putney or perhaps at London, & call'd something like Lave's & Drumme; but it afterwards changes names often. The Beautiful river Miosen seems to partake of the qualities of a lake as well as a river; and as the shores are formed all the way by the bases of hills & mountains, wherever the valley extends itself in breadth the water follows & becomes a lake. Below Minde it is always in the form of a river and is in the map call'd Vormens till the name is lost, with the river, in the Glomme, the principal branch of which runs to Frederickstadt. I was misinformed with regard to its dividing into two branches.

Soon after leaving Littlehammer we pass'd under a very fine wooded mountain to our right,[2] & came down a steep hill to a turn of the river which was incomparably beautiful, & led us into the most inchanting valley that can well be conceived.

black or dark brown in colour, and red about the eyes: the hen is much less brownish, with black spots…Their flesh is wholesome and well-tasted, and therefore they are very much followed by the sportsmen' (p. 64).

Dr Derry explains that *Aarfugl* = black grouse, *Lyrurus tetrix*, while *Aarhane* is black cock and *Aarhöne* grey hen. (See also the breakfast on p. 86.)

[1] Lillehammer, at the northern tip of Lake Mjösa, is now one of the principal tourist centres of Norway.

The Gudbrandsdal begins at Lillehammer; this valley is about 125 miles long, and is famous for architecture, wood-carving, and weaving, as well as the scenery. The highway through the Gudbrandsdal followed by Malthus was one of the most important in Norway, although for many years it was only passable on foot or with pack-horses; it was used by pilgrims going to St Olaf's tomb at Trondheim.

The river is the Laagen or Losna. *Laagen* means water; hence the same name for the river at Kongsberg.

[2] Balbergkampen, where British troops were to suffer the first of several defeats at German hands during the British-Norwegian fighting withdrawal through the Gudbrandsdal in April 1940.

The road hung over the river, which was studded with various islands, & on all sides rocks, mountains, grass fields, & picturesque cottages on the ridges of the hills, were combined in the most beautiful manner. The trees of all kinds were luxuriant in foliage,—the fields were of the finest verdure, which threw an air of softness over the whole picture, & made it appear one of the happiest & most enchanting spots that can well be imagined. The mountains however were still covered with clouds, & there was a little misling rain now & then which prevented us from seeing the valley in its greatest beauty. We could not help being astonished that none of our friends at Christiania had once mentioned the kind of country we were to pass thro. This perhaps made the pleasure we felt the greater, as it was almost totally unexpected.

After proceeding 2 or 3 miles thro this delightful vale, with the river sometimes running at our feet, we came into a more open part, where I was sorry to see that great ravages had been made among the firs by an accidental fire. This sometimes takes place when they cut & burn their firs in order to get their crop of rye.

Some way further we came to a fine fall of the river, & a rocky mountain which we had in view from the beginning of the valley reared its bold front on the opposite side. The latter half of the valley to Mosthuus (2 miles) was more open & had rather a wilder character, tho there were many houses & spots of cultivation scattered on the sides of the hills.

At Mosthuus we had eggs & bacon. Dinner & maid 2s. 6d.

From Mosthuus to Stav 1 mile. After leaving Mosthuus the valley closed again, & presented some most beautiful scenery—mountainous cliffs in alpine shapes rising one after another to our right. Left shore of the river not quite so fine. River about as broad as the Thames at Putney. In the two last stages passed frequent mountain torrents, some of which looked beautiful shining at a distance on the sides of the hills.

Had a conversation with the farmer who owned the horses, thro the medium of our servant as interpreter. There is a particular quantity of land that is calld a full farm; but I have not yet been able to learn what number of acres it contains. The man we talked with possessed half a farm, kept 32 cows, 2 housemen, & four horses. This he could do in a good year; but in a bad one he was obliged to sell some of his cows & horses. The farm was his own. There are not many we understand that rent farms.

The common price that is paid to a houseman per day is 4*d*. in summer & 2 in winter; but the farmer said that if he employed others besides his own housemen, which he generally did, he was then obliged to pay 8*d*. & sometimes for very hard work, 1*s*. with victuals. The farmers always give victuals. It is common for farms to be divided into halves & quarters. Some of the little clusters of houses that we had seen belonged to 2 or four farmers perhaps, who possess'd a full farm between them. We understand that all the sons inherit equally, & if the eldest cannot give his brothers an equivalent for their shares, they must either divide the farm or sell it. I do not understand why upon this principle all the farms in Norway have not become exceedingly small.

Bishop Pontoppidan wrote half a century before, 'These peaceable times occasion a great increase of people, and the ground belonging to one house, is often divided into three, four, or five parts, among as many families; which makes these new inhabitants see the necessity of being industrious in cultivating the ground in order to support their families.' The Bishop thought that in the past the peasants had been negligent, and chose to work in the woods or fisheries rather than on their land.[1]

To Loftnas 1½ miles.[2] Fells increase in height. (The Norwegians make use of the word Fiell, which answers to our northern term, & seems a good word to express something between a hill and a mountain.) Valley very grand on both sides. Rocky fells rising almost perpendicularly, & straining the sight to look to the top, each successive cliff appearing higher than the last. Firs & birches to the tops of the cliffs— below the road sometimes verdant banks to the river.

To Elstad 1 mile. Valley continued in the same grand style— Some sublime views back on the mountains we had passed. Towards the end of the stage we came to a mountain pass where the rocks were more than perpendicular & some tremendous masses had lately fallen.

[1] *Natural History of Norway*, p. 281.   [2] Loftnas is probably Lösnaes.

The road for the two or three last stages had still continued very good, tho with some steep pitches. It must have been formed in many parts at a great expence. I understand that the present road has not been finished above 7 or 8 years. It was almost impassable before.

We had determined to stay at Elstad, if it was as beautiful as the spots we had passed, to rest ourselves & enjoy the fine scenery, & its situation on seeing it did not make us alter our determination. We were received by the master of the inn, who was a considerable farmer, without stockings. The bed room which he shewd us was most extremely hot & close & none of the windows would open; but he goodnaturedly consented to take out one of the frames for us; and as the ladder employed for the purpose was very large & heavy, 4 or 5 men were engaged for half an hour in accommodating us. We had our usual supper of custard, the making of which we generally superintend ourselves.

Clarke and Cripps, in the autumn, travelled by the same road as Malthus and Otter, but in the opposite direction, coming south from Trondheim to Lillehammer. They found the names of Malthus and Otter in the post-book at Elstad, and on 24 October Clarke wrote to Otter most unreasonably from Christiania: 'We were surprised to learn that you halted a day or two at Elstad, instead of selecting a spot among the sublime scenery *you afterward visited* in the neighbourhood of Douvre fiel' (Editor's italics).

Clouds low, misling rain at times; at 9 in the evening a hard shower. Therm at half past 6 in the morning, 62; at 1, 65; at half past 7, 60.[1]

July 9 [Tuesday]. After breakfast, crossed the river to walk up one of the opposite fells. The river where we pass'd was rather broader than the Thames at Putney; but it seemed to be full rather beyond its usual state & was a little whitish in colour. The country looked beautiful from the river. The inn was situated on a most verdant knowl of green corn & grass which descended to the river, & behind rose high fells & rocky cliffs in fine shapes, forming at the same time a grand & cheerful scene.

[1] Malthus left a blank page after this.

Our walk up the cliff took us an hour & a half, & made us tolerably warm. It was by no means the highest in the neighbourhood; but we had some fine views from it of the surrounding country, & saw Doverfield, tho at the distance of near fifty miles, with his sugar loaf hills covered with snow.[1] In our way up the fell, not very far from the top, we passed a cottage belonging to a houseman with a little patch of cultivation. The sides of the fell high up were covered with a thick bed of Moss & the Hist plant; & on the rocks some very beautiful lichens. Firs & birches were the principal trees. Pyrola Uniflora in plenty. On the top we stood on rather a tremendous pinnacle of rock.

We descended by another way & called in at a cottage situated about the middle of the fell. A very old man & 3 old women besides 2 middle aged women & a little girl had excited our curiosity from looking very dirty & miserable; but we found the house much better than we expected. Wooden houses have a natural tightness & neatness about them, & they are in a manner wainscoated the moment they are made. One of the old women was making oaten cakes on an iron such as they use in Cumberland, & they were to be sure the coarsest that one could conceive to be eatable. They seemed to consist more of chaff, than of oatmeal. I brought a bit away for a specimen.

Bishop Pontoppidan has this to say of Norwegian baking: 'Oats, in most of the provinces, is the best grain, and is larger, whiter, and fuller, here than that of other countries. Of this the peasant makes his bread, but not in the form of the loaves of rye-bread, which they call stampe-brod, but in flat round cakes, about as big as a small dish, and extremely thin, this they call flad-brod. They bake it upon a round iron plate, or a flat stone set over the fire; they roll out a handful of dough with a rolling-pin, to the extent of the iron plate, and before it is quite enough on one side, they turn it with a small stick made for that purpose. These cakes are soon baked, so that the baker, who is generally a woman, can dispatch enough in one day to last a whole year; for this sort of bread will not mould or spoil, if kept in a dry place. Some reckon the oldest to be best; and

[1] Doverfield is Malthus's anglicised version of Dovrefjell, a high mountain plateau of almost 3,300 feet; the word is also used loosely to describe the whole of the mountainous district separating North and South Norway.

in former times, she used to be esteemed a good housewife that saved for her son's wedding, a piece of bread that she had baked for his christening.'[1]

Visitors to the Maihaugen Museum at Lillehammer in 1965 might eat, if they wished, some flatbröd made in 1914. At this museum there is also a sample of the very finely chopped straw which the peasants mixed with their meal when they made bread; it looks extremely like chaff.

The little girl was afraid of us at first. I held out a penny to her—she looked for sometime before she would take it; but when she found that her eyes did not deceive her she took it, & held out her hand to shake mine, saying, *many taks* in a very pretty manner.[2] Three or four cottages were scattered about on different parts of the fell. The cottage where we had called in contained (we heard) a houseman & his family, his own father & mother, & his wife's.

After dinner we talked to our Landlord who we found possess'd a full farm. He keeps 60 cows, 12 or 13 horses & 6 housemen. His cows are now gone to pasture on the mountains —to Saaters, as they seem to call it.[3]

Malthus might have remembered this passage from Pontoppidan: 'In the spring the cattle do not graze in the vallies and on the skirts of the mountains after Whitsuntide; for when the seed time is over, and the people can be spared, they are driven on the sides of the mountains to Sacters, or to Stols, as the country phrase is, which at that season afford them sufficient fodder, the snow being no sooner melted than the grass appears, at least a quarter of an ell high, grown under the masses of snow, from which it derived both warmth and moisture. When the distance is within a Norway mile, the milk is brought home twice a day; but if the distance be two or three miles to those pastures, they keep Saeterbo or huts on the mountains, where a maid-servant, distinguished by the name of Buedye, constantly lives, for the security of the cattle against wolves, bears, lynxes, and other wild beasts, who generally fly from such a weak keeper. She is at the same time employed in making butter and cheese, with which she goes down to the house once or twice a week. Regulations against disputes and quarrels with neighbours

---

[1] *Natural History of Norway*, p. 268.   [2] *mange takk.*
[3] The summer pastures of Norway are now spelt *seters* in English geography books.

or borderers, concerning this general right of common on the mountains, are laid down in the Norway Statute-book.'[1]

They had been gone about eight days, & have two men & two maids there to take care of them, and some very large dogs to defend them from the wolves. His housemen receive 2*d.* a day in the winter & 4*d.* in the summer which I understand now is a price regulated by law. I asked how a man could support a family on such sums. He said that they generally had land enough to keep 5 or 6 cows & one or two horses, & that the farmer assisted them always when in distress, & generally ploughed their land for them, if they were not able to do it themselves.

In this part of Norway the country seems to consist entirely of farmers and housemen. The housemen are always obliged to work for the farmer from whom they have their house at a stated price. From any person else they may ask what they please. Our landlord says he sometimes gives eightpence. Potatoes are much in use & much liked. I asked in the morning whether the housemen had generally some ground set to potatoes, & was answered that they had not always ground that would suit them. On the road yesterday we had talked to a man whose father had a quarter of a farm. He kept 16 cows & one houseman, & has about 25 tuns of corn yearly. The man who had half a farm had 50, so that the proportion seems to hold pretty regularly. Our servant thought it might be reckoned that they had an acre of ground in cultivation for every tun of corn which they grew. Mr Anker said that a tun was equal to half a quarter.

In the afternoon we again went down to the water, & were delighted with the beauty of the spot & of the evening. We bathed, & the water felt very cold, which I was rather surprised at, as the therm. immersed was 64, & the air was not then so warm—it was near seven in the evening. After bathing we went down the river in a boat & passed under the finest rocks imaginable rising directly from the water, & some of them hanging over it. Immense masses of dark rocks had apparently fallen from the summits, & a few not long since, as we could see

[1] *Natural History of Norway*, p. 109.

the places to which they had belonged. The rocks were jagged & of the finest forms & colours, & of a very great height. Birches & firs grew on every spot that was not absolutely perpendicular, which gave an extraordinary richness to the cliff. The opposite shores of the river rose directly from the water, but were not quite so perpendicular or in such fine shapes. We came back much delighted with our expedition.

On our way we called in at a cottage where a girl was weaving woollen for a petticoat. We saw some cloth that she had woven for shifts & shirts. It was most extremely coarse; but not very hard. The girl that was weaving had nothing but her shift & a single petticoat on. The women's shifts are made like shirts, long at the arms, & to button at the collar. The house seemed very comfortable. Near the ceiling was a frame of boards, which we understood they used for a bed chamber in the winter, on account of its greater warmth.

Archdeacon Coxe also noticed that the Norwegian peasant women about their work wore fewer clothes than their English counterparts; he writes, 'The women, while employed in their household affairs, frequently, as in Sweden, appear only with a petticoat and a shift, with a collar reaching to the throat, and a black sash tied round the waist. Their linen is remarkably fine; and as they are usually well made, this mode of dress sets off their shapes to the highest advantage.'[1]

When we came back to our inn the family were supping upon a kind of hasty pudding made of barley, a spoonful of which they seasoned with a little milk & cheese & then washed it down with a spoonful of beer.

Shower about 9; fine the rest of the day. Therm at 2, 66; at half past 4, 64.[2]

July 10 [Wednesday]. Paid bill for 2 nights, 4 dollars. Servants & man going up the fell, & boat, 2s. 6. When I gave the maids 6d. a piece, they shook me by the hand, & thanked me; & the man did the same. Cox takes notice of this mode that the

---

[1] *Travels*, v, 11.
[2] Malthus left another blank page here.

Norwegians have of expressing their thanks; but we had only met with it once or twice before.

Here is the passage from 'Cox' which Malthus remembered: 'The Norwegian peasants possess much spirit and fire in their manner, are frank, open, and undaunted, yet not insolent; never fawning to their superiors, yet paying proper respect to those above them.

'Their principal mode of salute is by offering their hand; and when we gave them or paid them a trifle, the peasants, instead of returning thanks by words or by a bow, shook our hands with great frankness and cordiality.'[1]

To Hundorp 1½. Valley rather wider—a very fine rocky fell to the right—the bottom near the river flatter & a little marshy. Part of it covered with large stones from a great inundation that happened about 8 years ago. Saw some very full crops of barley just in ear, & a good crop of hemp—Some of the land apparently very fertile.

The man who came with the horses was the son of a farmer who had half a farm. He kept 4 or 5 horses, 16 cows, & grew generally a hundred tuns of corn. His cows were at Saaters. The farmer at Elstad was in the practice of buying cattle in the spring, keeping them during the summer at Saaters, and selling them in the autumn at Christiania. His Saaters were at the distance of three Norway miles.

At Hundorp was a white round church finer than usual, roofed with sound tiles[2]—the hamlet larger than common but none of the houses contiguous. Many farms & clusters of houses were scattered on the sides of the fells. The wooden houses when old, look rather too dark at a distance, which prevents them from being so pretty as they otherwise would be from their shape.

To Kongsgaarden 1 mile. Valley continued rather wider. A very fine rocky fell on the right, intersected by perpendicular cliffs—birches luxuriant. The Scotch fir a little stunted & growing short & full of boughs. Road sometimes close to the river, which was become narrower & more rapid.

[1] Coxe, *Travels*, v, 10.
[2] Hundorp is between Ringebu and Harpefoss, and its octagonal stone church was built in 1787.

To Wig 1 mile. Valley closed again. Fells very high on each side; but some good land in patches, & many clusters of houses. At Wig a very fine amphitheatre of mountainous cliff on the right.

To Breedon 1¾. Many marks of the inundation. Valley wilder & less cultivated. At a spot where another valley branched from ours the mountains on all sides were particularly dark & grand—vally narrow. At Breedon, where we dined, some pretty grass fields & the rocky fells in fine shapes. The river which we passed in a boat to get to the inn (leaving our carriage behind us) was about the size of the Thames at Richmond. Paid for dinner & [c] 2s. 6d.

To Formoe 1¼. Valley at first quite narrow—Road cut out of the rock & hanging over the river. Soon afterwards we came to where the two principal streams that form the river joined— we pursued the smallest branch; & soon pass'd a beautiful cascade on the right, but not with a great body of water.[1] Towards the end of the stage we came to a very high range of cliff, with immense quantities of loose stones & rocks scattered in heaps every where over its sides, & the firs rising up amongst them.

At the place where we dined last we first began to observe that the shifts of the women reached only to the hips. They hang loose over the top of the petticoat, & on any motion of the person the bare body is seen.

To Haugen 1¾. The road continued for some time under the same rocky cliff which we called the crumbling mountain. Immense masses of loose rocks covered its sides, & many had fallen over the road. Some of the pieces were in regular shapes, & had a little the appearance of Basaltic columns, but we thought upon examination that they were not.—Crossed the river by a wooden bridge & proceeded up an alpine road on the side of the mountain, with very wild & sublime scenery all around. The woods were chiefly of firs,—not much birch. When we arrived at the top, which was not till after a walk of an hour & a half, we had a view of some of the highest mountains that we had yet seen, having their bases on the summits of others. In descending again to the river, we had a return of some fine verdure, cultivated spots & birches. The farmer

[1] The cascade was probably the 82-foot. fall of the river Laagen at Harpefoss.

who belonged to the horses kept 60 cows & 15 horses. He had sent one of his men with us, & met us half way with a fresh pair, fearing that the hills would be too much for the others.

To Tofte 1¼ mile. Road chiefly along the bottom of the valley through young firs. It was quite green & looked much like a road in a gentleman's parck. Mountains rose on all sides round us—that on the left had many patches of snow upon it. The man who was with us was a houseman, & we were surprised to hear that he kept himself, 3 horses, 6 cows & 2 bullocks, & generally grew 2 tuns of corn. He paid 8 dollars a year for his place (a certain rent is usual). He ploughs with his bullocks & generally sells one every year. Sometimes he sells some of his cows before winter or in the spring when fodder fails.

Passed some places that were marked by the inundation—cross'd the river again, & mounted a steep hill to Tofte. It was a little after ten, & the family were abed; but upon making a noise in the yard & opening a door where one of the maids was asleep, in two minutes 5 or 6 women were up, & were walking about the yard, with their hands under their short shifts rubbing their bodies very composedly while they were talking to us. We soon had a fire & our usual supper of custard, which we took in the kitchen as the dresser & every thing about was remarkably clean, & the presiding maid particularly agreeable in her manners & very good natured in endeavouring to find out our meaning when we tried to talk norse. The beds were so nice & the sheets so clean that we did not make use of our own.[1]

We have met with at the inns and seen on the road a number of very fine women in Norway, with fair complexions & agreeable countenances; & have been much struck with the superiority of the Norway women to the swedish.

The Houseman that we had talked with during the last stage said that potatoes had been but lately introduced, & were not generally used. He liked them himself but many people did not. They have increased much in general use about Christiania

---

[1] The lodging at Tofte has been famous since the time of Harold Fair-Hair (880–940), and almost every king of Norway has spent a night at this ancient farm. At the beginning of the eighteenth century the hall was decorated by Paal Veggum. It seems a pity that Malthus and Otter remained in the kitchen.

137

during the last 7 or 8 years, & now form a considerable part of the food of the common people in that part of the country, but are probably not much in use in the interior parts of the country.

July 11 [Thursday]. Paid a dollar for supper, beds & coffee. About Tofte there is more cultivated land together than usual in the valley; but the general appearance of the country was wilder & had fewer trees—the view back was on a mountain of considerable height much streaked with snow.—We could not see its top while in the valley. In mounting the hill to the inn we began the ascent of Doverfield. The master & mistress of the inn were gone to a wedding, which we understood is kept with much feasting & revelry in this part of the country. It lasts generally 8 or ten days. As many housemen as possible attend the bride to church.

The farmers all along the vale which we had passed are reckoned rich, & a very good sort of people. The country is also said to be remarkable for the tallest people of Norway. We remarked that they were in general well made. The Landlord of the house where we dined at Breeden was one of the stoutest & strongest-made men I ever saw. He had light long hair, & put us in mind of some of Ossian's heroes. The men in general cherish a great length of hair—this perhaps may be owing to their being constantly liable to be called out as soldiers.

In mounting the hill we intirely quitted our friendly river, the shores of which from our first crossing at Minde we had pursued for near 170 English miles, & I doubt whether any river in the world can show such a constant succession of beautiful scenery. The subjects would be difficult; but a vast number of spots might be chosen which would make the most beautiful landscapes. There would only be wanting distance.

To Fockstuen 1½.[1] The first Norway mile was all the way a steep hill.—the scene wild & bare. on the sides of the mountain we observed very little heath.—grass & moss, the juniper, a dwarf species of willow, the vaccinium, & the wild myrica's

---

[1] Fokstua is 3,120 feet above sea-level. The Fokstumyrene (bogs) on the Dovre plateau are described in the guide-books as a paradise for ornithologists and botanists.

were its principal covering besides innumerable flowers. Otter found it by far the best place for botanizing that he had ever seen, & picked up a great many new plants, among the rest the Primula Norvegiensis. In disending a little again to Fockstuen a few scrubby birches made their appearance. They were remarkably dark in leaves & branches, & looked almost like blackthorns. About Fockstuen there were some tolerable grass fields. Before we descended to Fockstuen we had some fine views of sugar-loaf mountains covered with snow; but as there was no foreground to them, & as their apparent height was not so great as their real height, on account of their rising from a flat which was itself a mountain, the view was not so interesting as we expected, & not to be compared even in point of grandeur with the shores of our delightful river.

We had taken 3 horses from Tofte on account of the hill we had to mount,—they were remarkably fine horses, all without shoes, though part of the road was stony. I was surprised to see such a large breed of horses among the mountains. They had been improving in goodness & size ever since we left Christiania. The worst pair that we have had in Norway was the pair from Christiania. In general we have found the Norway horses larger, better, & in better condition than those in Sweden—the condition may a good deal depend upon the summer being further advanced, but in general both the people & country seem to be richer. At Tofte a very thin oat cake was the only kind of bread we saw in use. The barley they eat moist, in the shape of a hasty pudding.

To Nedre Jarmen 2¼. Rather dreary—passed a valley in the mountains with some small lakes, surrounded by scrubby birches. Saw some poor-looking houses which we were told belonged to Saaters.[1] The Saters must be bad on the part of Doverfield that we passed, as there seemed to be very little for cattle to eat, tho we met a few that did not look ill. The cows that we have in general observed in Norway have been about the size of the scotch cattle, but prettier, & in good condition. We hear there is plenty of grouse on Doverfield, but they are never killd except in the winter when they can be sent to a distance.

---

[1] The wooden 'houses' of the seters, with turf roofs on which flowers grow, are still outwardly the same as they were in 1799.

At Nedre Jarmen we dined upon fish & bacon & eggs. They charged us 3 shillings which was higher than we had lately paid.[1] The tables, chairs & frames of the beds were very white & clean. We are almost always introduced into a room where there are two beds, & in general it is the only company room they have. We should often have been puzzled had we continued four in the party. The wooden houses are many of them built either with porches or a kind of collonade & before they get too dark by age look very neat. All over Doverfield are poles by the side of the road to direct the traveller in the snow.

To Kongsvold 1¼ miles. Wild dreary country enlivened only by alpine hills of snow. Descended a steep hill to the inn. At Kongsvold we saw the horses that had been ordered come galloping up by themselves to the door of the inn, where they were fed with salt which they seemed to eat very greedily. The Norwegians themselves seem to be as fond of salt as their horses. They have no idea of eating any thing quite fresh. The moment the butter comes from the churn it is salted; & at the house where we stopped a day a very fine trout was caught which we intended to have for supper, and the man asked as a matter of course whether we would not have it salted first.

The family at the inn at Kongvold were all fair, fat & rather handsome—the children particularly plump. One of the men was eating a dinner very comfortably on sower milk, oat cake, cheese & butter, which he either mixed before he put them into his mouth, or took them one after another. We had remarked for 4 or 5 stages that almost all the men had the same coloured coats on, cut in the same fashion. It was a kind of livery of grey cloth & green worked button-holes. The coats were made in the form of full dress, with long waists, short skirts, & very long flaps to the pockets, with 4 buttons below, & the button-holes worked with green.[2]

We understood that it was no particular livery, but merely the fashion of the country. We had some thoughts of borrowing 2 of them to help us out with our full dress at Petersburgh, as the Emperor, we are told, will admit of nothing else, even in the morning.

[1] Malthus started to write *chardged* for *charged*.
[2] See Plate 4.

The Emperor was the mad Czar Paul I, who succeeded his mother, Catherine the Great, in 1796, and was assassinated on 11 March 1801. His obsession was summed up by Princess Lieven in a single sentence: 'Waistcoats were forbidden, for the Emperor said that they had made the French Revolution.' Round hats (instead of tricornes) and frock-coats were also regarded as Jacobinical forms of dress, and three hundred special police, detailed for this work, had orders to tear them off their wearers in the streets. Paul also forbade the import of all printed matter, including music.

Clarke wrote of the Colletts' party in Christiania: 'A considerable part of our mirth was caused by the anecdotes related of the Emperor Paul of Russia; at this time the subject of general conversation in most parts of Europe...Almost every one has heard of his famous ukase against different articles of wearing apparel.'[1]

Malthus and Otter did get to St Petersburg, whence they sailed for England, but were 'detained' at Viborg on their way there.

To Drivstuen 2 miles. Descended by a grand rocky valley with a roaring stream at the bottom, the road winding in very steep pitches up & down the sides of the mountainous cliffs, the precipices below some times rather tremendous, & the road in places very steep & bad. This was the first bad road that we had met with. We had been advised at the inn to ride; but we told them that we should walk up & down the hills; however, we were obliged to take 3 horses to the carriage. The mountainous cliffs on each side of us were the highest we had yet seen. Snow was on the ridges of all that had a north & north-east exposure. Their sides were still enriched by the hardy birch, & nearer the bottoms some willows, wild cherries, & the sorbus in flower, but no firs. The birches, tho more flourishing than on Doverfield, looked still dark both in their leaves & branches, & had lost that character of softness by which they are in general distinguished. We were near 5 hours coming this stage of 2 miles. At Drivthuen we found civil people, took our supper of custard, & with the assistance of our own sheets went into tolerably comfortable beds.[2]

Fair & fine. Therm at 7, 50; at 4, 58. Wind. S.E.

[1] *Travels*, VI, 18.
[2] The inns at Fokstua, Kongsvoll, and Drivstua are the successors of three of the Dovre shelters that existed in Saga times: they now belong to the State. According to legend King Öystein provided property to maintain these refuges, which

July 12 [Friday]. Had tea for breakfast for the first time. Paid for supper, beds & breakfast 3 shillings. The man asked only something above 2. Our servant is engaged to board himself; but we rather suppose that his eating goes into our general account.—very cheap living—but we have our own bread & liquor with us.

In the kitchen at Drivthuen we saw seven men eating a most comfortable breakfast, of fried bacon & veal, some fried fish, large bowls of milk, & oat cake & butter. Each had his knife & fork & spoon—the bowls of milk were in common. We enquired of the master of the house afterwards whether they were all his men—he said they were, and lived in his house, besides others. He had, he said, 20 altogether in family, tho he had but little ground round the house, but a farm higher up the country. None of the men that lived with him were married. We did not learn how they were employed. The appearance of the master was quite that of a common peasant. The establishments of the farmers in this country appear to be much larger than with us, and it is probable that the sons of housemen & small farmers become the servants of farmers, and do not marry till they are able to obtain a houseman's place.

To Hiess 1½ miles. Continuation of the rocky valley, with mountains on each side. On the ridges of that on the left, which had a NE exposure, there was snow—that on the right was an extraordinary fine cliff of great height with steps of perpendicular rock fringed with birch, the birches beginning to be rather softer than they were. Scarcely any houses or cottages were to be seen. Towards the end of the stage the valley became more open & bare. Round the inn some good looking barley & oats not in ear. House very neat—the tables, chairs & frames of the bed, clean washed & white.

To Oftne 1 mile. Valley broader—road in the bottom thro firs, but not flourishing, & many of their boughs appearing as if killed by the frost. We observed also much dead Juniper. On the right was a very fine round mountain. Before the end of the stage we came to the termination of the valley which

were later taken over by the Church; after the Reformation the land was given to farmers on condition that they kept the hostelries and provided pack-horses for travellers.

branched off into two. We turned into that which went to the NE; and the river which we had brought down with us from Doverfield pursued the N. western valley. On the hill near Oftne was a church, which was the first we had seen since we left Tofte at the foot of Doverfield.[1] There were many scattered houses about, and a considerable quantity of land in cultivation. The barley & oats looked very well & were just in ear— some enclosures of stone walls—many aspens, the boughs of which are used for the cattle in winter. The aspen, which is a frequent tree in Norway, appears to me to have larger & finer leaves than with us. The mountains were more distant & bare & had some of them much snow on their tops.

We sate in the kitchen waiting while the horses were getting ready. The sides of the room & the beams of the cieling were painted various colours—the house & people not quite so clean as those we had met with lately. Both the shifts and the hair of the women were now grown longer—the first was tucked into the petticoat; & the second, plaited with a bit of red list or ribband, hung low down the back.[2]

To Stuen 1¼. The round mountain which we had on our right in coming down the valley presented now another front to us, different in shape—when we had passed it the valley became more open and the hills less perpendicular. We pass'd thro a wood of large firs, but the timber was knotted & not straight—young birch were intermixed. We observed again much of the dead Juniper, & upon enquiring the cause of the man that was with us, were told that tho the frost was very severe last winter, yet that the snow was scarcely above the shoes. They had not had so little snow for many years, & it was with difficulty that they could use their sledges. They had all their springs frozen & were much distressed for want of water.

Towards the end of the stage there was a fine view back on the mountains & in the distance one that we had not seen before appeared above the rest, entirely covered with snow, & touching the clouds which were not very low. At Stuen we found nothing to eat but 4 eggs & milk; but with the help of

---

[1] The church was probably that of Oppdal, built in 1650. The little town is now a centre for winter sports.

[2] According to the *O.E.D.* *list* is a band or strip of any material.

some dryed beef which we had with us, & some sugar to the sower milk, added to a little punch from the last remains of our rum, we contrived to make a very good dinner. The rooms were painted and all the women had long tails. We paid 1*s*—6 for our dinner.

To Sundfat 1¼. Appearance of the country much changed. The hills were sloped gradually & covered with firs & birches —the birches were chiefly on our side & the firs in the vally & on the opposite hill. We pass'd a foresty kind of ground with birches & shrubs mixed with grass. We understood that these grounds were saaters, & belonged to some farm at a distance. There appeared to be very good feeding for cattle. The farmers generally have much more cattle in the summer than they can keep over the winter. In the autumn they are bought up by people who make it their business, & sent in great numbers to Christiania to be killed and salted for winter provision. The Farmers also, & people in the country, kill what they want for their own consumption at that time. During this and the last stages, the stones we saw on the sides of the roads were of granite, which we had not seen for some time. Towards the end of the stage we entered a grove of spruce firs which conducted us to a fine valley covered with firs, with a stream at the bottom & some rich spots of grass & cultivation, particularly on the knowl on which the inn was situated.[1]

To Birkhagen 1⅛. Passed on the side of the hill near the top thro birch in grass grounds—crossed over the hill and saw some fine mountains rising before us towards Trondhiem—came to a beautiful wooded valley, of a softer character than those we had lately seen, tho not without rocks. The view in descending a steep hill to a bridge over the river was particularly pleasing. Fields of the finest verdure were mixed among the trees, and the birches had regained their wonted softness. We crossed the bridge & mounted part of the way up the opposite hill to the inn where we intended to sleep.

One of our horses was without shoes but the man rode him full trot down the stony hills without fear. It is not the custom for the men to ride; but as these 2 horses belonged to 2 different people & as both came with us, each to fetch his own horse

---

[1] Here Malthus stops writing in his first leather-bound notebook, with about an inch of paper to spare, and starts on the second.

back, one of them rode, as we could not let both sit on the carriage, being in great fear of our axle tree, which had been for some time in a perilous state.

We found but a very poor inn & the people very little inclined to trouble themselves about us. They said that they had not even fresh milk; but we fortunately saw a girl at a neighbouring house with a pail, & got some for our custard there. The greatest part of the family, we understood, were gone to Saaters, & those that remained were left without cows. —Our own sheets made the beds tolerable.

Fine & fair. Therm at ½ past 6, 52; at 10, 68; at 1, 71; at ½ past 9 in the evening, 60.

Paid for beds & supper 1s. 6d.; we had nothing from the house but the eggs & sugar.

Wollen caps instead of hats are universal.[1] They are in general red worsted knit, & are imported, we understand, from Copenhagen. Almost every other part of the dress of the peasants is made by them selves, & is in general very neat & tight, & I think superior to the dress of our english labourers.

Bishop Pontoppidan has an account of the self-sufficiency of the Norwegian farmers of the mid-eighteenth century; he wrote that the peasants never employ 'any hatters, shoemakers, taylors, tanners, weavers, carpenters, smiths, or joiners; nor do they ever buy any goods in the towns: but all these trades are exercised in every farm-house...Many of these polypragmatic peasants bring their work to such perfection, that it is hardly distinguishable from town-made goods.'[2]

July 13 [Saturday]. Round the house at Birkhagen & in other spots near, there were some very rich crops of barley—the soil appeared to be a dark mould & very good. At the side of the house were some scythes which were remarkably short & small in the blades, & long in the handles.

To Hoff 2 miles—The road soon passed out of the valley where we had slept into another, where the hills were lower, & the ground foresty, chiefly of birch—the latter part of this

---

[1] Malthus originally wrote *Nightcaps*, and altered it later, with a different ink.
[2] *Natural History of Norway*, p. 245.

vally was deeper with some fine rocks, & remarkably luxuriant in trees. We then pass'd into another very fine valley, many parts of which were well cultivated & the soil rich. A fine mountain rose over the nearer hills to our left. A small patch of grass was cut which seemed a good crop but rather weedy— It was not natural grass. Both the horses were without shoes tho the roads were rather stony. Entire horses are in general use here—they are sometimes a little inclined to kick & bite.

To Soknas, 1 mile.[1] Road chiefly thro a most beautiful valley, with rocks, hills & trees disposed in the most picturesque manner, & a stream in the bottom. Here & there some rich spots of cultivation, & slopes of the most verdant grass enriched by birches—The horses were again without shoes & entire.

To Foss 1 mile. Continuation of the same rocky valley, which closed in about midway, to the river, which we passed on a kind of raft pulled over by a rope. The temperature of the water was 60. In the valley we observed many little patches of potatoes which looked very well. At Bye we took some eggs for dinner, & found some bread & cheese that we could eat. The man of the house had either from ignorance or intention kept the paper written for the Feerboo, & not sent it on as he ought to have done.[2] He made some lame excuses, and assured us that we should find horses ready at the next stage; but it appeared upon our arrival at Leer that he had told us a lye, & had made us pay for a message which he had not sent—He moreover charged us 2s. 10d. for our eggs & bread & cheese; which we began now to think dear, tho in Sweden we should have thought it very cheap.

To Leer 1 mile. Continuation of the same rocky valley, but broader & not quite so beautiful. We have observed more cultivated land in this valley, particularly in the latter part of it than we have seen, lying together, since we crossed the great river at Minde. Near the road we saw a bear's head stuck upon a pole—we understand that there are many about. The peasants sometimes catch them in pits baited with a dead horse. We observed yesterday some cows running violently

---

[1] *Sognaes* on C. J. Pontoppidan's map of 1785, and so called by Clarke.
[2] *Forbud*, an advance notice of post-horses required, sent on from stage to stage, so that there should not be long delays while horses were fetched from distant pastures, and so on.

after a dog & making a great noise—we heard that they generally did so, mistaking him, as is supposed, for a wolf whom they consider as their great enemy. There are no wild boars in Norway; but the pigs that we saw had a little that air, having very high bristles & long legs.

To Meelhus 1 mile. Valley broader, & flatter at the bottom —still closed in by rocky hills. The country put me a little in mind of those bason-like vallies in Sweden which we took notice of, tho much superior in beauty. Some barley & oats were in full ear—the soil seemed very good & the crops fine. A few houses painted red were scattered about. Wells work'd by levers, such as we had observed in Holstein, and had frequently seen since, were general. They work very quick & easily—for a well not very deep the plan seems to be a good one.

We had waited above 2 hours for horses at Leer, the man at Bye not having sent either Feerboo or message, & were in fear that we should not get to Trondhiem that night; but by paying a little more at Meelhus we got the horses belonging to the innkeeper out of their turn, & by that means set off again pretty soon.

To Oust ¾ mile. Country more open & less interesting— at Oust rather an extensive view back on the mountains that we had passed. On the left before we came to Oust, we had a view of a bay of the Trondhiem river, with rocky shores, but not particularly fine.

To Tronhiem 1¾. In approaching Tronhiem we expected to see the cultivated grounds increase; but were rather surprised to find this last stage the most barren of any we had pass'd except Doverfield, & there were no mountains to make up for the deficiency—it was chiefly heathy ground & hardly hilly. A few smart looking houses with red tiles were scattered about. When we were desending towards Tronhiem, we thought the bay, the town & the shape of the country a little like Christiania, but wanting that softness which is particularly striking there. The bay is much larger & surrounded in parts by higher mountains. It looks in the same manner like a lake, but is not studded with so many islands. There is one small island on which a fort is built which commands the entrance of the harbour.

All the houses in the town are built of wood; but some of

them are large & handsome, & the streets broad & airy.[1] We found a pretty good inn and a large comfortable room with two beds—the bed rooms always serve for eating as well as sleeping.

On the journey we regularly paid 8*d.* a Norwegian mile for each horse. When we sent a fireboo forwards we had to pay for 3 horses, when we travelled without one for 2. The horses are always at grass & sometimes at the distance of a Norway mile from the posthouse—A Norway mile is longer than the Swedish & near 6¾ english. The man who came to take back the horses had about 4*d.* a mile, & the person at the posthouse who bespoke them 1 penny for each horse. We travelled one day near forty english miles without a fireboo, & calculated that our living & post horses together came to about 14*s.* 6*d.*, 7*s.* 3*d.* each. When the stages are divided into 1½ & 2 miles, one may get on tolerably well without a fireboo if you are not in hurry; but when the stages are a mile, 1 & ¼ & ¾ as they frequently are, it is necessary to send a fireboo, as you are liable to wait 2, 3, & even 4 hours for horses at every change.

We were rather surprised to see many parts of the road between Christiania & Drontheim almost covered with grass, & apparently very little used.[2] The whole way from Minde to within 2 or 3 stages of Drontheim we did not meet a single traveller. Some parts of the road were excellent & beaten like a smooth turnpike road in England, & those parts that were grown over with grass were in general very good. Within 3 or 4 stages of Drontheim the road was a little cut up by the carts loaded with copper from Rorraas, many of which we overtook. They were all small & drawn only by one horse. The habit of using such small carriages of all kinds is probably the reason why the roads of Sweden and Norway, when they are once made, continue good so long, without requiring much constant repair.

[1] The broad and airy streets of Trondheim were the result of what we should now call town planning by a General Cicignon, after a great fire in 1681. In modern guide-books the distance by road between Oslo and Trondheim, by way of the Gudbrandsdal, is given as 348 miles.

[2] The road was 'very little used' because pilgrimages to St Olaf's shrine ceased with the Reformation, and it had not been needed for military purposes for over half a century; people in the ordinary course of business went to Trondheim by sea.

Fair & fine all the morning—a few drops of rain about 8 in the evening. Therm at 6, 58; at 12, 72—at 4 with a clouded skye, 71. Wind S by W. rather high.

On entering Drontheim we observed that the grass on the ramparts was cut for hay.

Drontheim is always called Trondheim by the people of the country, & spelt so in Pantopidan's map. I wonder how it ever came to be call'd Drontheim.

During the journey our servant drove, & the peasant to whom the horses belonged rode behind—this is the general custom. The peasants are remarkably careful of their horses & dont like that they should be driven fast. They sometimes run the whole way themselves that they may not increase the weight for their horses. When the horses belong to two different persons, they will both sometimes go with the carriage; but unless they happen to be idle ones they seldom ride much. During the five or six last stages to Drontheim we had some remarkably tall & stout men who came with their horses. I expected to see the people a little stunted in their growth so far towards the North; but the contrary rather appeared.

The medieval name of Trondheim was Nidaros, Trondheim (Trondhjem) being the name then used for the surrounding district. Drontheim is a German form.

Clarke, in the preface to the first section of the account of his Scandinavian travels, is very scathing on this question of nomenclature: 'It is not a more low and vulgar barbarism to write *Lunnun* instead of London, than it is to substitute Drontheim or Dronton, in lieu of Trönyem.' He said, 'It was the wish of many of its literary inhabitants, that this should be duly stated to the *English* Nation; with a view, if it be possible, to abolish the nick-names of Drontheim and Dronton, bestowed upon this city by the *Irish*; who, from their intercourse with Norway, first gave rise to these appellations.'[1]

On the map 'prefixed to the English edition' of Bishop Pontoppidan's *Natural History*, Trondheim is called Dronthem, but in the text both Tronhiem and Drontheim are used. Clarke calls this 'a map quite disgraceful to geography', and one cannot but agree with him. I think, however, that 'Pantopidan's map', to which Malthus refers here, is the very fine one made by Christian

[1] *Travels*, v, ix.

Jochum Pontoppidan (1739–1807) which was printed in 1785, and which Malthus and Otter might well have used. We know from the accounts of the continental tour of 1825 and the Scottish holiday of 1826 that Malthus seems to have liked buying maps and guides. On C. J. Pontoppidan's map Trondheim is given as Trondhiem.

July 14. Being sunday, we saw the people going to church all very neatly dressed—the 3 or 4 carriages which we observed, belonging to the fine people, were remarkably heavy & old fashioned. We sent Mr Anker's letters to Count Molk who appointed between 12 & 1 for us to call upon him;[1] & in the mean time we took a peep into the church. We had got a boy of the inn with us to let us into a pew; but he broke the key & could not get in; so we stood for a little time in the aisle. The clergy man was preaching in a very high tone of voice with much energy & some action. We often heard the name of Christus pronounced. Most of the people appeared to be standing during the sermon. They all joined in a psalm afterwards, with a very loud organ. There was a lady sitting at a small table near the communion, with a white cloth upon it & some children standing round. After the psalm the clergyman went there and was reading something in a low tone of voice while the people were coming away. We have not yet heard an explanation of the ceremony—we though it might be churching but it is not.[2]

We afterwards called upon Count Molk who received us very politely & said that if we were not engaged he would take us with him to dine with a lady who was at her country house a little way out of the Town.[3] We accepted the invitation, &

[1] Count Gerhard Moltke was born in Copenhagen in 1764. He held the post of Stiftamtmann (provincial governor) in Trondheim from 1796 to 1802. He died in 1851.

[2] This passage, from 'There was a lady', was quite methodically crossed out at a later date, with a different ink. Perhaps Malthus did not wish Clarke to include it in his book.

[3] The lady who gave the dinner-party Malthus calls Madame Lisholm; see p. 167. She was the widow of a Trondheim merchant, Broder Brodersen Lysholm, who was born at Flensburg in 1734, and died in 1772, only nine years after their wedding. Mrs Lysholm was Catherine Meincke, the daughter of another Trondheim merchant; when Malthus met her, and described her as 'a very agreeable old woman', she would have been fifty-five; she died in 1815. In 1799 she was living at Havsteen, Byaasen. See Plate 6.

called upon him again at half past one, when we were introduced to the countess, & set off altogether in a Holstein waggon
& four fine horses to the house where we were to dine. The
countess was a pretty, fair woman with much vivacity[1]—she
talked french very fluently but with a pronunciation that it
was very difficult to understand, particularly while the carriage
was rattling over the stones.

We found a large party, & sat down to dinner two or three
& twenty, besides a table in an adjoining room. The dinner
was one of the most solid that we had seen, consisting of soup,
fowls, ham, fish, & almost half a roasted calf, besides inferior
dishes. For the desert we had a profusion of wood strawberries,
& abundant bowls of cream. The mistress of the house, at
whose left hand I sat, was a very agreeable old woman &
talked a good deal in middling french, tho she was frequently
interrupted by her cares as a hostess. On my left was an old
lady who I learned afterwards was the Countess Smittau.[2] She
had une bouche affreuse which prevented my talking to her
much. The mistress of the house told me that strawberries
had been gathered here 10 days ago which was as early as
they had them at Christiania. She said that in general about
the 27th of June was the time of their first ripening; but that
one year she had had them as early as the 20th.

At the end of the dinner, I suppose upon some sign from
the mistress, the company bowed to her, & drank her health,
& then suddenly rising, pushed their chairs with a very great
noise to the sides of the room. They then stood for a short time
silent, appearing as if they were saying a grace, & then bowing
to one another the ladies were assisted out of the room by the
arms of the gentlemen. We had observed the ceremony of
rising & moving the chairs altogether, before, & the grace
we had remarked at Professor Brunnick's at Kongsbergh; but
the process all the way thro was more intense here, & the

---

[1] The Countess, formerly Bertha Sophie Bille-Brahe, came from Odense. She
was twenty-five, and had married Count Moltke when she was seventeen. She
died in 1833.
[2] This old lady would have been seventy-one. Her maiden name was Eleonore
Frederica von Bassewitz, and she was the widowed mother of Count Gottfried
Wilhelm Christian Schmettau (1752–1823), at that time a Lieut.-Colonel in
Trondheim. His mother outlived him, dying in 1830 at the age of a hundred
and two.

noise almost put me in mind of the rising of the great concil in Milton.[1]

From Count Molk after dinner I heard that when he first came to this government which was about 3 years ago, there were many discontents among the peasants, & much disposition towards the french; but that that spirit was nearly over now since they had heard that the lower classes of people in France had gained nothing by the revolution. They now rejoice at the victories of the English. There was at that time also a little difficulty about corn, & the people assembled in parties, & were not without some trouble, prevailed upon to disperse. He seems to have adopted always the most mild measures which he has constantly found to answer better than force. The people have now great confidence in him.—He is Grand Bailiff of the government of Drontheim.

He said that the popn had lately increased very considerably in his government, partly from their being fewer impediments to marriage from the military regulations. Cultivation also had been proceeding very rapidly—they had for some times had very fortunate years; but he was not without apprehensions that should a bad year come, the people in consequence of the increased popn would suffer most extremely. He has published a kind of proclamation to the farmers desiring that they would all keep a certain stock by them beyond their yearly consumption; & declaring that those who did not should receive no benefit from the publick stores in the event of a scarcity. It is supposed that in consequence of this proclamation most of the farmers have kept a stock by them which they were otherwise in the habit of selling to Sweden.

From the remote situation of Drontheim it is extremely difficult to obtain relief in time by importation, in case of the failure of the crops; and the uncertainty of the climate renders a failure of the crops always possible, however flattering appearances may be. There are 3 nights at the end of august & beginning of september that are particularly dreaded, & I think he said were call'd the iron nights. These sometimes

[1] Clarke describes the after-dinner ceremony in a little more detail: after 'bowing to the master of the house, and to each other, they shake hands with their host, and kiss the hand of their hostess, when the ladies are assisted out of the room by the arms of the gentlemen' (*Travels*, v, 663).

destroy at once the fairest promise. It is now however 15 years since there was an actual famine in the Drontheim government.[1] The regular importation of corn into Drontheim is about 300,000 tuns. The population has greatly increased of late years; but the importation has not increased—a proof that cultivation is going rapidly forwards.

The people on the sea coast are the poorest & suffer the most. They in general marry very young & have large families which they hope to support by fishing, and in a bad year when the fisheries are unsuccessful they are reduced to extreme poverty. The people in the interior parts of the country seldom marry till they can get a place in which they can support a family, and this does not always happen while they are very young, particularly as they in general wish to be quite free with respect to the military before they settle themselves. More however have married early since it has not been necessary to obtain the permission of the officer, and Count Molk expressed some fears of the consequences. I have understood from 2 or 3 authorities that the country girls generally have sweethearts for a considerable time before they marry. A marriage seldom takes place but when a child is about to appear.

The Odels right which has been supposed with justice to impede the cultivation & population of Norway is not yet ablolished—The term has been only shortened.

The Odels law concerned the inheritance and buying of land, and it is perhaps difficult for the urban reader of today to appreciate the intense interest taken in this in the eighteenth century. Bishop Pontoppidan's *Natural History of Norway* closes with a dissertation on the subject; Archdeacon Coxe sums it up as follows:

'A curious custom prevails in Norway, called *odels right*, or right of inheritance, by which the proprietor of certain freehold estates may re-purchase his estate, which either he or any of his ancestors have sold, provided he can prove the title of his family. But in order to enforce this claim, his ancestors, or he, must have declared every tenth year, at the sessions, that they lay claim to the estate, but that they want money to redeem it; and if he, or his heirs, are able to obtain a sufficient sum, then the possessor must, on receiving

[1] There were serious famines in 1772 and 1784.

the money, give up the estate to the *odels-man*. For this reason, the peasants who are freeholders keep a strict account of their pedigree. This custom is attended with advantages and disadvantages. As to the advantages, it fixes the affections of the peasant on his native place, and he improves with pleasure those possessions which are so strongly secured to him: it increases the consequence and excites the industry of his family. On the contrary, the estate loses its value when sold to another person, because, as he possesses only a precarious estate, which he may be obliged to resign, he is not inclined to improve the lands, as if they were irrecoverably his own.'[1]

At present if a farm has been sold, any lineal descendant of the original possessor (the eldest having always the prior right) may within ten years repurchase the farm, at the price which was paid for it. Formerly the period was 20 years. It was instituted at a time when there was emigration from Norway, & was meant to encourage those who had acquired property in other countries to return, & also to prevent an advantage being taken of the necessities of a farmer in a particular year, to buy a farm for little or nothing. The law has at present many advocates. Count Molk is not decidedly against it. I understand that 5 or 6 years ago there was an endeavour made by Government to obtain the sense of the people upon the subject of the abolition of it, & the event was that it was retained; but it was doubted whether the sense of the people was really for its being retained. As might be expected there were two parties—those who had bought estates, and the ancient possessors.

The total abolition of it is still talked of. It has occasioned more processes at law than any other subject of dispute whatever, & this is considered as one reason for its abolition. The commission of conciliation in every parish has very greatly contributed to put an end to these processes and indeed to most others, & it turns out to be a most useful institution. The lawyers have suffered by it, but they were in general considered as not a very honest race, & are not therefore much pitied.

The general law of Denmark & Norway with respect to succession is that the sons shall share equally, & have double

---

[1] *Travels*, v, 9.

the portion of the daughters. The reason that the farms in Norway have not been more divided is, that the population has increased very slowly till of late years; and that the eldest son has always the option of paying his brothers & sisters in money and reserving the estate, which he is generally able to do by mortgaging. Of late years however since the cultivation & population have been increasing it has been more the custom to divide the farm itself, which is the reason that we heard in our journey of many half farms & quarters of farms; but I understand now that there is no particular quantity of land which is call'd a complete farm.

The sons of housemen & small farmers generally go out to service, either in farms or with gentlemen, till they can get a houseman's place, which may enable them to marry. The Farmers sometimes, as we saw in our journey, have many unmarried servants.

The younger sons of farmers, when they have received their portions from their eldest brothers, either buy a part of a farm with it, or lend it out to interest. The legal interest of money is 4 per cent on landed security & 5 per cent on bond.

Part of this information was the result of conversations with some other gentlemen besides count Molk. After coffee we walked about the garden, in different parties, till tea time, & afterwards again till supper, which was conducted in the same form & with the same noise at rising as the dinner. The place had no great beauty but the view of the bay which was fine. We returned about 11 and Count Molk was so good as to send us the English papers the same evening, one of which I read at midnight with ease, tho the sky was very clouded. Therm at 12 at night, 60.

Fair. Therm at noon, 69. There had been a little rain in the night. Wind rather high S.[1]

July 15 [Monday]. A very rainy morning—passed most of it in writing—Took a walk before dinner in the environs of the town & saw some very fine crops of grass, & some extraordinary heavy crops of barley in full ear, laid by the wind of the preceeding night. One field of grass was cutting. Apples ripen at Drontheim; but not apricots, which we heard ripened pretty

---

[1] Here Malthus resumes his habit of leaving a page blank.

well in Christiania. There is not however upon the whole so much difference in the climate as I expected, which perhaps may arise from the greater proximity of Drontheim to the sea.

The Bay of Drontheim never freezes. The cold is not nearly so great here as at Roraas, which is further south. Last winter at Roraas the mercury in the thermometer & Barometer froze naturally; but this intense frost lasted only 3 days, & in the northern part of Norway it was generally considered as a mild winter, tho they were in much apprehension on account of the small quantity of snow, that everything would be kill'd. They complain much of the uncertainty of the weather in the summer —one day perhaps may be excessively hot & the next quite cold—the transition is sometimes in the space of an hour. In winter the climate is much more regular, & they have in general a clear sky.

Dined at the inn, & took a walk in the afternoon. The bay & the mountains on the other side form the chief beauty of the place—the immediate environs are bare of trees, & the rocky hills look rather cold & barren; but there is nothing cold in the appearance of the cultivated soil in the neighbourhood, which seems to be peculiarly rich. I think I hardly ever saw heavier crops of barley & oats. The rye was in full bloom. The first I observed in bloom was at Elstad.

Rainy the greatest part of the morning—fair except a few slight showers in the afternoon. Therm at 3, 54. Wind. N.

July 16 [Tuesday]. Count Molke called upon us in the morning & in the course of conversation gave us some information which we had reason to think was more correct than what we had obtained before on the same subjects. The institution of the Odels right is of very ancient date, but the exact period the count was not informed of. At first there were absolutely no limits, & an estate might be claimed at any time by either the lineal or collaterel descendants. Afterwards the limit was 20 years, but the date of that limit the Count was not acquainted with. In 1771 the period was limited to ten years, and the collateral branches were all excluded.[1] It must however be

---

[1] Malthus is not quite clear on this point. Struensee's ordinance of 1771, based on earlier inquiries, gave the direct line of heirs 15 years in which to claim an estate, where the Odel right had been established by a minimum period of 10 years' ownership.

ten years of uninterrupted possession; for if before the expiration of the ten yrs a person who has a right to claim under the Odels law, gives notice to the possessor that he does not give up his right, tho he is not then in condition to make the purchase, the possessor is obliged to wait 6 years more before he is perfectly secure. The eldest in the lineal descent may reclaim an estate that has been repurchased by a younger brother.

The Count has taken some pains to inform himself of the sentiments of the people in his government respecting this law; & thinks they are in favour of it with proper restrictions: but the reasons that the Count gave us in favour of it, the principal of which I have mentioned before, did not appear to us convincing.

With regard to the descent of property, he informed us that at present the father has a right to divide his property among his children as he pleases, during his life time, provided he leaves to his eldest son a part of the farm sufficient to enable him to bring up a family. If he does not, the son has a power of claiming his right by law. When a father dies without having disposed of his property, a kind of commission in the district meets, and values the farm at a very moderate price—the eldest son has the option of taking it at that price, and the sum is divided among the brothers & sisters—the sisters having half the portion of the brothers. It has lately been more the custom to divide farms, & it is very common for the father to give up to his son if he wishes to marry, the possession of the farm, and to live with him without interfering in the management of it.[1]

With regard to the Courts of Justice we heard that the Juries now only consist of four, and are confined to the smaller courts of justice in the Bailliages. The high court has no jury; but consists only of one Judge & two Assesseurs; the High Bailiff or Governor has no voice in it. The Juries in the smaller courts have a right to record their sentence, & when a difference occurs between the Judge & the Jury, the parties, if they please, may abide by the sentence of the Jury; except in criminal cases when, on such a difference occuring, the affair must be referred to the high court. Formerly the Juries consisted of 8. (Story of their ignorance).

---

[1] At the Folk Museums visitors are shown, in several large farms, 'the room belonging to the old people'.

The Count is in the commission of conciliation with a peasant who is reckoned an oracle by the common people. If one of the parties cites the other to appear before the commission of conciliation, & he refuses to come, the party so refusing must pay all the costs of suit, even tho he gains his cause: but after the affair has been stated to the commission either party is at perfect liberty to refuse to abide by its decision, & to appeal to the courts of law. The expence of bringing a cause before the commission is only 1s. 4d. each. The institution is of three years date in Norway, & about 5 years in Denmark, & it has been found to answer in the highest degree.

A merchant to whom we had a letter call'd upon us afterwards—he had been settled above 30 years at Drontheim, & came from near Flensburgh as most of the merchants here do. They are almost all of German extraction. He said that since he had been here a very marked change had taken place, & that the winters were much less cold & the summers less warm than formerly. When he first came the land round Drontheim was very little cultivated & almost entirely covered with woods. The road to Christiania was quite impassable with any kind of carriage. The cold is never so severe at Drontheim as in the interior of the country—the lowest that he recollected the thermometer last winter was 18, & the highest this summer 18; but sometimes they have it as high as 21.[1] 300,000 shippunds of Copper are exported at Drontheim from the mines of Roraas only.[2] Fish, wood & copper are the chief exports.

In the afternoon we went to the fort in the little island, in which there was not much to see.[3] There were not long since 80 pieces of cannon there; but the greatest part of them have been removed—they are however to be replaced by others. This fort is the principal defence of the harbour tho there is only 25 men there at present, but more could be obtained immediately on their being wanted. We saw one man who had been confined here near eleven years for forging notes. 2 more

[1] Malthus means that the lowest winter temperature was −18° R (−8·5° F). 18° R = 72·5° F and 21° R = 79° F.

[2] According to the O.E.D. a 'shippound' (1545) was 'a unit of weight used in the Baltic trade, varying from 300 to 400 pounds'.

[3] This is the island of Munkholm, where Canute founded a monastery in 1028.

had been placed here by their families; one of them had been lately taken away & the other, who had remained in the island 48 years, refused to go. These men seemed to have been placed by lettres de cachet exactly similar to those in France; but these are now quite at an end.

The Governor, who was a fine hearty old Norwegian, was puffing & blowing with the heat & told me that his thermometer was 23. I was rather surprised, as mine was only 62; but I found afterwards that his was in the sun.

The man who was confined for forging notes had the liberty of amusing himself on the island in any way he pleased. We did not see the old man who had refused to go.

The breadth of the bay across from the town is a mile & a quarter Norway. On our return from the island the water was quite calm & smooth & some dark clouds in the horizon gave the distant shores of the river the true mountainous tinge of blue, & made them look very fine. The distance of the fort from the shore is about an english mile & a half.

In the evening we went to a rout & supper at Count Molk's. It was but a little after six when we got there & all the company were already assembled. There were many card tables at whist & Ombre; but not being very fond of cards, I accepted the proposal of the Count to try a game of chess. He beat me the first game & I beat him the 2 next—the fourth was interrupted by a most substantial supper, one dish of which was a quarter of a calf. Veal, fowls, ham & fish came on one after another—the ham is not eaten with the fowls or veal. During supper I learnt that the price of veal was 5d. or 6d. & the price of beef & mutton 3d. & 4d. Housemen who are found in victuals receive 1s. in summer & 8 in winter. Butter 6d. & sometimes 8d. a pound.

Fine & fair, Therm at 3, 62; at midnight, 54.

There are many grounds about the town planted to potatoes, & they have been much used by the common people within this last ten yrs. There is no wheat & not much rye sown; but barley & oats thrive very well. Rye is the chief corn imported. The most common food of the peasants is the oaten cake. Enough is in general grown in the country for its consumption, & it is seldom necessary to import much either of barley or oats.

July 17 [Wednesday]. The Count called upon us to shew us the publick institutions for the poor, & both the rooms and the people appeared to be very neat, tho there were rather too many crouded together in the same room. There is an hospital for the old & infirm; & a house of industry where any person may be employed & receive a proper price for his work. In the house of industry also, a certain number of young persons are instructed in weaving, making stockings, & are paid a dollar a week. The house of industry costs yearly about 800 or 1,000 dollars. The Count makes it a rule not to admit any person into the hospital for the old & infirm till they have done something, or at least tried to do something, in the house of industry for 2 years. All that we saw in the house of industry were employed in spinning, weaving & making stockings, & most of the old women in the hospital were spinning.[1]

These establishments are supported chiefly by some large legacies which were left for the purpose, aided by voluntary contributions. The number of poor in Drontheim has in consequence of these establishments greatly increased. The popn of Drontheim is about 10,000 & it is said that 1,200 receive assistance. The institutions however seem to be very well inspected & great care seems to be taken not to admit any but real objects of charity into the hospital. The dress of the people in the hospital was neater than in the poor houses of England. We saw also a kind of house of correction where persons who had committed small offences were confined, & obliged to work. This house had been only established half a year—the count did not think it would answer, as they corrupted one another from being all in the same room, & he hoped to hit upon some better plan. He spoke of the prison at Philadelphia as an excellent institution.[2]

In all parishes there are voluntary contributions for the poor —every person declares what sum he is willing to contribute yearly, and the funds are managed by persons appointed for that purpose. This seems to be a little upon the plan of the management of the poor in Scotland.

---

[1] The beautiful old people's home is still there, outwardly much the same, but in 1965 spinning has given place to knitting.

[2] Here under Quaker influence, in 1790, solitary confinement had been introduced, as a long-term remedial measure.

Went to his excellency the General [blank] to dinner in the Holsteen,[1] with Count Molke & his lady, where we found a large party, & as usual a very solid dinner which lasted no inconsiderable time. After coffee we walked to see two very fine cascades which are in the General's grounds, & of which he seemed not a little proud. The scenery around is pretty, but not grand, & he assured us that on account of the extraordinary small quantity of snow which they had last year, there was hardly the 20th part of the water that they usually had. They are however in their present state very well worth seeing—one is 80, & the other 98 feet—the highest is also the broadest & when full of water must be the grandest, tho it is not so perpendicular as the other. The general admires the lowest the most, & one great advantage it certainly possesses, that of being without saw mills. At the upper fall, by way of being rural & picturesque, we drank punch at a table in the sawmill.

The country is oddly intersected, as if by old entrenchments, but are supposed to have been formed in some way or other by the water.—The views are some of them very agreeable, & one of the distant mountains grand, but there is a general want of wood.

The rooms of the house were large & handsome; but the sides were merely the bare wood, & the general seeing me looking round perhaps with some little air of surprise, said that if any body was to offer him the richest tapestry, he would not accept it. They praise much the warmth & dryness of their wooden houses.

We found the General a most mild, pleasing, gentlemanlike man, & the youngest looking man in the face for 68 that I ever saw. He told me that last year, till the 1st of Feby, the thermometer was never lower than 10.—in the beginning of March there were 2 days as low as 21. He did not always keep a regular account.

Between coffee & tea & tea & supper we walked about the grounds in different parties. There is much ceremony in all their meetings & salutations. They bow much upon all

---

[1] The General was Georg Frederik von Krogh, Commandant in Trondheim. He lived from 1732 to 1818; when Malthus met him he would have been sixty-seven, and was virtually viceroy in northern Norway. This country-house was probably at Bakland, where the General owned a tileworks. See Plate 7.

occasions & stand a considerable time with their hats off, even when two persons meet in the grounds, who had perhaps been talking together not ten minutes before. In passing the streets of Drontheim Count Molk pulls his hat off completely to every person that bows to him, and his hat is necessarily twisted into all kind of shapes.

About 10 we sat down to a very solid supper; but I confined myself chiefly to strawberries & cream which were in tolerable plenty. In going & returning in the carriage, I learnt from Count Molk that every cause that concerns life & death must go to Copenhagen, & that a sentence of death never passes without the absolute confirmation of the King. A governor is responsible in every particular for his conduct, & if he arrests a person without sufficient reason, that person may have a process against him in the courts of law & recover costs for false imprisonment.

There are 4 bailliages in the government of Drontheim. The different Bailiffs have nothing to do in the courts of law, except to see that everything be conducted properly, & to refer a cause to the high court if they do not think the sentence of the inferior court just. This they have the power of doing at any time, even tho the criminal be satisfied with his sentence.

In the other governments of Norway there are generally 6 or 7 Bailliages.

I endeavoured to get at the height of some of the mountains in Norway; but could only obtain the height of one which is however reckoned one of the highest in Norway, & is nearly a perpendicular rock situated on the coast between Drontheim & Bergen. The height of this I heard was 6,600 Norwegian ells which equals 2 of our feet.[1]

Fair & fine. Therm. at 1, 66; at midnight, 60.

When we were on the subject of antiquities with the General, he told us that he had dug not long since on an island mentioned by Snorrostreslisius, & found there a curious confirmation of a story that he relates respecting two Norwegian chiefs & brothers—Harold—&c:[2]

[1] The nearly perpendicular rock cannot be identified, but Malthus was badly misinformed; the highest mountain in Norway is only 8,090 feet. See p. 200 for another instance of this kind, which shows how different travelling in the eighteenth century was from touring today.

[2] Malthus left three pages blank, presumably for the story of 'Harold—&c:'.

Clarke was also told about the General's excavations some three months later, and was rather sceptical of the identity of a skull and other relics, found by von Krogh in a tumulus on the island of Lekoe.[1]

Snorri Sturluson was an Icelandic historian who lived from 1178 to 1241, and wrote a chronicle of the Kings of Norway. This work was edited, with Latin and Danish translations, by Gerhard Schöning (3 vols. 1777–83), and was quoted by Archdeacon Coxe.[2]

July 18 [Thursday]. Took a walk on the shore, & bathed—temperature of the water 57. There are no machines here for bathing. The custom of bathing does not seem to prevail either among the higher or lower ranks.[3]

Dined at home & in the afternoon about 6 went to tea & supper at a Mr Knutzon's, a merchant,[4] where we met the Count & Countess Molke & many of the same persons that we had seen before, only a smaller party. The countess told me that there was but one society at Drontheim, & that the reason of their having in general such large parties was, that people were offended if they were not all invited. She complained of the early hour at which their societies met for the evening. When she came first to Drontheim, which was 3 years ago, it was five; at present it is about 6. As she is not fond of cards, she thought that from 5 to 11 was rather too long to remain in one party.

At supper, after 3 courses of soup, fowls, ham, fish, lobsters &c: &c, a quarter of a calf came to astonish us; but we could only admire, & had no strength left to eat.

From Mr Knutzon & another gentleman I heard that the present price of rye per tun is 6 dollars, of barley 4 & of oats 3. These are reckoned high prices. In general, Rye is 4, Barley 3,

---

[1] Clarke, *Travels*, v, 645.
[2] Coxe, *Travels*, v, 188–98.
[3] Some Norwegians must have bathed occasionally, if Archdeacon Coxe is to be believed. Writing of the Norwegian fisheries he says, 'Mackerel might also be taken in much larger quantities, if many of the Norwegians were not prejudiced against eating them, from a strange notion, that shoals of mackerel often attack and devour the human species, when bathing in the sea' (*Travels*, v, 19).
[4] Hans Carl Knudtzon (1751–1823) was a native of Schleswig. His son, Broder Lysholm Knudtzon, would have been 11 years old at the time of Malthus's visit; he lived in England from 1808 to 1814, and became a friend of the future Lord Durham, and of Byron.

& oats 2 & sometimes 1½. A tun & a half equals our english quarter. Mr Knudson told me that more barley than rye was imported—the rye comes from the baltic & the barley & oats from England & Scotland. When there is a plentiful year in Scotland much oatmeal is imported & is much valued, & greedily bought up here.

I heard from Count Molke & another gentleman 2 extraordinary instances of the rapidity of vegetation in some spots, & in some years in this country. On a farm some way to the south of Drontheim a farmer had reaped two crops of barley in the same year; & a similar instance occurred last year on a farm 10 norway miles south of Drontheim. It is not uncommon for barley to be reaped 6 weeks after it was sown. Some of the vallies have a most fertile soil, & being shut out from all winds, retain the heat very much; & as the sun is so long above the horizon, & the thermometer during the short night often does not sink lower than 60, it may easily be imagined how rapid must be the vegetation when not interrupted by frosts.

Fine & fair except a few drops of rain about 6 in the afternoon. Therm at 3, 70; at midnight, 60.

The butter that we eat at the inn has great lumps of salt in it as big as hailstones, which makes it extremely disagreeable, but we understand that there is no better to be got in the town. The fine people have their butter from Holstein for the winter —in summer they make fresh butter themselves, but their fresh butter is always pretty well salted.

The servants & lower classes of the people dress rather neatly, & many of the women are handsome. Their caps are generally a mob with the caul close to the head, & a black handkerchief or broad fillet bound tight round over the forehead & under the pole,[1]—the broad fillet is sometimes additionally bound with narrow pink ribband.

There are some, but not many, ragged people in the streets —on the ramparts we have always seen some slaves working in chains, & they are in general dressed very miserably. They are condemned to this species of slavery according to their crimes, some for a certain number of years & some for life.

---

[1] The *O.E.D.* gives 1834 as the earliest date for the use of 'pole' in biology as 'each extremity of the main axis of any organ of more or less spherical or oval form'.

Horse-stealing is slavery for life. For lesser thefts it is seldom till after the second or third offence that they are condemned to work on the ramparts. Persons who have deserted three or 4 times receive this species of punishment.

July 19 [Friday]. A gentleman called upon us by Count Molke's desire to shew us the chamber of natural history & the Church. The collection in natural history is small & poor & does not seem to be much attended to. The society was set on foot about 30 years ago, by a bishop whose name I have forgot, & supported by a Monr Summ of Copenhagen who made a present of a collection of books. Each member on being elected presents some books, but there is no annual contribution. The society consists of about forty and the present Bishop, who is considered as a man of letters, is president. He is unluckily absent & we had not an opportunity of getting any information respecting the curiosities of the collection, or any Runic inscriptions that might remain, as the gentleman who went with us professed himself ignorant on such subjects.

The 'chamber of natural history' was the Trondheim Scientific Society, founded by Johan Ernst Gunnerus in 1760 on the model of an institution at Jena. Gunnerus had studied at Halle and Jena as well as at Copenhagen University, and became Bishop of Trondheim in 1758.

The interests of the Society ranged from 'the writing of Norway's history, so as to show its separateness from that of Denmark, to propaganda for the more scientific agriculture which might enrich its soil. For fifty years this remained the only centre of learning in the country above the level of the old cathedral schools.'[1]

Peter Frederick Suhm was a historian who lived from 1728 to 1798. He was born in Copenhagen, but was in Trondheim from 1751 to 1765, where he married Karen Angell.

The Bishop of Trondheim in Malthus's time was Johan Christian Schönheyder (1742–1803). He was a learned and energetic man, but perhaps too preoccupied with ecclesiastical affairs to have much time for the Scientific Society.

The expences of the society are supported by funds which have arisen from legacies. There is an old gentleman now alive

[1] T. K. Derry, *A Short History of Norway*, p. 115.

who has bequeathed 20,000 dollars to the use of the society after his death. The room is a large handsome room in a brick building which was erected 10 or 12 years since for a publick school, from a large legacy left by a Mr Angel, a merchant, for that & other purposes. In the room besides the portraits of the Bishop & Mr Summ, is a portrait of Tycho Brahe which seems to be very well executed.[1]

We afterwards went to see the church which was built in the tenth centuary & has a mixture of Gothic & Saxon architecture—the body chiefly gothic & the two wings saxon, tho sometimes they are mixed together in the same part of the building. A well which they shew'd us was called the well of St Olav—the bishop who first introduced Christianity into Norway. A monument that had rather a poor appearance related the merits & travels of bishop Pantopidan:—the date of his birth was 1616 & of his death 1688.

Malthus was not very well informed here. Christianity did not come to Norway until quite at the end of the tenth century, 'introduced' by King Olaf Tryggvason, who was christened in the Scilly Isles and confirmed at Andover, and is believed to have founded the city of Trondheim in 997. St Olaf was not a bishop but King Olaf II, who was killed by his heathen subjects at the battle of Stiklestad in 1030. The well was built on the site on which a healing spring gushed from the earth where the saint's body was buried.

The Cathedral, partly Norman, partly Gothic, was built over a long period, between 1150 and 1320. The kings of Norway were crowned and buried there.

Among the cemeteries was the vault of Mr Angel who had left so magnificent a legacy for charitable purposes.[2] He died in 1767. His legacy exceeded 200,000 dollars, & consisted in part of a share in the copper mines at Roraas which produced

---

[1] Tycho Brahe was a famous Danish astronomer, who lived from 1546 until 1601. He built the observatory of Uraniborg on the island of Huen, six miles off Zealand, where he worked for many years under the patronage of Frederick II. Malthus would have read a long account of him in Coxe's book, including a description of the golden nose that he wore to replace his natural one, which had been cut off in a duel (Coxe, *Travels*, v, 237–61).

[2] Thomas Angell was a native of Trondheim who lived from 1692 to 1767. He left £150,000, two-thirds of the interest going direct to the poor, and one-third remaining to enhance the capital sum.

at that time 500 dollars annually. It does not produce more than 300 now. Part of the sum is employed in those establishments which we saw with Count Molke, part has been employed in publick buildings, & another part supports a society of old women above the lower class,[1] who besides house, firing, &c &c, have 50 dollars a year a piece.

In the course of conversation with the gentleman who was with us, we learnt that there were two free schools in Drontheim for the children of the common people, besides 2 for the higher classes. In the country parishes there are no regular schools; but it is the custom for itinerant schoolmasters to go about, & reside for 2 or 3 months in different hamlets, supported by the farmers in the neighbourhood, by which means almost all the common people are able to read, & most of them to write.[2]

There are no sects in religion at Drontheim. Much indifference on religious subjects seems to prevail, & we were assured that the churches are by no means well attended. The sacrament is however administered twice a week, on fridays & sundays.

We have observed both at Christiania & here that Sunday is the great day for parties of all kinds. Mr Anker's balls are always on a sunday, & the largest fétes here are on the same day.

Dined at home, & went to see a philosopher & conjurer who came from Copenhagen, in the afternoon, where I met Count Molke & his lady, & many of the party that we had been in the habit of seeing. Otter was sick in bed from something that had disagreed with him & could not be of the party. Both the conjuring and the philosophy were very poor. Supped with Madame Lisholm, the lady with whom we dined the first day, —a small family party.

The only piece of information I gained was that a Norway cow was reckoned a good one, which produced cream for 36 pounds of butter during the summer, or 3 months, which

---

[1] Malthus at first wrote *old women rather above the lower class*.
[2] The rite of Confirmation (based on the English service) was legally established in 1736; it became a recognised preliminary to grown-up life, to employment, marriage, and rights of inheritance. The children learnt to read in order to follow a course of instruction in Luther's catechism, organised by the parish priest—hence the itinerant schoolmasters. See also p. 175.

they consider as synonimous. Madame Lisholm's daughter kept 15 cows for making butter, & made only 36 pounds a week. She has four children & an establishment of 20 persons. A Norway pound is to an English pound as 100:112.

First part of the morning fair & fine—slight showers the rest of the day. Therm at 12, 68; at 11 at night, 57.

The grass is pretty generally cutting. This morning I saw 2 loads carrying. When the weather and ground are moist they sometimes hang it up on poles & rails to dry.

Madame Lisholm's daughter was Catherine Sara Marie who, in 1782, at the age of eighteen, had married a native of Trondheim, Carsten Gerhard Bang. There is a local tradition to the effect that they fell in love when he was a student and she still only a little girl. When Malthus and Otter met the couple, she would have been thirty-five and her husband forty-three. He had established a regiment of volunteers at Röros in 1788, and in 1797 was made a lieutenant-colonel.

On 10 April 1802, when he was on his way back to England, Clarke wrote to Otter from Mount Hamus: 'My greatest Happiness would be to marry...If you will agree, we will both advertize for a Wife, in all the Gazettes of Europe; stating our Requisites, & Qualifications—our Situation, &c. I am afraid my Adventures in Turkey must not be included in the Notice; not a Syllable said in your Statement about Mrs Banks of Trönheim. Don't be savage! I will not ask you to compare Notes—'

Mrs Banks is presumably Mrs Bang, but it is hard to see how Otter could have managed more than a casual flirtation. Or was he really a little in love, and retired to bed on purpose to avoid the 'small family party'? We can but conjecture, and it is just possible that it might have been romantic effusions about Mrs Bang, in his journals, that made Otter reluctant to ask his wife to copy them out for Clarke some fifteen years later.

July 20 [Saturday]. Took a walk on the other side of the back river, & had a fine view of the bay & surrounding mountains from a rock situated near an old house which is said to have been the ancient residence of some of the Norway kings.[1] It

[1] The 'back river' is the Nid, the old city of Trondheim being on a sort of peninsula, with the Nidelv on one side and the fjord on the other. The 'rock' is now in the grounds of the Folk Museum.

had rained in the morning, but we found it one of the most sultry days that we had felt at Drontheim.

Saw a fieldfare in a copse. I had seen one or two before. On the shore we found a great quantity of the Triticum Junceum growing in a very flourishing manner & just in bloom.

Dined at home, & spent the evening with a gentleman who has a house under a bare rock on the shore with a fine view of the bay. We heard afterwards that on this rock in the spring there are sometimes 200,000 fish drying, & there are huts built about in different parts for the women & children to attend to them. Freights of fish are sometimes worth 30 or 40 thousand dollars, & a cargo of fish & copper is often worth 50,000.

The party was nearly the same as we had met before, & the supper as long & as solid. The ladies play their parts in general extremely well.

Morning rainy till 10. afterwards fine. Therm at 3 in a back yard, 71; at a west window in a narrow shade, 78; at 12 at night, 59.

The result of what we have heard about the army is that,

There are 2 regiments of infantry in the government of Drontheim, & one of Cavalry, each consisting of 18 companies, of 120 men each. These are a part of the national army & are embodied & exercised for a certain number of days every year. But 2 companies of the regiments of infantry are kept constantly embodied; & the men who form these companies are regularly enlisted, & no person is obliged to serve in them that does not chuse it. It is even unlawful to enlist the sons of farmers into them. The regiment of cavalry has no part of it constantly embodied; but both the men & horses are said to be nearly as well disciplined as the most regular troops. The men have a constant allowance for the keep of their horses which is however very trifling, not more I think than 5 dollars a year.

Beside these three regiments there is a smaller regiment of Chasseurs consisting of about a 1000. This is not always stationary in the government of Drontheim.

Of the 2 regiments of infantry one is commanded by Gen. F de Krogh, & the other by Count Smittau.[1]

The Grand Bailiff or Governor of Drontheim is call'd

[1] See note 2 on p. 151.

Stiftamptman, & the inferior bailiffs Amptmen.[1] Of these there are 4, or rather 3 besides Count Molke, who is Amptman in the immediate bailliage of Drontheim. Under each of the Amptmen there are 3 or 4 Sonescrivers,[2] according to the extent of the division, who are the judges, & before whom, assisted by a Jury, all causes come in the first instance. We were told by an Assesseur that in civil cases the jury sat chiefly as witnesses to the trial, & did not give their opinion except in matters relating to Odels right, & confines, when they generally consisted of 8, & much weight was attached to their opinion. It is in these cases probably that the opinion of the Jury has the preference to that of the Judge. In criminal causes the Jury consists of four—at any time when the criminal is not content with his sentence it goes before the superior court, & in all cases where the punishment exceeds 2 months imprisonment. Every sentence must be confirmed by the superior court, tho the cause, when the parties are content with the sentence, is not pleaded a second time.[3]

July 21 [Sunday]. Went to the church & had an opportunity of copying Bishop Pantopidan epitaph, over which is a picture containing the portraits of himself his wife, his son & a young daughter.[4]

D. O. M. S.

Nobilissimi celeberrimi admodum reverendi DN. Erici Ericii Pantopidani P.L.C. Philosophiae & SS. Theologiae doctoris olim 16 annorum [*sic*] spatio Regia Aulae Antboschoviensis

---

[1] The *Amtmann* was a county governor and chief local official; their establishment dates from 1660.

[2] A *Sorenskriver* is a country justice or district judge.

[3] Malthus left a blank page for an addition which he never made.

[4] Malthus probably confused Erik Erikssön Pontoppidan (1616–78), Bishop of Trondheim, with the writer of the *Natural History of Norway* published in 1751: this was Erik Ludvigsen Pontoppidan (1698–1764), Bishop of Bergen, who wrote, 'The diocese of Drontheim is the only one I have never been in' (*Natural History of Norway*, p. xviii).

The picture and memorial tablet are still in the Cathedral at Trondheim, high up on the west wall of the south transept. It is hard to read, but I saw that *annorrum* was correctly spelt, and in addition to this, Malthus has made other slips in copying: on p. 171 lines 5–6 should read *non domi minus in Academis Ecclesiis et Scholis*...and line 10 should be *famam posteritati commendarunt*; the Bishop's son was *filius supertis*. Malthus has also anglicised all the dates.

Concionatoris hinc 7 annorum et 9 mensium decursu prepositi Ramsoensis et pastoris Coagiensis tandem 5 annorum curriculo Trondhiae Norlandiae et Finmarkiae Episcopi Capituli Nodrasienses Decani Pietate Prudentia Justitia Integritate Singularique Inserviendi voluntate non domi minus in Academia Ecclesiis et Scholiis quam foris in meliori orbe Europeo variis obitis peregrinationibus et monumentis editis nobilitati Pantopidan in Bringaard 21 Jany. anno 1616. nati Nidrosiae 12 July 1678 denati effigium huic tabulae, nomen saxo, cineres conditorio famam posteritati commendarum Vidua relicta Catherina Valentina Koler et filius superstes Valentinus Ericius.

We saw many old fashioned figures driving from Church in little one horse chairs made very clumsily. The old women had very large gauze caps and looked as if they were about a century behind-hand in fashions. Old fashioned one horse chairs are very common & are used for making visits &c &c:

At 2 we went to dine at Count Molke's, where we met a smaller party than usual, all gentlemen. Among the rest was a curious little philosopher from Copenhagen, who came when the dinner was half over, dressed in a blue jacket and blue silk sash, with leather pantaloons laced before with blue laces ornamented with tassels. He had very long hair tucked into his coat & had altogether very much the appearance of a woman.[1]

We understood from Count Molke that he was employed as a Botanist to make a collection in Norland & Finmark for the King's library at Copenhagen. He was in Finmark for the same purpose last year; but was too late in the season & did very little; and now on the second expedition he is likely to be in the same predicament. He afterwards called upon Otter & seemed to know most of the plants that O had found on Dover-field, & those that he did not know he took without asking leave, & opened all our books on the table in the coolest & most nonchalant manner.

---

[1] I have to thank Dr Albert Fabritius of Copenhagen for identifying this philosopher as Martin Friedrich Arendt (1773–1823). He was the son of a tobacco merchant in Altona, and studied botany at Göttingen and Strasbourg, but later became more interested in Norwegian coins, runic inscriptions and the like, and was known as the Wandering Antiquary. The Danish poet Oehlenschläger described his appearance as 'fantastically slovenly' and his manner as brusque and inconsiderate.

He was recommended to Count Molke by Count Ravenclos; but Count M. found him so extremely intrusive and troublesome that he was heartily tired of the introduction. He receives only 200 dollars a year for his travelling expences. On taking leave of Otter, he was going to kiss him, but luckily could not reach so high without some effort, which gave Otter time to mark his disapprobation, on which the little philosopher observed vous ne faites pas cela en Engleterre.

In conversation at dinner I heard from an officer who lived to the Northward that only 13 miles from Drontheim the sun may be seen for 2 or 3 nights following the whole 24 hours above the horizon. The situation where he saw it was at a considerable farm in a valley near the top of some high mountains. The country below is sometimes quite green when the grounds of this farm are covered with deep snow. It is the custom to throw ashes on to snow to hasten its melting— the grass grows under the snow; & it generally happens that the ground is prepared, the seed sown, & the harvest got in, in the course of 2 months.

I understood from Count Molke & another gentleman, that much irregularity prevails among the common people before marriage, & that in some districts, it is even approved of & sanctioned by the parents. In general however it is not thought creditable to have more than one Sweetheart at a time.[1]

We rose from table early to drink coffee at Count Smittau's country house about half a mile from the town; but before we went the Count shewed us again the two Jaloux's which we had seen when we first called. They appear to be something between the cat & the leopard and are found in the woods of Norway tho they are not common. We found Count Smittau's much the finest situation that we had seen in the invirons of Drontheim. It was not deficient in wood, was more retired, had a finer foreground & a better view of the bay & mountains than the others that we had visited; but no taste in laying out grounds prevails any where.

Count Smittau is a great farmer, & talked much of the prejudices he had had to encounter among the peasants; but

---

[1] Malthus wrote, *it is not thought right to have more than one Sweetheart at a time. Creditable* is an afterthought, added in a different ink.

hoped that now some of them were coming over to his opinions. He showed us his house & grounds with much self-satisfaction & a little ostentation. He said his cows were fed in stalls for nearly 8 months in the year, and that it was the same almost all over Norway. He plants a great many potatoes & peas, has tried most of the artificial grasses, & intends now to take to turnips, for sugar.

We drank coffee & tea with a large party of ladies in a kind of wilderness in the garden. The day was extremely warm & beautiful—the warmest I think that we have felt at Drontheim, but unluckily I had not had an opportunity of looking at the thermometer. I fell into conversation here with a gentleman who seemed to be a very sensible & intelligent man. He told me that he generally observed the thermometer & that the greatest heat this year was at the latter end of June when his therm (Reaumur) was at 20. He had seen it as high as 21 & 22 & had heard of it as high as 24 some years ago. He assured me that his therm. was always in a deep shade. He had not observed it at the proper time today, but supposed that it would be about 20. Yesterday his therm was 18, & mine in a deep shade was 71. The greatest cold in winter he said was in general about 17 or 18; for 2 days last year it was 20. He believed that the quicksilver had frozen at Roraas.

He praised very much the government of the Prince Royal, tho he seemed himself to be a little of a Democrat, & said that Norway was increasing very fast in cultivation & population; and that in a few years it would be a very different country from what it had been. He praised very much the new regulations about the army, & said that formerly the priest had the power of refusing to marry a couple who could not shew that they could support a family, even tho the man was not enrolled in the army: and those who were enrolled to serve, found it so difficult and expensive to get married, on account of the permission necessary from the priest & officers, which was not always obtained without douceurs, that they scarcely ever thought of it before their service was expired. He said that the country wanted hands now, that the wages of labour were high, & that the peasants were rich & lived much at their ease.

He seemed to think that we had but little liberty at present in England, & said that the freedom of the press that had been allowed in the Danish dominions had been of the greatest service to the government.

About half past 8 we set off for another Country house of Count Smittau's on the other side of the town, where we were to sup—On the way we call'd at our inn to send off a fireboo, & prepare matters for our departure the next morning. The other country house of the Count is very near the town & has no beauty—he only lives in it to be near the place where the soldiers exercise.

At supper, which was in the same style as usual, I sat by a Major of the Chasseurs who was the only officer I had met with who approved of the new regulations in the army about taking the youngest always first. He seemed to think that it was better for the country & not worse for the army. The Regiment of Chasseurs consists of 600 men, one battalion of which only is in the government of Drontheim. Each battallion consists of 300. They are exercised 8 days in the summer & four in winter. In the winter they always exercise with snow skaits—long pieces of wood with which they slide & support themselves in the deepest snows.

Malthus struggled for an English word to describe skis, and first wrote *pattens*; *snow skaits* was written later. He may have remembered the account of them in Pontoppidan's *Natural History*: 'When they have a long way to go, they put on scates about as broad as the foot, but six or eight feet long, and pointed before; they are covered underneath with seals-skin, so that the smooth grain of the hair turns backwards towards the heel. With these snow-scates they run about on the snow, as well as they can upon the ice, and faster than any horse can go.'[1]

The major spoke highly of the prince's government, & said that the great movement was given in the cabinet by Count Woronzoff. I am not quite sure however of the name.

The Countess Smittau was very gracious & seemed to take great care of her guests.

We walked home with Count Molke & a large party. The Count very kindly desired to hear from us when we reached Petersburgh & hoped to see us at Copenhagen in our return.

[1] Pontoppidan, *Natural History of Norway*, p. 274.

He talks of leaving Drontheim in about a month—perhaps not to return.[1] From all we could hear he will be very much regretted—Every body speaks most highly of him, and it is universally allowed that he has done much good during his government of 3 years. The income is only 2,000 dollars, but having a private fortune he spends six. We thought him a very sensible unaffected & amiable man, & felt ourselves much indebted to him for his civilities. We had found the Countess also very polite, & very lively, and were only distressed sometimes at not being able to understand her very fluent french.

Fine, very warm. Therm, 12 at night, 57.

The gentleman that I talked with at Count Smittau's confirmed what I had heard about the education of the common people. He said that they could all read & most of them write, & that in every parish there were 2 or 3 schoolmasters according to the size of it, selected from the most learned of the peasants, by the Clergyman, & confirmed by the Bishop.[2] The farmers read the gazettes & talk on political subjects. They are at present contented; which was not quite the case at the commencement of the French Revolution.

One of the most powerful reasons of the present prosperity of the country he thought was, that the people now depended less upon fishing, & more on the produce of the earth. In Norland still there is little or no cultivation, & the people go from the interior to the shores during the fishing season.

July 22 [Monday]. Left Drontheim about 8 & called in our way on Colonel Bang, Son in law to Mrs Lisholm, to breakfast. He had promised to write out the route for us, & insisted upon our not passing his house without calling. Mrs Lisholm & the Colonel's wife & family were ready to receive us. They took

---

[1] Count Moltke had put a notice in the issue of the *Trondhjemske Tidender* of 12 July to the effect that he was shortly going to Copenhagen, and that all bills must be sent in to him before 1 August, as he would not pay any received after that date. He did, in fact, return to Trondheim, where he was Stiftamtmann until 1802.

[2] Bishop Pontoppidan wrote with endearing partiality that the children of Norway 'take their learning extremely fast, and are capable in a very short time to get a book by heart, and to comprehend the meaning of it; especially since schools are upon such a good footing, God be praised, as I have every where found them on my annual visitations, with equal joy and surprise' (*Natural History of Norway*, p. 248).

us round the grounds which we found the finest next to Count Smittau's, gave us a most abundant meat breakfast, & overwhelmed us with all kinds of civilities. We received the route that was promised & some other letters, & then with some difficulty got away [in] time enough to save double shutes.

For nearly the first 5 stages the road was the same that we had pass'd before; and we again admired the beauty of the valley which was much superior to any thing we had seen about Drontheim.

The Barley & oats had made great progress while we were in Drontheim & looked very fine. Hay was almost every where making & the scene in consequence very cheerful as well as beautiful.

At Bye, or rather Foss, we were again detained for horses. The man at Melhuus instead of sending the note with a horse on purpose had given it to a man on the road with a loaded cart, who did not arrive at Foss till after us. We had paid notwithstanding for the fireboo's horse at Melhuus. There is a book in every post house where any complaints may be written against the postmasters, but as we had now passed the guilty person two stages, we had not an opportunity of lodging our accusation against him.

Between Foss & the next stage we crossed the river again that we had passed in coming. The temperature of the water was 62½. We turned off a little before we came to Socknas in a very beautiful part of the road where two vallies met. There was a large farm near & the peasants were very busy making hay. The hay is all carried in sledges, & housed immediately. The horses draw the sledges up a kind of platform into the loft or barn.[1] We have never seen any ricks either of hay or corn. The men in mowing stand nearly upright, & take a very short & narrow stroke. They mow extremely close, particularly when the crop is light, as it very often is, in the higher grounds, that are sprinkled with shrubs & trees.

We have wondered that they do not take more pains to grub up these trees in the grounds that they mow; but it would be a disadvantage in a picturesque light, as the mixture of trees & verdure in the Norway vallies certainly adds greatly

---

[1] We should now call this 'platform' a ramp; it is still a feature of many Norwegian farms.

to their beauty. We waited near 2 hours & a half at Storermoe (not far from where we turned off,) for horses, & were obliged to send to Socknas for them. The distance from Foss to Storermoe was 1 mile & ¼.

To Bogen, 1½ mile, thro a close rocky valley, by the side of a river, which had a broad bed but not a great quantity of water. The road was in parts very steep & stony, & hung over the river with little or no defence against falling down the rocks in case of a startlish horse. The hills were much varied in shape & richly covered with firs. One or two of them perfect Cones.

To Kirekevold, 1¼, a continuation of the same valley, & much the same kind of scenery—the road very bad in parts. On account of our being so long detained for horses we did not arrive at Kirekevold till half after one. We had been observing that since we had been in Norway we had not felt any of the cold nights which we were told sometimes succeeded their hottest days. To night however, we found the therm. 45, & felt some inconvenience from the cold, as the Therm during the day had been 73.

At Kirekevold, tho but a poor inn we slept tolerably well, after having got a little boiled milk for supper. We had not time to turn it into Custard.

Fine. Therm at 2 in a deep shade, 73.—in the carriage in a narrow shade, 78. Between 12 & 1 at night, 45. Wind Easterly.

July 23 [Tuesday]. Hay was going forwards all round our inn. When the crop is heavy they always hang it up on cross poles to dry; when it is light they suffer it to dry on the ground. We had some tea & biscuits that we had taken with us for breakfast & paid 3 shillings for the milk, beds & trouble.

To Gaare 2½. The road lay chiefly thro fir woods, in the same valley, but not so close as before, and the hills less perpendicular. The man who came with the horses had a small farm, for which he paid a rent to the Crown. He kept 2 horses & 11 cows. The woods in the neighbourhood all belong to the King; but those who had farms were allowed to cut as much timber as they wanted for their private use. We heard at Drontheim that except the Crown & Church lands, there were very few rented farms in Norway. Almost all the farmers are proprietors. Some of the Crown lands are now selling. When we were at Christiania, Mr Peter Anker was going up the Country for that purpose. Our servant told us that a Sonescriver in the neighbourhood of the inn where we spent a day in Goldbransdale had been commissioned to sell three farms there, & had taken a bribe of 2,000 dollars to let the possessors have the farms at a very low rate.[1] It is also very generally asserted that the officers are bribed to let off the rich peasants from serving; & formerly they received douceurs for giving a permission to marry, & it is said that these may be among the reasons why they disapprove of the present regulations. These reports seem to indicate that there is either as much dishonesty in Norway as in other places, or more calumny.

The road during this stage was in many parts made by trees laid across, as in Russia, & was in general very bad. We were near 5 hours going the 2 miles & a half. In the first part of our way strawberries were very plentiful.

To Hof 2 miles. First part of the valley more open & cultivalted—much hay going forwards.—Afterwards mounted a steep hill covered with firs, & had a view of the surrounding mountains which in the vallies had been hid by the nearer cliffs & hills—Descended & cross'd the river by a smelting furnace, the environs of which looked very barren & desolate. The latter part of the way was again smiling & full of haymakers. Some of the grass that is mown is very light & fine, & seems hardly worth the trouble; but it is necessary to get all the hay they possibly can for their cattle during the long winter. The road was in parts made with trees as in the former stage.

Clarke, in his account of his travels, records how he and Cripps saw the names of Malthus and Otter in the post-book at Hoff exactly two months later. He takes the opportunity of paying Malthus a characteristic tribute when he writes of 'our two friends ...One of them had been collecting, in this, as in other parts of Norway, facts, to elucidate a work, which, after the opposition it experienced from half-witted writers, has at length classed him in that degree of eminence as a philosopher, to which, by his great abilities, he is so justly entitled'. The name of the Rev. Professor Malthus and the title of the book are given in a footnote.[2]

---

[1] The 'day in Goldbransdale' was Tuesday 9 July; the place was Elstad. See pp. 130–5.
[2] *Travels*, v, 617.

From Hof to Roraas 3½ miles. For this very long stage we had a horse that could scarcely go at first, & in half a mile he stood completely still. Luckily at a neighbouring farm we were able to get fresh horses, by which means we at last got to Roraas, tho not till half past one. The road was chiefly on those high grounds, where the cattle are fed in Summer, & which are called Saters. We passed some cows lying together in a small enclosure with a fire in the middle of them, which we were told was to keep the bears off, which are common in this part of the country. The bells which all the horses have about their necks are supposed to be of use for the same purpose.

About half a mile before we came to Roraas we pass'd a river in a valley on the mountains which we found afterwards was the Glommen very near its source. The bottom of the valley near the river was covered with a most thick cold mist which we found very uncomfortable in passing thro. The river issues from some lakes a little higher up, which we could not see for the fog. The therm after getting out of the fog was only 38. In the day it had been 71. The change was not pleasant to our feelings.

At Roraas we found rather a cold reception, as the people were not well pleased at being disturbed. It was with great difficulty we got a little milk for supper, & not till after we had been assured 2 or 3 times that we could have nothing. The master of the Inn, an old gentleman of 80, whom they unfortunately called up, was rather cross.

Fine. Therm at 2 in deep shade, 71; in carriage, 75; at 1 in the morning, 38. Wind easterly.[1]

Röros is about 97 miles from Trondheim, 2,060 feet above sea level. It was founded in 1646, when the copper-mining had just begun, and was three times burnt by the Swedes, in 1678, 1679 and 1718. Only one mine is now worked, but there are conducted tours still, not only of the mines, but also of the houses in which the miners used to live at Sleggveien. The old buildings are all of timber, except for the church built in 1780. It is a delightful place, and deserves to be better known, for it is a living example of what towns were like in the eighteenth century; in the two straight unpaved main streets the elegant wooden houses are contiguous,

[1] Malthus left another blank page here.

but behind them are yards and barns (equally picturesque) where cattle and sheep are kept in winter, sometimes until the end of May, if the snow lies very late.

Clarke gives an account of the inn, which he reached on 20 September: 'We were received by an old and intelligent Apothecary, who had attained his eighty-fourth year; a very worthy man, with a young wife, whose house had long afforded accomodations of the very best kind to travellers...In the *Livre des Etrangers* we found, to our great joy, the names of our two friends, Otter and Malthus, from whom we parted at the Wener Lake, upon our first coming into Sweden, and received from our host the only intelligence we had since received of their welfare...These tidings, and the welcome we experienced from the good old apothecary and his family, made us regard his house as a home...There was, in this house, an entire library of books condemned to supply waste paper for the drugs, grocery, &c. sold by the old apothecary; it had been the property of an English gentleman of the name of Hammond, who died here; but nothing further could we learn of his history.'[1]

July 24 [Wednesday]. This morning we found the features of the old gentleman rather relaxed & the hearts of the whole family softened. We had some most ixcellent coffee for breakfast, some rusks of white bread, & butter that was not bad. The director of the mines to whom we had letters being at a friend's house in the country, we were obliged to wait all the morning before we got his answer. When it came, we found that he could speak no other language but his own, and that he could not be at home before the next day in the evening; but that he had sent word to an inferior superintendant who would shew us everything as well as if he was with us himself.

Tho it was rather a smart inn, we could only get for dinner salt fish & potatoes, besides a kind of soup made of preserved cherries which was not bad. The master of the Inn told us that if he would give any money, he could not buy a bit of meat in Roraas; yet it certainly is the most considerable place that we have seen in Norway, except Christiania & Drontheim & perhaps Kongsberg.

In the afternoon we went with the superintendant to see the smelting houses. The ore undergoes five processes before the copper is brought to the state in which it is generally exported.

[1] *Travels*, v, 601, 602.

The first is simple roasting with wood; the rest are repeated smeltings with charcoal. It did not appear that any flux was used. We saw the last process, which was rather curious. When the copper is sufficiently melted, & is all boiling together in the furnace in a perfectly liquid state, the man at the furnace throws a part of a pail of water on the top of the liquid copper, which hardens the surface about an inch or two deep, & enables him to take off a solid tho red hot cake, which is immediately plunged into a cistern of water near, & is then in the state in which it is carried to Drontheim for exportation. We waited to see this process, but gave the men no kind of trouble, & were therefore rather surprised, when we asked the superintendant what we ought to give them, at his mentioning two dollars.

We could only get information thro the medium of our servant as interpreter. In this way we learnt that the mines produce about 3,000 shippunds of copper yearly. There are nearly 600 men employed, nearly 400 of which are at the mines, & the rest at the smelting houses. The wages are different according to the nature of the employment, and the time that a man has worked as a miner. A ten years apprenticeship is necessary before full pay is given. The highest of the common wages is 1s. a day. There is a public magazine of different kind of corn & other necessaries, to furnish provisions for the workmen; but they receive no very great advantage from it besides the convenience. The prices of all the articles are fixed twice in the year by the proprietors at Drontheim, according to the average prices of those articles at the time, and they always continue the same for the half year—a regulation by which sometimes the Magazine may gain as well as lose. The prices of grain for the last half year have been 6 dollars the tun for rye, & five for barley. Very few oats are consumed. The only advantage besides their wages that the workmen have is a house, and ground enough generally to keep two cows, rent free. The town of Roraas is made up of a great number of poor looking scattered cottages, with a little enclosure round each for hay. In the summer the cows are on the commons. Scarcely a single cottage has anything like a garden.

In the evening we walked to the Glommen, at the distance of a quarter of a Norway mile, & were very near getting bogged

in our way. Roraas and its environs are most extremely dreary
& miserable, the country consisting entirely of a barren heath,
in parts dry & in parts boggy. The mountains that seperate
Norway from Sweden are seen at no great distance, but they
do not appear very high, from Roraas itself being situated on
very high ground. Over all these mountains that seperate
Norway from Sweden, we understand, are a number of wandering Laplanders who are sometimes on the Swedish & sometimes
on the Norway side of the mountains. In winter they sometimes
come down into the villages to sell their skins & buy a little
grain; but in the summer they are seldom seen or heard of
except now & then by the peasants who are with their cattle
at Saters.

Fine & fair. Therm at 1, 64.

In walking about the environs of Roraas we observed a
number of small wooden houses without windows, dotted about,
in the different enclosures. We were informed that these were
all places for hay, which belonged each to a different person,
& that as many of these houses as we observed in one enclosure,
among so many different persons was the ground divided.
These divisions were marked by stones that were not then
visible for the grass.

July 25 [Thursday]. At 6, in company with the intendant, we
set off for the mines at ¾ of a mile distant. We were told that
we must have 3 horses to the carriage, tho it appeared afterwards that 2 would have done perfectly well, tho the superintendant whom we carried with us was none of the smallest.
We pass'd over a dreary stony heath with a chain of small
lakes in a bottom to the right, which form one of the small
rivers that run into the Glommen.

The entrance to the mines of Roraas is not by a shaft as in
all other mines, but is a gradual descent under a vaulted arch
by a road which horses and carts may go up & down without
much difficulty. We descended for a considerable time, the
arch high, low, broad or contracted, according to the extent
of the vein, when it was worked. When we were about 50
Norway yrds perpendicular we stopt, to hear three reports
from the blowing up of the ore, which sounded rather tre-
mendously & continued to vibrate for a long time on the ear.

We afterwards examined the places from which the rocks had been broken, & the ore that they were then working appeared very rich. It is all the yellow copper:—there is no grey which is in general reckoned the richest.

The gradual descent down which we came was not formed to answer any particular purpose, but merely in pursuit of the vein which led from the top in that line, & in places appears to extend on all sides, & to be very irregular both in thickness & direction. We afterwards descended lower & walked about among different excavations, lighted by torches made of bundles of split fir held by men who looked very much like devils. Among the men who were at work in making holes for the powder we observed some very fine large Vulcanian figures; but from the thick cover of black in their faces we could not distinguish whether they looked healthy or not.[1] We were told however by the superintendant that the miners seldom ailed much, & had not even colds often, notwithstanding the miserable dampness of the vaults in which they work. One man who attended us was 70, but he was nearly worn out.

The men that we saw working, were employed entirely in making holes for the powder & charging them. The holes are a Norway yrd (2 feet english) deep & 7 ounces of powder are put in each, which is confined with dryed clay driven in with much force. From 10 to 12 are the hours of shooting, & those which are not absolutely necessary for this part of the work, are allowed to remain above ground for these two hours. Before the explosions begin, one of the superintendants examines all the holes, & if they are not of a proper depth, they are filled up again, & the man who made them is obliged to bore another. The stated labour of each man is two holes a day; for which, when they have served their apprenticeship of ten years to the mines, they receive 5 dollars a month. Those who have not worked ten years received only 4 or $4\frac{1}{2}$ dollars even tho they do exactly the same quantity of work.

[1] Although Clarke used quotation marks here, he embellished Malthus's text as follows: 'We afterwards descended lower, and walked about among different excavations, lighted by the torches of deal splinters, held by men black as the eternal night of these caverns. Among the miners, who were at work in making holes for the powder, we observed some athletic figures, of stature and appearance fitted to call to mind the poetical descriptions of Vulcan's associates, the Cyclops.'

Besides the stated labour, there are odd jobs by which a man may add to his earnings. The miners work from monday morning till friday noon. They remain in a house by the mines during these days, & go home to Roraas to their wives & families on the friday. Sometimes, by working harder they do their appointed work before the time, & are allowed to go home sooner. They generally work from 4 in the morning till 5 in the afternoon, except meal times & 2 hours from ten to 12.

While we were in the mines explosions were continually going off, & those at a distance rolled so exactly like thunder, that they were not to be distinguished from it. There are generally 150 explosions during the hours of shooting. The ore is carried in small carts with horses in the lower parts of the mines, & brought to shafts to be taken up. The shaft we saw was only 50 yrds deep,—we heard that there was another about 100 yrds. These shafts serve to give fresh air to the mines, & up these the water is pumped by Engines. The greatest depth of any part of the mine is 150 yrds. or 300 English feet, We were not lower than 60 yrds. The mines extend in a straight line about 1500 yrds, but they are of considerable extent in other directions.

After coming out of the mines we went to see the house where the men live & sleep during their working days, & a more miserable place I think I never saw. Near a hundred men are crowded together in a room not more than 8 or 9 yrds square. They sleep on narrow boards in a kind of frame that goes all round the walls—the breadth of each board did not appear to be 2 feet, & on those that we saw there was neither bed nor covering. Many of the men were sleeping while we were in the room. They never pull off their cloaths from the monday to the friday. During two months in Summer a great many of the children of the miners are employed, in washing the smaller parts of the ore, & receive from 4d. to 5d. a day.

The mine is divided into 172 shares—each share last year produced 400 dollars clear; formerly a share produced 500 or 600 dollars. The greatest proprietor possesses 18 shares. Mr Angel who left his property to the poor at Drontheim possessed that number, & one or two more at present possess the same.

We brought back the Superintendant to dine at the inn with us, & the landlord killed his fatted calf on the occasion & let us have a bit of veal. In the afternoon the Intendant, Mr Knoph,[1] called upon us, but as he spoke only a very few words of french & no english, we could not reap all the advantage from his conversation that we wished. He promised however to send in the course of the evening a little account of the mines in writing, & answers to some of our questions.

By means of our servant I asked him about the freezing of the quicksilver last winter. He said that the account which was put in the papers was from a Lieutenant Dram who lived about 7 miles from Roraas.[2] The quicksilver that was frozen, was not in the thermometer or Barometer; but was some that Lt Dram had exposed in a cup, & Monr Knoph had doubts about its purity. On the 5th of Feby this year Mr Knoph's Therm sunk into the ball; but when the glass was broken the quicksilver was found liquid. Mr K was so good as to send for the thermometer that he had broken to shew me. It was graduated to 30 degrees below o—Reaumur's scale, & there was a space above the ball not graduated, which seemed as if it would answer to 15 degrees more, so that the cold must at any rate have been excessive.[3]

In the letters that we had delivered to Mr Knoph it had been mentioned that we wished very much to see the Laplanders, and he was desired to put [us] in the best way of accomplishing our purpose. He said he would give us a letter to a gentleman at Tolgen about 4 miles from Roraas who would probably be able to direct us where to find them; but that they remained for so short a time in the same place during the summer that it was difficult to catch them.

Mr K informed us that the population of Roraas was between 1750 & 1800.[4] The latitude, 62°. 34'. 40".

There are many poor & a poor house in Roraas but I did not hear the nature of the institution. There is certainly an air of poverty both in the houses & people.

[1] Erich Otto Knoph had been Director of the Röros mines since 1789.
[2] This was probably Nicolai Hersleb Ramm (1756–1830) who had left the army as a lieutenant in 1785 on becoming an Inspector of Forests, and in 1801 was elected to the Trondheim Scientific Society. I am indebted for this suggestion to Mr Olaus D. Schmidt, through the kind offices of Professor Magne Skodvin.
[3] Yes indeed! $-45°$ R $= -69°$ F, or 101 degrees of frost.
[4] The population of Röros today is 2,795.

The wood used is floated down the rivers, the charcoal brought in sledges during the winter.

Fine & fair. Therm at 2, 65. Wind Northerly.

Mr Knoph sent us the paper which he promised, from which it appeared that the products of the mines in the different yrs. [were:]

1796. 2,295 shippds. at 8d. the Shipp.[1] 183,000 dollars
1797. 2,530 Sh. at 8o. ditto. 202,400
1798 2,583 Sh. at 84. per Shipp. 216,972.

The expences of the mines are between 107,000 & 120,000.

Men & boys employed at the mines	430
At the furnaces	220
in the whole	650

The substances that are found mixed with the copper are the Pyrites cupreus Quartz, Hornblende & Mica.

Between 12,500 & 13,000 tuns of copper are smelted yearly at the 4 different furnaces of Roraas, Tolgen, Dragaas, & Freminds Mitter. From 24 to 26,000 Carts of charcoal.

July 26 [Friday]. Paid six dollars for sleeping 3 nights, breakfasts, dinners & coffee &c: which we thought reasonable, particularly as we expected to be made to pay rather severely; but the old gentleman who was so cross at first, turned out afterwards to be a very civil sort of person.

Left Roraas about 8. Therm at starting, 45. Crossed the Glommen & got soon into a forest of birch which was rather a relief after the bare scenes of Roraas. The road to Oust, 2 miles, very good, & on a descent all the way.[2] Mountains with large fields of snow in the distance, & a little in the shape of Doverfield.—latter part of the stage a return of fir woods. Oust is a village rather larger than usual. The tops of the houses were so flourishing in grass that we asked if they did not sometimes mow them, & were answered in the affirmative.

From Oust to Tolgen 2 miles. The road thro a foresty country of birches first, & afterwards of firs, by the side of the Glommen, & on the opposite shore a fine mountain wooded half way

[1] '8d. the Shipp.' must obviously be a slip of the pen for 8od.
[2] Oust is Os.

up & bare the rest. Passed some farms on which were some very heavy crops of grass. The best land is very frequently extremely uneven in its surface, having mole hills & little dips almost all over it. We have been quite astonished at the manner in which such ground is mowed, the mole hills being shaved quite close & the dips hollowed out with the greatest nicety. When the crop is heavy they generally spread a part of it rather thinly over the ground, & the rest they hang up upon rails. Sometimes all is put upon rails. The hay seems to be made well, & carried in a very good state before it has lost its colour.

We arrived at Tolgen, at which there is a smelting furnace,[1] about 2, & not finding anybody at home at the Inn, delivered our letter to the superintendant of the works, & took possession of his house & some bacon & eggs with all convenient speed. The roofs of the house & outhouses here had evidently been mowed.

The superintendant of the Smelting furnaces to whom Mr Knoph's letter was addressed, & at whose house we were, advised us to order 3 saddle horses immediately & go to a farm house about a Norway mile distant among the mountains, where we were likely to get intelligence of the Laplanders, or Lap fins as they are called, sleep there, & the next morning go in pursuit of them. This advice we adopted, & in consequence about 4 o clock set off, with our servant mounted on the third horse, to act as interpreter, & a peasant on foot as our guide.

We crossed the Glommen by a wooden bridge that had given way in the middle & appeared as if it would not bear the horses, but our guide seemed not to think of it. On the opposite side we mounted a steep hill of firs & afterwards birches, by a rocky path. On the top we came into the grounds that are used for Saters, which are call'd Satermark. Here & there was some tolerable grass, but the greatest part was extremely barren, & covered chiefly with the rein deer moss. It was still, however, a wood of birches, tho they were not flourishing—Beyond the birches were bare hills & mountains, which gave us a good idea of the higher grounds of Norway, & formed a strong contrast to the beauty & fertility of the vallies. In the lower parts of these high grounds were many small lakes.

[1] Tolgen, now called Tolga, is about twenty miles from Röros. It was famous for copper smelting from 1670 to 1870.

After not an unpleasant ride, tho we went a foot's pace all the way, we arrived at the Farmer's house where we were to lodge. With the outhouses & cottages of the housemen, it formed a little hamlet; but was in too dreary a situation to look cheerful. Some of the fields round the house, & particularly the tops of the houses, were tolerably fertile in grass,—the environs in general extremely barren. On the tops of the houses the hay was in cock. In so wild & distant a situation we enquired about the bears & the wolves; & were told that the wolves did much mischief; but that the bears were of the small kind & seldom killed any cattle. The cows, sheep & goats are brought up every night, & either housed or placed in enclosures near the house. During the light nights the wolves will seldom come near a house, & an enclosure at home is a sufficient defence; but before october all of the cattle must be housed every night. We saw a number of goats, which they milk regularly with the cows, & make cheese from them. The farmers generally have goats with their cows at Saters.

We could get nothing to eat but very coarse oaten cake & milk—no eggs were to be had. There was only one bed & one sheet & a quilt made of cows' skins; this, as Otter was the worst sleeper of the two, I gave up to him, & having laid a cow's skin upon the dresser & spread a great coat over it, & taken another for a pillow, I laid myself down not uncomfortably & slept at intervals till half past 3—

[*July 27*, Saturday]—when we rose, took our milk & oat cake for breakfast, & at 4 mounted our horses in pursuit of the Lapfins. The first part of the country we passed thro was very barren, & much covered with the reindeer moss, but generally among woods of scrubby birches. On the left in the bottom was a chain of lakes, one or two of considerable size. When we arrived at the foot of the mountain on the side of which the fins were last heard of, we came into some woods of birches, the intervals between which were filled up with some very good grass, & we passed 5 or 6 houses where the people who attend the farmers' cattle live during the summer; but unluckily there were none of them properly inhabited, & the reason, we were told, was that the grass in these saters was late & that the farmers to whom they belonged generally sent their cattle to some other saters first.

There were a few men, however, at some of the saters, employed in mowing the grass round the house previous to the coming of the cattle. In general there is a part inclosed near every Sater house for hay; but round these there were no enclosures & it was necessary therefore to mow before the cattle came. The hay made at Saters is carried home in the winter on sledges. In general there are only women at the Sater houses to attend the cows; but it is the custom for their Sweethearts to go not unfrequently to comfort them in the retirement.

We enquired of the few people that we found at these houses if they had heard anything of the Lapfins, as we had been much alarmed the night before with a report that they just flitted, & that we might search for them perhaps for 4 or 5 days among the mountains without finding them. A man that was mowing at one of the Saters at last told us that he had seen them the night before & that they lay on the side of the mountain not far beyond Satermark. Much pleased with this information we pushed forwards, & when we were getting out of the woods looked with great eagerness round in search of Laps—the man who first view'd one, was to have 6 pence. The first symptom of our approaching them was the barking of dogs; & shortly after I saw the hut; but could not claim the reward till, after coming in view of the hut a second time, I saw a she Lap peep out.

She proved to be the mother of the whole party, & after asking us some questions in Norse, which she spoke tolerably well, desired us to walk in, tho she said that they had ly'd abed very late that morning & were not yet all up. She said the deer were out at feed & would not come back in less than an hour. I lifted up the bit of sailcloth that covered the little opening for the door, and saw the party rather in an undress'd state sitting up on the skins that were placed round the hut. On receiving a second invitation from a man within, we entered, & the old woman folded up some skins &c: for us to sit on.

We sat here for near an hour & a half, finding the smell very little offensive on account of the fire, & opening at the top of the hut for the smoke. The party at first consisted of the old lady, a married daughter with three children, & her husband who was principal spokesman; & a son & 2 daughters unmarried. They finished their dressing while we were there without any ceremony. The women wear stockings of rein deer skins that reach to the ankles, & these meet some high shoes made of the same kind of materials only thicker. Their shifts were in the short fashion that we observed in some parts of Norway & reached only to their hips. A coarse woollen petticoat & a woollen jacket formed the rest of their dress. The men wear pantaloons of reindeer skins, & shoes meeting them & tyed at the ankles like the women, a common coarse shirt, & coarse woollen jacket or coat. One of the women had no shift, & all the children were sleeping quite naked under their coverlids of rein deers hides.

The hut was formed of large branches of birch stuck in the ground & meeting at top, leaving a hole for the light, the air & the smoke. On these large branches were matted closely the smaller boughs & leaves of the birch so as to exclude all winds. On the floor also was strewed the small boughs of the birch, & over these round the sides of the hut were spread the rein deers hides for their beds. In the middle was the fire, & over it hung a brass pot suspended from a cross pole. The breadth of the hut at bottom was about 3 yrds. & a half. Many rather good looking kettles & pots & wooden plates & bowls were poked about in different corners.

After conversing some little time with the old lady & her son in law, the patriarch whom we had not seen before, & who they told us was the father of them all, entered the hut. He was the shortest, & most complete fin of the party; but they were all short & had the characteristic features of the Laplanders, high cheek bones, hollow cheeks, a prominent chin, & small flat eyes. The old man appeared to be about 4 feet 10.—the other men were 2 or 3 inches taller.

When the old man came in, breakfast was prepared, which consisted of some very fine looking trout that had been boiled before we came in, & two sorts of cheese from the Reindeers milk one white, & the other yellow & soft. The old woman prepared the fish by cutting it in pieces of a proper size, pulling out some of the bones, taking off the head & fins & laying it very neatly on a trencher. It certainly looked very nice & as it was a fine fish I should certainly have been tempted to eat some of it, had not I seen the mode of preparation which was chiefly by the fingers, & these were frequently licked clean in the mouth. Otter eat a little, & tho he said it was remarkably good he was almost sick afterwards with the idea. I eat a bit of both the sorts of Reindeer cheese by way of curiosity; but it had not any predominant taste that I can describe. When the fish was handed round it was pulled to pieces & eat with the fingers. In the water in which the fish had been boild we saw them putting some very good looking oatmeal, & thought that it was a mess for themselves; but they told us it was for their dogs which they are obliged to keep to drive in the rein deer.

The old man told us that he was 62,[1] & had had 13 children, 7 of which were dead & 6 alive; 4 daughters & 2 sons, who all lived in the family, besides the Son in-law who was married to one of the daughters & had 3 children. The business of milking & taking care of the rein deer was performed by the sons & daughters assisted by one servant. The old man had formerly lived with his brother; but they had within these 3 or 4 years parted on account of the increase of the families.

The relationship was curiously mixed among them. The Son-in-law was originally a Swedish Lap; but his mother & the old man's father were brother & sister; & his mother also was half-sister to the old woman (his wife's mother). The brother of the old man had also married the son-in-law's sister. We spoke of the Laps that we had heard of at Roraas, & they said they knew them & were related to them. It appears from this that they do not increase much & generally inter-marry with one another. We had heard at Roraas that the Laps wandered on the Norway or Swedish sides of the hills just as they pleased; but the son-in-law told us that a Norway lap must not go into Sweden, nor a Swidish lap come into Norway.

The old woman was only 52, tho she looked much older than that in the face. She had however a very good set of teeth. The son in law was 33. The old man was rather infirm & looked

[1] Malthus wrote *The old gentleman*, but changed it to *man* immediately afterwards.

more than 62. We asked the name of the old woman & were rather diverted at hearing that it was Maria Sophia Anders daughter. The old mans name was Jonas Anderson.

As we passed an hour & a half in the hut we saw all that was going forwards & were a little surprised at seeing the mother wash her children's faces, & still more at seeing the man wash his. This was certainly above the mark of many of the Norway maidens; but perhaps it was done in compliment to us. I am persuaded that we could not have sat so long in a bed room of a Norway farm house with half so many people in it, without feeling much more inconvenience. This is to be attributed however to the fire smoke & apperture at top rather than the cleanliness of the Laps.

Being almost tired of sitting we went out, & luckily the deer were just then coming home, & looked with their branching horns like a moving forest.[1] We were desired not to go near them till they were in the enclosure, for fear they should take fright at us & run back. When they had been driven into their pen which was a circle not above 15 or 20 yrds in diameter, made of the boughs & large branches of birch, we followed them, & were present for above an hour at the business of milking, which is a work of considerable time & trouble. There were about 600 in the pen as the old man told us, tho the son-in-law had before said that they never counted them. They seemed all inclined to lie down as soon as they came in—the bottom of the pen was almost entirely covered with them. It appeared rather formidable at first to walk about among so many large branching horns, which we were sometimes obliged to push aside to get along; but they were all perfectly quiet & did not shew the least disposition to butting. They were fat & in fine order, & appeared to me about the size of the red deer. I measured two of the largest with my stick, & should conjecture that they were about 3 feet 6 inches high. The horns are nearly a yard high from the head besides the great circle that they make. They are covered with a skin & soft hair which gives them a very novel appearance, & the branches immediately over the forehead are varied in almost every deer.

With the deer came home 2 daughters & a son who had been

---

[1] It is interesting to see that the *O.E.D.* gives 1829 as the earliest date at which the word 'antler' is popularly used for 'the branched horn of a stag, etc.'.

out to watch them. The business of milking very soon began, which was performed chiefly by the women, while the men were employed in catching the does & tying them to 2 or 3 little birch trees in the pen. The does seemed very unwilling to be caught, particularly the young ones who had not been milked before this year. Sometimes the men by a sudden spring were able to catch them by the leg or round the neck; but in general they were obliged to throw a cord over their horns which they did at some distance with considerable skill. After they were caught the young does sometimes resisted much the being led to the birch to be tied up.

The women milked in thick round bowls of wood, & sometimes struck the udders very hard between the legs behind to get down the milk. The son-in-law afterwards came out to assist in milking, & said that as they had not women enough for that work the men were obliged to help. A good deal of hair generally gets into the milk, & to get rid of this they strain it thro a wooden cullender covered with a little wisp of hay, in putting it into the large vessel that stands on the other side of the inclosure. The does when they have lately calved yield about a pint of milk; but the quantity soon falls off. Out of the six hundred deer there were about a hundred in milk, which perhaps yielded on an average half a pint a piece.

It was 9 o'clock when they began to milk. The deer had been at pasture on their moss since 12 the night before, with little bits of sticks in the mouths of the young ones to prevent their sucking. They stay in the pen near five hours, & are then turned out again without bits in the mouths of the young ones. They are brought up again at 7 or 8, & we were rather diverted at hearing the old woman say that then only milk enough was taken from them for coffee or tea. At 12 they are turned out for the night. Whenever they go out, 2 or 3 persons & 2 or 3 dogs attend them. When so attended they are not in much danger from the wolves; but they sometimes lose many, if the attendants are careless, particularly in the winter. They are turned out in the same manner both winter & summer, & have nothing but what they can find for themselves on the mountains, which in the winter is only the lichen Rangiferimus. In summer they eat a little grass sometimes, but the farmers are jealous of their coming near the Saters. The old man said that when they had enriched a piece of ground with their rein deer that the farmers immediately drove them from it. They now pay a tax to the King (a dollar) which I believe they did not before, & hope they shall have their rights better secured.

The Sonescriver came the other day to take an account of the number of the deer; but it is supposed that the old man did not shew them all. Our guide indeed told us that he did not shew them all to us, for that he was sure that he had above a thousand. In the winter they sometimes, but not often, kill their deer & sell the venison—the finest haunch for six shillings. The great coats which they make of the skins & sow together with the sinews as threads, they sell for 15 or 16 dollars. It is reported by the farmers in the neighbourhood that they are very rich & hide their money on the tops of the mountains. The old lady indeed told us that many of the farmers' sons had offered themselves for one of her daughters, & had enquired what portion she meant to give them; but that she had sent them away without satisfying their curiosity or accepting their offers.

The deer are not milked after september. They then begin to rot of the hair & skin from their horns, & shed them at Candlemas. The deer that are used in the sledges are all cut and generally grow the largest. They never harness more than one at a time. In the summer they put on them little oval boxes made of birch, & lined with birch bark to carry their children & utensils in when they move from place to place.

After watching the milking for above an hour we went again into the hut, as a shelter from a little shower that came on, & the old lady very kindly went to fetch 2 or 3 of the sweetest skins that had been airing, & made a bed for us; asking us if we would not take a nap. We had made them a present of 2 pound of tobacco & 2 bottles of brandy, one of which they drank very soon, & the other they finished just as we were going away, upon the supposition that we wanted the bottles again. The old lady seemed much pleased when we refused to take them & attended us part of the way back for fear we should get into a bog. When we went out of the hut to go away we heard a horn blowing at the pen very prettily. Upon going down again we found that one of the girls had been sounding a little horn with 3 stops, which they use to call the deer together when they are going to drive them home to the pen. She gave us a little more of the music for the stivers that we presented her with. The milking was still going forwards, & it was then 2 hours since they had begun. We left them about 11, and it was about 7 when we arrived.

There were many more questions that we wished to ask, but our servant naturally thought so many questions trifling & foolish & shewed a little unwillingness to repeat them; but upon the whole we had reason to be satisfied with him. We heard from Mr Knoph & at Tolgen that the number of fins on these mountains had remained nearly the same for many years. On my asking Mr Knoph what became of their children, he said that when they had no deer they became the servants of others, & that very frequently they wandered about the country begging. Sometimes the fins who had only 8 or ten deer, joined 4 or 5 families together, to make up a tolerable herd. The brother of the old man had about the same number of deer as himself & was encamped about 2 or 3 miles distant. We endeavoured to get at the period when this colony of fins first settled on these mountains, but could get no satisfactory answer. The Son in law said that the old man's father was born upon the mountains, & that was all he knew. Mr Knoph said that they had inhabited these mountains before Roraas was known.

In returning from the Fins we went up to an eagle's nest which we had seen at a distance in coming with some intention of taking it; but we found the tree so very rotten that we did not chuse to venture up—The old bird flew over us; it did not appear to be of a large kind. In coming also we had seen what we took to be the large snipe of Linnaeus flying round us & making a great noise, & sometimes perching on a tree, as if it had a nest somewhere near. We lamented much that we had not a gun. By the by, when we were with the laps we saw a gun, & would have borrowed it to shoot the eagle; but they refused to lend it, saying that it was a bird which often took revenge.

On our way home we saw 2 or 3 of these snipes. They were about the size of a woodcock with a longer neck, & were in colour & manner of flight exactly like a common snipe; but the circumstance of pitching on a tree is rather unlike the habits of this genus. When we arrived at the farmer's, we found nothing but the milk & oat bread, which we could not relish much, & therefore wished to get on as fast as we could to Tolgen; but the peasant insisted upon having an hour to rest his horses. We eat however little or nothing, tho we had breakfasted at 4, reserving our appetites, which had a great craving for something more solid than milk, for our host at Tolgen, where we at last arrived about 5, & were immediately calling about us for something to eat, when we were told that our host had got some venison for us for supper. Not wishing to disappoint him, we determined to wait a second time, tho sorely against our inclinations, & put off our dinner till his supper.

At half past seven we sat down to some trout & a piece of Reindeer venison, which we thought a very lucky finishing to our Laphunting day. It was very tender, & not badly flavoured; but had no fat, & no very high or marked taste. We understood that it was a young one. Our host told us that we should take some with us cold the next day; but we were so hungry with our long expedition that we left very little remainder. We found very comfortable beds, which was rather a treat after the dresser.

Fair in the morning—slight showers from 10 till 5—fine afternoon. Therm at 4 in morning, 42; at 2, 50.

In our afternoon's walk at Tolgen we saw a lamb feeding on the top of one of a house that had been mown; so that it might be fairly said that in Norway they mow the tops of their houses, & turn their cattle in for the aftergrass.

July 28 [Sunday]. Found most excellent coffee in the morning, & set off about 7. We could not offer anything to the gentleman of the house at Tolgen; but gave the wife 3 dollars with which she did not seem ill pleased. We had been treated very hospitably & civilly, & the best of everything had been produced for us.

To Tonset $2\frac{1}{2}$.[1] Thro a forest of firs with the river to the left, & some fine hills on the other side, & mountains with patches of snow in the distance. A little before we came to Tonset we entered a broad rich valley much cultivated, with one of the

---

[1] Tonset is now called Tynset, and is only about thirteen miles from Tolga. The new church which Malthus describes was built in 1793 and is still there.

fine snowy mountains not far from us. At Tolgen [Tonset] I found out that I had left my watch behind me, which we were obliged to send back for to Tolgen, & hearing that there were no beds & nothing to eat further on we determined to stay to night & set off very early the next morning, & here I am in a tolerably comfortable room just finishing my journal before I go to bed.

We had a most delightful bathe in the Glommen before dinner, & afterwards walked up to the church, which is prettily situated on a hill. It is a new building entirely of wood. The covering is of wood in the shape of tiles. In the inside are very large wooden pillars, & the whole being of unpainted deal nearly new has an odd effect. There was unluckily no service or we should have attended it; but we understood that on those sundays that the clergyman did not come the clerk read a part of the service in his stead. The Clergyman comes only once a fortnight, tho the church & parish seem to be very large. The men all wear grey coats trimmed with blue; and the women blue woollen jackets & striped or checked petticoats & a blue checked handkerchief either bound tight or thrown loosely round the head; all are nearly alike.

Fine & fair. Therm at 7, 50; at 2, 67. The river, 56. Wind N. by W.

In the fir wood that we passed thro between Tolgen & Tonset there was some fine red deal timber. There are but two species of fir mentioned in the Flora Scandinavia—the Pinus abies & the Pinus sylvester. The Pinus abies is certainly the common spruce fir, tho when they grow very high they have rather a different appearance, particularly a variety of it (samulis pendentibus) which is mentioned in the Flora Scandinavia.

The Pinus sylvester appears to be the scotch fir, at least looks exactly like it when it is young, or left to spread; but when it grows in the crouded Norway woods, it has smaller branches on the sides & has a more spire like top, than any scotch firs that I have seen in England. The red deals are from the Pinus Sylvestris but they are not all of equal redness. The Pines that make red deals, appear much redder & darker in their outward bark—in other respects they grow exactly the same.[1]

---

[1] The next page is blank except for the single word *July*, which has been crossed out.

July 29 [Monday]. Paid two dollars for our day & night, and a piece of cold lamb & of veal, to serve us for dinner two days—a new and unexpected treat. While on the road in Norway we never hoped to find anything like fresh meat;[1] but our host at Tonset had been in England & had learned to prepare a Sunday's dinner.

To Moe 2 miles. We crossed the Glommen immediately & took leave of it for some time. We mounted for near half a Norway mile a hill of fir woods having the great Trons fiel streaked with snow on our right. It did not appear lower for our ascent. Tron's Fiel is reckoned the highest in Osterdale.[2] On the top of the hill we came to the Saters of the farmer where we slept at Tonset. He had 43 cows, a herd of goats, 3 maids & 2 boys at his Saters. From this hill we descend by a wild rough valley, with hills & mountains on each side to Moe, the other village where the clergyman of Tonset preaches every fortnight. The covering of the church was in the same manner, wood in the shape of tiles. The old wooden churches look rather dark & melancoly—otherwise they are built rather in a pretty form & with a neat spire.

To Midskaw: 2½ miles. Green road thro fir woods in the valley.—a fine rocky mountain to the right—on the left some crumbling cliffs with the rocks covered with a white lichen. Many of the firs on the cliffs dead.

To Berset 2¾ miles. Continuation of wild wooded valley with cliffs on each side. So many of the firs appeared dead & blasted, that we inquired the reason & were told that there had been a great fire in the woods about 40 years, & that its effects were not yet worn out. Almost all the ground was Satermark —latter part of the stage more cultivated. At Berset we dined on our cold meat. Gave 6*d.* for the use of the room.

To Agre 2¾ miles. The same wild foresty valley—in some places marks of the ravages of torrents from the mountains—

---

[1] Bishop Pontoppidan gives some idea of the meat Malthus and Otter may have been offered on the road. He writes of the Norwegian peasants' cows, sheep, and goats killed for their winter stock: 'They do not pickle and smoak all, but cut some of it in thin slices, sprinkle it with salt, then dry it in the wind, and eat it like hung-beef. This they call Skarke, and it requires a ploughman's stomach to digest it' (*Natural History of Norway*, p. 270).

[2] Tron's Fiel, now called Tron, is 5,460 feet high.

they had scattered sand & stones widely over the valley. At Agre we were stopt for horses, which the postmaster said was because there was no date to the note for the Fireboo; but I believe it was because he wished to keep us there that night or make us pay more for his own horses. On our telling him to send for 2 horses immediately he said that the stage was so hilly that we must have three: this at last we consented to, & he then put two of his own horses to the carriage, & said that we must pay as for three for that they would do the work of three. This we thought rather extraordinary; but agreed to it rather than wait 2 or 3 hours longer, and we afterwards found the stage as hilly as he had represented it.

While we stopt at Agre we sent a girl out to gather some strawberries, & she brought back a little dish full pretty soon, which with some cream we found a pleasant bait. We had been told at Drontheim that we should get plenty of them on our journey, if we would write, Iorebar med Flödde, (that is, strawberrys & cream) on the note which we sent forwards with the Fireboo. We had tried the experiment however, once or twice, without success, & this was the first time that we got any, & then not by the assistance of the Fireboo.

In the kitchen we saw a child about 5 weeks old swaddled & bound up almost like a mummy. The mother told us that she kept them in that state for nearly a year, & we were much surprised therefore to hear that she had had 12 children, 9 of which were alive.

Round Agre the hay was mostly in. We bought a young grouse for 4d.

To Westgaard 3 miles. Ascended a very long & high hill of fir forests for a mile & a half. The lad who attended us to bring back the horses was the farmer's son, & dressed out by his mother very smartly for the purpose. He was a lively intelligent young man of 24, tho he did not look so old, & gave us some information. He said that there were a great many wolves all along the valley of Reindale that we had passed, & that the farmers were obliged to house their cattle every night at Seeters; tho he said that higher up the country he knew that an enclosure near the house was thought sufficient. The bears were of the small kind and did not do much mischief. There were many grouse & Orehens. The Orefowl kept chiefly towards the tops of the Fiels. The wild turkies sold for about 1*s*. & 1*s*. 4*d*. apiece in winter. They are seldom or never killed but in that season.

In going up the hill, as I was walking before at some distance from the carriage I saw a very fine black cock get up within 15 or 20 yards of me. I longed much for a gun; but very few opportunities had occured before of using one, & there would have been some trouble & care attached to the carrying it. The fir forests that we had passed today seemed all to have been extremely neglected & ill used. Many trees had been cut & left to rot on the ground, many had been barked & had died & were dying in consequence, many had been cut half way thro & left in that state, & many had been half burnt. After seeing the forests in this state we were rather surprised to hear that on this hill & in the latter part of the valley they belonged to Mr Rosencratz, who has the largest property of any man in Norway, & it chiefly consists in timber.[1]

The young farmer informed us that there were some wild rein deer & many Elks. We were told that there were many wild rein deer on the high fiels to our left when we went to see the Laps. They are supposed to have escaped from the herds of the Laps, & to have spread themselves over the mountains in the neighbourhood. I had not heard of any Elks before. Mr Rosencratz has offered ten pounds for a young one but cannot get one. The farmer said that in the summer they keep to the forests under the highest Fiels, & that the young one follows as soon as it is born, & is very difficult to be taken. In the winter they come down lower into the vallies and are often seen & shot.

The Fiel that we had been gradually ascending was very high & the top was too barren for Saters. It was chiefly covered with mosses, particularly the Lichen Rangiferimus & scattered firs. On the top we had a fine view back on a very high mountain which occupied a great space in the horizon, & was streaked with snow & capped with clouds. On asking our farmer the name of it he said it was the Sone Fiel, & was reckoned the highest mountain in Norway.[2] We asked him if

---

[1] See p. 105 n.

[2] Sone Fiel is now called Sölen, and is 5,744 feet high. The farmer must have been influenced by local patriotism, for Snöhetta, the highest peak in Dovrefjell is 7,500 feet. The highest mountain in Norway is Galdhöpiggen, 8,090 feet, in the Jotunheim.

it was as high as Doverfield, & he said much higher. I had never heard it mentioned before in talking of the mountains of Norway. It was at the distance of 6 Norway miles, & certainly appeared to be the highest that we had seen.

We descended gradually, but by a very rough road to the Glommen, which we had crossed at first setting off in the morning, & now crossed again in the evening after a journey of 13 Norway miles which is above 80 english miles. We got in soon after 9 oclock, tho we had been delayed on the road twice, an hour & a half each time, & the last stage was very hilly & bad road. The expences of the day, including 2 shillings for the ferry and 2 shillings for an extra horse for one stage, were 1.16; 18s. a piece which for living a day & night, & travelling 80 miles, was not dear. Our expences in eating & beds only came to 3s. 10d. At Westgaard we found a tolerable house & clean beds. The Glommen had received some tributary streams during our absence, & was about the size of the Thames at Richmond. A village & 2 or 3 clusters of houses were near its banks, & the hay was cut & carried on the meadows.

No sweet milk or cream was to be obtained at the inn. The cows were all at Saters 2 or 3 miles off, & not a single one left at home. Sower milk & cream which had been sent from the Saters were to be had in great plenty; but we had not yet come to a relish of them. All the Innkeepers or Postmasters are farmers. They get little or nothing by keeping the house as a profession but they are allowed certain privileges which makes it desireable to some. These I believe are chiefly the liberty of distilling spirituous liquors, & the selling everything that they please. Many of the inkeepers keep shops as well as farms.

Therm at 4, 44. Morning fine & fair till 11; slight showers the rest of the day. Therm at 1, 54; at half past 7 in the evening on the Fiel, 40½. Wind. N.

At Westgaard we were very glad of a fire, & liked it the better for not being in a Stove.

July 31 [Tuesday *July 30*]. Paid 3 shillings for supper & beds. Set off about 7—a very fine morning, to Mycklebye 1¼ miles. A flat valley between high hills with some pretty grass meadows on this side & a range of woods which we understood were

Mr Anker's, on the other—the grass not so fine or so forward as that which we passed before we entered Osterdale.

To Krogen 2 miles. Valley narrower, & less cultivated—woods close to the river,—many parts just rescued for cultivation. When the firs are cut down for this purpose the birches & Aspens are generally left on account of the use which their leaves are put to for the cattle. Observed 2 or 3 large black woodpeckers about the size of a Jackdaw.

At Krogen the farmer's men & boys were eating in the kitchen. They seem always to have a great plenty of butter & cheese which they generally put together between 2 pieces of oatcake. This the men that we observed were washing down with two soups, one made from a kind of yellow looking mixture of cheese & butter which we had seen once or twice before, & the other a black looking soup of peas. We are told that in the farmers' houses they generally eat 6 times a day. We have almost always seen something of that kind going forward, and if the men are not taking a regular meal, the bread & butter & cheese are standing about, & they take a mouthful whenever they feel inclined. The Norwegians in general have appeared to us as if they were well fed. The women have plump round faces; & most of the boys who have been with us to take back the horses have been very good looking lads, & stouter & with better calves to their legs than those of the same age in England.

No sweet milk to be had. All the cows at Saters.

To Satre 2 miles. The woods on the right had been ravaged dreadfully by a fire, & little else than the bare poles were remaining. On enquiry we found that the fire had happened 20 years ago from the carelessness of the girls at Saters. It burnt for 2 days & was only stopt by cutting down the trees. The woods for most of this stage reached to the borders of the river, & there were not many spots of cultivation. The hills lower than in the first part of the valley.

Skins of calf or sheep or goat are the general bed covering. Sheets are seldom used but for company, & some of the inns that we passed had none. In most of the houses of the vale we have observed fire-places, & not stoves. This is probably a consequence of the great plenty of wood. At Satre we made our second dinner on the cold meat which our friend at Tonset had furnished us with, & we felt ourselves much indebted to him for supplying us with 3 excellent dinners, coffee, supper, beds & breakfast for 2 dollars. At Satre we saw a pair of snow skaits, one of which was near 7 feet long & the other about 6—the bottom covered with reindeers' skins. We understand that one is always longer than the other.

To Sorknas 1 mile, chiefly thro fir woods with a bottom of heath & Rein deer moss—hills lower.

To Navsat 1 mile. Valley cultivated—broad meadow ground by the river, tho not very rich in grass—many goodlooking houses—the inn at Navsat remarkably neat & nice with a fine verdant cultivated hill opposite, but no want of wood—the richest & prettiest part of the valley that we had seen.

To Brunset 2 miles. River broader than the Thames at Richmond—Sandy road thro firs & barren heath, & some land lately taken in. The stumps of the firs are always left one or two feet or more high, & the aspens & birches are preserved. Passed thro some woods of tall firs, chiefly spruce. We asked the farmer who was with us how high he supposed them to be—he said about 40 ells, or a little more than 80 english feet; but that he had seen some as high as 80 aunes, or 160 english feet.[1] These were the spruce firs.

We have found Osterdale much less cultivated & the land less rich than we expected. We had heard that in Osterdale were the richest farmers in Norway. We have indeed observed many very goodlooking houses, & some that we have Stopt at have been much handsomer than usual, but the riches of the farmers must arise from the profits on their woods rather than from cultivation, as the land is certainly poorer, & there is more uncultivated ground than in many other parts that we have seen. In the cultivated spots there are but very few enclosures except round the houses; & the grass and corn have in general no fences to divide them. This is the case in most parts of Norway.

Fair and fine. Therm at 7, 51½; at half past 2, 56½. Wind Northerly.

At Brunset we found a very good house & tolerable beds.

---

[1] According to the *O.E.D.* an aune is an old French word, corresponding to an ell, and used chiefly in the measurement of woollen cloth. The ell varied in different countries: an English ell was 45 inches, a Flemish ell only 27 inches. The Norwegian *alen* was 0·6275 metres, or 24·7 inches.

We intended to have our young grouse dressed for supper, but unluckily it turned out to be magotty, & we were obliged to content ourselves with our custard. The postmaster was one of Mr Rosencratz's stewards.

On the banks of the Glommen Mr Anker & Mr Rosencratz possess many woods, besides which they buy much of the Farmers, who also have extensive possessions of this kind which form the principal source of their riches. The King has also timber woods by the Glommen, & it is said that the farmers now & then borrow a little of his timber, by means of a little douceur to the Steward that looks after it; but this may be only scandalous report. The farmers cut their timber in Autumn after the harvest, carry it to the river in the winter on sledges, where it is sold to the Merchants, & floated down in the spring at the breaking up of the frost. The water of the Glommen is at present low & there are many rocky places, & shoals of sand that would stop the timber in its passage; but in the spring these are covered—much of the timber, however, still stops on the rocks & on the shores, & there are persons regularly employed at certain periods to walk down the banks of the river, & set the timber afloat again that had stopt.[1]

July 31 [Wednesday]. Paid a dollar for our beds & supper & set off about 7 for Oone which is called only a mile but we found it certainly above a mile & a half. Passed for half a mile thro a fir wood to the Glommen which we crossed by a ferry for which we paid 5*d.* to the village of Grunset, where a large fair is annually kept the first tuesday in March.[2] We saw a number of booths for shops which are kept constantly standing. The fair lasts a week & sometimes 2 or 3 thousand people are present. The little merchants lodge & eat at a large house situated near, & pay a dollar a day. The booths let at from 2 to ten dollars. Round the village of Grunset is much cultivated ground, & many scattered houses, among which are some that appear to belong to substantial persons.

To Lunbye 1½ miles Road all the way thro fir woods.— the inn on a hill to the left with some cultivation.

[1] The following page is left blank.
[2] The site of the Grundset Fair is near the town of Elverum, notable for the Glomdal Museum of houses, costumes, and farming tools of the Österdal.

To Melbye 2 miles. Road chiefly thro fir woods with but few openings—valley wide—hills not high. By the side of the road we saw a boy surrounded by a number of cows who were licking his hands, & caressing him very much—on enquiry we found that he was feeding them with salt which is a very general practice. In descending from Doverfield we had observed the horses fed in the same manner.

Most of the ground in Osterdale & Riendale is Sater mark. Riendale is properly only an inferior division of Osterdale, tho they are certainly different vallies, & in coming out of Riendale into Osterdale we crossed over a very high fiel. Before we arrived at Melbye on the left was a fine rich hill much culti-vated. Round Melbye much corn & cultivation—some fine crops of rye.

To Oustad 1 mile. Country much cultivated till we came to a tributary stream of the Glommen about an english mile from Melbye, which we crossed on a raft of firs—a very convenient kind of ferry boat. This river comes from Sweden & much Swedish timber is floated down it to the Glommen, tho the laws of Sweden do not permit the exportation of timber to Norway. Rest of the stage a straight sandy road thro firs almost all very young & low. Many of the woods that we have passed thro have been cleared of all their good timber, & none but young & in some places very young trees remain. We have observed the stumps of many firs not three inches in diameter —these must have been either cut for firewood, or parts of the wood may have been cut for cultivation & returned again to firs as we have remarked in some other spots. Valley wide, hills not high.

To Wold 1½ miles. Straight sandy road thro small firs.— hills distant.

To Brandvold 1¾. Richer & more cultivated country. Hay carried in many parts—some good crops of rye. We observe rye here more common than further North about Drontheim. Drank some of our own tea at Brandvold, & the woman of the house furnished us with some fresh cream, which we hardly expected, as the man of the house, who was a small farmer & kept 2 horses & 14 cows, told us that his cows were at Saters 3 Norway miles off. Some of the Saters are very distant from the farms to which they belong. At Brandvold & the last stage

Wold we observed a few shoes made of the plaited rind of the birch. They are not very general as they will not last above 8 days. The last stage had a little the appearance of those basonlike vallies we observed in Sweden only more extensive.

To Kongswinger 2 miles. At first fir wood, afterwards by the banks of the river, which were rich in grass, & the immediate shore fringed chiefly with the Betula Incana—(the hoary alder) of which we have observed great quantities in Norway. The hills rich in trees & in parts cultivated—some sandy shoals in the river, which appeared broader than the Thames at Richmond. Crossed the river by a ferry & mounted rather a steep hill to Kongswinger. At the ferry lived one of Mr Anker's Clerks, to whom he was to send our Portmanteau if he could recover it, by advertising it & offering a reward. Our hopes were here at an end as the Clerk had had no letter whatever from Mr Anker.[1]

In Kongswinger we luckily met a gentleman whom we had seen at Mr. Anker's, & who was going to sleep that night at a house close to Professor Thaarup, whom we had determined to call upon the next morning, & talk about Statistics, altho we had no letter of introduction to him. This gentleman was so good as to say that he would prepare the Professor for our coming, & give us an introduction to him; & we thought it therefore a very fortunate rencontre.[2] Found a very good inn.

Rain in the morning till 8.—afterwards fair & fine. Therm at 7, 53; at half past 2, 62; at 9 in the evening, 57. Temperature of the water on crossing at 9, 59.

We have thought in general Osterdale very much inferior in beauty to Gobrensdale, which we passed in going to Dover-field. In Gobrensdale every spot that was capable of cultivation, from its situation, seemed to be fertile & good land; but in Osterdale the soil is chiefly a very light & barren sand. The hills of Osterdale are also very inferior in richness, grandeur & picturesque beauty to the mountains of Gobrensdale; yet Osterdale was often mentioned to us both at Christiania &

---

[1] The portmanteau was lost on the way back from Kongsberg to Christiania on 3 July; see pp. 116–17, 120.

[2] Mr Olaus D. Schmidt, of the Royal Norwegian Scientific Society, thinks that this gentleman, whom Malthus calls Mr Leeson, might be Niels Lasson (1762–1853), for many years a confidential agent to Bernt Anker. (See also pp. 215–16.)

Drontheim as extremely well worth seeing; but not a single person ever mentioned the other dale, which is perhaps one of the most beautiful vallies in Europe. The flatness & goodness of the roads in Osterdale & the richness of some of the farmers must I think be the chief reasons of the preference.

Many of the churches were rather large in Osterdale, & round most of them we observed a row of sheds for shelter to the horses of the farmers who attend church, as many of them must necessarily come a long way. The churches in the Country we have understood are well attended, tho those in the large towns not so.

Almost every district has a little difference in the form of dress; but the coats of the men are generally grey cloth, & the difference is chiefly in the colour of the worked button holes & the form of the pockets—among the women the shape of the cap, jacket & petticoat, length of the shift, &c. At Lunbye we observed some of the short shifts again. At Roraas we observed a kind of jockey cap, square before, made of cloth; & this kind of covering to the head has prevailed all along the vale more or less; but is not so general as the red woollen caps.

In Oterdal & all the way from Drontheim many of the horses were entirely without shoes, & none of them had shoes on the hind feet. In Oterdale we found a larger breed of horses than usual. The general size of the horses we have met with is from 13 to 14 hands high but some of these were nearly or quite fifteen. They were in general geldings.

July 1 [Thursday *August 1*]. The gentleman that we met yesterday promised to call upon us this morning at 9 and walk with us to the ramparts.[1] We waited till after 11 & then took the walk by ourselves. A centinel followed us into the fortifications to where a party of officers were standing; but they could none of them talk french or English. We however made them understand that we wished to walk round the ramparts, & they immediately assented & sent a corporal or sergeant with us.

The view from the ramparts is on every side over a fine rich varied country of hill, dale & wood, but none of the grander

---

[1] The fortress of Kongsvinger, built in 1683, still stands, and 'the fine view from the ramparts' is praised in modern guide-books.

features of Norway. The Glommen looks very much like the Thames from Richmond hill & there is a lake of some size on one side of it, which adds to the beauty of the water scenery. The fortifications seem to be strong & mounted with some good cannon, particularly on the side of Sweden.

Soon after we returned to the inn Mr Leeson, the gentleman we met yesterday, came to us & said that Professor Thaarup expected us to dinner, & that he should meet us there. This was rather lucky as the Professor sent us word by Mr Leeson that he could not express himself well in English or french tho he understood them both a little.

After waiting some time for Mr L to do some business in Kongswinger, we set off for the Professor about 1, & for half a mile passed thro a very richly wooded & hilly country with a narrow valley & chain of small lakes, immediately below us on our left. We arrived before Mr L, & on the Professor's coming out to meet us were struck a little with his awkward appearance, & found it but too true that he could not express himself in French, & but with great difficulty understand it.[1] When we made him understand that we had heard of his fame as a Statistic writer, & had purchased his work in Copenhagen even tho we did not understand Danish or German—& that we wished to beg the favour of an answer to a few questions on the subject of his enquiries, he was so much alarmed, & seemed to feel so awkward that we were rather in pain for him. We got on so slowly & heavily that we congratulated ourselves that we did not call so unexpectedly as we at first intended, as we should have found it very difficult to explain who we were & what we wanted.

Mr Leeson soon after arrived; & a very good dinner with plenty of strawberries & cream afforded us great relief. During dinner Mr Leeson who spoke English very well, served as our Interpreter; but even by this means we could not get much out of the professor; & when we asked about the causes that had impeded or promoted the population of Norway, he always

---

[1] Frederik Thaarup was the same age as Malthus: he was born in Copenhagen, and wrote his first statistical work in 1790. From 1793 to 1797 he was Professor of Statistics, but quarrelled with his colleagues; it will be remembered that a statistician in Copenhagen had told Malthus 'that Professor Thaarup had stolen from him' (see p. 61). From 1797 to 1804 he was *Fogd* (Sheriff) in Solör and Odal. He died in 1845.

refeered us to some other works, & said that that particular part of statistics had not made the subject of his enquiries.

The only piece of information we got, which was chiefly from Mr Leeson, was with respect to the revenues of the Clergy. The tenth of the produce is divided into three parts between the King the Church & the Clergyman. The compositions for these revenues have been settled long ago, & are now much below their real value. The clergyman has the power of taking his third part of the tenth in kind; but it is a power that has lately never been exercised, as the clergyman would probably lose more than he would gain by it, on account of a great part of his revenue depending upon voluntary contributions. Woods are not subject to tithes, & as there are many parishes in Norway that consist almost entirely of wood, in these the greatest part of the clergymans income depends upon contributions.

These contributions are not entirely voluntary—every person is obliged to give a certain sum, & he may give as much more as he likes. The offerings are six times in the year. A Houseman is obliged to give 4d. It is also customary for all the persons present at a marriage or a Christening to make an offering to the Clergyman, & this is so general that it is reckoned rather disgraceful to omit it. Mrs Thaarup, who is the sister of the clergyman, said that her brother often lent his parishioners money for the offering to himself.[1]

The third of the tenth which is appropriated to the church is paid to the person to whom the ground & the building belong, & these are in general private property. The owner is obliged to keep the church in repair; but not to lay out all the money he receives upon it.

The third of the tenth that is due to the King has not been raised for many years, & is in the same manner a trifle compared with its present real value. There is a land tax to the King besides this.

Tho we could not get much out of the Professor in the way of information, he was most extremely civil & obliging. He

---

[1] Mrs Thaarup was Christine Cold Rynning, ten years younger than her husband. She was his second wife; they were married on 12 September 1798, his first wife having died eight months before. Professor Thaarup obviously could not live without a wife, for when Christine died in May 1806 he married again on 1 September of the same year.

promised to get for me from Copenhagen the lists of the births, deaths & marriages for the last 7 or 8 years, & some older ones to compare them with; & would make me take some new Russian statistical tables which he said were highly esteemed, & from which he had abstracted what he wanted. The lists he was to send to me in England.

The Professor has been appointed Fute[1] or collector of the King's money, which induced him to settle in Norway. His former residence was at Copenhagen. The office of Fute is reckoned rather profitable. The professor has bought a farm house with ground to it, has made a very large & handsome kitchen garden & is going to pull down the greatest part of the old offices, & build a new house. He has been twice married & both times to Norwegian ladies. What tells very much in his favour is that tho he had two children of his own he adopted the orphan son of the farmer who possessed the house he lives in, & brings him up with his own children. The impression with which we left the Professor was, that he was a very good sort of man; but did not quite answer our expectations as a professor.

We had a great desire to have a day's shooting in Norway before we left it, & had determined therefore to stay a day at Magnor, which we heard was a good place, for that purpose. On mentioning our intention to Mr Leeson who was himself a sportsman, he very obligingly said, he would send home for his dogs above 2 miles off, sup with us that evening at Magnor & the next morning shew us a specimen of the Norway hunting & shooting. He set off from the professor's before us to arrange these matters. After expressing our obligations as well as we could to the Professor for his civilities, we left him about 5 to proceed to Magnor, within an english mile of the borders of Sweden.

We changed horses about ¾ of a mile from the professor's— the country hilly & rich in wood—a chain of small lakes to our left, & towards the end of the stage a rocky cliff rising on the other side from the water. The evening was very pleasant after the rain, & the country, particularly about the place where we changed horses, very pretty. At this place, the name of which I do not recollect, I saw a number of little bundles of

---

[1] This is Malthus's version of *Fogd*.

birch boughs stuck on poles to dry.[1] This we understand is a very common winter provision for cows & sheep.

From —— to Magnor 1¾ miles. The country at first of the same kind as that we had passed; afterwards we entered a range of woods belonging to Mr Anker, which lasted almost to Magnor. We observed much timber lying near the road in a state ready for floating. This would not be carried to the river till next winter, & as it was carried from the place where it was cut last winter, it will have been two years before it gets to the river. This we hear is not unfrequently the case.

At Magnor we found all the rooms and beds occupied by those Swedes who had been staying beyond the territory of Sweden to avoid their creditors.[2] We hear there is much of this running backwards & forwards on both sides, & the different governments seldom interfere to claim deserters except in very particular cases.

The master of the inn was out shooting when we arrived, & as the rooms & beds were absolutely occupied we began to despair about getting a lodging, till fortunately for us the master returned, & hearing from our servant that we were great people, without much ceremony turned the poor Swedes into the hay loft, & gave us their rooms, where we got some supper ready for Mr Leeson who came about half past ten.

Upon taking out my thermometer this evening, I had the extreme mortification to find it broken.[3] I had in some way or other lost the little case in which I carried it at Drontheim, & for this I was obliged to substitute the case of my Cambridge Thermometer, which I found broken with the jolting on taking

[1] The place whose name Malthus had forgotten was probably Edsbroen; here Clarke found on 31 October, 'a single house, almost as wretched as the shed at Malmagen...We were however induced to halt for dinner, upon finding in the Post-book, in the hand-writing of our friend Professor Malthus, the words "*good treatment*"...The good woman of the house was moreover tidy in her appearance, and brought forth some excellent butter' (*Travels*, VI, 87).

[2] Magnor is nineteen miles from Kongsvinger, and now has 717 inhabitants. A note in a guide-book says: 'Lively border trade.'

[3] Malthus's mortification at finding the thermometer broken might well have been extreme. His interest in such matters was known to his friends: we find Clarke writing to Otter, 'Tell Malthus we have regularly estimated the thermometer;' it was Cripps's task to take readings each day at noon throughout their travels. These were published in an appendix to each volume, and listed beside them for comparison were those taken daily at 2 p.m. in the 'Apartments of the Royal Society in London'.

it out at Drontheim. This case did not at all fit the little Them: yet by wrapping it well in paper I was in great hopes of getting it safe to Stockholm; but from what cause I could hardly conjecture I found it cracked & entirely spoilt to night.

Slight showers in morning—hard shower at 4, & small rain in the evening. Therm at 1, 67. Temperature of water, 57. Wind Southerly.

The man of the Inn who had very much the air of an old English gamekeeper had been detained later than usual by the loss of his dog, which he had reason to think had been killed by one of those wild cats (Jaloux) which we saw at Count Molke's. The dog opened upon some scent, & he thought he heard a baying at a distance. He had remained for some time on the ground calling but in vain; and when he returned he said he was sure the dog would never come back any more. There was a wild cat in the neighbourhood that had killed some of the largest dogs that followed the cows. A report however was brought soon after that a bear had taken off two foals the night before & the loss of the dog was then attributed to the bear.

August 2 [Friday]. Mr Leeson's dogs not being come, after waiting some time for them we determined to defer our hare & ore fowl shooting till the afternoon, & take a little duck shooting before dinner. We went about half an english mile to a small pond with a marshy end to it, & with one dog which Mr Leeson had with him, which was an excellent one, we soon found 5 or 6 ducks, & might perhaps have killed one or two but that we had only one gun between us & that hung fire. We returned therefore without success. These ducks breed about all the ponds lakes & rivers during the summer, & leave Norway, except sometimes near a cataract, in the winter.

We dined at a common table with the Swedes, & heard that they attributed their misfortunes to the injudicious regulations of the King which had forbidden the importation of allmost all foreign goods, & had consequently ruined all the merchants that dealt in those articles.

One excellent part of our dinner was a plenty of good strawberries & cream. The strawberries are I think larger & finer than ours.

Mr Leeson's dogs had arrived & in the afternoon we went into the woods for hare & Ore hens, which we conceived to be the same as the black game. The manner of hunting hare is by turning 2 or 3 couple of hounds into the woods &, when the hare is found, waiting for her, as she makes her rings, with a gun, in the most likely places. We told Mr L that we were much more interested about the Ore fowl than the hares; but he would shew us the hare hunting & said that we should find the Ore fowl at the same time. We were rather entertained at the noises that he made to encourage his dogs, which were more intense & more vociferous than ours.

There was only one moment of interest during our whole chasse, & that was when Mr L who had gone a little forward, called us to him, & told us to walk very softly; for that the dogs had disturbed some Ore fowl who were now up in the trees all round us. We looked very eagerly and anxiously all about, & Mr L & the Gamekeeper began imitating the noise of the young ones, saying they should very soon have the old hen down within ten or fifteen yrds, & that this was the way they always killed them at this time of the year. All efforts however were vain—no hen came & no young ones were seen on the trees, & thus ended our only interesting moment.

The dogs during the whole evening never came upon any more fowl, & with four men, four guns, 2 men to assist, & 3 dogs we with great difficulty killed a squirrel between us; & afterwards a young hare ran into a hole among some rocks & was caught. We left Mr Leeson in the woods at 9 oclock straining his throat, & calling his dogs off; and we were in some apprehension that he would lose one of them, as our host had done the preceeding evening. Mr L returned with his dogs about 11, & seemed very much hurt that we had had no sport, & only wished that we had been at his house instead of where we were.

The woods that we had hunted were some of them very thick, but without very fine timber. Bogs & deep mosses & much rotten timber lying across rendered the walking not very easy. We came to 2 or 3 housemen's places among the woods, where the ground had been cleared round the house. While we were waiting for Mr L we went into one of them, which was most picturesque in form & most extremely neat & nice. Some of the grass round the house which was mowing was pretty good, & we were told that all the spots we had seen had been cleared in the course of the last three years or a little more.

Mr Leeson informed us that the original divisions of the land for farms in Norway were called gores;[1] & that since they have been subdivided, & call'd half gores, & end gores or quarters of farms; but that a gore did not consist of any specific quantity of land; but was probably determined formerly by accident, or what was thought sufficient to support a family. Many End gores are now very valuable estates. Mr Peter Anker's is one. The farm, part of which we walked over to day, had been a gore, & was now divided into 12, & supported 12 families, besides 14 housemen who each perhaps had one or two horses & 6 or 7 cows.

These divisions the timber merchants consider as very prejudicial to the woods; for the right in the woods being divided among the different children or grandchildren, each will endeavour to cut as much as he can, by which means the timber is cut before it is fit & the woods are spoilt. To prevent this, the Merchants such as Mr Anker Mr Rosencratz &c. buy large tracts of woods of the farmers; but by law, the farmer is obliged to reserve to himself the right of pasturing his cattle, & of cutting timber sufficient for his house repairs & firing. A contract however is in general made by the merchant, that the farm shall not be any further subdivided, or more housemen placed upon it; at least that if there are more families, they shall have no right in the woods. It is said that the merchants are not very strict on this point, provided the smaller farmers & housemen do not take timber for the houses. Wood for firing & fences is not regarded.

A piece of ground such as we saw to day round the housemen's dwellings cannot be taken in from the woods for cultivation, without an application first to the proprietor of the woods, declaring that the part is not fit for timber, & then a further application to the Sonescriver. On leave being granted by both these, the wood is cut in the autumn of one year, lies to dry for the next, & is burnt & sown almost immediately after in the July or August following. After the crop of rye, cattle are

[1] *Gaard*, but Malthus used *gores* in the chapter on Norway in the 1803 edition of the *Essay on the Principle of Population*. See Appendix 1 (pp. 286–8).

turned in upon what grass may chance to grow; but when the land is bad, wild nature often again asserts her rights & the firs return. We certainly saw many spots covered thickly with firs, all young, which had been burnt & had a crop of rye some years before.

From other conversation with Mr Leeson, who appeared to be a sensible well informed man, we learnt that the reason of the great preference that people in general gave to Osterdale, was on account of the richness of the farmers & the cleanness & neatness of their houses; & that they were besides reckoned more honest, not being much in the habit of buying & selling, from dealing in nothing but timber like the gentlemen who have large woods. They seldom or never sell corn, butter cheese &c.—all they have of this kind they consume at home.

We had seen some of the Snow skates in Osterdale & Mr Leeson described to us the manner of using them. The long skait, which is generally 6 or 7 & sometimes 8 feet long, is always worn on the left leg & on this leg the skaiter chiefly rests—the short skait, which is generally one or two feet shorter than the other, is worn on the right, & serves principally for pushing the other forwards & directing it. For this purpose the short skait is covered with rein deer skin, the hair of which lies smooth while going forwards, but becomes rough on going backwards & therefore serves as a hold on the snows. The bottom of the long skait is smooth wood with a hollow groove within the surface, to make it lighter & assist the spring, as sometimes in going very rapidly down hills, very great leaps must be taken over the rocky & rough ground that may be above the snow. Mr L shew'd us about the distance that they sometimes leaped, & we thought it about 12 or 15 yrds. A stick, flat at the end to prevent its sinking in the snow, is always held in the hand as a director, & the position in going down hill is always with the knees very much bent, leaning forwards & bearing on the left side with the two hands on the stick, which they in a manner drag after them & at the same time support themselves with. In this way they go down the steep hills with a velocity greater, Mr L said, than any bird could fly.

The Regiments of Hunters are all exercised in these skaits every year. Mr Ln himself was in the horse chasseurs when the Norwegian army marched into Sweden. The Prince gave him a Lieutenancy without his consent & in three days sent him into Sweden. He was soon afterwards made captain; but quitted the service at the end of the war.[1]

The mode of bear hunting is by tracking the bear in the snow a few days before the time that he is going to lye in (as it is called). When he comes near the place where he intends to rest during the winter he goes backwards and forwards, & makes much work to prevent his being tracked—as soon as this work is perceived, the hunters take a very large circuit round, so as to be sure that they have him in the ring, & mark the trees in the circle that they may know it again. After it is supposed that the bear has been asleep 2 or 3 days, they go again & contract their former circle & so on successively till they are sure that they have him in a circle of small diameter, & having marked this, they let him have his nap out till the spring; & then 3 or 4 days before his usual time of rising go with dogs & guns. They generally see his breathing place thro the snow; & sometimes kill him in his bed; at other times he gets up & runs off; but not being in a strong state, & with his feet soft & sinking a little in the snow he cannot get on so fast as his pursuers with snow skaits, & is generally over taken & shot. A man in the neighbourhood of Kongswinger kills 4 or 5 in this manner every spring. Mr Leeson has been present once or twice. A bear which the man once suddenly met in a narrowish path, as he was passing, caught hold of his skait behind & held it for a moment, till by taking hold of a birch he forced it from his claws, & turned round & shot him.—The man thought he had had a narrow escape.

The wolves are in much greater plenty than the bears, & do much more mischief; but there is no successful way of taking. They are sometimes caught by pitfalls made for them in the snow, but not very often. Mr Leeson said that in the district round Magnor he supposed that the wolves killed sheep, goats & cattle to the amount of 6000 rix dollars a year; yet in the number of journeys that he had made in Norway he never saw wolves but twice in his life, & once was, seven together, very near Mr Peter Anker's house, as they were taking a ride before

[1] Mr Leeson's active service must have been during what Malthus called the 'little affair in 88' on p. 58. This was when Denmark, because of her alliance with Russia, reluctantly declared war on Sweden.

dinner in sledges. The other time was, as he was walking one evening with a large dog belonging to a farmer, which was attacked by four wolves at once. The dog had a steel spiked collar on, & being very strong & active defended himself against all four, & had them down one after another, & was never under himself. On Mr L's coming up to his rescue the wolves ran off into the woods. They often fight & devour one another in winter—& at all times whenever blood is drawn from one of them the rest fall upon him immediately. The dog before mentioned one evening returned very bloody to the farmer's to whom he belonged, which they attributed to a battle that he had had with some wolves; & the next morning they found the tails & scalps of some wolves which they supposed to be the remains of those who, after being wounded by the dog, were devoured by their companions.

Some of the yellow looking substance of which we had seen some soup made in Osterdale was brought in for supper, & we heard from our host with the assistance of Mr Leeson, that it was made from a kind of goats' milk wey mixed with cream. From the skim milk of the goats' milk a white kind of cheese is first made, the way is afterwards boiled till it becomes of a thick substance & the cream which had been skimmed is then added to it, & forms this mixture which is called something like misosmeure.[1]

The harvest last year had been tolerably plentiful in Norway but in Sweden it had fail'd extremely, approaching almost to a famine. Much corn had been consequently exported from Norway to Sweden, & the people on the borders were much in want. Mr Leeson said that he himself knew above thirty families that since two or three weeks after last Xmas had not tasted any other than bread made of the bark of the firs. On the borders of the two countries there is a race of fins who do not live in a wandering state like those we saw; but have the housemen's places in the woods, & among these the want has been most severely felt; but some who possessed gores have been obliged to live upon the bark bread, with a little mixture of oat flower perhaps only sprinkled with it. We collected some specimens of the bark bread that were only sprinkled during the making with a little oat flower.

---

[1] *Mysostsmör*, a soft cheese made of whey.

Morning very cloudy—rest of the day fine & fair except a few drops in the evening—warm. Wind Southerly.

There are three rinds to the fir, the outermost brown or yellow, then one of green, & then of white, and it is the white bark of the best red firs that is used for bread. Many of the finest trees are spoilt in this way; but it is only in times of scarcity & no punishment can be inflicted upon men who are driven to such a resource by famine.

Bishop Pontoppidan writes about bark-bread, in a paragraph in which it is difficult to reconcile the last sentence with the first: 'If grain be scarce, which generally happens after a severe winter, the peasants are obliged to have recourse to an old custom, as a disagreeable, but sure method of preserving life. Their bread, in time of scarcity, is made thus, they take the bark of the fir-tree, boil it and dry it before the fire, then they grind it to meal and mix a little oatmeal with it; of this mixture, they make a kind of bread, which has a bitterness and a resinous taste, and does not afford that nourishment, that their usual bread does. However, there are some people, that think it is not right to disuse this sort of bread entirely, and even in plentiful years they sometimes eat a little of it, that they may be prepared against a time of scarcity, which by the goodness of providence, does not happen in a century'(*Natural History of Norway*, p. 268).

Bark-bread was in fact used in 1800–2, when the harvest failed in many parts of Norway, and again from time to time as a result of the British naval blockade during the latter part of the Napoleonic Wars.

The Bishop also describes the 'Finlaplanders' whom the Norwegians looked upon 'in a despicable light'; they commanded them 'like slaves, and treat them with such contempt, as in other countries the people do the Jews'. He explains that 'these Finlanders are quite a distinct nation from the Norwegians, and they do not only inhabit the north-side of the mountains, but likewise the south-side, and particularly those rocks, that part Sweden and Norway...They are good marksmen, and live partly by hunting, and partly by cutting down the woods, clearing the ground, and sowing rye, from which they are called Rye-Finlanders. They do their country a good deal of damage by this practice, for many fine woods are destroyed by them, and the overseers connive at it for a small bribe'(p. 286).

August 3 [Saturday]. As there were two hares said to lie close round the house, Mr Leeson insisted upon our killing them before we went, and as the horses by mistake were not ordered so soon as we intended, we consented to make the attempt; but were again unsuccessful. As a last effort Mr L accompanied us a second time to the pond where the ducks were, which was on our route, about half an english mile, & we ourselves thought that as we had now better guns we might as well kill one or two en passant, but fortune still proved unfavourable, & tho we got one or two fair shots, we came out of Norway guiltless of the blood either of bird or of beast. The Norwegians shoot with shot almost like Swanshot, & very little of it; but they sometimes by that means kill at a very great distance— they talk of 80 or 100 yrds very familiarly.

Mr Leeson gave us some letters into Sweden, & tho he had shewn us no sport in the shooting way, we felt ourselves extremely obliged to him for his extraordinary attention & civility. In about a quarter of a mile we came to the line of demarcation that divides the two countries which, in the place where we passed it, was a kind of avenue cut in the fir woods about 10 yrds across, half of which line belongs to Sweden & half to Norway. The firs are cut down every ten years by a united operation, & constantly kept low to mark the line of boundary. The Entrance from Sweden to Norway is here nearly flat—in all the parts further north it is mountainous, & the chain of mountains is call'd the grindstone or boundary mountains. Near the road we observed many ravages of fire & were told that they were occasioned by the fires made in the woods by people who were running from one country to the other. A temporary exchange of subjects in this way is constantly going forwards.

We took leave of Norway with regret, having been delighted with many beautiful scenes in it, & having received the most agreeable & flattering attentions from the inhabitants.

At Magnor Tull, about half a mile from the boundary, the first village in Sweden, we had our pass examined, & might have had our potmanteaus searched, but as they gave us no trouble in that way, we gave a 12 schilling note. The custom house officers spoke french tolerably well which rather surprised us.

The Economic Notes, 1810

These jottings on economic subjects take up less than 15 pages of a small leather-covered notebook, 4 in. × 6⅛ in., which contains 96 pages altogether, and which Malthus afterwards used for the diary and cash account of the continental tour of 1825. On the outside, on the top right-hand corner, the book is inscribed in his own handwriting, 'T. R. Malthus—journal'. If the book is turned over 'upside-down', which is what Malthus did for his accounts, the top right-hand corner is clearly marked 'George Holland', but this has been crossed out.

The notes are undated, but obviously relate to a northern tour, which I think he may have made in 1810. He starts with some information he received from 'Mr Otter': it seems reasonable to assume that this was William Otter's elder brother Edward, who was also at Jesus, and who on 14 February 1810, was instituted as rector of Bothal-with-Hebburn in Northumberland;[1] Malthus may have known Edward Otter fairly well, as his sons, like Henry Malthus, went to a school at Richmond, in Yorkshire, kept by the Rev. W. Tate; William Otter's eldest went to Rugby and Charterhouse, and the young Clarkes to Eton.

There are two further clues as to the date. On p. 222 Malthus refers to 'the last load of timbers for Covent Garden new house'; Covent Garden was burnt down on 30 September 1808 and the new house opened (with the violent 'Old Prices' campaign) on 18 September 1809.[2] On p. 224 he writes about 'the breaking out of the Spanish business', which sounds like the beginning of the Peninsular War in 1808 and could hardly have been used with reference to that war much later than 1810.

The only thing we know for certain about Malthus's doings in 1810 is that on 13 July he was a witness, at Claverton, of the wedding of 20-year-old Anne Eliza Eckersall and 24-year-old Henry Richard Wood,[3] and that he also witnessed the marriage

---

[1] I am indebted for this information to the Rev. R. M. Henderson, the present rector of Bothal.

[2] *Oxford Companion to the Theatre*, ed. Phyllis Hartnoll (London, 1951).

[3] Claverton Parish Register.

settlement.[1] Henry Wood was the heir of Colonel Wood of Hollin Hall, near Ripon; travelling in those days was expensive, and the sharing of post-chaises was very common, so it seems to me quite possible that Malthus had a month's holiday in June, without his wife and three little children, and then journeyed south with the bridegroom to pick up the family party and go on to Claverton.

The notes give little idea of Malthus's itinerary, but it is just possible to make out a faint list of names written in pencil at the 'back' of the book which was later used for the 1825 accounts:

'Taymouth   Breadalbane
Berceau Walk
Temple of Venus
Lion and Tay
Kenmore Church
Taymouth to Killin 16
Tundrum 20 Glenorchie 12
Inverary 16 Luss 30
North side of Loch Tay very populous.'

It is not unlikely that Malthus, like Dorothy Wordsworth, was charmed by the 'princely gaiety' of Inverary, for he subsequently tried to go there with his family on 3 July 1826, but 'stopped at Dumbarton on account of the weather'.[2] He also writes, on p. 264 of the Scottish diary, 'came into the road from Dalmally and Tyndrum', as though he knew it.

On p. 223 Malthus writes of the cotton mill at Lanark, and one assumes that this is David Dale's establishment which his son-in-law, Robert Owen, was to make famous.

In his autobiography, published in 1857, when he was 86, Robert Owen wrote: 'By this period of my life (from 1810 to 1815), my four "*Essays on the Formation of Character*," and my practice at New Lanark, had made me well known among the leading men of that period.' He gives a list of seventeen names, beginning with the Archbishop of Canterbury, and goes on: 'But I must not forget my friends of the political economists—Messrs Malthus,—James Mill, —Ricardo,—Sir James Mackintosh,—Colonel Torrens,—Francis Place,—&c., &c. From these political economists, often in animated discussions, I always differed. But our discussions were maintained to the last with great good feeling and a cordial friendship...It was a singular circumstance that in my discussions with Mr Malthus,

---

[1] I am indebted for this information to Mr A. H. Boynton Wood, the couple's great-great-grandson, who lives at Hollin Hall.
[2] See p. 260.

which were frequent, (and my own impression was that at last he became very doubtful of the truth of principles which he had so ingeniously maintained), Mrs Malthus always took and defended my side of the argument.'[1]

It would seem that the acquaintance was not begun on this visit, since on p. 224 Malthus leaves a blank for Mr—, 'the owner of the works'; on the other hand, he may simply have forgotten Mr Dale's name for the moment.

Heard from Mr Otter that the jobbers of Cattle from their extensive communications, immediately hear of the slightest variations in the prices of cattle at the different fairs, which they are accustomed to frequent, and arrange their purchases and sales accordingly, so as to buy where they are cheap, and sell again almost immediately at some distance where they are dearer.

It is probably from practices of this kind that the level of currency is so accurately kept, and any country bank is prevented from filling its district of circulation too full. If for instance the Lincoln district was too full of notes and prices had experienced the slightest rise in consequence, cattle and other commodities would be purchased with Lincoln notes in the neighbouring districts, and these notes, which will be received by other banks, will be immediately sent to be exchanged for bank of England notes, and reduce the circulation of the Lincoln notes to their proper level.[2]

It is the custom for the bankers of neighbouring districts to send their clerks once a week or oftner mutually to exchange their notes. In general, probably, the balances will be nearly equal, but if one issues a greater proportion than the rest, he will have to pay a greater number of Bank of England notes, and on notes returned thus soon, he can make no profit.

The last load of timbers for Covent Garden new house, was purchased at Glasgow—another proof how soon, and to what a distance, the effect of even accidental low price extends.

The Hinds, or bond servants in Northumberland have in general 2 bolls of rye, 2 of pease, two of barley and two of oats

---

[1] *Life of Robert Owen*, by Himself (London, 1857), p. 103.
[2] Malthus was rector of Walesby, near Market Rasen, Lincolnshire, from November 1803 until his death, although he never resided there. (See p. 9.)

in the year, the keep of one or two cows, a cottage, and about five guineas and a half in money   Lrd Gr.[1]

The farmers in Northumberland do not in general get $\frac{3}{4}$ of rent as profit, and in consequence suffer much by the income tax. In the new leases the tenants' share of the income tax is in general calculated, and falls of course chiefly on the Landlords.

This has occasioned a little check in the rise of rents during the last two or three years.

Heard at Edinburgh that the whole of the farming profits of the Lothian farmers seldom amounted to more than 5 per cent on the capitals they employed.

This seems incredibly low.

The improvement of Scotch husbandry has arisen principally from the improving capitals and skill of the tenantry, and not from the capitals of Landlords.

The tenants in Scotland pay income tax on half of the rent, but this is considered as above their clear profits, and they feel much oppressed by the tax.

Labour about Edinburgh half a crown and two shillings— a day, for all the summer half year, and about 20 pence and sometimes 2 shillings in winter.   M.

At Lanark wages were lower, and 20 pence seemed to be the common price.

About 15 hundred people are employed at the Cotton mill, and great debauchery prevails among them. The hours of working are from 6 in the morning to 7 in the evening. A good school is established in the village, but the spinners cannot have much leisure to attend it, as after their day's work they will naturally want some recreation. Sunday is therefore the only day on which they can be expected to give much attention to reading.

All the work is done by the piece, and no apprentices are now taken.[2] Highlanders with large families contribute to the peopling of the village.

[1] Possibly Charles, second Earl Grey of Howick, Northumberland (1764–1845).

[2] By 'apprentices' Malthus must mean the orphan pauper children who were sent to the mills by the poor law authorities, and housed by the employers in

Not many children from Lanark are employed, and none from other places.

A great check to trade was felt before the breaking out of the Spanish business, but the people were kept together, and employed at reduced prices.[1] Each family subscribes one shilling a head a year for a surgeon, for which sum he endeavours to cure all their disorders.[2] The children looked tolerably, but they are apt to be very sickly in winter.

There are no poors rates at Lanark but a person who had worked at the mills if belonging to Lanark might receive something from the Church subscriptions, but this would be very trifling.

A piece of land of eight acres near the mills is rented by the owner of the works at 120£ a year. It is dressed and properly prepared, and then let out in small patches to the families employed at the mill, to be planted with potatoes. In this way Mr — is supposed to make more than the rent of it, altho it is so enormous.

One of the parishes of Edinburgh has a regular assessment for the poor; and a poor house; which is held out as a threat to those who ask relief. In the poor house no animal food is allowed, and it is meant only to be considered as a refuge from starving. Even where assessments are known the poor are considered as having no right to relief.

During the scarcity the rates amounted to nearly 1s. 6 in the pound, but now they are reduced again to 4d.

Sr H. Moncrieff.[3]

barracks. Robert Owen discontinued this practice as soon as he could after becoming manager at New Lanark.

The new school, which we should now call 'progressive', for children from the age of one upwards, was not opened until 1816.

[1] By the 'breaking out of the Spanish business', Malthus must mean the Peninsular War, 1808–12. In 1806 there was an embargo on the export of American cotton, and Robert Owen spent over £7,000 giving his workers their full wages, although they had no work to do for four months, other than 'keeping the machinery clean and in good working condition'.

[2] The account of the surgeon does not quite tally with what Robert Owen's son, Robert Dale Owen, wrote in his autobiography. He said that when he was about nine years old (he was born in November 1801) he had leave 'to go on a shooting expedition with a young man who had a salary from the New Lanark Company as surgeon of the village, and who attended the sick there gratuitously' (Robert Dale Owen, *Threading My Way* (London, 1874), p. 47).

[3] Sir Henry Moncreiff, Bart., D.D., 1750–1827, was an Edinburgh divine noted for his benevolence, so it may well have been he who supplied Malthus with information about the poor in Edinburgh.

The pensioners were reduced by telling them they might go to the work house, and only 9 old people accepted the offer.

At Glasgow, price of labour nearly the same as at Edinburgh, but if anything rather lower. Weavers at Paisly chiefly engaged in fancy patterns, and earn more than at Glasgow.

The most skilful weavers are able at times to earn 4 or 5 shillings a day, but the average earnings at Glasgow are not above ten shillings and at Paisley above 12.

NB probably below the mark.

A weaver with only common skill, and at com work, must labour from six in the morning till 9 at night to earn 2 shillings a day.

Many of the weavers single men, and much deb. prevails among the weavers, tambourers and master manufacturers. Abor frequently procured—Instrument:

Weaving by steam does not seem likely to succeed, on account of its still requiring a person to attend each loom.

During the late check to trade the weavers were still employed, but at very reduced prices.

It is at these seasons that the capitalists lay in great stocks, and on the return of a demand make extraordinary [profits]. The weavers are apt to do more work when the prices are low in order to enable them to live in the same manner as before.

Labour about Loch Lomond 2s. 6 a day without victuals, and 20d. or 2s. with victuals.

An old soldier that Dr Stewart employs almost constantly the year round he pays 20d. a day and victuals.

At Arrochar the price of labour about the same. Inverary about two shillings. The Duke's people who are employed most of the year and have cottages given them and a cow kept at an under price, 14d., and 16d.

Dalmally—price of labour the summer half year 2

The Continental Tour, 1825

This diary of a tour of the Low Countries and the Rhine has at times a perfunctory feeling about it; churches and picture galleries and castles seem listed with more conscientiousness than enthusiasm, although Malthus does note his preferences, and anyone contemplating such a sight-seeing holiday today may be amused to compare his own tastes with those of an English party only ten years after Waterloo. One cannot help feeling that it must have been a technical concern which made the Rev. Professor Malthus so very interested in baroque pulpits.

On 23 May 1825 Malthus's youngest child and second daughter, Lucy, died 'of a rapid decline', according to Louisa Bray. I have not been able to find where she was buried; she may have been taken to London, to be near a particular doctor, and died there. Payne says that she died at Hatfield,[1] but this mistake is obviously the result of an error in the *Gentleman's Magazine*, where, in the obituaries in the June issue, she is described as daughter of the 'Rev. R. Malthus of Hatfield'—a very natural mistake for 'Hertford' in the days before typewriters. Lucy's death is recorded in the weekly *County Chronicle* for Tuesday 31 May and here she is described as 'second daughter of the Rev. T. R. Malthus, professor at the East India College, Haileybury'.

Malthus's diary begins with the party already at Dover on Saturday 4 June, less than a fortnight after Lucy's death; the accounts show that they left Haileybury on the 2nd. From Otter onwards, biographers are agreed that this tour was undertaken to comfort Mrs Malthus in her grief. I think it is possible, however, that the holiday was planned before Lucy was taken ill, and that Malthus, with what some would call heartlessness and others commonsense, had decided that foreign travel would be the best thing for the four remaining members of the family, who accordingly set off as had been previously arranged.

Hal at this time was 20; he had been admitted to his father's old college on 18 January 1822 but, a vacancy occurring at Trinity

---

[1] J. O. Payne, *Collections for a History of the Family of Malthus* (privately printed, London, 1890). Payne's family tree.

before one at Jesus, he went there instead—a practice quite common in those days. Emily was 19 on 5 July, when the family were at Breda, but Malthus makes no reference to her birthday. We know that the two children were with their parents, on this and the Scottish tour, because the 'spending money' given them by their father is entered in his accounts.

Modern readers may find these accounts unendearing; to keep such a detailed record nowadays smacks of meanness, so it is perhaps only fair to Malthus to point out that in his time such a practice was quite common, especially on holidays abroad. The accounts themselves are revealing in small ways; they show, for instance, that Malthus not only had no objection to travelling, but also none to changing money, on a Sunday, something of which a later generation would have strongly disapproved. The expenditure on the outward journey begins with 'coach to London &c: Hampstead stages & coach', and it is possible that Malthus called on his widowed sister Mrs Bray, who was then living in Hampstead and who had also lost a daughter at the age of 17, almost exactly six years before.

The tour lasted just over two months, from the beginning of June until 5 August, when the party were back in London again; the ground they covered is familiar to modern tourists, as far as the ancient monuments and works of art are concerned, but the political situation was quite different. It is as well to recall that, although the Protestant Dutch declared themselves independent in 1581, Catholic Belgium remained under Spanish domination until 1713, when, by the Peace of Utrecht, she was handed over to Austria. In 1792–5, however, the French Revolutionary armies were welcomed as liberators by many citizens in both countries, though Belgium was annexed to France and Holland formed into a satellite 'Batavian Republic'. This lasted until 1806, when Napoleon made his brother Louis King of Holland; he abdicated in 1810, as a protest against the commerce of his country being ruined by the 'continental system', whereupon Napoleon annexed the satellite state and made it part of France. In 1814 the Congress of Vienna detached the two countries from France, but not from each other, and they became an independent kingdom under William I of Orange. Belgian revolts began to be serious in 1830, but it was not until 1839 that the great powers finally established Belgium as an independent country under her own king, Queen Victoria's Uncle Leopold.

It is also as well to remember that Malthus and his party saw the Rhineland pretty much as Byron did, where ruin greenly dwelt: Dorothy Wordsworth wrote at Bingen on 25 July 1820 about the 'human distress and poverty' of the villages and small towns, and of the castles, the 'melancholy thought which will attend the traveller along the ever-winding course of the Rhine—the thought that of those buildings, so lavishly scattered on the ridges of the heights, or lurking in sheltered corners, many *have* perished, all *are* perishing, and *will entirely* perish!'[1] She was wrong. During the war, the smaller states of Germany had been reorganised by Napoleon as the Confederation of the Rhine; one result was that in 1815 the Rhineland was transferred to Prussia. The Gothic Revival and the energy and organising ability of the Prussian royal family were completely to alter the 'old and retrograding appearance' of the Rhine towns and villages;[2] the castles, so far from perishing, were all either restored, or carefully preserved as permanent, picturesque, and orderly ruins. In 1825 the Rhine legend had not been fully established; Clemens Brentano had invented the Lorelei in 1802, but Heine's song was not published until 1827. The young Karl Baedeker would have been living in Coblenz when Malthus visited the town, but his first guide-book—to the Rhine country—was not published (in conjunction with John Murray) until 1834. As for Richard Wagner, in 1825 he was a schoolboy at Dresden, and only twelve years old.

June 4 [Saturday, 1825]

Dover. New buildings towards the Cliff. Would make an agreeable bathing place. Passage to Calais by Steam boat £1. 1. each. Hotel de Paris—pretty good & cheap.

Calais

June 6 [Monday]. Improved since 1803. New buildings. Not so characteristically marked as formerly. Hotel Meurice. Rue de la Prison—not very well situated but good and reasonable.

Diligence to Dunkirk in 4 hours, 4 francs each.[3] Much sandy heath. Sand hills by the sea. Exchange at Calais in gold 24.75. Labour about 30 Sous. White bread about 3 sous lb. Labour and bread near Dunkirk about the same.

June 7. Dunkirk—a well built clean & cheerful Town, one of the best in France. Harbour—Road—Front of the Church a

---

[1] Dorothy Wordsworth, *Journals*, ed. William Knight (Macmillan, 1925), p. 438.
[2] Malthus's diary, see p. 241.
[3] A diligence was a public stagecoach, and Dorothy Wordsworth, in July 1820, described one in Dunkirk as 'heavy, dirty, dusty' (*Journals*, ed. E. de Selincourt (Macmillan, 1941), II, 15).

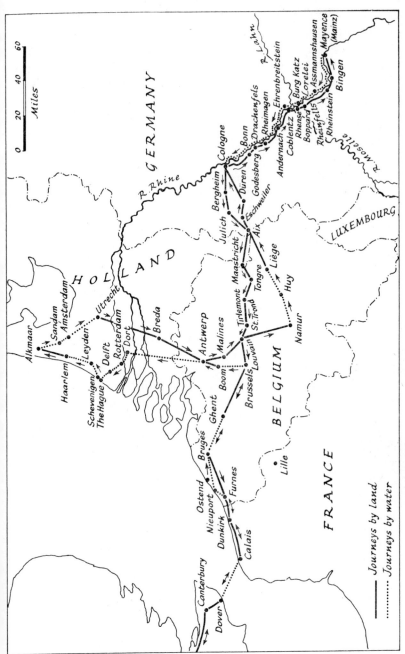

2 Sketch-map of the Continental Tour, 1825

Journeys by land
Journeys by water

229

Pediment with ten very large fluted corinthian columns.—
Hotel de Flandres excellent. Calush to Furnes over the sands
25 francs.[1] Visite at a small village on the frontier of Belgium;
luggage untied but not a strict search. No search afterwards.
Stopped before by two men on the sands who made enquiries
but did not search. Breakfasted at Furnes. Tea Coffee and
Strawberries 5 francs. Barque to Nieuport middling—fare only
1 franc each. From Nieuport to Bruges 2 francs each. Dinner
2.f.—a bottle of most excellent claret for 1½ f.

Country for the most part a dead flat common field—dreary,
though interspersed with cattle, and tolerably neat farm
houses. Cultivation looking sometimes good, sometimes very
indifferent. Crops apparently favourable. After joining the
great canal about 3 miles from Ostend—more wood—chiefly
different kinds of poplar—aspen & Arbele.[2] Country in
general very low and not well drained—grass rushy. Woody
and agreeable on approaching Bruges. Baggage to the Hotel
de la fleur de Bled. 2.f.

June 8 [Wednesday]. Bruges at 8 o'clock. Hotel nearly full.

June 9. Tower in the Market Place. Church of Notre Dame:
Carved Pulpit. Statue of the Virgin by Michaelangelo. Tombs
of Charles the Bold & his daughter. St Salvador. Baptism of
John by Van Os. Resurrection not yet put up.

Church of Jerusalem not worth going to. Black Manteau's.[3]
Some of the whitened houses do not suit the antient character
of the Town.

At the Hotel Fleur de Bled Vin de Bordeaux ordinaire 2.f.

June 10. To Ghent by the Grand Barque. Passage 5½ francs
each. dinner included, wine excluded. Vin de Bordeaux
ordinaire 3 f. Claret at 4 f. not better.—rather approaching
to the wine at 1½ f.

For a great part of the way the banks were so high that the

---

[1] A *calèche* (also *calash* in English), was a light carriage with low wheels and a re-
movable folding hood. Furnes, 13 miles from Dunkirk, is the Flemish Veurne.
[2] The *abele* is the white poplar, *Populus alba.*
[3] Dorothy Wordsworth also noticed the black cloaks worn by the women of
Bruges and Ghent (*Journals*, ed. de Selincourt, II, 21).

country was not visible—wood on each side—chiefly poplar of different kinds, and beech—Latter part of way banks lower—neat houses—good deal of rye the main food of the common people. Labour 14 sous, 28 French Sous. White bread $3\frac{1}{2}$ pounds for 4 Sous or *pence*.

June 11. Town—marks of the wealth and splendour of the middle ages. Cathedrale de St Bavo rich in marble.[1] Pulpit by Delvaux. Statue of Bishop Trieste by Quesnoy. Ch[ch]. St Michael. Crucifixion by Vandyke—a very fine picture, but dirty, and not distinct.—another copy in Academy in better order, but not reckoned so good. Van Kraeger. Boxon sculptor —single portrait of himself.

Nunnery. Town Hall Gothic side superb.

Sabots. women without stockings. Blue Carters frocks. Cotton cloaks

June 12 [Sunday]. Feats of swimming from the bridges of the Schelde and the Leys, numerous barges laden with Coals chiefly from Charleroix.

In the afternoon to Brussels by the Diligence—premiere caisse.[2] Pavè the first half of the way between two rows of beeches. Country flat but not unpleasing from the number of trees—chiefly different kinds of poplar, and beech,—no large timber. Much rye in full ear, and good crops, some barley turning yellow,—but little wheat—just coming into ear. good crops flax. From Alost the crops of wheat and rye forwarder, and the finest and fullest I ever saw.—the first half of the way the houses the neatest,—last half thatched cottages, and a waving country much like England. Alost and Assche very white and cheerful. Blue frocks. women without shoes. Hotel Belle Vue. Place Royale. Park—splendid.[3]

---

[1] It is interesting that Malthus does not mention the famous 'Ghent altar-piece' in St Bavon's Cathedral, by the brothers van Eyck; the central picture had been sent back by the French in 1816, under the terms of the second Treaty of Paris.

[2] Possibly a mistake for *classe*?

[3] Dorothy Wordsworth also stayed at the Hotel Belle Vue, in the Place Royale, 'which looked like a square of palaces'. She described the park as 'a very large open space, with shady walks, statues, fountains, pools, arbours, and seats, and surrounded by palaces and fine houses' (*Journals*, ed. de Selincourt, II, 24).

For this park, of just over forty acres, Belgium is indebted to the Austrian occupation; it was laid out by the Austrian architect, Zinner, in 1776.

June 13 [Monday]. St Gudule. Pulpit. Statues of Quesnoy. two beautiful statues by Delvaux. Park. Coffee House in Park.

June 14. Old Orange Palace—now Musaeum Natural History. Collection of Paintings. Rubens.
Fine Statue of Hercules by Delvaux. Rivage. Allee Verte.[1]

June 15. Waterloo Mont St Jean. La Haye Sainte Belle Alliance. Mound of Earth. & Golden Lion where the Prince of Orange was wounded.[2] The Wellington tree removed.

June 16. Eglise de notre dame de la chapelle. Statues of Duquesnoy. Tomb of Spinoler by Plumiers.

June 17. Left Brussels in the barque for Boom. Rows of beech and poplar. King's Palace. chiefly grass.—making hay. Complaints of the weight of taxes—Capitation tax. House tax. Taxes much heavier than in the time of the French; but the french taxation introduced the present system. Complaints of the low price of corn. Farmers cannot purchase manure. Competition of the North. Labour about 7 sous Holl. a day. Antwerp. Hotel du Grand Laboreur. Place de Meir. Grand and stinking. Tower of the Great Church the most beautiful I have ever seen—466 feet. Houses high—Gable ends. Marks of great former wealth.

June 18. Eglise de Notre Dame. Spoliation in 1797.[3] Rubens. Elevation of the Cross. Decent from it. Ascension of the Virgin. —the second very fine, the first not so fine, and the 3rd inferior. Other pictures not remarkable. Statue of the Virgin by

[1] Dorothy Wordsworth, in July 1820, describes the Allée Verte as the Hyde Park of Brussels, 'with streams of carriages of every description from the chariot of my Lord Anglais to the lowest of the Bourgeoisie (whose awkward vehicles were much more amusing) crammed like Johnny Gilpin's chaise with whole families, from the grandmother to the babe at its Mother's breast...On one side of the drive a Fair was held;—smoking and drinking-booths—stalls of eatables and abundance of toys and trinkets' (*Journals*, ed. de Selincourt, II, 27).

[2] The Lion Mound at Waterloo had only been made the year before, in 1824. The lion was of cast iron, not gold.

[3] According to Nagel's *Guide*, the spoliation by the French of Notre Dame at Antwerp was in 1794, and it was reopened for worship in 1802. Rubens's pictures were replaced in 1816.

Quesnoy. Mausoleum of St Ambrose and Pulpit by Verbrugen. Church of St James.[1]

Statues of St Peter by Verbruggen, and St Paul by Willemsens. Caudela family Vervoort. Putin family. Figure emblematical of Eternity by M. Vervoort very good.

Balustrade G. Coshx. Otto Venius. Chapelle de la famille de Ruben. Church of St Paul. Scourging of Christ by Rubens —an exquisite picture—Adoration of the Shepherds Rubens— The grand Altarpiece—descent from the Cross by Sers.[2] Grand Altar Verbruggen. Musaeum. Crucifixion Rubens. Chef d Oeuvre Vandyke. Trinity Rubens bad.

June 19 [Sunday]. Service. Music. quite full, at the mass for the Soldiers. Great attention.

Church St Charles Borromée.
PP Jesuites.[3]
St Augustin.

Baptism of St Augustin by Van Bree quite modern.— some merit. Cels.

Maitre Autel Verbruggen.
Rubens

Private Collection Van Lanker. Dutch pieces.

June 20. Tower of Notre Dame. Steam Boat to Dort.[4]—first Dutch Town—peculiar. Brick neat Houses out of the perpendicular. Church. Basons.

June 21. Rotterdam first appearance Quay and large Canals

---

[1] The church of St James at Antwerp is famous for its private family chapels with their burial vaults and tombs. The 'Putin family' is the Plantin family, whose chapel was decorated by Rubens. Malthus was possibly muddled over the 'Figure emblematical of Eternity by M. Vervoort': there is a haut-relief of the 'Raising of the Cross', carved by van der Voort, in the south transept, and a statue by Geefs of 'A Dying Christian and Eternity' in the ambulatory near the Rubens chapel. 'G. Coshx' is G. Kerricx.

[2] 'The Descent from the Cross' over the high altar of St Paul's church is by Cels.

[3] The former Jesuit church at Antwerp, St Carolus Bonomaeus Kerk, was rebuilt after being burnt in 1718.

[4] Dort is an abbreviated form of Dordrecht.

with fine trees and lofty houses very striking.[1] Small bricks very thick.

June 22 [Wednesday]. Tower. Country Houses. Canals crowded with vessels, apparently much business doing. The most active town we have seen. Yet from Mr Anderson we learned that no new house had been built upon a fresh site during his residence of 20 years. Taxes double what they were under the French. Clergy paid by the government—very regularly. No tithes. All sects equally admissible to Offices—lately a Jew. Protestants and Catholics live very amicably together. Bonaparte took the funds which had been appropriated before to the payment of the clergy. Wiped off two thirds of the national debt— sanctioned by the present Government. The clergymen of English Presbyterian Congregation equally paid by the government as those of Holland. Government professes to assist all Sects who are not able to pay their own clergy.

June 23. To Delft by the Boat to dinner, 2 hours, 9 miles—neat Dutch Town. Churches. Monuments of William 1st. and Grotius in New Church,[2] and Van Tromp in the old.[3] Fair.

Large Canal part of the way—meadows coarse & entrenched with ditches. Country houses.

To the Hague 5 miles—about an hour. Borders of the canal wooded and country houses very frequent. Canal Smaller— latter part of the way green with duck weed.

The Hague. Belle Vue.

June 24. Museum.[4] Cattle by Paul Porter as large as life very

---

[1] According to Baedeker, the wide quay on the Maas at Rotterdam, known as the Boompjes, 'owes its name to a vanished avenue of elms'.

[2] The Nieuwe Kerke at Delft was built in the fifteenth century. The William I who is buried there is William the Silent, assassinated in 1584 by a Catholic fanatic. Hugo Grotius, born at Delft in 1583, was sentenced to life imprisonment in 1619 for being a republican. His wife contrived his escape to France where, in 1625, he published his classic work on international law, *De Jure Belli et Pacis*.

[3] The Oude Kerk was built in 1250. Admiral van Tromp, who was killed in battle off the Texel in 1653, is memorable for having hoisted a broom to his masthead after defeating the English off Dungeness in the previous year.

[4] The Museum at the Hague is the Mauritshuis, built in the seventeenth century for Count John Maurice of Nassau, and used since 1821 as a picture gallery, for works from the collections of the Princes of the House of Orange. Paul Potter's bull is still there, and examples of Gerrit Dou.

good. Gerard Dow. Imitations of the French school. King's palace.[1] Palace in the Wood.[2] Scheveling.[3]

June 25 [Saturday]. To Leyden by Boat; 1st part of the way the same as from Delft after turning—the canal crowded with country houses on the left. meadows on the right—latter part of the way meadows—no corn. Lion d'Or. *26th* [Sunday] Church of St Peter. Tomb of Borehane. Sacrament sitting round the table. French Church—Sermon. Botanic Garden.[4]

June 27 [Monday]. Musaeum.[5] good collection. Birds still at Amsterdam. New buildings to be prepared for them.

Broad Street a handsome and picturesque Street. Rappenburgh disappointing—by no means equal to some at Rotterdam.[6]

Professor Tyddeman. Rector of the University—a magistracy. Annual Election. Farms in general small 10, 20, and 30 arpents.[7] Price of labour in the Summer about a florin. Want of work in the winter. Great complaints since 17 and 18 of a want of vent for the produce of the land. Woollen trade declining. Masters will not take from their workmen all that they can do—only a piece of a certain size in a certain number of days. Leyden—diminished in population like most of the Towns of Belgium and Holland.

Right of succession according to the Roman Law.

Professor Tyddeman Professr of Law gives a course in Political Econy. Latin disquisition—not very good.

Mutton 3*d* Beef 4*d* a pound Bread 1½.

[1] The 'King's palace', built by Peter Post in 1640, is now the International Institute for Social Studies.

[2] The 'Palace in the Wood' is Huis ten Bos, also seventeenth-century, with wings added in 1748; it stands in a thickly wooded park.

[3] Scheveling is Scheveningen, then a fishing village.

[4] St Pieterskerk at Leyden contains memorials of professors of the University, established in 1575. Herman Boerhaave was a famous teacher of medicine in the eighteenth century. The Botanic Gardens were laid out in 1587.

[5] The Natural History Museum was well known for its collection of animals from the Dutch colonies, especially the Temnick Collection of Birds.

[6] Broad Street is Breestraat, the wide main street of the city of Leyden, which still contains many baroque gabled houses. The Rapenburg is a wide thoroughfare on each side of a canal; the University of Leyden is on the west bank.

[7] An arpent is an obsolete French measure of land, a hundred square perches, varying with the size of the perch from about five-sixths of an acre to an acre and a quarter (*O.E.D.*).

To Harlaem by boat 4 hours Golden Lion, kept by a french family.

Canal—chiefly meadows on each side—latter part of way—ground rather higher. good trees. Sand Hills conspicuous. Neat cheerful Town. Houses Red ornamented with white. Gable Ends. Largest Church in Holland. Finer Canal than at Leyden (Rappenburgh) but houses not so large.

June 28 [Tuesday]. Statue of Koster. 5 specimens of his printing in the Town Hall. 2 first wooden plates the next three moveable types, supposed to be in metal. Is said to have begun printing in 1420 and to have died in 1439.—Doubtful. Date of this print it is said is not earlier this [*sic*] 1440.[1]

Revelations. Speculum Salutis.

Organ.[2] Mutton and Beef 5*d.* a pound.

Environs of Harlaem more varied and agreeable than any Town in Holland we have seen.[3]

June 29. Voiture to Alkmaer. Sand Hills. Fine trees of all kinds and many large country houses to the left. Beverwick—Alkmaer—cheerful Dutch Town. Gable Ends. Walk in Wood. Ramparts[4]—Canal to the Holder and Amsterdam.

Voyage characteristic of Holland, Rivers Salm & Y.[5] Long line 2 or 3 miles of neat and peculiar houses Green red, blue white terminating in Sandam.[6] Peter the Great's Cottage. Crossing the Y. View of Amsterdam. French Theatre.

July 1 [Friday]. Palace. New Church.

---

[1] The statue of Laurens Janszoon Coster still stands at Haarlem in the Grote Markt, a meeting-place of ten streets. He was born at Haarlem in 1370 and died in 1440. According to the Dutch, it was he who really invented printing from movable type; after his death an apprentice is said to have gone off to Mainz and set up business there with Gutenberg (*c.* 1400–68) who is generally regarded as the father of printing.

[2] The organ of the Grote Kerk at Haarlem, built in 1735–8, has five thousand pipes.

[3] The 'Environs of Harlaem' still 'abound in gardens, parks, and attractive country houses'. It was famous for its tulips at the end of the fifteenth century, and by Malthus's time was well established as the centre of the bulb industry.

[4] The ramparts of Alkmaar have now been replaced by public gardens.

[5] The river Y is the Ij, pronounced 'eye'.

[6] Sandam is Zaandam, where Peter the Great studied shipbuilding in 1697; the 'Czaar-Peter-Huisje' is still preserved.

July 2 [Saturday]. Museum. Collection of pictures—all the rooms not open. Rembrants night watch. Gerard Dows Schoolmaster. Vander Helsts Repast. VandrerVelde [*sic*] Sea pieces River Y. Port of Amsterdam. Battle of De Ruyter and Monck 1666. Le Pendant, another Battle of De Ruyter &c Woosermans Teneirs &c &c

Brock. Inundations very extensive. Great numbers have been employed to repair them—Receive about one florin 4 stivers, or two shillings a day—reckoned the general price of day labour in the Summer. Sabots common, and women without shoes and stockings not very infrequent throughout Holland. Dress of the common people on the whole tolerably good. Average prices of wheat of average quality free on board at Rotterdam for 11 years from 1814 to 1825. 34*s.* 8*d.* per quarter (lowest price not included). Average for 5 years from 1820 to 1825 31*s.* 3*d.* for 1825 22*s.* 8*d.* Mr B.

July 3 [Sunday]. Episcopal Chapel.[1] *Sermon.*
Amstel Bridge. Keyser Graft. Heeren Graft.[2] Plantage.[3] Gardens by Haarlem Gate. Beau Monde. Every man with his pipe.

July 4. To Utrecht by boat. Amstel fine River—Country houses. River Vecht. Extensive meadows divided by ditches—land lower than the Canal. Lock Elevation about a foot. large and agreeable country houses. latter part inferior Entrance to Utrecht bad.
    Tower. View.[4] Walks. Wood.

[1] The 'Episcopal Chapel' was probably the Arminian Protestant Church of the Remonstrants; Simon Episcopius was a follower of Arminius (1560–1609), who opposed Calvin's doctrine of predestination, and held that 'forgiveness and eternal life would be given to all those who repented of their sins and unfeignedly believed in Jesus Christ'. This church is between the Prinsengracht and the Keizersgracht: it contains portraits of preachers by T. de Keyser, and Hendrik de Keyser built two near-by churches in the early seventeenth century, which may account for Malthus's confused spelling.

[2] Gracht, which Malthus calls 'Graft', is the word for a canal in a town, usually with a roadway on either side. According to Baedeker, the Herengracht, lined with trees, still affords 'a good idea of what an aristocratic Dutch street was like in the 17–18th c.'.

[3] The Plantage is the name of the district where the Botanic Garden is situated, east of the old Jewish quarter of Amsterdam.

[4] The Cathedral Tower of Utrecht is the tallest church tower in Holland; it is detached from the main body of the building, and is 367 feet high. At 328 feet, says Baedeker, there is 'a splendid view from the platform...(458 steps, tiring)'.

July 5 [Tuesday]. To Breda in the Diligence. Ground higher. at first Pastures divided by ditches. afterwards fine crops of hemp potatoes rye & c:—pass the Lock—the Waal, and a small arm of the large water formed by the difft branches of the Rhine and Maes. Latter part of the way a more common kind of country—part heath firs and inclosures.

Breda. Church. Tomb of Engelbrecht the second Count of Nassau. Michael Angelo.[1] Rampart—fortifications. Walks.

July 6. To Antwerp by Diligence. Country common in its appearance fine crops of rye, some enclosures some heath. Trees, particularly oaks, without leaves, apparently from catterpillars. Great Church and Musaeum.[2] Rubens and Vandyke. Labour lower than in Holland—almost all articles cheaper—people said to be indolent—commonest workmen do not earn above 5 franks in the week.

July 7. To Malines in voiture. very fine crops of rye, wheat, and flax, some rye cut, country not quite flat. Thatched cottages. children running after the carriage—not in Holland.

Malines[3]—a very clean agreeable looking Town with good houses and open place's. Jubilee of St Rombold Great Church —very fine Tower.[4] Crucifixion Vandyke. Church of St John. Pictures of Rubens. Adoration of the Magi, Martyrdom of St John,[5] Decollation of John the Baptist [a space is left here for about three words] all at Paris and returned.

Church of Notre Dame Ruben's miraculous draft of fishes, very fine.[6]

---

[1] The alabaster tomb of Count Engelbert II of Nassau (died 1504), who was Stadholder of the Netherlands under the Emperor Maximilian I, is still the show-piece of the Grote Kerk at Breda. It is now attributed to either Tommaso Vincitore of Bologna or Pietro Torrigiano of Florence.

[2] It is pleasant to find the Malthus family party going back to the 'Great Church and Musaeum' at Antwerp on 6 July, after previously visiting them on 17–18 June. See pp. 232–3.

[3] Malines is the French form of the Flemish Mechlin (or Mechelen).

[4] The Cathedral of St Rumbold at Mechlin was meant to have the highest tower in Christendom, 570 feet, but was left unfinished at 318 feet; William the Silent, in 1578, requisitioned the building materials for fortifications.

[5] In St John's Church, the 'Martyrdom of St John' shows the Evangelist being thrown into boiling oil.

''The Miraculous Draft of Fishes' is in the church of Notre-Dame-au-delà-de-la-Dyle: there are two other churches of Notre Dame at Mechlin.

To Louvain—country not quite flat. very fine crops of rye wheat and flax—many children following the carriage without great appearance of poverty, thatched cottages, appearance of the country like England, except the straight road which shews the tower of Malines 15 miles off exactly in the center of the avenue of trees which reaches from Malines to Louvain.

Hotel de Ville—a beautiful specimen of Gothic architecture —very peculiar.[1]—handsome church.[2] Library of the University fine room. 4 classes. 16 Professors—None in Theology.[3]

July 8 [Friday]. To Namur,—more hilly—agreeable country a good deal like England—rather more common fields, and more white poplars.—cottages inferior, and some delapidated —more appearance of poverty. Had excellent coffee and a good breakfast at a small Auberge on the road—steep hill going down to Namur.

July 9. Namur the junction of the Sambre and the Meuse. Samble very small—Meuse low in water and smaller than expected. Shores of the river rocky woody and sometimes picturesque, but not high. Huy. Chateau Choquier, Prince Bishops former palace. frequent villages and Campagne. Country full of Iron mines & Stone quarries Cutting Ordinary labour about a france. at present a movement in manufactures. Government approved as being more favourable to liberty than those of their neighbours, but the prohibitory system adopted between France and the Netherlands much complained of—begun by France—has subsisted 2 years.

July 10 [Sunday]. To Aix la Chappelle in the Diligence. Liege situated a little like Bath, and the country the first part of the way to Aix like the Bath country—hilly small enclosures chiefly grass, thatched cottages, and rich hedge rows.

[1] The Stadhuis of Louvain, begun in 1448, has façades much ornamented with sculpture; on the corbels are reliefs of stories from the Old Testament, 'some of truly medieval Flemish coarseness' (Baedeker).
[2] St Pieters-kerk, opposite the Town Hall, was probably the 'handsome church'.
[3] The University of Louvain was founded in 1425, and occupied the Cloth Hall from 1432 until this was burnt down by the Germans in 1914. In the sixteenth century the University had six thousand students in fifty colleges; it was said in the eighteenth century that, in the Austrian Netherlands, no one could hold an official post without having been educated at Louvain.

Altogether the country between Liege and Aix fine and varied, like some of the best parts of England, part resembling a little the hogs back. some heath on the hills after passing the Prussian Frontier. Blue frocks almost universal.

Aix. Crowded Streets—Exhibition of Relicks once in 7 years.[1] Church Carolo Magno.[2] Town House, Statue of Charlemagne.[3] Walks.[4]

July 11 [Monday]. To Cologne by Dueren Bad road. First part of the way varied and rather pretty. Woods. Streams. Dueren manufacture of Cloth. The Streams support the Town. Mills. common labour in the manufacture from 20 to 24 and 30 sous a day. after Dueren a vast flat common field—bad soil and bad agriculture. a dry sand. Plain of Cologne again good crops. barley cut.

Cologne. Church of St Peter Crucifixion of St Peter by Rubens. Fine, but too dark to see it well. Rhine. Bridge of Boats.

July 12. To Coblentz by voiture. Breakfast. Bonn.—no beauty before Godesberg.—7 mountains. Drachenfels. Some of the views after passing the Drachenfels the finest and most picturesque. Rheimagen—dinner. Convent fine view. Andernach Valley open and the country flatter to Coblentz—Vines covering most of the hills wherever they can be planted. The vin du Rhin ordinaire at Rheimagen, from Bingen. Coblentz. Fortifications. Bridge of the Moselle—walk to the confluence of the Rhine. Ehrenbreitstein.

[1] The 'Relicks' of Aachen (Aix-la-Chapelle) are now in the Treasury.
[2] The Cathedral was built round Charlemagne's octagonal Chapel Palatine; it was begun in 796 and consecrated by Pope Leo III in 805. *Carolo Magno*, on a marble slab on the floor, probably does not mark Charlemagne's actual burial place.
[3] The Town Hall of Aachen was built in the fourteenth century on the site of Charlemagne's ninth-century palace.
[4] The party's 'Walks' may have been in the Elisengarten, which had been laid out behind the neo-classical pump-room built in 1824, and called after Princess Elisabeth of Bavaria. She was the wife of the Crown Prince who, in 1840, became Frederick William IV of Prussia; he is known chiefly for his extremely illiberal views, but it is worth remembering that, at the time of Malthus's tour, he was a young man of thirty doing much to build up both the prosperity and popularity of the Rhineland. In 1842 he set about finishing Cologne Cathedral, which was begun in 1248 and completed in 1880.

Fortifications destroying. Towns and villages on the Rhine have an old and retrograding appearance—people looking poor—women and children without stockings and shoes.

July 13 [Wednesday]. To Mayence—The finest part of the Rhine for picturesque beauty from Coblentz to Bingen—full of ruined castles, and towns and villages in picturesque situations. —the villages all look extremely well at a distance, and the frequency of the old castles gives a very peculiar and striking character to the scenery—the great Theatre of German Transactions in the middle ages. Junction of the Lahn Old Castle of Lahneck Ruins of Stolzenfels.[1] Rhense. the Konigstuhl (Royal Seat. Disposition of the Emperor Wenceslaus. Castle of Markusburgh[2]—Old Castles Lebenstein and Sternfels—the brothers. Boppart.—palace of Kings of the Franks. Convent of Manenburgh. Old Castle of Katz Ruins of the Antient fort of Rheinfels. Rock—Lurleyberg.[3] Castle of Schonberg. Overwesel. Castle of Gutenfels near Caub.—Old Castle of Stalberg. Convent of Furstenthal. Village of Asmanhausen—red wine.[4] Rheinstein. Castle of Falkenberg. Whirpool of Bingerlock.

From Bingen the road leaves the Rhine and the country is comparatively uninteresting, chiefly common fields in cold not very fertile

July 14. Mayence. Collection of paintings (indifft). Roman Antiquities found in the Neighbourhood of Mayence.[5] Cathedral Church Red stone.—Evening Music. Roman Aqueduct Citadel. Drusner Garden—fine view of the Rhine the Mayn and Mayence. people not contented with the Prince

---

[1] The 'Ruins of Stolzenfels' had been given to the Crown Prince Frederick William by the citizens of Coblenz in 1823. His restoration of them is a wonderful example of nineteenth-century Gothic; he used the castle as his summer residence, and his widow lived there until 1873.

[2] Marksburg, in 1825, was made into a home for disabled veterans of the Napoleonic wars.

[3] The 'Rock—Lurleyberg' would have had no special significance for Malthus. Clemens von Brentano invented the Lorelei in 1802—there was a strong current below the rock, and a five-fold echo—but Heine's song did not appear until 1827.

[4] Assmannshausen is still famous for its red wine.

[5] Mainz was the Roman Moguntiacum, founded in 11 B.C. by Drusus—hence the Drusner Garden.

of Hesse Darmstadt. Better under the French (Cocher). Town garrisoned by 3,000 Austrians and 3,000 Prussians Fortifications very strong.

July 15 [Friday]. To Coblentz by Boat.[1] Rhine broad and the shores pleasing, but not high before Bingen. Castles of Psalzberg & Rheinstein on left[2]—Ehensfels on the Right. Oberwesel walls with Towers. St Goai with stone fort of Rheinfels above a striking part of the Rhine. Boppart Convent & castles. Kapelle opening of the Valley of the Lahn with Church—and castles, and Castle of Pstolsenfels. Therm. Reaum 25.

July 16. Coblentz Notre Dame Chartreuse View. Landing of Crown Prince of Prussia at Kapelle well received. New fortifications, and old everywhere repairing Casernes. Ehrenbreitstein nearly finished.

July 17 [Sunday]. To Cologne by boat. Some fine views but not so marked as those above Coblentz except near Drachenfels, one of the seven mountains, where perhaps there are some views as fine as any on the Rhine. Nonenvert-island where we stopt to dine a beautiful situation looking to Drachenfels.[3] Town of Bonn looks well on approaching it, but interior bad.

July 18. Cologne. Chathedral unfinished but very fine. To Juliers in the afternoon. very hot. The master of the hotel Rheinberg Cologne said that the day before the Thermometer in the shade had been as high as 27 Reaumeurs—99 of Farenheit.[4]

July 19. To Aix la Chapelle. Rye and Barley generally getting in. Wheat not cut. From Cologne chiefly a champaign country till near Aix.

---

[1] Like many other tourists, the Malthus party went up the Rhine by road, and then down again by boat.

[2] Psalzberg is the Pfalz, a fortress on an island in mid-stream.

[3] Nonnenwerth, an island of about a hundred acres, is now a girls' school. The nunnery, founded in the twelfth century, would have been sequestrated by Napoleon, but Josephine got his permission for the nuns then living there to stay until they died—and the Prussians honoured the arrangement. In about 1823 the island was sold, and the convent became a 'commodious hotel'.

[4] 27° R is, in fact, equal to 93° F, not 99.

July 20 [Wednesday]. To Maestricht, by a bad road—nearly overturned from a precipice—Horses rolled to the bottom, but escaped without much injury—a very young coachman. Some rather pretty country, near Maestricht common field. Harvest getting in. Meuse low—walk by the side. Town House. Churches, 2 squares—good private houses. Did not see, except at a distance St Peters Hill, and excavations.[1]

July 21. To Bruxelles by the Diligence through Tongre St. Tron, Tirlemont and Louvain. Rich Common fields varied with some low hills and woods—prevailing tree white poplar.—latter part of the way rye all got in, wheat cutting.

CASH ACCOUNT

The Cash Account gives in complete detail the expenditure of the Continental Tour amounting in all to a few shillings less than £200, of which £155 was spent abroad in either francs or florins, respectively 25 and 11·8 to the £.

Franc expenditure is shown in 3 columns, Napoleons (equal to 20 francs or 16 shillings), francs and centimes (from 8 July sous at 20 to 1 franc replace centimes). Florin expenditure is similarly shown in Williams (equal to 10 florins or 17 shillings), florins, and a lower denomination equal to 1/20 florin.

Until 23 June 'Receipts' are shown in sterling only and no attempt is made to balance these against expenditure recorded in other currency. On that date Malthus counted his cash and thereafter both sides of the account are kept in currency and balances are regularly struck.

Unfortunately the record of 'Receipts' appears to be incomplete since it appears to show net drawings of £160 only against expenditure of £200.

Omitted receipts would explain why the cash counted on 23 June was £10 (in sterling equivalent) more than appears warranted by the account, and also why there was an increase in his holding of francs from 528 at the 23 June count to 1270 on 8 July—an increase of just under £30 in sterling equivalent—without any intervening

---

[1] St Peter's Hill, the Petersberg, 404 feet high, is 2½ miles south of Maastricht; it is honeycombed with stone quarries, worked from Roman times until the end of the nineteenth century. The soft stone is easily sawn, but hardens on exposure to the air; stone pillars were left to support the roof, and there is now a labyrinth of over three hundred galleries.

16-2

recorded receipt, and after a period in which his recorded expenditure in florins almost equalled his holding of them.

The heading £. s. d. above the expenditure beginning on 10 June is clearly and unambiguously there in Malthus's accounts. But it is evident from the right-hand column and from the whole method of his accounts that this is a mistake and the figures are in Napoleons, francs and centimes.

RECEIPTS				EXPENDITURE			
E I Coll* *June 2* [Thursday] *1825*					£	s.	d.
	£	s.	d.	Coach to London & c:	0	9	0
In hand.	21	7	6	Hampstead stages & coach	0	6	0
Draft on Hoare	50	0	0	Premium Insurance	1	10	0
				Mrs M.—3 from Emily	2	0	0
	71	7	6	Trunk	1	6	0
Expenditure				Mrs Woodward	2	0	6
To *June 5*	24	0	6	Places to Dover	3	0	0
				Sts†		12	6
	47	7	0	Edith	5	0	0
20£ from Hal				Passport	0	5	0
				Pls. turnpike	0	3	0
				Letters Parcels	0	8	0
				2. Tours	0	16	0
				Map.	0	17	0
				Pocket & c:	0	5	0
				Parcel.	0	2	0
				Coachm. Glass coach, & porter	0	5	6
				Teas	0	8	0
				Coffee, oranges	0	3	6
				Coachman to Canterbury	0	7	0
				Guard & 2nd Coachman	0	8	6
				Remaining fare	3	8	0
					24	0	6

* East India College. † Malthus's abbreviation for 'servants'.

1825

RECEIPTS				EXPENDITURE			
	£	s.	d.		£	s.	d.
	71	7	6	*June 5* [Sunday]	24	0	6
	[29	10	0*]	Bill at Dover Paris Hotel. Sts.	2	14	6
	[41	17	6*]	Commissioner		5	6
From Hal	20	0	0	Ladder		1	6
				Passage	2	2	0
	91	7	6	Steward	0	4	0
	29	10	0	Ladder	0	2	0
	61	17	6		29	10	0

* Crossed out.

					Fr.	
June 7 [Tuesday]						
In hand. Calais	61	17	6	Bill at Meurice's Calais	2 14	0
Expenditure	14	0	0	Places	0 16	0
	£47	17	6	H.E & M.	3 5	
				Commissionaire	0 10	0
				Church. Calais	0 2	0
				Sts at Meurice's	0 8	0
				Conducteur	0 4	0
				(£50 and 7. Louis.)		
				Bill at hotel de Flandre	2 11	0
				Sts. & Carriage to Furnes		
				Cotter.* Commssr.	1	50
				Visites Frontier		
				Postillion. Barriers	8	30
				Breakfast at Furnes, Portier	6	0
				Barque to Nieuport	4	20
				To Bruges	8	0
				Dinner	8	0
				Wine. excellent	1	50
				Steward		50
				[*June*] 9. Books	2	50
				Churches	4	0
				[*June*] 10 Bill at Fleur de Bled		
				Sts. Portrs.	2 16	50

		Centimes	To Ghent	1 2	0
Changed 9£			Wine & Steward	0 8	0
Exchange en Or	24	70	Coach. to Hotel & c.	3	50
[*June*] 10 Bruges	24	50		17 4	50
In Boat from Bruges	25	0			
At Ghent	24	60			

* Possibly a mistake for *cocher*.

1825

RECEIPTS	£	s.	d.
	61	17	6

EXPENDITURE	£	s.	d.
June 10 [Friday]	17	4	50
10. Plan of Ghent	0	2	0
St. Bavon Cathedral	0	1	50
11th St. Michael. Academy			
Library	0	4	50
Voiture Commissionaire	0	7	0
Lettres affranchis	0	1	50
Washing at Ghent	0	5	0
Bill at Hotel de la Post 2 days	4	3	50
Sts		6	0
Baggage to Diligence	0	1	50
Conducteur	0	4	0
Places to Brussels. 1re Caisse	1	5	0
12th. Coach to Belle Vue with			
luggage	0	3	0
13 Eglise de St Gudule	0	5	0
Shoes Mrs M.	0	5	0
14 Museum, loan of book,			
pictures.	0	0	50
Coach and bath	0	4	50
Coach. afternoon	0	5	0
Hal	1	1	16
Mrs M.	1	1	16
Church Place de Sablon	0	0	50
	27	10	82

[Sunday, *June*] *12th.*
Changed 20 sovereigns at 25 f.
Received 23 double ducats or
pieces of 10 florines each worth
in French money 21 f. 16 centimes
and f 13...23 c

15 June [Wednesday].			
EXPENDITURE	27	10	82

RECEIPTS

	£	s.	d.
June 16	61	17	6
Brussels	30	0	0

	£	s.	d.
15 Dinner at Mont St. Jean			
Waterloo	0	8	0
Wine & Sts	0	7	0
Guide	0	5	0
Sights at Waterloo Belle			
Alliance & c:	0	6	0
Carriage & Coachman	1	2	0
16 Limonade. Eglise	0	2	0
Coach	0	4	0
Places Comedie	1	1	16
Bill 5 nights	9	9	75
Sts	0	15	0
17 Boots and passport	0	2	0
Coach Luggage	0	3	0
Passage to Boom	0	5	0
Breakfast & places	0	5	0
Places. Luggage Schelde	0	3	0
Diligence	0	6	0
Conducteur	0	1	0
Luggage to Hotel Antwerp	0	2	0
	42	17	73

June 16 [Thursday]
Received the change of 30£
at fr. 25·05 the £. = 35 pieces
of 10 florins each, and 6 f. 26 c.
4 f. 50 c was deducted for Commissn &
brok'ge.
Friday Evening. *17th.* Had 42 Piece d dix
florins, 1 sovereign and 4½ franks.

RECEIPTS

1825
June 18 [Saturday]

	EXPENDITURE	42 17 73
Pocket omissions & Eglises		
Notre Dame. St. Jaques.		
St Paul	15	0
Musaeum....	4	50
Hal repaid.	1	50
M. Van Lancker's pictures.	1	0
Augustins	0	80
Lemonade & Coffee	2	0

Holland Money	Florins	
Places in Steam Boat	36	80
Letter	0	50
Tower	1	0
Bill and Sts. at Grand Laboureur	63	0
Luggage	1	0
Dinner in Steamboat and wine.	10	50
Luggage	0	50
Dort one night tea & bst,*		
and passage to Rotterdm.	14	0
Bill Sts and Porter at		
Hotel D Angleterre 2 nights	36	0
Tower fruit & c:	2	
Passage boat to Delft & c:	3	50
Dinner & c:	7	0
To the Hague, 1 f. Porter 1 f. & c:	2	0
	florins 1 77	8

Paid for Mr B's Places Fl. 18 – 40.
June 23 Drew for 30£. Received
10 Williams, 26 Napoleons and 2 Florins.
In hand *23rd* at night 34 Williams 7
florins & 26 Napns 8 francs french
money

With French money even.

* Malthus's abbreviation for 'breakfast'.

Dutch Money	34 7	*June 25* [Saturday]	
Expend.	21 6	Hotel at Bellevue Hague 2 nights	42 0
	——	Carriage for Park & Scheveling	2 50
July 1	13 1	Porter	1 0
		Boat to Leyden	2 0
		Porter Leyden	1 0
		Roef—engaging it	1 0
		26. Churches Musaeums pocket	
		& c	2 0
		Commissionare 2 days	4 0
		Bill at Lion d'Or	50 0
		Balance to Mr B for sights &	
		boat to Harlaem	6 13
		Bill at Harlaem with organ and	
		carriage to Alkmaer.	56 0
		Coachman & Churches	17
		Bill at Alkmaer	22 0
		Porters Passage to Amsterdam	
		& c:	10 7
		Palace. dome.	1 0
		Spectacle.	10 0
		Letters	1 0
			——
			216 7

	w. f.	*July 2* [Saturday].	
Remainder *July 2*	13 1 0	Carriage boat & c: to Brock	0 6 10
Change of 10 Sovereigns	11 8 10	Musaeum Anatomy	1 10
Silver from Draft	9 3	Washing	6 5
	——	3. Bill at Amsterdam 4 nights	97 6
	25 8 13	Washing	3 16
Change of 5£ note	5 9 5	Gardens and Coach	6 0
	——	Coffee & c:	0 7
	31 7 18	Boat to Utrecht	7 4
Expend to *July 5*	18 4 6	Porter	1 0
	——	Tower Utrecht	1 0
	13 3 12	Commissionaire	1 5
		Bill	20 0
		Breakfasts	2 16
		Places to Breda in Diligence	25 12
		Conducteur	1 0
		Porter	0 15
Ns 26		Church Breda	1 0
36		Pocket	1 0
—			——
62			184 6

July 5 Eveng. Remr.	13	3	12
[Tuesday]			

6. Bill at Breda	15	18
Sts	1	0
Places to Antwerp	16	8
Conducteur	1	4
Musaeum		15
Bill at Antwerp	13	0
Coffee. Sts	1	0
Malines breakfast & Waiter	4	10
Eglises & Commissre.	2	0
Bill at Louvain & Waiter	18	0
7. Breakfast on the road	2	3
Voiture from Antwerp to Namur	48	0
	123	18

W
12   3 18

Left in Silver
22 francs. Had before 8 f

	Nap's		
Remainder	63	10	0
[Bill at Namur	1	15	0
Boat and breakfast to Huy	0	10	0
Boat from Huy to Liege	0	5	0
Breakfast at Huy	0	6	0
Porter Liege	0	2	0
Places for Aix la Chapelle. 6	2	14	8]*
	16	19	18
	46	10	2

July 8 [Friday]			
Bill at Namur		1	15	0
9 Boat and Coffee		0	10	0
Breakfast at Huy		0	6	0
Boat from Huy to Liege		0	5	0
Porter Liege		0	2	0
Coach to Aix. 6 places		2	14	0
Bill at Liege & Waiter		1	11	0
Porter		0	2	0
10 Conducteur		0	6	0
Porter		0	2	0
Douane & cherries		0	2	0
Bill at Aix la Chapelle		1	4	0
11 Breakfast at Ashwelt†		0	3	6
Dueren		0	3	6
Commissn.			1	6
Voiture to Cologne from Aix		2	0	0
Bill at Cologne & Sts.		2	0	0
12 Breakfast at Bonn & Sts & Letter		0	8	0
Dinner Sts. and Convent		1	0	0
Voiture to Coblentz		2	5	0
		16	19	18

* The above six items of expenditure, which were obviously written in the wrong place, have all been vigorously crossed out; Malthus used four vertical lines, a large X, and a smaller diagonal stroke to the right of it.
† Ashwelt is Eschweiler.

July 12 [Tuesday]

Remdr.							
46	10	2		Bill at Coblentz & Sts	0	16	0
18	0	9	*13*	Breakfast Boppart & c	.	5	0
				Dinner at Bingen & Sts	1	0	13
28	9	13		Music. Cherries & c	0	1	10
			14	Voiture to Mayence	2	11	0
				Voiture in Mayence	0	10	0
				Washing	0	14	0
				Sights	0	2	0
				Valet. Porter. Ices	0	6	0
				Bill at Mayence & Sts	3	5	0
			15	Diligence par Eau to Cologne	2	6	0
				Mats & c:	0	4	0
				Breakfast in boat	0	5	0
				Apricots cherries	0	2	0
				Umbrella Chain		1	6
			16	Bill at Coblentz	3	8	0
				Hal	1	0	0
				Sts. Voiture Valet Cocher⎱ Baggage ⎰	0	10	0
				Fruit	0	1	0
				Dinner cold & tea.	0	7	0
				Wine & Mats	0	5	0
					18	0	9

Remainder							
28	9	13	*17*	[Sunday] Bill at Cologne	2	0	0
16	3	3	*18*	At Bercheim*	0	8	7
				At Juliers	1	0	0
12	6	10	*19*	Voiture to Aix.	2	2	0
				Cocher		4	6
				Pocket fruit & c. & c	0	12	0
				Stockings Mrs M.	0	7	0
				Bill at Aix & Sts.	2	6	0
			20	Bringing voiture	0	2	0
				Breakfasts	0	3	0
				Bill at Maestricht	1	13	10
				Voiture to Maestricht	1	0	0
			21	Luggage	0	2	0
				Breakfasts at Tongre	0	3	10
				Wine & water	0	1	10
				Dinner & waiter		10	10
				Diligence from Maestricht	3	3	10
				Conducteur	0	6	0
				Luggage & Coach to Bellevue	0	4	0
					16	3	3

* Bercheim is Bergheim.

Remainder	12	6	10	22 [*July*, Friday]. Mrs M	3	0	0
Part of draft of 20£				Places for Ghent	1	10	0
at Brussels.	12	0	0	Spectacle	1	1	0
				Ices	0	0	15
	24	6	10	Coffee	0	1	10
	18	19	5	23 Bill at Belle Vue			
				2 nights	3	10	0
	5	7	5	Sts. fille & Porter	0	7	0
				Conducteur & porter		3	10
				Wine & cherries on road	0	2	0
				24 Bill at Ghent & c:	0	18	0
				Dinner & c boat & c:	1	6	0
				Porter	0	1	6
				Coffee & c: Bruges	0	5	0
				Voiture to Furnes	2	12	0
				Bill at Furnes & c:		11	10
				Coach to Calais & Porter	1	18	0
				Conducteur	0	5	0
				Dunquerque breakfast & c:		6	10
				Spectacles & Seal & brush	1	1	0
					18	19	15*

* The total here has been added in pencil.

Remainder in French money	5	7	5	Bill at Calais	2	1	0
From Emily	.	11	0	Sts. Commissre & Porter			
	£			ladder & c:	0	14	0
Remainder E Money	10	1	0	Part of passage	2	0	0
	5			Part of dinner	0	18	0
				Mrs M. Cloak	0	5	0
	15	1	0				
	10	17	6		5	18	0
	4	3	6	£			
Remainder of Expences				[Remainder English Money*]			
in Town & Journey				Remainder Passage	5	0	0
of Mrs M down	3	15	0	[dinner*]			
				Remainder dinner		1	6
		8	6	Tea	0	6	0
				Stewards	0	3	0
				Boat. Coach.	0	4	0
				Emily.	3	0	0
				Hal.	1	0	0
				Coach place	0	4	6
				Remainder		4	0
				Chaise from Waltham Cross		12	6
				Breakfast in Town		2	0
					10	17	6†

* Crossed out.   † The total here has been added in pencil.

Remainder	4	3	6	*August*		
Draft Hoare	10	0	0	5. Coach to Town	0 7 6	
Insurance returned	1	10	0	Coach	0 1 0	
				Eye Water	1 8	
	15	13	6	Mr Alexander	1 1 0	
	3	1	8	Arcquebusade	0 10 0	
				Neale's man	7 6	
	12	11	10	Coach down	8 0	
				Luncheon	1 0	
August 9				Pocket	4 0	
Actual remainder	12	11	6			
					3 1 8	

The Scottish Holiday, 1826

Francis Jeffrey wrote on 6 January 1826: 'My dear Malthus—I ought to have thanked you before for making us acquainted with the Eckersalls, to whom we take mightily, &c.

'It is long, my good friend, since we have met in quiet and comfort; for these little glimpses during my fevered runs to London are not the thing at all. Will you not bring down Mrs Malthus, and stay a few weeks with us next summer at Craigcrook? I have a great deal of leisure after the middle of July, and I am persuaded we could find sufficient employment for you, both at home and on our travels. I was not at all surprised to learn how severely both you and she had suffered from the great affliction which has befallen you.[1] I never look at the rosy cheeks and slender form of my own *only* child, without an inward shudder at the thought of how much utter wretchedness is suspended over me by so slight a cord. You have still two such holds on happiness, and may they never be loosened, &c.

'God bless you, my dear Malthus. I have long been accustomed to quote you as the very best example I know of a wise and happy man. I should be sorry to be obliged to withdraw either epithet, but I would much rather part with the first than the last.—Believe me always, very affectionately yours.'[2]

The Francis Jeffrey who wrote this sympathetic letter was a wealthy lawyer and a famous man of letters, fifty-three years old; he would become a Member of Parliament for a short time, after the advent of Lord Grey's Whig government in 1830, and Lord Jeffrey and a Judge in the Court of Session some six months before Malthus's death in 1834; he would also become the most doting of grandfathers. But he is now chiefly remembered for founding the *Edinburgh Review*, in 1802, with Henry Brougham, Francis Horner, and Sydney Smith. Brougham and Horner soon went to seek their fortunes in London, and Sydney Smith also left Edinburgh—whither he had only come because the French war had prevented his taking a pupil (Michael Hicks-Beach) on the

---

[1] The death of Lucy Malthus in May 1825.
[2] Henry Cockburn, *The Life of Francis Jeffrey* (London, 1852), II, 220–1.

usual grand tour. Jeffrey therefore remained sole editor of the *Review* until 1829.

Malthus and his family did not stay a few weeks at Craigcrook, and were on their way home again by the middle of July, but it seems likely that Jeffrey's invitation led them to think of a Scottish holiday.

This diary is a small book of 76 pages, $5\frac{3}{4} \times 3\frac{3}{4}$ in., with a paper cover in blue and a little brown, which might be described as marbled or mottled. The accounts take up 20 pages, and the diary $25\frac{1}{2}$. The holiday lasted from 12 June to 26 July, and just as the journal of the Continental tour seems largely a list of places and pictures, so this Scottish diary is largely a list of people.

The first person the Malthuses met in Edinburgh was not Jeffrey, but Leonard Horner (1785–1864), the younger brother of Francis; he ran his father's linen business, but his hobby was geology, and educational reform his mission in life. He was one of the founders of the Edinburgh Academy, but his most important work was the setting up, in 1821, of a 'School of Arts for the instruction of mechanics', the forerunner of all such institutions. Later he became 'Warden' of the University of London at its opening, and then an energetic chief factory inspector. A few months before Malthus's visit, Horner had befriended a first-year medical student of seventeen, who recorded years later that 'Mr Leonard Horner...took me once to a meeting of the Royal Society of Edinburgh, where I saw Sir Walter Scott in the chair as President'. The student's name was Charles Darwin, and while Malthus was in Scotland, Darwin was on a walking tour in North Wales.[1]

The first 'outing' in Edinburgh was to the Courts, which was characteristic of the period; in the words of Michael Joyce, 'it was not the University, but the Courts of Law, that gave the Northern capital its distinctive flavour: it was not the professors, nor even the clergy, but the forensic luminaries that shone forth conspicuous and superior'.[2] Dorothy Wordsworth, when writing her diary for 17 September 1822, said, 'Writer's Library—Advocate's Library—very handsome, but more resembling rooms for promenading or Balls than the Libraries of Scholars.'[3]

Sir Walter Scott was at his most unhappy at this time; it was in January 1826 that he became his creditors' vassal for life, and on 15 May his wife died. Mr Mackenzie, on the other hand, although eighty-one, was still the life of the company, with anecdotes and

---

[1] Charles Darwin, *Autobiography*, ed. Nora Barlow (Collins, 1959), pp. 52, 53.
[2] Michael Joyce, *Edinburgh, The Golden Age, 1769–1832* (Longmans, 1951), p. 147.
[3] Dorothy Wordsworth, *Journals*, ed. de Selincourt, p. 345.

fun, and enjoyed some quiet shooting, fishing, and a game of bowls. Henry Mackenzie (1745–1831) is chiefly remembered for *The Man of Feeling*, published anonymously in 1771, and for his report on James Macpherson's 'Ossian' poetry. According to Cockburn 'he was thin, shrivelled, and yellow, kiln-dried with smoking, with something—when seen in profile—of the clever wicked look of Voltaire'. Normally he used an ear-trumpet, but in 1826 he experimented unsuccessfully with 'Wellington Ears', of silver and papier-mâché, with ribbons attached, to be tied round the back of the head.[1]

Of the other people whom Malthus met in Edinburgh, Mr Murray, Mr Rutherfurd, Lord Alloway, Mr Cranstoun and Mr Craig were all successful Whig lawyers—so also was Henry Cockburn (1779–1854) whom Malthus spells Cobourn or even Colbourn, and of whom a little more should be said, since he shared with Jeffrey the leadership of the Scottish bar. He was 'below the middle height [Jeffrey was "diminutive"] with a handsome and intellectual face, fond of outdoor exercises, and a devoted lover of nature. Among friends he was a delightful companion, and his general unconventionality and genial familiarity with his country-men of every class contributed to make him one of the most per-sonally popular of Scotsmen.'[2] His memoirs and his *Life of Jeffrey* are among the best accounts of Edinburgh at this time.

Malthus also met Count Flahault, who had been aide-de-camp to Napoleon; he had been educated in Britain, was allowed to take refuge here on the restoration of the Bourbons, and on 20 June 1817 —two years and two days after Waterloo—married Margaret Elphinstone, Viscountess Keith and Baroness Nairne in her own right, friend and confidante of the Princess Charlotte. Later Count Flahault returned to France, and served as ambassador in Rome, Vienna, and London.

'Mr Maculloch' was John Ramsay M‘Culloch (1789–1864), famous as a disciple and populariser of Adam Smith and Ricardo, a chief contributor of economic articles to *The Scotsman* and the *Edinburgh Review*, and as one of the original members of the Political Economy Club. Since 1820 he had removed his quarters from Edinburgh to London, where in 1824 he delivered the Ricardo lecture. In 1826, the year of Malthus's tour, he published his Wages Fund theory in Edinburgh, in the 'Essay on the Circumstances which determine the rate of Wages and the Condition of the Labouring Classes'.

[1] Michael Joyce, *Edinburgh, The Golden Age*, pp. 182–3.
[2] *D.N.B.*

It would be pleasant to think that 'Mr Wood' was John Philip Wood of Cramond, the deaf-and-dumb antiquary and biographer, who so overcame his handicaps that he also obtained the appointment of Auditor of Excise in Scotland.

Mrs Laing, widow of the historian Malcolm Laing (1762–1818), was a Miss Carnegie of Forfarshire; as her husband spent the last ten years of his life as a recluse in the Orkneys, and she had no children, she was probably glad to return to Edinburgh society. Sir William Hamilton (1788–1856) studied medicine in Edinburgh, got a first in classics at Oxford, and then returned to Edinburgh to become an Advocate; in 1821 he became Professor of Modern History: according to the *D.N.B.* his salary was £100 a year, 'payable from a local duty on beer, and after a time not paid at all...When his pay ceased he gave up lecturing.' In 1826 he was reading papers on phrenology to the Royal Society of Edinburgh; he began to make his name as a philosopher in 1829, with articles in the *Edinburgh Review*, and in 1836 became Professor of Logic and Metaphysics. Andrew Coventry (1764–1832) was Professor of Agriculture from 1790 to 1831. His annual salary was only £50, but he also made money by arbitrating on land questions and advising on drainage. Towards the end of his career he lectured in alternate years only, telling his students to go to chemistry and botany classes in the meantime.

On his return to Edinburgh at the end of his tour, Malthus writes 'Dr Gordon' as the sole entry for Sunday 16 July. This was probably Robert Gordon, D.D. (1786–1853), a very popular preacher who was also interested in science, which would have endeared him to Malthus: he wrote articles in the *Edinburgh Encyclopaedia* on 'Euclid', 'Geography', and 'Meteorology'. The next day Malthus met Captain Basil Hall (1788–1834) a naval officer who would have been at home in 1826 after marrying the daughter of the British Consul-General in Spain in 1825, and before setting out on a tour of North America in 1827; he had written interesting accounts of his naval engagements and travels all over the world. 'Mr Hall' might have been his elder brother John, who became the fifth baronet and a F.R.S., or his younger brother James, who was later well known as a patron of art and an amateur painter.

Perhaps the most interesting house Malthus visited was that of 'Mr Naismith'. It would certainly have been full of pictures, for Alexander Nasmyth (1758–1840), his son Patrick, and his six daughters were all artists; when he lost his aristocratic patrons on account of his Whig opinions, Alexander turned from portraits to landscapes, and scenery for plays. His son James, eighteen at the time, would have been responsible for the 'Models of Steam Engines' —one was actually used for grinding his father's colours; he became a famous engineer, the inventor of the steam-hammer and a number of machine-tools.

I cannot identify 'Mr Morehead' of Corstorphine, but he may have been a connection of Jeffrey's. According to the *D.N.B.*, Jeffrey's uncle, William Morehead, who died in 1793, turned him into a philosophical Whig; the uncle was a genial man, whereas Jeffrey's father, a high Tory, was 'of a gloomy temper'. The other people Malthus met in Scotland are described in notes with the text.

The accounts for the Scottish holiday cover the whole period from the Malthuses' departure from Haileybury to their return, although expenses on the journey northwards are not given in as much detail as those on the way home. They throw an interesting light on the cost and slowness of travel before the introduction of railways; when they were abroad, the previous year, the family had used what we would now call 'public transport', but on this tour they used their own carriage, hiring post-horses (and a boy to walk them back) as they went along.

The diary starts at Hollin, near Ripon, reached, as the accounts show, from Haileybury by way of Cambridge and Ockenbury Hill. The Malthuses stayed at Hollin for a short time both on the out-ward and homeward journeys; on the way back they stayed three nights and Malthus gave the servants six shillings. Colonel Wood had died in 1815, so the master and mistress of Hollin Hall were Harriet's brother-in-law and sister, who had been married at Claverton in 1810.[1] In 1826 their family would have consisted of a little girl of ten, and boys of nine, twelve, and fifteen; the eldest went to Manchester Grammar School before going up to Magdalene College, Cambridge.[2]

Hollin *June 17* [1826]
To Northallerton 20. m.
Darlington 16. m. dined. Rushyford 9. Durham 9. slept.

June 18 [Sunday]. Cathedral. Walks. College. Newcastle 15. m. dined. Morpeth 15.
Weldon Bridge 10. m. Brinksbourn Priory. River Coquet.— slept.

June 19. Whittingham 10. m. breakfasted. Cornhill. 12. m. crossed the Tweed Scotland Coldstream. Kelso.
Melrose. 16. Abbey moonlight, Eildon Hills. slept.

[1] See pp. 220–1.   [2] *Burke's Landed Gentry* (1952).

June 20 [Tuesday]. Torsonce 12. banks of Tweed. Gala water. Fusie Bridge. Edinburgh. Dinner. Mr L Horner.

June 21 [Wednesday]. Courts, Advocates Library.[1] Writer's Library.
College.[2] Musaeum.
Dinner Mr Murray and Mr Rutherforth.

June 22. Courts. Sir Walter Scott. Dinner Lord Alloway Mr Mackenzie. Mr. Cranstoun. Mr Cobourn evening

June 23. Ruthvens presses. Holyrood House Dinner Mr & Mrs Rutherforth. Mr Horner's in the evening. Calton Hill ½ past two next morning.[3]

June 24. Craig Crook.[4] Bowls. Dinner. Mr Cobourn. Mr Mackenzie. Mr Rutherforth. Count Flahaut. Mr Craig. Mr Murray.

June 25 Sunday. St Georges Church. Dinner Mr Maculloch.

June 26. Courts. Mr Wood. Sessional School. New Academy.[5] Dined at Lord Alloway's. Mrs Laing widow of the Historian. Sir Wm Hamilton. Lord Mackensie. Dr Coventry. Professor of Agriculture.

June 27. Visits. Courts. No company at Dinner.

June 28. To Anstruther. Mr & Mrs Bruce. Drive in Carriage. Mr & Mrs Smith. Dr Jackson.

---

[1] The Advocates' Library is now the National Library of Scotland.
[2] Malthus crossed out 'University' and wrote 'College' because Edinburgh University was founded in 1582 by the town council as 'the Town's College'; it became the College of King James when James VI became patron. The building designed by Robert Adam in 1789 was not completed until 1827.
[3] The erection of the National Monument on Calton Hill had been started four years before Malthus's visit, in 1822; it was intended to reproduce the Parthenon, to commemorate the Peninsular and Waterloo campaigns: the money ran out after twelve columns had been built, at a cost of £1,000 each.
[4] Craig Crook Castle, 'beautifully situated under Corstorphine Hill', belonged to Francis Jeffrey from 1815 until his death in 1850. When he took it over, it was 'an old keep with a disorderly kitchen-garden', which he delighted in improving (*D.N.B.*).
   For biographical notes, see the Introduction.
[5] The 'New Academy' was the Edinburgh Academy, founded in 1823 by Leonard Horner, Henry Cockburn, and other Whigs.

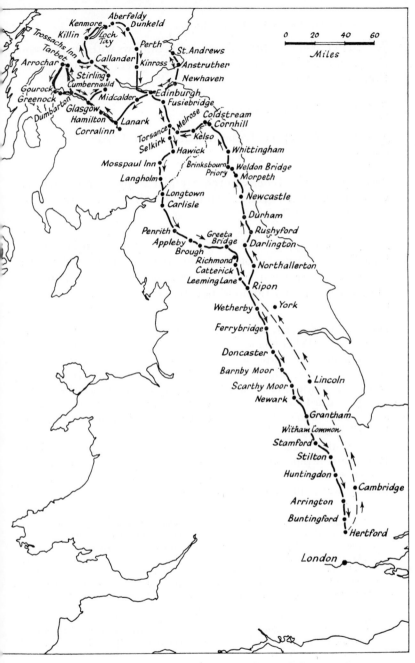

3 Sketch-map of the Scottish Holiday, 1826

17-2

June 29 [Thursday]. Breakfasted at St Andrews with Dr Jackson Dr. Chalmers.[1] Cathedral. Square Tower. Dinner. Mrs Douglas and Sister.

June 30. Returned to Edinburgh.

July 1 [Saturday] To Lanark. Falls of the Clyde Bonington. Corra Lynn.

July 2 [Sunday] Relief Church Mr M'Farlane. Mouse River. Cartland Craigs. Bridge. Hamilton. Glasgow. Drank tea with Mr & Mrs Brown.[2]

July 3 [Monday]. Set off at 9 in the George Canning Steam boat for Inverary. Stopped at Dumbarton on account of the weather. Dumbarton Castle. Luss. Boat in the evening to highest island. Ben Lomond not free from Clouds.

Dorothy Wordsworth wrote in September 1822 of the early Glasgow steam-boats: 'What a labouring of smoke in the harbour from many steam-boats! one, close to ours, taking in its cargo, and crew, chiefly mechanics and peasants. Women's white caps very lively, with a few scarlet shawls, among the grimly-attired men. We move swiftly forward carrying with us our own beating, rushing sound and black volume of smoke...Fast we glide away—heaving and labouring below—and smoking above.'

She made the same trip as the Malthus party, and found at Rob Roy's cave a piper in full Highland dress, boys selling nuts, and tourists scrambling through 'to say they have been there'.[3] Scott's *Rob Roy* was published in 1817.

---

[1] Dr Thomas Chalmers (1780–1847), a noted theologian, preacher, and philanthropist, was at this time Professor of Moral Philosophy in the University of St Andrews. As a minister in Glasgow he had been much concerned with 'home heathenism' and the degradation of pauperism; he was 'intensely attached to the old Scotch method of dealing with pauperism, not by assessment but voluntary contribution, believing that to give the poor a legal right to parochial relief was sure to destroy the spirit of independence, and to impair the readiness of children to help their parents in old age'. He wrote about his own highly organised system of parish relief in the *Edinburgh Review* (*D.N.B.*).

[2] Mr and Mrs Brown were probably Dr and Mrs Thomas Brown; Mrs Brown was Marion Jeffrey, the sister of Francis, who married her 'physician in Glasgow' in 1800. See pp. 262–3.

[3] *Journals*, ed. de Selincourt, II, 351–4.

July 4 [Tuesday]. Hill by Turnpike before breakfast. Small hill the other way after breakfast. Down to Stoney river and wooden bridge. View of Luss & Ben Lomond. Steam boat. Rowerdennan. Tarbet. Invernaith. Rob Roy's cave. Tarbet. Walk on a shoulder of one of the mountains in the evening.

Heard at Luss that the wages of the man who worked in the slate quarries were about 20*d.* a day. All had been employed, and there had been little or no fall.

In Fifeshire, from Mr Bruce the same account. Wages had risen in 1825, and had not fallen again—no want of agricultural work. In 1811, 12 and 13 the price of labour for single men had been 12*s.* a week. In 1823, they had fallen to 9*s.* and in 1825 rose to 10*s.* at which price they remained, June 30th 1826. For about 3 months of the year the wages are only 9*s.*; and during the harvest much is done by piece work.

Married men are paid by the keep of a cow, a house, potatoe & flax ground, with a certain yearly sum in money. At one period of the war unmarried ploughmen paid by the year received 18£, and 6½ bolls of meal with milk. In 1816 the money wages fell to 9£. At present. 12£. Altogether what the married men receive is worth more than the earnings of the single man. Their wages in money are about half those of the single man.

The boll of wheat is rather above 4 bushels, of barly six, of oats six.

Farms are now for the most part let in Scotland so as to vary with the price of corn. Sometimes the whole rent varies with the price of corn, and sometimes a part is reserved in Money.

The average produce is calculated according to the quality of the land and the rent is paid according to the price at the fiars.[1]

The average prices of corn at the Fiars from 1800 to 1821 were

	s	d
Wheat per boll	41.	6
Barley	32	¾
Oats	25.	¼.

[1] According to the *O.E.D.* 'fiar' is a Scots word for the owner of the fee-simple of a property, as opposed to the life-renter. This does not make sense in this context, and it seems likely that Malthus really meant fairs.

At present the price of wheat is about 30s. per boll. Lord Abercrombie's estate formerly let at 5£ per acre, that is during the high prices of the war.

At present a lease has been granted at a boll & a half of wheat, and a boll and a half of barley per acre scots.

1½ bolls of wheat at 30s.	£2.	5
1½ bolls of barley 6 bushels at 29.	2.	3
	4.	8
In 1825. Wheat.	1.	16
barley	1.	7
	3.	3

Great difference in the rent.[1]

July 5 [Wednesday].

Mountain behind Tarbet before breakfast. Cobler, Ben Inn.[2] To Arrochar. much superior to Tarbet. Fine trees round the Inn. Rain. Dinner. Walk in the evening by steep road from Tarbet to Head of Loch Long. Mountain's looking very high and picturesque, particularly the Cobler or Ben Arthur.

Malthus might well have found Arrochar superior, for according to Dorothy Wordsworth there was at Tarbet 'a villainous Inn, that for scolding and dirt, and litter and damp, surely cannot be surpassed through all Scotland...The Father has been lamed, the Mother is a whisky drinker...Two or three black, big-faced servant maids trail or slash about without caps...Ceilings fallen down—windows that endanger the fingers, and only to be kept open by props.'[3]

July 6. Walk before breakfast up the hill by Manse, rocky stream. Rain. Walk with party by Church and Manse and along the hill. Stations for sketching. Steam boat at ½ past 2. down Loch Long opening to Loch Goil Head. Mr and

[1] The next page is left blank.
[2] 'The Cobbler' is the popular name for Ben Arthur, 2,891 feet. Ben Ime is 3,318 feet high.
[3] *Journals*, ed. de Selincourt, II, 355–7.

Mrs Brown and daughters. Isle of Bute. Granite mountains of Arran. fine outline. Gourlock. Raising the comet Steam boat.[1] Rose Neath Helensburgh. Greenock. Port Glasgow. Dumbarton Castle. View of Ben Lomond. Erskine House. 100000£. Erskine Ferry. Campbell House.
Swimming boys. Glasgow.[2]

July 7 [Friday]. Ship Bank. New House. Garden Square. Number of new streets and elegant houses on the hill to the West. Exchange. Statue of King William. Trongate. High Street at right angles. College. Old, and new buildings. Cathedral. Pillar, John Knox. Dr Brown said that the introduction of Steam boating had quite altered the habits of the people of Glasgow, and given them strong locomotive propensities. This has been assisted by the Captains not charging for children, which has encouraged parents to take pleasure jaunts with all their family. Dr Brown's daughter of 12 years of age was not charged for.

The crash, and check to credit and confidence, much greater and of longer duration than was ever remembered. To Stirling by Combernald. To Callender in the evening. View back on Stirling Castle. Line of mountains to the West, Ben Ledi, Ben Venue & c: Heavy shower latter part of the way.

July 8 [Saturday].
To Trosachs Inn. Stuart. by Lake Vennachar. Turk Bridge, Loch Acray. Trosachs. Views of Ben Venue rising over them. The finest views of the lake from the Northern shore with Helens Island and a peninsular promontory in the middle distance. Much beautiful detail among the rocks and birches on the North side of the lake. The fine birches on Ben Venue were all cut by the Duke of Montrose about 8 years ago—a great loss. Dined on Helens Island and spent the greatest part of the day on the lake and its environs.[3] The rocky & woody

---

[1] The *Comet*, launched on the Clyde by Henry Bell in 1812, was the first practical passenger steamer in Europe.

[2] Dorothy Wordsworth described Glasgow in 1822: in spite of its 'quick walkers and busy streets, characteristic of a commercial town', it was 'finer than any town I have seen in England except Oxford' (*Journals*, ed. de Selincourt, II, 350).

[3] The lake here is Loch Katrine. Helen's Island is usually called Ellen's Isle, after Ellen Douglas, The Lady of the Lake. Scott's poem was published in 1810. In the accounts for Saturday 8 July there is the item 'Boatmen—3 shillings'.

accompaniments to Ben Venue render the views of it more picturesque and beautiful than perhaps any other *single* mountain we have seen.

Labour from 9 to 12 shillings a week The Crash at Glasgow has not affected the Trosachs. Mr Stuart greatly disapproves of the poor Laws and Tithes of England.

July 9 [Sunday].

To Callender to breakfast. Fine morning. Shadows on Ben Venue. View over Loch Acray. Callender. Fine view of Benledi from the Bridge. Gaelic preaching in a field adjoining to the Town. Sacrament in the kirk. Influx of people from all quarters; a few proper highland dresses. Church overflowing, and great numbers at the Gaelic sermon sitting on the grass round a pulpit near a grassy mount. Another pulpit in the same field was occupied subsequently by a preacher in English.

Brachlin Bridge.

Pass of Leni in the road to Loch Erne Head. Waterfall. Benlidi with fine accompaniments. Trosachy. Loch Lubnaig. Further end, where an Inn was projected, and given up when half built, very picturesque, much superior to Loch Earne Head. Rain. Dined and slept at Loch Earne Head.

July 10. To Killin to breakfast 8 m. Mountainous road, half ascent and half descent. View back to Benvoirlick, forward to Ben More. Came into the road from Dalmally and Tyndrum. Entrance to Killin very striking Rocky river rough bridges, Mill. MacNab's burying ground.[1] Ben Lawers. Mr & Mrs Kennedy.[2] Walk up the hill. Fine view of the lake. Lord

---

[1] The rocky river is the Dochart, and the MacNab burial ground is the lower of the two islands by the bridge. The hill was probably Stronachlachlan (1,708 feet) 'easily ascended in 1 hr.', whence 'the beauty of the surrounding country is well surveyed'.

[2] Mr and Mrs Kennedy were Thomas Francis (1788–1879) and his wife Sophia, whom he had married six years before; she was the only daughter of Sir Samuel Romilly, and her brother John (1802–74) married Otter's daughter Caroline in 1833. Thomas Kennedy was M.P. for the Ayr burghs from 1818 until he retired from politics in 1834, owing to 'financial embarrassment, due in great measure to his voluntary assumption of responsibility for his father's debts'. A strong Whig, Kennedy was concerned with the removal of religious disabilities, the extension of the franchise, the reform of the poor law, and the reduction of corn duties. He was also interested in sanitation, stock-breeding, and the application of science to agriculture on his Ayrshire estates.

Glenorchy's house. Ben Lawers. Boat to the halfway house towards Kenmore. Fine view back on the head of the lake and Ben More. Great complaints of the drought. The crops of oats and barley near Killin looking extremely ill. Wages in summer 1*s.* 6 – 20*d.* and 2*s.* but work not always to be had. Cottar system 2 acres of land, with keep for a cow. Rent with the house about 7 or 8£ a year. Sometimes the house is built by the tenant and no rent paid for the house for a certain term of years. Tasks for 13 or 15 yrs. Many houses without chimnies; thatched with fern. Killin a good specimen of a large highland village.

The small trades people generally rent two or three acres of land with pasture on the mountains for a cow or cows.

Dine on cold meat under a rock by the lake.

Barley and oats near the road on the side of Loch Tay after we joined the carriage looking better.

Slept at Kenmore, shared the large room with Mr & Mrs Kennedy for tea and breakfast next morning.

Landlord at Kenmore complained of the drought, the fall in the price of cattle, and the overpopulation of the country. Many small farms of 15 or 20£ a year, mountain pastures for their cattle. No great sheep farms. These prevail more to the Westward.

Dined at Aberfeldi. Falls of Moness. The labourers working at the quarries for the bridge which is building earn 20*d.*, & 22*d.* without victuals. The rent for two acres and a cottage generally 8£. the land apparently very indifferent.

Inn at Inver a mile from Dunkeld. Walk in the evening by the Tay.

July 12 [Wednesday]. Breakfasted at Dunkeld with Mr and Mrs Kennedy. Dunkeld Grounds.[1] Larches; Cathedral; Church; Walks by the River. American Garden.[2] Ferry. Hermitage. Ossian Fall.[3] Fine views from the hill going to

---

[1] The Grounds were those of Dunkeld House, then the seat of the Duke of Atholl. The cathedral is a ruin, desecrated in 1560, but the choir is used as the parish church.

[2] Could the American Garden be the precipitous slopes of Craigiebarns? On the advice of Alexander Nasmyth, the fourth Duke of Atholl had them planted with seeds which were fired at the hillside in canisters out of a small cannon.

[3] The Hermitage is still there, near the waterfall on the Bran, now National Trust property.

Hermitage. Much might be seen from Inver without a guide. Dined at Dunkeld with Mr & Mrs K. To Perth in the evening. Mr K informed me that in Ayrshire the labourers at present earn from 6 to 9 shillings a week; average hardly more than 7. without victuals. The price of labour much affected by the influx of the Irish. Town of Perth. Tay. Hill [an illegible word] of Square.

July 13 [Thursday]. To Kinross. View back on Perth. Crops much burnt.
River Earn. New Bridge. Mineral Waters.[1] Loch Leven. Kinross. N. Queens Ferry. Hill. view of Edinburgh & Frith of Forth. S. Queens Ferry. Hill. Western mountain's. Craigh Crook.

July 14 [Friday] Barley cut on the road to Edinburgh. Excellent cultivation. The farm next to Mr Jeffrey lets for a boll of wheat, a boll of barley, and £3. 15. an acre. seems to have suffered but very little from the drought.

July 15 [Saturday]. Courts. Heard an excellent speech from Mr Jefferey and a good reply from Mr Colbourn. Cause—a libel on Professor Alexander of St Andrew's Insubordination in the Greek class.

The case of the libel on Professor Alexander was reported at length in *The Scotsman* for Wednesday 19 July 1826. The professor was suing Alexander Macdonald, printer and publisher of the *Dundee, Perth and Cupar Advertiser* for £1,000 damages in respect of a report published on 24 March 1825; this stated: 'The Senior Greek Class is in a state of insubordination. The Professor appears to have lost all control over the students and to be in extreme perplexity.'

The Rectorial Dispute, which was the cause of the commotion, does not concern us, but Jeffrey's speech on behalf of Macdonald is of interest. He said he could prove that the students sang during the class ('Auld Lang Syne' and 'Highland Laddie') and that the Professor shed tears and threatened to resign his Chair, but this did not mean that he was unfit for his duties. He was surprised,

---

[1] The mineral wells of Pitkeathly (or Pitcaithly) are about a mile to the west of Bridge of Earn.

Jeffrey continued, that the Professor should stoop to ask damages for a 'paltry incidental paragraph in a provincial newspaper': Dugald Stewart and John Millar never did that sort of thing, and 'it would be long ere they heard of the great Malthus, a man with whom Professor Alexander never could be compared, seeking reparation in damages for the innumerable and gross attacks made upon him for want of religion and other ridiculous charges'.

Cockburn's speech on Professor Alexander's behalf was concerned with the effect the report would have on the Professor's reputation; the class consisted of very young lads, and parents would not wish to entrust their children to someone who could not keep order. This seems to have swayed the jury, for after fifty minutes they found unanimously in favour of the Professor, but he only got £50 damages.

The Scotsman reported that 'Professor Malthus and his family were in court during the whole trial'.

July 16 [Sunday]. Dr Gordon.

July 17. Captain B. Hall. Mr Hall.
Arthur's Seat. Mrs Trotter, Upholsterer. Provost of Edinburgh. Tables. Cabinets. Curious Elm.
Calton Hill Camera Obscura.
Mr Naismith Pictures. Models of Steam Engines. Lectern. Invention for securing the safety of High Pressure Engine.

July 18. Village of Costolphen.
Mr Morehead.

July 19. Waterloo Hotel. Castle. Grass Market. Leith. Newhaven

July 20. To Selkirk—Valley and banks of the Tweed. Crossed both Tweed and Ettrick.

July 21. To Penrith
Source of the Teviot between Hawick and Mospaul Inn. Another stream running the opposite way from the same source joins the Esk. Green mountains. Not burnt. To Langholm— same kind of country chiefly. From Langholm to Long Town. Vale of the Esk.

July 17
   Durham. Walks by the river near the Cathedral. Fine views from the bridge, and the other side. Fine stone. parts repaired.

18th. Cathedral service. To Newcastle. Main street large and broad. Fine valley. To Morpeth. Weldon Bridge. Brinkbourn Priory on the river Coquet.
   July 19. Whittingham. Cornhill. Cross the Tweed. Coldstream 1st Scoth Town. good pretty country to Kelso. To Melrose by the Tweed. Eildon Hills in the distance.[1]

---

[1] This page, which has been crossed out with four vertical strokes, was obviously written by mistake on the third opening of the section of the notebook devoted to the accounts of the Scottish Tour. On the facing page is written *July 3* followed by an ornate capital *R* and the figures *32.14.0.*

CASH ACCOUNT

EXPENSES

Haileybury *June 12* [1826]	52	2	0	Journey to Cambridge		
June 17 from Mrs M.	10	0	0	Ockenbury Hill & Ripon	7	3	6
July 1 from Sir Wm Forbes.	20	0	0	Journey to Edinburgh	22	2	0
				Expenses in Edinburgh		
	82	2	0	Road book & c:	2	10	0
	40	6	6	*June 28* to Newhaven		
				Coach & Toll		8	6
	41	15	6	Passage to Anstruther	0	18	0
				Boats embarking & landing	0	4	0
				Breakfasts—	0	6	0
				Sts* at Grange Muir	0	10	0
				Return	1	9	0
				Fergus bills & c:	1	10	0
				July 1. Hal	3	0	0
				Black Handkerf:		5	6
					40	6	6

* Malthus's abbreviation for 'servants'.

July 1 [Saturday]

Remainder	£41	15	6	To Mid Calder 12 miles.	0 18 0
	9	1	0	Boy & Turpikes	0 5 0
				To Lanark 20 miles	1 10 0
	32	14	6	Boy & Turnpikes	0 10 0
				Falls of the Clyde	0 2 0
				Bilat Inn & c:	1 12 0
				Ju^y 2nd. Church	1 0
				Mouse & bridge	1 6
				To Hamilton 16 miles	1 4 0
				Boy & Turnpikes (5s.)	8 6
				To Glasgow 11 miles	15 6
				Boy & Turnpikes	5 0
				3 July. Bag	11 0
				Soap. pills & paper	2 6
				Noddy to Steam boat.	2 6
				Passage to Dumbarton	8 0
				Landing	2 6
				Castle	2 0
					9 1 0

July 3 [Monday]

R.	32	14	6	To Luss from Dumbarton	
	8	15		13 miles	0 19 6
				Turnpikes & boy	0 5 6
On returning to Glasgow	23	19	6	Boat	5 6
July 6 [Thursday]				*4th* Bill at Luss & c:	1 16 0
				Steam boat & landing ⎫	0 15 0
				Tarbet ⎭	
				5. Bill at Tarbet & servts.	1 7 0
				Cart and boy to Arrochar.	0 3 0
				Bathing	0 1 0
				Bill at Arrochar & Sts.	1 12 6
				Steam boat to Glasgow	
				by Loch Long	1 0 0
				Noddy to Inn.	2 6
				Dinner on board.	7 6
					8 15 0

Remr. July 6 [Thursday]	£23	19	6		Bill at George. Glasgow	£ 3	8	6
7th Draft on Hoare					Mrs M.	1	0	0
at Glasgow	25	0	0		Washing		5	8
	———				Strawberries		1	0
	48	19	6		Waiter & Chamberd		9	0
	10	18	2		Hostler. Carriage. Porter		6	0
	———				Stamp for draft.		2	0
	38	1	4		Horses to Combernald. 14 m.	1	1	0
					Turnpikes & driver	0	5	0
					Horses to Stirling 3. m.		19	6
					Turnpikes & driver		6	0
					Dinner at Stirling & Waiter		12	6
					Turnpikes to Callendar		1	10
					Turnpike to Loch Katherine		2	0
					Boatmen.		3	0
					9th. Bill at Trosachs Inn	1	10	8
					Sts.		4	6
						———		
						10	18	2

Remainder July 8 [Saturday].	38	1	4		July 9. Bill at Callendar	0	19	0
	7	5	2		Sts	0	5	0
	———				Brachlin Bridge	0	1	0
	30	16	2		Turnpike	0	2	0
					10 Bill at Loch Erne Head ⎫ and Sts. dinner tea & beds ⎰	1	6	0
					Bill at Killin & Sts. ⎫ Tea beds lunch boat. ⎰	1	10	0
					Turnpike	0	2	0
					11 Bill at Kenmore ⎫ Tea beds Breakfast. ⎰	0	17	8
					Waiter Chambermaid. & c:	0	5	6
					Dinner at Aberfeldi & c:	0	12	0
					Guide to falls of Moness		1	6
					Turnpikes.		3	0
					Post boy in advance	1	0	0
					G.		1	0
						———		
						7	5	2*

* The total here should be £7. 5s. 8d.

July 11 [Tuesday]. R.	30	16	4	*12th.* Bill at Inver & sts.	0	11	6
July 18 [Tuesday]	20	17	2	(Tea and beds).			
	———			Guide & ferry	.	6	0
	9	19	2	Bridges & Turnpikes	0	5	8
				Bill at Dunkeld. Sts. ⎫			
				Breakfast & dinner ⎭	1	3	6
				Postboy in advance	1	0	0
				13th Bill at Perth & Sts.			
				Tea beds breakfast	1	6	0
				Job horses for 7 days.			
				at £1 12	11	4	0
				Driver at 5s. £1. 15			
				Return Turnpikes. 2s. 6.	.	.	.
				Paid in advance 2£			
				Post Horses from Kinross			
				to Queens Ferry	1	4	0
				Turnpikes & driver	0	6	0
				From Queens ferry to Edinburgh	0	15	0
				Turnpikes & driver	0	6	0
				Dinner at Ferry & Sts	0	10	0
				Ferry.			
				(carriage 6. 6) &c: Persons 6d.		9	6
				Edinburgh Carriages & c:			
				to *July 18.*	1	10	0
					———		
					20	17	2

July 18 [Tuesday].	9	19	2	*July 18* Hal.	2	2	0
19th from Ed. B.	40	0	0	Repaid	0	5	0
	———			*19* Coachmaker	0	6	0
	49	19	2	Tailor		2	6
	13	15	0	George Street		3	6
	———			Coaches: Newhaven.		4	0
	36	4	2	Peggy.		10	0
				Fergus's bills washing & c:	1	0	0
				G.	1	0	0
				Standing & washing Carriage		16	6
				20 To Fusey B from Craig Crook			
				with tolls & boy 16 miles.	1	9	6
				To Torsonce 14 m.	1	6	0
				To Selkirk 14 m.	1	7	0
				21. Bill at Selkirk & sts			
				tea and beds	0	15	0
				To Hawick. 12 m.	0	18	0
				Boy & Tolls.	0	5	0
				To Mosspaul Inn 13 m & c:	1	5	0
					———		
					13	15	0

July 21 [Friday]	36	4	2		To Langholm 10. m. & c:	0	19	6
	15	12	6		To Long Town 12 m & c	1	4	0
	—	—	—		To Carlisle 9. m. & c.		17	6
	20	11	8		Breakfast at Hawick.		9	0
					Dinner at Carlisle	0	13	0
					To Penrith. 18 m.	1	7	0
					Boy & Turnpikes	0	6	0
					Mrs M.	0	2	6
					22. Bill at Penrith. & c:	.	18	6
					To Appleby 14 m.	1	6	6
					To Brough 8 m.	0	16	0
					Breakfast	0	9	0
					To Greeta Bridge 19 m.			
					4 horses for 7 miles	2	7	6
					Dinner		7	6
					To Catterick B. 14 m.	1	6	6
					To Leeming Lane. 11 m.	1	1	0
					To Hollin 12. m.	1	1	6
						15	12	6

July 23 [Sunday]	£20	11	8		July 25 Sts Hollin	.	6	0
	16	7	0		To Wetherby 17.m.			
	—	—	—		15d [per] m. Boy & turnpikes	1	7	6
	4	4	8		Breakfast	0	9	0
					To Ferry Bridge 17. m.			
					1s. 6d [per] m. & c:	1	12	0
					To Doncaster 15 m.	1	7	0
					To Barnby Moor. 14 m.	1	6	0
					Dinner	0	12	6
					To Scarthy Moor 13 m.	1	4	0
					To Newark 11. m.	1	0	6
					To Grantham 14.	1	6	0
					Tea sleeping & c	0	18	6
					To Witham Common 10.	0	19	0
					To Stamford 11. boy & Turn-pikes	1	0	0
					Breakfast	0	9	0
					To Stilton 15	1	7	6
					Huntingdon.	1	2	6
						16	7	0

July 26. R.	4	4	8		July 26 To Arrington 15.^{m}	1	7	6
	4	7	8		Dinner & maid	0	19	0
	—	—	—		Buntingford 12^m	1	4	8
Borrowed James 3s					Haileybury 14	1	6	6
						4	7	8*

* The total here should be £4. 17s. 8d., so Malthus ought to have needed 13s. from James. Perhaps 'Dinner & maid' at Arrington were only 9s. and not 19s. (Dinner at Barnby Moor was 12s. 6d., and at Greeta Bridge only 7s. 6d.)

Appendices

Appendix 1

The chapter on Norway in the *Essay on the Principle of Population* ('sixth edition',[1] that is, the fifth version of the second edition of the *Essay*, with Malthus's own footnotes) is here reprinted in parallel with the relevant source passages of the Scandinavian Journal.

The *Essay* chapter is printed continuously on the left-hand page; the Journal passages, with added references and notes, are opposite.

OF THE CHECKS TO POPULATION
IN NORWAY

In reviewing the states of modern Europe, we shall be assisted in our inquiries by registers of births, deaths and marriages, which, when they are complete and correct, point out to us with some degree of precision whether the prevailing checks to population are of the positive or preventive kind. The habits of most European nations are of course much alike, owing to the similarity of the circumstances in which they are placed; and it is to be expected therefore that their registers should sometimes give the same results. Relying however too much upon this occasional coincidence, political calculators have been led into the error of supposing that there is, generally speaking, an invariable order of mortality in all countries: but it appears, on the contrary, that this order is extremely variable; that it is very different in different places of the same country, and within certain limits depends upon circumstances, which it is in the power of man to alter.

Norway, during nearly the whole of the last century, was in a peculiar degree exempt from the drains of people by war. The climate is remarkably free from epidemic sicknesses; and, in common years, the mortality is less than in any other country in

---

[1] London, 1826.

274

Students of Malthus will know that by preventive checks to population he meant either prudently delayed marriage, of which he approved, although 'it must be allowed to produce a certain degree of temporary unhappiness', or vice—of which, of course, he did not. Positive checks to population were such as prematurely destroyed those already born; under this head he included 'all unwholesome occupations, severe labour and exposure to the seasons, extreme poverty, bad nursing of children, great towns, excesses of all kinds, the whole train of common diseases and epidemics, wars, plague, and famine'.

Frederik Thaarup, modern readers will note with amusement, is here quoted as an authority. Apart from Clarke, few people would have known that 'he was a very good sort of man; but did not quite answer our expectations as a professor' (p. 210). Malthus had bought Thaarup's work in Copenhagen (p. 208); this was probably when he discovered that there 'Every thing in the shops is remarkably dear, & books particularly so' (p. 62). He must have studied Thaarup's statistics *en route* for Norway or he could not have written, as soon as he reached Fredrikshald, of the Norwegian population 'increasing so slowly, tho the people live so long' (p. 89).

Europe, the registers of which are known to be correct.[1] The proportion of the annual deaths to the whole population, on an average throughout the whole country, is only as 1 to 48.[2] Yet the population of Norway never seems to have increased with great rapidity. It has made a start within the last ten or fifteen years; but till that period its progress must have been very slow, as we know that the country was peopled in very early ages, and in 1769 its population was only 723,141.[3]

Before we enter upon an examination of its internal economy, we must feel assured that, as the positive checks to its population have been so small, the preventive checks must have been proportionably great; and we accordingly find from the registers that the proportion of yearly marriages to the whole population is as 1 to 130,[4] which is a smaller proportion of marriages than appears in the registers of any other country, except Switzerland.

One cause of this small number of marriages is the mode in which the enrolments for the army have been conducted till within a very few years. Every man in Denmark and Norway born of a farmer or labourer is a soldier.[5] Formerly the commanding officer of the district might take these peasants at any age he pleased; and he in general preferred those that were from twenty-five to thirty, to such as were younger. After being taken into the service, a man could not marry without producing a certificate, signed by the minister of the parish, that he had

---

[1] The registers for Russia give a smaller mortality; but it is supposed that they are defective. It appears, however, that in England and Wales during the ten years ending with 1820, the mortality was still less than in Norway.

[2] Thaarup's *Statistik der Danischen Monarchie*, vol. II, p. 4.

[3] *Id.* Table ii, p. 5.

[4] Thaarup's *Statistik der Danischen Monarchie*, vol. II, p. 4. The proportion of yearly marriages to the whole population is one of the most obvious criterions of the operation of the preventive check, though not quite a correct one. Generally speaking, the preventive check is greater than might be inferred from this criterion; because in the healthy countries of Europe, where a small proportion of marriages takes place, the greater number of old people living at the time of these marriages will be more than counterbalanced by the smaller proportion of persons under the age of puberty. In such a country as Norway, the persons from 20 to 50, that is, of the most likely age to marry, bear a greater proportion to the whole population than in most of the other countries of Europe; and consequently the actual proportion of marriages in Norway, compared with that of others, will not express the full extent in which the preventive check operates.

[5] The few particulars, which I shall mention relating to Norway, were collected during a summer excursion in that country in the year 1799.

Malthus uses almost verbatim the entry in his journals giving the information he obtained from General Mansbach and Mr Niels Anker (p. 89): 'Every man in Denmark & Norway born of a farmer or labourer is a soldier. Those born of sailors are sailors. Formerly the officer of the district might take them at any age he pleased and he generally preferred a man from 25 to 30 to those that were younger. After being taken the man could not marry without producing a certificate signed by the minister of the parish that he had substance enough to support a wife & family, & even then it was at the will of the officer to let him marry or not. This, & the uncertainty in respect to the time of being taken has hitherto operated as a strong preventive check to population in Norway, & accounts for their increasing so slowly, tho the people live so long. No man could consider himself as perfectly free to marry, unless he had solid possessions, till he had served his time which, from their being taken sometimes at thirty, might not happen till he was 40 years old.'

substance enough to support a wife and family; and even then it was further necessary for him to obtain the permission of the officer. The difficulty, and sometimes the expense, of obtaining this certificate and permission, generally deterred those who were not in very good circumstances, from thinking of marriage till their service of ten years was expired; and as they might be enrolled at any age under thirty-six, and the officers were apt to take the oldest first, it would often be late in life before they could feel themselves at liberty to settle.

Though the minister of the parish had no legal power to prevent a man from marrying who was not enrolled for service, yet it appears that custom had in some degree sanctioned a discretionary power of this kind, and the priest often refused to join a couple together when the parties had no probable means of supporting a family.

Every obstacle, however, of this nature, whether arising from law or custom, has now been entirely removed. A full liberty is given to marry at any age, without leave either of the officer or priest; and in the enrolments for the army all those of the age of twenty are taken first, then all those of twenty-two, and so on till the necessary number is completed.

The officers in general disapprove of this change. They say that a young Norwegian has not arrived at his full strength and does not make a good soldier at twenty. And many are of opinion that the peasants will now marry too young, and that more children will be born than the country can support.

But, independently of any regulations respecting the military enrolments, the peculiar state of Norway throws very strong obstacles in the way of early marriages. There are no large manufacturing towns to take off the overflowing population of the country; and as each village naturally furnishes from itself a supply of hands more than equal to the demand, a change of place in search of work seldom promises any success. Unless therefore an opportunity of foreign emigration offer, the Norwegian peasant generally remains in the village in which he was born; and as the vacancies in houses and employments must occur very slowly, owing to the small mortality that takes place, he will often see himself compelled to wait a considerable time, before he can attain a situation, which will enable him to rear a family.

Detailed information about the certificate of permission to marry was obtained at Trondheim, from the sensible and intelligent man whom Malthus met in a kind of wilderness in Count Schmettau's garden, drinking coffee and tea with a large party of ladies (p. 173). 'Those who were enrolled to serve, found it so difficult and expensive to get married, on account of the permission necessary from the priest & officers, which was not always obtained without douceurs, that they scarcely ever thought of it before their service was expired.' 'Formerly the priest had the power of refusing to marry a couple who could not shew that they could support a family, even tho the man was not enrolled in the army.'

At this point Malthus would have turned back in his diary to Fredrikshald and General Mansbach (pp. 90–1). 'These laws however are just now at an end. The liberty of marriage is allowed without any certificate, or permission of the officer, & all the young men of 20 are taken first, & if that is not enough all of 22, & so on, & it is no longer in the breast of the officer to chuse the men at what age he likes. Formerly any person under 36 might be taken; & the oldest were generally taken first... The General disapproved of the new regulation, & said that the peasants would probably now marry without any prospect of being able to maintain a family, & that the consequence would be that more would be born than the country could support...He thought that 20, tho it might suit very well France, was too young for a Norwegian, as the northern peasant was much later in attaining maturity.'

Colonel Bielefeldt, in Christiania, agreed with General Mansbach: 'He thought that very young men did not make good soldiers, & he had besides apprehensions that they would all be tempted now to marry so early, that they would not be able to provide for their families, & the country be much more distressed than formerly' (p. 103).

The Norway farms have in general a certain number of married labourers employed upon them, in proportion to their size, who are called house-men. They receive from the farmer a house, and a quantity of land nearly sufficient to maintain a family; in return for which they are under the obligation of working for him at a low and fixed price, whenever they are called upon. Except in the immediate neighbourhood of the towns, and on the sea-coast, the vacancy of a place of this kind is the only prospect which presents itself of providing for a family. From the small number of people, and the little variety of employment, the subject is brought distinctly within the view of each individual; and he must feel the absolute necessity of repressing his inclinations to marriage, till some such vacancy offer. If, from the plenty of materials, he should be led to build a house for himself, it could not be expected, that the farmer, if he had a sufficient number of labourers before, should give him an adequate portion of land with it; and though he would in general find employment for three or four months in the summer, yet there would be little chance of his earning enough to support a family during the whole year. It is probable, that it was in cases of this kind, where the impatience of the parties prompted them to build, or propose to build a house themselves, and trust to what they could earn, that the parish priests exercised the discretionary power of refusing to marry.

The young men and women therefore are obliged to remain with the farmers as unmarried servants, till a houseman's place becomes vacant: and of these unmarried servants there is in every farm and every gentleman's family, a much greater proportion, than the work would seem to require. There is but little division of labour in Norway. Almost all the wants of domestic economy are supplied in each separate household. Not only the common operations of brewing, baking, and washing, are carried on at home, but many families make or import their own cheese and butter, kill their own beef and mutton, import their own grocery stores; and the farmers and country people in general spin their own flax and wool, and weave their own linen and woollen clothes. In the largest towns, such as Christiania and Drontheim, there is nothing that can be called a market. It is extremely difficult to get a joint of fresh meat; and a pound of fresh butter is an article not

The 'gentleman who had been at school in England', whom Malthus met at the inn at Wennersburg, had told him about housemen in Sweden (p. 80) but the actual word is not used in the journals until the useful conversation with Mrs Collett in Bernt Anker's garden (p. 117). Malthus's three main sources of information about housemen were the farmer who owned the horses at 'Mosthuus' (pp. 128–9), the landlord of the inn at Elstad (pp. 132–3) and the man who came with the horses on the way to Tofte (p. 137); in each of these cases he must have used 'our servant' as interpreter.

The first insight Malthus had into the difficulties of Norwegian housekeeping came from 23-year-old Mrs Niels Anker (p. 89): she told him that 'baking, brewing & every thing must be done at home, which required rather a large household of servants, particularly as the servants were rather proud, & would not turn their hands to different sorts of work'. At Christiania he learned from Bernt Anker that 'it was absolutely necessary for a man to have every thing within himself in Norway; for that scarcely any thing could be bought. Those who live handsomely in this country must collect a store themselves from all parts of the world, for the whole year...He keeps thirty servants & told us that his brother kept 60' (p. 99).

Malthus saw a girl weaving in a cottage at Elstad (p. 134) and towards the end of his journey to Trondheim he wrote, 'Wollen caps instead of hats are universal...imported, we understand, from Copenhagen. Almost every other part of the dress of the peasants is made by them selves' (p. 145).

With regard to the difficulty of buying fresh meat, Malthus would have remembered 'The master of the Inn told us that if he would give any money, he could not buy a bit of meat in Roraas' (p. 180), and the landlord at Tynset who gave them 'a piece of cold lamb & of veal' (p. 198). He noticed himself 'There is not a pound of fresh butter to be bought at Christiania. All persons use what they make themselves or salt it for keeping' (p. 118).

to be purchased, even in the midst of summer. Fairs are held at certain seasons of the year, and stores of all kinds of provisions that will keep are laid in at these times; and, if this care be neglected, great inconveniences are suffered, as scarcely any thing is to be bought retail. Persons who make a temporary residence in the country, or small merchants not possessed of farms, complain heavily of this inconvenience; and the wives of merchants, who have large estates, say, that the domestic economy of a Norway family is so extensive and complicated, that the necessary superintendence of it requires their whole attention, and that they can find no time for anything else.

It is evident, that a system of this kind must require a great number of servants. It is said besides, that they are not remarkable for diligence, and that to do the same quantity of work more are necessary than in other countries. The consequence is, that in every establishment the proportion of servants will be found two or three times as great as in England; and a farmer in the country, who in his appearance is not to be distinguished from any of his labourers, will sometimes have a household of twenty persons, including his own family.

The means of maintenance to a single man are, therefore, much less confined than to a married man; and under such circumstances the lower classes of people cannot increase much, till the increase of mercantile stock, or the division and improvement of farms, furnishes a greater quantity of employment for married labourers. In countries more fully peopled this subject is always involved in great obscurity. Each man naturally thinks, that he has as good a chance of finding employment as his neighbour; and that, if he fail in one place, he shall succeed in some other. He marries, therefore, and trusts to fortune; and the effect too frequently is, that redundant population occasioned in this manner is repressed by the positive checks of poverty and disease. In Norway the subject is not involved in the same obscurity. The number of additional families, which the increasing demand for labour will support, is more distinctly marked. The population is so small, that even in the towns it is difficult to fall into any considerable error on this subject; and in the country the division and improvement of an estate, and the creation of a greater number of housemen's places, must be a matter of complete notoriety. If a man can

The English wife of a Christiania merchant, whom Malthus calls Mrs Clareson (p. 121) must have inspired part of his account of Norwegian domestic economy. This poor lady 'expatiated much on the inconveniences which persons of moderate fortunes were subject to, from not being able to lay in those stores which Mr Ancher spoke of. She said that nothing was to be bought, if you had ever so much money; & that she was really sometimes ready to cry with vexation' (p. 103). It was Mrs Collett, 'reckoned a pattern to all the wives in Norway' (p. 102), who told Malthus 'that the housekeeping in Norway from its peculiar nature, & the largeness of the establishments necessary, took up so much time, that the ladies had not leisure for many other employments after marriage' (pp. 119–20).

On page 142 of the journal Malthus wrote: 'In the kitchen at Drivthuen we saw seven men eating a most comfortable breakfast...We enquired of the master of the house afterwards whether they were all his men—he said they were, and lived in his house, besides others. He had, he said, 20 altogether in family, tho he had but little ground round the house, but a farm higher up the country. None of the men that lived with him were married...The appearance of the master was quite that of a common peasant. The establishments of the farmers in this country appear to be much larger than with us, and it is probable that the sons of housemen & small farmers become the servants of farmers, and do not marry till they are able to obtain a houseman's place.'

This matter was obviously discussed at Mrs Lysholm's dinner-party on the first day in Trondheim, with Count Moltke and 'some other gentlemen', as Malthus notes in the course of the entry for 14 July: 'The sons of housemen & small farmers generally go out to service, either in farms or with gentlemen, till they can get a houseman's place, which may enable them to marry. The Farmers sometimes, as we saw in our journey, have many unmarried servants' (p. 155).

obtain one of these places, he marries, and is able to support a family; if he cannot obtain one, he remains single. A redundant population is thus prevented from taking place, instead of being destroyed after it has taken place.

It is not to be doubted, that the general prevalence of the preventive check to population, owing to the state of society which has been described, together with the obstacles thrown in the way of early marriages from the enrolments for the army, have powerfully contributed to place the lower classes of people in Norway in a better situation, than could be expected from the nature of the soil and climate. On the sea-coast, where, on account of the hopes of an adequate supply of food from fishing, the preventive check does not prevail in the same degree, the people are very poor and wretched; and, beyond comparison, in a worse state than the peasants in the interior of the country.

The greatest part of the soil in Norway is absolutely incapable of bearing corn, and the climate is subject to the most sudden and fatal changes. There are three nights about the end of August, which are particularly distinguished by the name of iron nights, on account of their sometimes blasting the promise of the fairest crops. On these occasions the lower classes of people necessarily suffer; but as there are scarcely any independent labourers, except the housemen that have been mentioned, who all keep cattle, the hardship of being obliged to mix the inner bark of the pine with their bread is mitigated by the stores of cheese, of salt butter, of salt meat, salt fish, and bacon, which they are generally enabled to lay up for the winter provision. The period in which the want of corn presses the most severely is generally about two months before harvest; and at this time the cows, of which the poorest housemen have generally two or three, and many five or six, begin to give milk, which must be a great assistance to the family, particularly to the younger part of it. In the summer of the year 1799, the Norwegians appeared to wear a face of plenty and content while their neighbours the Swedes were absolutely starving; and I particularly remarked, that the sons of housemen and the farmers' boys were fatter, larger, and had better calves to their legs, than boys of the same age and in similar situations in England.

It was also at Mrs Lysholm's party that Malthus heard that 'The people on the sea coast are the poorest & suffer the most. They in general marry very young & have large families which they hope to support by fishing, and in a bad year when the fisheries are unsuccessful they are reduced to extreme poverty. The people in the interior parts of the country seldom marry till they can get a place in which they can support a family' (p. 153).

On the same occasion Malthus gleaned some information about the climate: 'There are 3 nights at the end of august & beginning of september that are particularly dreaded, & I think he [Count Moltke] said were call'd the iron nights. These sometimes destroy at once the fairest promise' (pp. 152–3). He did not hear about the bark bread until he was staying on the Swedish border with 'Mr Leeson' (pp. 217–18). On this memorable shooting party he also supplemented the detailed information he had collected on his way up the Gudbrandsdal about the size of housemen's holdings and the actual number of horses and cattle they kept (p. 214). For the concluding sentence on page 284, Malthus went back in his diary to the journey along the Österdal (p. 202): 'The Norwegians in general have appeared to us as if they were well fed. The women have plump round faces; & most of the boys who have been with us to take back the horses have been very good looking lads, & stouter & with better calves to their legs than those of the same age in England.' This is a point to which Malthus obviously attached importance: on p. 73 of the 1798 edition of the *Essay on the Principle of Population* he wrote that in England 'The lads who drive plough, which must certainly be a healthy exercise, are very rarely seen with any appearance of calves to their legs; a circumstance which can only be attributed to want either of proper, or of sufficient nourishment.'

It is also without doubt owing to the prevalence of the preventive check to population, as much as to any peculiar
healthiness of the air, that the mortality in Norway is so small.
There is nothing in the climate or the soil, that would lead to
the supposition of its being in any extraordinary manner
favourable to the general health of the inhabitants; but as in
every country the principal mortality takes place among very
young children, the smaller number of these in Norway, in
proportion to the whole population, will naturally occasion a
smaller mortality than in other countries, supposing the climate
to be equally healthy.

It may be said, perhaps, and with truth, that one of the
principal reasons of the small mortality in Norway is, that the
towns are inconsiderable and few, and that few people are
employed in unwholesome manufactories. In many of the
agricultural villages of other countries, where the preventive
check to population does not prevail in the same degree, the
mortality is as small as in Norway. But it should be recollected,
that the calculation in this case is for those particular villages
alone; whereas in Norway the calculation of one in forty-eight
is for the whole country. The redundant population of these
villages is disposed of by constant emigrations to the towns, and
the deaths of a great part of those that are born in the parish do
not appear in the registers. But in Norway all the deaths are
within the calculation, and it is clear, that, if more were born
than the country could support, a great mortality must take
place in some form or other. If the people were not destroyed
by disease, they would be destroyed by famine. It is indeed
well known, that bad and insufficient food will produce disease
and death in the purest air and the finest climate. Supposing
therefore no great foreign emigration, and no extraordinary
increase in the resources of the country, nothing but the more
extensive prevalence of the preventive check to population in
Norway can secure to her a smaller mortality than in other
countries, however pure her air may be, or however healthy
the employments of her people.

Norway seems to have been anciently divided into large
estates or farms, called Gores; and as, according to the law of
succession, all the brothers divide the property equally, it is a
matter of surprise, and a proof how slowly the population has

Gore, as we have seen, is Malthus's version of *Gaard*, a word which he picked up from Mr Leeson (p. 214). A farmer who provided horses in the Gudbrandsdal (pp. 128–9) was his first informant about inheritance and the division of farms, and he learned more at Mrs Lysholm's first party (pp. 154–5): 'The general law of Denmark & Norway with respect to succession is that the sons shall share equally, & have double the portion of the daughters. The reason that the farms in Norway have not been more divided is, that the population has increased very slowly till of late years; and that the eldest son has always the option of paying his brothers and sisters in money and reserving the estate, which he is generally able to do by mortgaging. Of late years however since the cultivation and population have been increasing it has been more the custom to divide the farm itself, which is the reason that we heard in our journey of many half farms & quarters of farms.'

The subject was further discussed with Count Moltke two days later (p. 157): 'With regard to the descent of property, he informed us that at present the father has a right to divide his property among his children as he pleases, during his life time, provided he leaves to his eldest son a part of the farm sufficient to enable him to bring up a family. If he does not, the son has a power of claiming his right by law. When a father dies without having disposed of his property, a kind of commission in the district meets, and values the farm at a very moderate price—the eldest son has the option of taking it at that price, and the sum is divided among the brothers & sisters—the sisters having half the portion of the brothers.'

hitherto increased, that these estates have not been more subdivided. Many of them are indeed now divided into half gores
and quarter gores, and some still lower; but it has in general
been the custom, on the death of the father, for a commission
to value the estate at a low rate, and if the eldest son can pay
his brothers' and sisters'[1] shares, according to this valuation, by
mortgaging his estate or otherwise, the whole is awarded to
him: and the force of habit and natural indolence too frequently
prompt him to conduct the farm after the manner of his fore-
fathers, with few or no efforts at improvement.

Another great obstacle to the improvement of farms in Norway is a law, which is called Odel's right, by which any lineal
descendant can repurchase an estate, which had been sold out
of the family, by paying the original purchase money. Formerly collateral as well as lineal descendants had this power,
and the time was absolutely unlimited, so that the purchaser
could never consider himself as secure from claims. Afterwards
the time was limited to twenty years, and in 1771, it was still
further limited to ten years, and all the collateral branches
were excluded. It must however be an uninterrupted possession
of ten years; for if, before the expiration of this term, a person
who has a right to claim under the law give notice to the
possessor, that he does not forego his claim, though he is not
then in a condition to make the purchase, the possessor is
obliged to wait six years more, before he is perfectly secure.
And as in addition to this the eldest in the lineal descent may
reclaim an estate, that had been repurchased by a younger
brother, the law, even in its present amended state, must be
considered as a very great bar to improvement; and in its
former state, when the time was unlimited and the sale of
estates in this way was more frequent, it seems as if it must have
been a most complete obstacle to the melioration of farms, and
obviously accounts for the very slow increase of population in
Norway for many centuries.

A further difficulty in the way of clearing and cultivating the
land arises from the fears of the great timber merchants respecting the woods. When a farm has been divided among children
and grandchildren, as each proprietor has a certain right in
the woods, each in general endeavours to cut as much as he

---

[1] A daughter's portion is the half of a son's portion.

288

Odels right was another important matter first mentioned at Mrs Lysholm's (p. 154) and elaborated later in a private talk with Count Moltke: 'At first there were absolutely no limits, & an estate might be claimed at any time by either the lineal or collaterel descendants. Afterwards the limit was 20 years, but the date of that limit the Count was not acquainted with. In 1771 the period was limited to ten years, and the collateral branches were all excluded. It must however be ten years of uninterrupted possession; for if before the expiration of the ten yrs a person who has a right to claim under the Odels law, gives notice to the possessor that he does not give up his right, tho he is not then in a condition to make the purchase, the possessor is obliged to wait 6 years more before he is perfectly secure. The eldest in the lineal descent may reclaim an estate that has been repurchased by a younger brother' (pp. 156–7).

The conflict between cultivation and forestry is not touched on until the 'very fortunate rencontre' with Mr Leeson. Writing of the continual splitting-up of farms (p. 214) Malthus notes: 'These divisions the timber merchants consider as very prejudicial to the woods; for the right in the woods being divided among the different children or grandchildren, each will endeavour to cut as much as he can, by which means the timber is cut before it is fit & the woods are spoilt. To prevent this, the Merchants such as Mr Anker Mr Rosencratz &c. buy large tracts of woods of the farmers; but by law, the farmer is obliged to reserve to himself the right of pasturing his cattle, & of cutting timber sufficient for his house repairs & firing. A contract however is in general made by the merchant, that the farm shall not be any further subdivided, or more housemen placed upon it; at least that if there are more families, they shall have no right in the woods. It is said that the merchants are not very strict on this point, provided the smaller farmers & housemen do not take timber for the houses. Wood for firing & fences is not regarded.

A piece of ground such as we saw to day round the housemen's dwellings cannot be taken in from the woods for cultivation, without an application first to the proprietor of the woods, declaring that the part is not fit for timber, & then a further application to the Sonescriver.'

can; and the timber is thus felled before it is fit, and the woods spoiled. To prevent this, the merchants buy large tracts of woods of the farmers, who enter into a contract, that the farm shall not be any further subdivided or more housemen placed upon it; at least that, if the number of families be increased, they should have no right in the woods. It is said, that the merchants who make these purchases are not very strict, provided the smaller farmers and housemen do not take timber for their houses. The farmers who sell these tracts of wood are obliged by law, to reserve to themselves the right of pasturing their cattle, and of cutting timber sufficient for their houses, repairs, and firing.

A piece of ground round a houseman's dwelling cannot be enclosed for cultivation, without an application, first, to the proprietors of the woods, declaring, that the spot is not fit for timber; and afterwards to a magistrate of the district, whose leave on this occasion is also necessary, probably for the purpose of ascertaining, whether the leave of the proprietor had been duly obtained.

In addition to these obstacles to improved cultivation, which may be considered as artificial, the nature of the country presents an insuperable obstacle to a cultivation and population in any respect proportioned to the surface of the soil. The Norwegians, though not in a nomadic state, are still in a considerable degree in the pastoral state, and depend very much upon their cattle. The high grounds that border on the mountains, are absolutely unfit to bear corn; and the only use, to which they can be put, is to pasture cattle upon them for three or four months during the summer. The farmers accordingly send all their cattle to these grounds at this time of the year, under the care of a part of their families; and it is here, that they make all their butter and cheese for sale, or for their own consumption. The great difficulty is to support their cattle during the long winter, and for this purpose it is necessary, that a considerable proportion of the most fertile land in the vallies should be mowed for hay. If too much of it were taken into tillage, the number of cattle must be proportionably diminished, and the greatest part of the higher grounds would become absolutely useless; and it might be a question in that case, whether the country upon the whole would support a greater population.

With regard to the *seters* or summer pastures, Malthus had first heard of them from Mrs Collett: 'The farmers who live higher up the country go for two months, from June to August, up into the mountains to pasture their cattle. The[y] live in little wooden sheds built at the time, & it is during these 2 months that they make the greatest part of their butter, which is salted, & brought to the fair at Christiania in the winter on sledges' (p. 118).

Malthus learned the word 'Saaters', and more accurate details of the system, from the landlord at Elstad (pp. 132–3) as well as from his own observation on his travels. He gives his readers here none of the picturesque touches, of the defences against bears and wolves, any more than he expatiates on the inconvenience of this arrangement to those who could not relish 'sower milk'.

Notwithstanding, however, all these obstacles, there is a very considerable capacity of improvement in Norway, and of late years it has been called into action. I heard it remarked by a professor at Copenhagen, that the reason why the agriculture of Norway had advanced so slowly was, that there were no gentlemen farmers to set examples of improved cultivation and break the routine of ignorance and prejudice in the conduct of farms, that had been handed down from father to son for successive ages. From what I saw of Norway I should say, that this want is now in some degree supplied. Many intelligent merchants, and well informed general officers, are at present engaged in farming. In the country round Christiania, very great improvements have taken place in the system of agriculture; and even in the neighbourhood of Drontheim the culture of artificial grasses has been introduced, which, in a country where so much winter feed is necessary for cattle, is a point of the highest importance. Almost every where the cultivation of potatoes has succeeded, and they are growing more and more into general use, though in the distant parts of the country they are not yet relished by the common people.

It has been more the custom of late years than formerly to divide farms; and as the vent for commodities in Norway is not perhaps sufficient to encourage the complete cultivation of large farms, this division of them has probably contributed to the improvement of the land. It seems indeed to be universally agreed, among those who are in a situation to be competent judges, that the agriculture of Norway in general has advanced considerably of late years; and the registers show, that the population has followed with more than equal pace. On an average of ten years, from 1775 to 1784, the proportion of births to deaths was 141 to 100.[1] But this seems to have been rather too rapid an increase; as the following year, 1785, was a year of scarcity and sickness, in which the deaths considerably exceeded the births; and for four years afterwards, particularly in 1789, the excess of births was not great. But in five years from 1789 to 1794, the proportion of births and deaths was nearly 150 to 100.[2]

[1] Thaarup's *Statistik der Danischen Monarchie*, vol. ii, p. 4.
[2] *Ibid.* table i, p. 4. In the *Tableau Statistique des Etats Danois*, since published, it appears that the whole number of births for the five years subsequent to 1794

The professor in Copenhagen was Peter Abildgaard of the Veterinary College, with whom Malthus had a long conversation in French; he 'spoke of the state of agriculture in Norway as very miserable, on account of the very few people of education that there are there. It is now however thought to be improving' (p. 60).

The intelligent merchants would include, of course, the Ankers: on p. 106 we learn that Peder Anker kept fifty cows for his own household, and on p. 103 that Bernt Anker killed a fat ox generally once a fortnight; Frogner was surrounded by 'some very fertile grass fields' (p. 99). John Collett, however, described as 'a great farmer', was one of the most important Norwegian improvers, and his methods are described in detail on p. 101. There were two well-informed officers who were also agriculturalists: General Mansbach of Fredrikshald was 'a cultivator as well as warrior, & farms himself a considerable quantity of land which belongs to the castle' (p. 87). The other was Count Schmettau of Trondheim, also 'a great farmer', who 'talked much of the prejudices he had had to encounter among the peasants; but hoped that now some of them were coming over to his opinions... He said his cows were fed in stalls for nearly 8 months in the year, and that it was the same almost all over Norway. He plants a great many potatoes & peas, has tried most of the artificial grasses, & intends now to take to turnips, for sugar' (pp. 172–3).

It was Mr Collett who first told Malthus that 'Potatoes thrive remarkably well. They have been introduced into Norway about 30 years, and are coming daily more into use' (p. 101). Malthus noticed some potato patches by Lake Mjösa (p. 124) and the landlord at Elstad said they were 'much in use & much liked' (p. 133); the houseman on the way to Tofte, however, said that 'potatoes had been but lately introduced, & were not generally used. He liked them himself but many people did not. They have increased much in general use about Christiania during the last 7 or 8 years, & now form a considerable part of the food of the common people in that part of the country, but are probably not much in use in the interior parts of the country' (pp. 137–8).

Many of the most thinking and best informed persons express their apprehensions on this subject, and on the probable result of the new regulations respecting the enrolments of the army, and the apparent intention of the court of Denmark to encourage at all events the population. No very unfavourable season has occurred in Norway since 1785; but it is feared that, in the event of such a season, the most severe distress might be felt from the rapid increase that has of late taken place.

Norway is, I believe, almost the only country in Europe where a traveller will hear any apprehensions expressed of a redundant population, and where the danger to the happiness of the lower classes of people from this cause is in some degree seen and understood. This obviously arises from the smallness of the population altogether, and the consequent narrowness of the subject. If our attention were confined to one parish, and there were no power of emigrating from it, the most careless observer could not fail to remark that, if all married at twenty, it would be perfectly impossible for the farmers, however carefully they might improve their land, to find employment and food for those that would grow up; but when a great number of these parishes are added together in a populous kingdom, the largeness of the subject, and the power of moving from place to place, obscure and confuse our view. We lose sight of a truth, which before appeared completely obvious; and in a most unaccountable manner, attribute to the aggregate quantity of land a power of supporting people beyond comparison greater than the sum of all its parts.

was 138,799, of deaths 94,530, of marriages 34,313. These numbers give the proportion of births to deaths as 146 to 100, of births to marriages as 4 to 1, and of deaths to marriages as 275 to 100. The average proportion of yearly births is stated to be $\frac{1}{55}$, and of yearly deaths $\frac{1}{48}$ of the whole population (vol. II, ch. viii).

Count Moltke told Malthus that round Trondheim 'The population has greatly increased of late years; but the importation [of corn] has not increased—a proof that cultivation is going rapidly forwards' (p. 153). The 'sensible and intelligent' fellow-guest at Count Schmettau's also said that 'Norway was increasing very fast in cultivation & population; and that in a few years it would be a very different country from what it had been' (p. 173).

The most thinking and best informed persons who feared too great an increase in population were General Mansbach and Colonel Bielefeldt, whose views have already been quoted on p. 279. Count Moltke also expressed much the same opinion (p. 152): 'He said that the popn had lately increased very considerably in his government, partly from their being fewer impediments to marriage from the military regulations. Cultivation also had been proceeding very rapidly—they had for some times had very fortunate years; but he was not without apprehensions that should a bad year come, the people in consequence of the increased popn would suffer most extremely.'

As may be noted in Appendix 2, 'the danger to the happiness of the lower classes of people' caused by a redundant population were 'in some degree seen and understood' in Switzerland as well as in Norway.

Appendix 2

An extract from Harriet Eckersall's journal of 1802, describing an episode in Switzerland used by Malthus in the second edition of the *Essay on the Principle of Population*.

The extract is dated Sunday 4 July; the scene 'a delightful glen' somewhere near the Lac de Joux.

We found in our way quantities of the finest wood strawberries & at the source bought an immense provision of them of some young girls—while we sat on the grass to eat them, were much entertain'd with the Philosopic discource of the driver of our char on the over-population of his country; he complain'd much of the extreme early marriages, which he said was the 'vice du pays,' & a custom that had originated in a prosperous time & when a good deal of money could be earn'd by polishing stones, & that now when the case was altered & the means of subsistence less, they still continued, 'de se marier au sortir de l'Ecole': they had large families of children who owing to the extreme healthiness of the air never died but from actual want —he concluded with observing 'qu'on ne devoit se marier qu'a quarante ans, et encore alor's qu'a des vielles filles'—les *jeunes* filles who were sitting near us were much diverted but did not look as if they would take his advice. The Author of a late Essay on Population with whom he held the conversation was greatly interested to hear many of his own ideas in the mouth of a Swiss peasant—Some of our party wishing for milk to drink after their strawberries, rather shamefully it must be own'd, seiz'd upon one of ye Cows by force & milked her—no bribe being able to corrupt the fidelity of the little Boy who kept them; they did not belong to him, he said, & he could not sell any of the milk—he endeavour'd to drive his cows away— even after the mischief was done & the cow milk'd, they could hardly make him take any money for it—the milk was not his

& it would do him no good—The theives while they robbed him praised his honesty & commended his conduct but his example produced no effect; those who had no concern in the seizure of the Cow shared her milk.

Malthus's account of this incident is in chapter VII of book II of the 1803 edition of the *Essay on the Principle of Population*, pp. 281–3:

I was very much struck with an effect of this last kind in an expedition to the *Lac de Joux* in the Jura. The party had scarcely arrived at a little inn at the end of the lake when the mistress of the house began to complain of the poverty and misery of all the parishes in the neighbourhood. She said that the country produced little, and yet was full of inhabitants; that boys and girls were marrying who ought still to be at school; and that, while this habit of early marriages continued, they should always be wretched and distressed for subsistence.

The peasant, who afterwards conducted us to the source of the Orbe, entered more fully into the subject, and appeared to understand the principle of population almost as well as any man I ever met with. He said, that the women were prolific, and the air of the mountains so pure and healthy, that very few children died, except from the consequences of absolute want; that the soil, being barren, was inadequate to yield employment and food for the numbers that were yearly growing up to manhood; that the wages of labour were consequently very low, and totally insufficient for the decent support of a family; but that the misery and starving condition of the greater part of the society did not operate as a warning to others, who still continued to marry, and to produce a numerous offspring which they could not support. This habit of early marriages might really, he said, be called *le vice du pays*; and he was so strongly impressed with the necessary and unavoidable wretchedness that must result from it, that he thought a law ought to be made restricting men from entering into the marriage state before they were forty years of age, and then allowing it only with '*des vieilles filles*', who might bear them two or three children instead of six or eight.

I could not help being diverted with the earnestness of his oratory on this subject, and particularly with his concluding proposition. He must have seen and felt the misery arising from a redundant population most forcibly to have proposed so violent a remedy. I found upon inquiry that he had himself married very young.

The only point in which he failed, as to his philosophical knowledge of the subject, was in confining his reasonings too much to barren and mountainous countries, and not extending them to the plains. In fertile situations, he thought, perhaps, that the plenty of corn and employment might remove the difficulty, and allow of early marriages. Not having lived much in the plains, it was natural for him to fall into this error; particularly as in such situations the difficulty is not only more concealed from the extensiveness of the subject, but is in reality less, from the greater mortality naturally occasioned by low grounds, towns, and manufactories.

On inquiring into the principal cause of what he had named the *predominant vice* of his country, he explained it with great philosophical precision. He said, that a manufacture for the polishing of stones had been established some years ago, which for a time had been in a very thriving state, and had furnished high wages and employment to all the neighbourhood; that the facility of providing for a family, and of finding early employment for children, had greatly encouraged early marriages; and that the same habit had continued, when, for a change of fashion, accident, and other causes, the manufacture was almost at an end. Very great emigrations, he said, had of late years taken place; but the breeding system went on so fast, that they were not sufficient to relieve the country of its superabundant mouths, and the effect was such as he had described to me, and as I had in part seen.

In other conversations which I had with the lower classes of people in different parts of Switzerland and Savoy, I found many who, though not sufficiently skilled in the principle of population to see its effects on society, like my friend of the *Lac de Joux*, yet saw them clearly enough as affecting their own individual interests; and were perfectly aware of the evils which they should probably bring upon themselves by marrying before they could have a tolerable prospect of being able to maintain a family. From the general ideas which I have found to prevail on these subjects, I should by no means say that it would be a difficult task to make the common people comprehend the principle of population, and its effect in producing low wages and poverty.

Appendix 3

A letter written by Malthus on the day of his son's birth.

The letter is addressed to Messers Cadell and Davies, Strand, London. There is no postmark. It was found inserted in one of several volumes which the Bath Libraries and Art Gallery Committee purchased from the Broadley Collection, and is now in the Municipal Library, Bath; it is printed here with the kind permission of the Committee.

December 16th, 1804   Bath.
                                              37 New King Street.

Dear Sir,

I have looked over the packet that you sent, though from being at present very particularly engaged I have not been able to give it the attention that I could have wished. Some of the notes appear to have merit, others not, and some of the most important points are not discussed at all. It is difficult however to pass any fair judgement upon the work as a whole; because the supplementary chapters evidently contain the discussion of those subjects which the writer thinks of the greatest consequence, and none of these supplementary chapters are sent. With regard to myself I can have no manner of objection to your publishing this edition before mine, as it would give me more time, which the more I think on the subject the more I feel is necessary, in order to produce an edition that would have any thing like the effect of giving you a new copyright. I had much rather that you would rely on the advice of any other friend respecting the eligibility of publishing the edition now offered, than on mine, particularly as I have not had leisure to read the manuscript very attentively, and this you will not be surprised at when I tell you that in addition to the engagements, I have been in a state of considerable anxiety about Mrs Malthus, who was brought to bed this morning before her time, but is now happily pretty well. Should the present offer that you have received or any other, make you wish to alter your plans, I beg that you will not consider yourself as tied by anything that has passed between us.

I am Dear Sir

Your obet huml St.

T. R. MALTHUS

In the advertisement, the last paragraph and the manner in which the French economists are spoken of do not give a favourable impression. The style is not very correct, and is written without punctuation; but such little errors may be easily amended.

The Author of the original work is always called *Mr* Smith; but Adam Smith, Dr Smith, or Smith are all preferable.

I am writing in the dark—Excuse great haste.

Messrs Cadell and Davies were a firm of London booksellers and publishers. Thomas Cadell, the first member of the family to trade in London (his father of the same name had been a bookseller in Bristol), was the publisher, jointly with W. Strahan, of the 1776 and 1778 editions, and several of the subsequent editions, of Adam Smith's *Wealth of Nations*. They never published for Malthus; the first two editions of the *Essay on Population* were published by J. Johnson and *The Principles of Political Economy* by Murray. But Malthus long contemplated an edition of the *Wealth of Nations* incorporating his notes. The history of the firm by Theodore Besterman—*The Publishing Firm of Cadell and Davies* (O.U.P. 1938, pp. 163-4)—contains a letter from Malthus about this, written in 1812 (see *The Works and Correspondence of David Ricardo*, ed. P. Sraffa, vol. VI, pp. 159-60.) It was clear that at this much later date Malthus was intending to publish his edition through Messrs Cadell and Davies. That letter contains the sentence: 'I most decidedly wished to give you the preference in any engagement I might form for notes to Adam Smith both on account of your being the original publishers of the work, and on account of what formerly passed between us on the subject.'

Since the letter is quite clearly dated in December 1804, it seems certain that Malthus had already had some discussion with them as early as that year, at latest, and that this is why Cadell and Davies consulted him about the book discussed in the letter.

Cadell and Davies did in fact publish in 1805 the eleventh edition of *An Inquiry into the Nature and Causes of the Wealth of Nations* by Adam Smith LL.D., with Notes, Supplementary Chapters and a Life of Dr Smith by William Playfair. Playfair's 'Advertisement to This Edition' lists 'the principal changes that have taken place since 1775'. Seventh and last of these changes: 'the French revolution, brought on in some measure by the *French Oeconomists*, has operated an almost total change on the face of Europe'. His preface also devotes a long paragraph to the French writers. His Life of Adam Smith, which follows it, is again concerned to discuss the French Oeconomists and their influence on Adam Smith. Finally a 'Supplementary Chapter II [By the Editor]' of eleven pages is entitled 'On the French Oeconomists'. Playfair's edition as printed calls Adam Smith 'Mr Smith' throughout, even when pages are (possibly belatedly) headed 'The Life of Dr Smith'.

It now seems certain that Cadell and Davies had sent Malthus part of the manuscript of the Playfair edition for his comments.

William Playfair (1759–1823) had a varied career. In 1780 he was a draughtsman with Boulton and Watt in Birmingham; subsequently he opened a shop in London for the sale of metal knick-knacks, and when this failed he went to Paris, where he became embroiled in a fraudulent company for encouraging emigration to America. From 1795 until 1815 he lived in London, chiefly as a journalist, writing pamphlets and translations: he had a brief period in Paris between 1815 and 1818 editing 'Galignani's Messenger', but had to flee back to England after a libel action over a duel.

The writer of Playfair's obituary in the *Gentleman's Magazine* said that 'The notes to Adam Smith's "Wealth of Nations" display considerable knowledge of political economy', and that 'In private life Mr Playfair was amiable and firm in his friendship as he was loyal in his principles'.[1]

[1] *Gentleman's Magazine*, June 1823, p. 566.

SACRED TO THE MEMORY
OF THE REV. THOMAS ROBERT MALTHUS
LONG KNOWN TO THE LETTERED WORLD
BY HIS ADMIRABLE WRITINGS ON THE SOCIAL BRANCHES OF
POLITICAL ECONOMY
PARTICULARLY BY HIS ESSAY ON POPULATION

ONE OF THE BEST MEN AND TRUEST PHILOSOPHERS
OF ANY AGE OR COUNTRY
RAISED BY NATIVE DIGNITY OF MIND
ABOVE THE MISREPRESENTATIONS OF THE IGNORANT
AND THE NEGLECT OF THE GREAT
HE LIVED A SERENE AND HAPPY LIFE
DEVOTED TO THE PURSUIT AND COMMUNICATION
OF TRUTH
SUPPORTED BY A CALM BUT FIRM CONVICTION OF THE
USEFULNESS OF HIS LABORS
CONTENT WITH THE APPROBATION OF THE WISE AND GOOD

HIS WRITINGS WILL BE A LASTING MONUMENT
OF THE EXTENT AND CORRECTNESS OF HIS UNDERSTANDING

THE SPOTLESS INTEGRITY OF HIS PRINCIPLES
THE EQUITY AND CANDOUR OF HIS NATURE
HIS SWEETNESS OF TEMPER URBANITY OF MANNERS
AND TENDERNESS OF HEART
HIS BENEVOLENCE AND HIS PIETY
ARE THE STILL DEARER RECOLLECTIONS OF HIS FAMILY
AND FRIENDS.

BORN FEB : 14 · 1766 .   DIED 29 · DEC : 1834.

Appendix 4. Memorial Tablet to Malthus in the Abbey at Bath. The tablet is in the north porch at the west end of the church.

302

Appendix 5

This family tree cannot claim to be either comprehensive or of unimpeachable accuracy: it is based to a certain extent on that of John Orlebar Payne, who printed his *Collections for a History of the Family of Malthus* in 1890, and who, in the words of the late Colonel Sydenham Malthus, 'made a great many mistakes'. I have naturally used the entries in parish registers wherever I know them, and have got what I can from such standard works of reference as *Burke's Landed Gentry*, for England and Ireland, Venn's *Alumni Cantabrigienses* and Foster's *Alumni Oxonienses*. Fortunately the Eckersalls were educated at Westminster, and the records of Barker and Stenning, and Whitmore and Radcliffe, have been of great assistance.

My chief aim has been to show the intermarriages of the Malthuses with the Daltons, Grahams and Eckersalls, and to provide a sort of who's-who for those who are interested in seeing a great man in his family setting. Louisa Bray wrote of her uncle, 'In private life few could equal him,' and in 1818, when the fatherless young Brays were scattered by illness, she wrote that the youngest sister was 'with the Robert Malthuses in Hertfordshire'; one feels that the Robert Malthuses would have taken the youngest and, presumably, the most troublesome.

Law and medicine preponderate among Malthus's ancestors, and this trend seems to continue. I must thank Dr Cecil Malthus of Christchurch, New Zealand, for telling me about the family there, descended from two of Malthus's great-nephews, Charles and Henry Perceval Malthus, who emigrated in 1860. Of Dr Malthus's five children, all graduates, two are doctors and one is a lawyer; his daughters are married to a lawyer and a professor; he has twenty-three grandchildren. There are now well over 200 members of the family in New Zealand, 'scattered right up and down the country from Kaitaia to Invercargill', of whom about half bear the name of Malthus. 'You will agree', writes Dr Malthus, 'that we conform very well to Pop's theory of what tends to happen in a young country where the means of subsistence abound.'

Select Bibliography

T. R. MALTHUS (1) *An Essay on the Principle of Population*. London, 1798.

T. R. MALTHUS (2) The Second Edition, 'very much enlarged'. London, 1803.

The First Essay, which Darwin read for 'amusement', and which is essential for the understanding of the young Malthus, has in recent years been extremely difficult to come by. The facsimile edition, published for the Royal Economic Society by Messrs Macmillan in 1926, has for many years been out of print. It is good to know that, to mark the bi-centenary of Malthus, it will shortly be reprinted. An alternative is the Ann Arbor Paperback, published in 1959 by the Michigan University Press (139 pages).

The Second Essay (577 pages) is printed by the Everyman Library. In the 1958 edition, Professor Fogarty has made an original and imaginative contribution to the Mistakes about Malthus: on page vi he says that Malthus 'married in 1805, and practised the principle of population to the extent of eleven girls'.

BOOKS ABOUT MALTHUS

OTTER, WILLIAM. *Memoir of Robert Malthus*. Published as an Introduction to Malthus's *Principles of Political Economy*, London, 1836.

EMPSON, WILLIAM. 'The Life, Writings and Character of Mr Malthus', *Edinburgh Review* (January 1837).

PAYNE, JOHN ORLEBAR. *Collections for a History of the Family of Malthus*. Privately printed, London, 1890.

BONAR, JAMES. *Malthus and his Work*. Allen and Unwin, 1924.

KEYNES, J. M. Essay on Malthus in *Essays in Biography*. Rupert Hart-Davis, 1951.

MCCLEARY, G. F. *The Malthusian Population Theory*. Faber and Faber, 1953.

SELECT BIBLIOGRAPHY

BOOKS ABOUT SCANDINAVIA

ANDERSSON, INGVAR. *A History of Sweden.* Translated by Carolyn Hannay. Weidenfeld and Nicolson, 1956.

DANSTRUP, JOHN. *A History of Denmark.* Translated by Verner Lindberg. Wivel, Copenhagen, 1948.

DERRY, T. K. *A Short History of Norway.* Allen and Unwin, 1957.

For guide-books to every country which Malthus visited, I have found Baedeker, Muirhead, and Nagel all extremely helpful.

Index

Aabenraa ('Abenrae'), 47, 48
'Aarehens' (Orehens), *see under* birds
Abildgaard, Professor Peter Christian
  (Veterinary College, Copenhagen),
  58–61, 293
accommodation
  beds, 32, 68, 81, 110, 137, 140, 141,
    145, 188, 202
  fires, 137, 201; fireplaces, 202
  see also inns
accommodation, prices of, at Berset,
  198; Birkhagen, 145; Brunset, 204;
  Elstad, 134; Engelholm, 68; Hamburg, 32, 36; Hogdal, 82–3; Kirke-
  vold, 177; Moe, 126; Moss, 95;
  Roholdt, 123; Röros, 186; Westgaard, 201 (for the Continental
  Tour and the Scottish holiday, *see*
  Cash Accounts on pp. 243 ff. and
  pp. 268 ff.)
'Adersleben', *see* Haderslev
administration, *see* government
Adolphus Frederick, King of Sweden,
  79, 79 n.
agriculture, in Denmark, 60, 61; in
  Norway, 60, 87–8, 100–1, 152–3,
  155, 172–3, 284–93
  enclosure, 65
  enclosures, 48, 49, 50, 51, 52, 71, 203
  land tenure, 64–5, 117–18, 265; *see
    also* housemen *and* rent
  mowing, 145, 196
  pasture, 52, 65, 87, 122, 125
  pasture (summer), 118, 132–3, 135,
    144, 179, 187, 188–9, 198, 290–1;
    of reindeer, 193–4; *see also* Seters
  ploughing, 133, 137
  see also animals (domestic), crops *and*
    farms
Aix la Chapelle, 239–40, 242
Akershus, 102–3
Albury (Surrey), 4, 5, 6, 9, 39
Alkmaar, 236

Altona, 31–2, 39; walks to, 34–7
Amsterdam, 236–7
'Ancher', *see* Anker
André, Major John, 102
Angelholm (Engelholm), 68
Angell, Thomas, legacy of, to poor of
  Trondheim, 166–7, 184
animals, domestic
  chickens, 41
  dogs, guard, 133, 189, 191, 193, 212,
    217; hunting, 210, 212–13
  geese, 52, 75
  goats, 188, 198, 202, 216
  pigs, 41, 52, 75, 147
  sheep, 41, 52, 189, 196, 211, 216, 265
  reindeer, 189–95, 200
  see also cattle *and* horses
animals, wild
  bears, 132, 146–7, 179, 188, 199, 212,
    216
  elks, 200
  frogs, 37, 44
  hares, 213, 219
  jaloux (wild cat), 172, 212
  lynxes, 132
  reindeer, 200
  squirrel, 213
  wolves, 132, 147, 188, 193, 199, 216–
    17
Anker, Bernt, 5, 96–7, 120–1, 123, 124,
  150, 202, 206; iron-works of, 94, 95;
  conversations with, 98–9, 105–6,
  281; country seat of, 99–100, 293;
  dinners with, 102–4, 108, 117, 120;
  library of, 107; gives a ball, 107–9,
  167; woods of, 124, 201–2, 211,
  214
Anker, Mrs Bernt, 99, 100
Anker, Jess, 119 n. 1, 121 n. 1
Anker, Niels (of Fredrikshald), 83 n. 2,
  277; two days with, 83–93
Anker, Mrs Niels, 84, 89, 281
Anker, Peder, 104–5, 106, 178, 216, 293